Traditions *and* History
of
Anderson County
South Carolina

By: Louise Ayer Vandiver

Southern Historical Press, Inc.
Greenville, South Carolina

This volume was reproduced from
an personal copy located in the
Publisher's private Library

All rights reserved. No part of this publication may be reproduced, stored in a retrieval system or transmitted in any form or by any means without the prior written permission of the publisher.

Please Direct All Correspondence and Book Orders to:

Southern Historical Press, Inc.
1071 Park West Blvd.
Greenville, SC   29611

Originally printed South Carolina 1928
New Material Copyrighted 2025 by:
         Southern Historical Press, Inc.
ISBN #978-1-63914-165-4
Printed in the United States of America

Dedicated to Anderson

O Anderson! Thou wert the scene of all
My glad young years. The place where I have dwelt
From girlhood's days, and where we children knelt
Around the altar at my father's call.
The home that ever must my heart enthrall,
Because 'tis there my woman's soul has felt
The joys and griefs that many a year has dealt—
Those sacred things my mind loves to recall.
O little town beside the Blue Ridge Hills!
Thy sons and daughters are among the blest,
No bloated wealth, nor cringing poverty
Rends brother's heart from brother's heart, nor fills
With bitter hate the souls of men oppressed.
Thy people work, and dwell in harmony.

PREFACE

*T*HIS *book is by no means a complete history of Anderson County, nor a full record of her people. It is merely a collection of sketches. The material has been gathered through a number of years; at first with no idea of publication, merely because the collector liked to hear the old people tell what they knew, or in their early days had heard from their elders about what went on in that long past day when other vanished people lived here, people forgotten except when some antiquarian became reminiscent.*

Numbers of men and women deserve mention of whom the narrator chanced to glean no information.

Most of the persons from whom the old-time gossip came have passed on themselves. Among them were Mr. T. J. Webb, who talked often and long to an interested listener; Mrs. Julia Daniels, Mrs. Lucy Langston, Dr. R. E. Thompson, Dr. R. F. Divver, Mrs. R. C. Hoyt, Misses Elizabeth and Margaret Morris, Miss Nellie Brown, Mr. C. W. Webb, Mr. J. B. Leverette, Mr. A. A. Dean, Colonel J. N. Brown, Dr. W. J. King, Mr. J. B. Lewis, Miss Jemima Nevett, Colonel Lewis Campbell, Mr. and Mrs. B. B. Breazeale, Reverend Mike McGee, Mr. John M. Hubbard, Miss Nora Hubbard, Mr. L. P. Smith, Miss Bettie Earle, Mr. J. Pink Reed, Mr. D. H. Russell, Miss Mattie McCarley, Mrs. Eliza Skelton, Mr. O. E. Horton, of Atlanta; Mrs. Kate Maxwell, Mrs. Margaret Van Wyck, Mrs. E. M. Rucker, Mr. R. E. Belcher and others. Among the notes from which the book has been written, there are some whose source is entirely forgotten.

General C. A. Reed had a most valuable bound volume of the old HIGHLAND SENTINEL *and* THE ANDERSON GAZETTE *which he lent several times to the collector. Also the Public Library was most indulgent in allowing a thorough study of the bound volumes of* THE INTELLIGENCER.

PREFACE—Continued

To the help and interest of Miss J. Lois Watson more is due than can ever be adequately acknowledged. For years she has brought to the collector of Anderson county data every item of history or interest that she found or learned, and in these last hurried days, she has replied promptly and fully to several S. O. S. calls, never failing to get in the quickest possible time the required information and sending it immediately.

Miss Carrie Pearman also has been a valuable assistant and has taken the trouble to furnish many interesting items, especially about Broadaway Township, which without her help would not have been included in the history of the county.

To Mrs. J. M. Paget, too, the writer is indebted for much that is interesting and important.

Without the help and sympathy in the undertaking of these friends, the collection could never have been made.

And after all the long years of accumulation, at last the book has been hastily thrown together. The hope of publication had been abandoned, and the material consisted of unarranged notes, when Mr. Wilton E. Hall, editor of THE ANDERSON INDEPENDENT, *wrote asking that the manuscript be sent him, he would have it published as a part of Anderson's Centenary—and he asked to have it in two weeks' time.*

The two weeks was impossible, but it has been put together by a slow typist in less than a month, and it shows it. The writer realizes that it is very faulty, but there is no time for revision; and such as it is, it is offered to the people of Anderson with the sincere love of the writer for the home of her best years.

CONTENTS

Page

Chapter I
The Days of the Indians _____ 1

Chapter II
Formation of Anderson County and Beginning of the City ____ 10

Chapter III
Some of the Pioneer People and Their Social Life _____ 18

Chapter IV
The Churches _____ 32

Chapter V
The Revolutionary War _____ 64

Chapter VI
Newspapers and Writers _____ 80

Chapter VII
Some of the Early Industries _____ 91

Chapter VIII
In Schoolroom Walls—The County _____ 95

Chapter IX
In Schoolroom Walls—The Town _____ 110

Chapter X
Some of the Early Citizens and Homes _____ 130

Chapter XI
Some of the Forefathers _____ 137

Chapter XII
Andersonville and Some Early Settlers _____ 161

Chapter XIII
Waters and Graveyards _____ 170

Chapter XIV
Railroads _____ 180

CONTENTS—Continued

	Page
Chapter XV	
Townships	188
Chapter XVI	
War Between the States	223
Chapter XVII	
War Time at Home	237
Chapter XVIII	
Reconstruction and the Aftermath	249
Chapter XIX	
The Middle Years	257
Chapter XX	
Some Public Buildings	277
Chapter XXI	
The Spanish War	286
Chapter XXII	
Manufactories, Mills and Other Industries	290
Chapter XXIII	
Highways and Byways, People and Things	303
Chapter XXIV	
Later Times	312

CHAPTER I.

THE DAYS OF THE INDIANS.

FOR more than a hundred years after the coast of Carolina had become a prosperous British Colony, and Charleston was the most elegant and cultured city of the New World, all the "back country," as it was called, was gloomy forest peopled sparsely by Indians, and abounding in wild animals.

The Red Men lived in rudimentary towns, and one of the chief of these was almost where Walhalla now stands. Many of the names of upper South Carolina are of Cherokee origin, Seneca, Tugaloo, Generostee are instances. Keowee or Kewhohee means the river of mulberries; Enoree is the river of muscadines.

It is doubtful whether the famous Keowee trail passed through what is now the city of Anderson, but smaller trails did. One started at about "Whitehall," which was very close to the residence of Mrs. Nelson Green, ran through North Anderson, through the grounds of the Anderson County Hospital and Fant Street School, ran back of where Mr. John Hubbard's house stands, went through Mr. Raymond Mattison's premises, through the grounds of "Arlington" and on towards Belton. It probably joined the Keowee Trail lower down. If that is truly the lines followed by the trail, the Indians did not travel as the crow flies, but followed devious and crooked paths.

Along this old trail are sometimes still found arrow heads, pipes, hatchets and other remains of Indian handiwork.

On the Williamston road near the Bailey home was an Indian town. The arrowheads found about there are different from most that have been picked up in the vicinity of Anderson. They are beautifully polished, and look almost like fish scales. It has been suggested that they were brought to the place by hostile Indians, and that there may have been a battle there between two tribes. Some of the articles discovered in this section have been sewing awls of stone and bone, stone pipes, remnants of pottery of a rude kind, flat stones with hollowed center, corn mills and stone knives.

The old Byrum place, now converted into a country club, stands on the site of an ancient Indian camp. On the plantation of Mr. Henry McFall near High Shoals they buried some of their dead. It is said that near that locality is still to be found a root of which the Indians made bread. At High Shoals also they had a burial place,

HISTORY OF ANDERSON COUNTY

and on the old Bailey Breazeale place between Anderson and Belton are to be seen several Indian burial mounds.

An Anderson man tells of having seen an Indian burial mound opened when he was a boy. Deep in the ground was a pen of pine piles filled with parched corn; but in wonderfully good condition considering its age, and the length of time it had been buried. There were in the grave tomahawks, white clay beads, colored glass beads, long stemmed clay pipes, decorated pottery, arrowheads, and knives of stone and bone—things which the savages thought would be serviceable to the departed spirit on its journey into the unknown. The gentlemen said that chickens killed on the place were frequently found to have swallowed some of the same kind of clay beads.

In 1908 a freshet changed the course of the Savannah River, and in the old bed were various pieces of Indian pottery. A government expert was sent from Washington to examine the things exposed by the river, and he discovered many interesting relics.

The old Johnson University buildings were erected on a spot where many Indian articles have been found; among them pieces of stone so hard that ordinary tools were broken in trying to cut it. It is supposed that the stone must have been brought to the locality by Indians, as none like it has been found anywhere else in the county. Pieces of this stone were used for stamping Confederate money for the short time that the Confederate Treasury occupied the University buildings.

Most of the Indian mounds were burial places, but the very large ones were probably community dwellings; whole tribes being herded into one mound for shelter. The red people usually lived in squalor and thrived on dirt. Some mounds bear evidence of having been places of public meetings, sort of council chambers.

Some very small ones were probably picket posts where sentinels were stationed to guard the settlements.

Between Anderson and Walhalla run several creeks bearing singular names. One Mile, Six Mile, Twelve Mile, Eighteen Mile, Four and Twenty, Six and Twenty, and farther down the line of the Keowee Trail lies the town named Ninety-Six. These names are accounted for by an Indian tradition about which there has been some controversy. Iconoclasts loudly proclaim the whole story a fabrication, but Dr. J. W. Daniell, South Carolina's highest authority on Indian lore, thinks the story is founded on truth. At any rate it is a pretty legend, and if the annals of a people or a land be shorn of legend and tradition, none but the Gradgrind family will ever read its history.

It is said that long ago a young Englishman named Allen Francis taught an Indian school at Keowee. Among his pupils was Cateechee, a Choctaw maid, captive of Kuruga, the Cherokee chief. In her own tongue her name was Issaqueena. Both words mean deer's head. The two fell in love with each other, and when Allen left the Indian settlement it was with a promise to return for his dusky sweetheart at some future day. He went to Fort Cambridge and established himself there in a trading business with his father and brother.

One night Cateechee overheard Kuruga and his warriors planning an attack on Fort Cambridge, intending to massacre all of the white people living there.

The girl determined to save her lover. After the Indians were asleep she stole away to go to the fort ninety-six miles from Keowee, and warn the white people of their danger. When morning came she was missed, and the Cherokees, suspecting her errand, started in pursuit.

As she ran, a succession of mountain streams crossed her path, and she named them as she sped on, comforting herself with the sound of the number of miles she had thrown behind her. At nightfall, footsore and exhausted, she told her tale. When a little later the Indians reached the place the fort was garrisoned, and the attack was easily repulsed.

Naturally Cateechee remained among the people whom she had saved, and she and Francis were married. For several years they lived in peace among the people of the little town, then called Ninety-Six in memory of her race with death over ninety-six miles of forest.

But in far off Keowee, Kuruga had not forgotten nor forgiven. He waited his chance for vengeance—and one night when a violent storm was raging, preventing cries from being heard, the Indians descended upon Francis' cabin and bound both Allen and his wife, taking them back over the dreary miles to Keowee. Cateechee carried in Indian fashion her infant daughter on her back. When the Indian town was reached the mother and child were sent to the wigwam of the chief, there to resume her life of servitude. Francis stood bound in the midst of the Indian council, awaiting whatever cruel fate they chose to mete out to him. But so stoical and indifferent did the young man appear that he won the admiration of Kuruga, who in place of putting him to death, determined to adopt him as his son. Henceforth the little family was united; they, however, were so closely watched that two years had passed before they found an opportunity to escape. Then one wild night when the Indian women were returning late and in confusion from a nutting expedition, the opportunity occurred; Cateechee, hampered by the weight of her child, lagged behind the women who were hastening to reach home before the fury of the tempest burst upon them.

Francis had gone to meet the returning party, and finding themselves alone, in spite of the storm they determined to escape. They were too wise to attempt to reach their home immediately, and for a time hid in the forest, making a big hollow tree their shelter. The Indians, suspecting that they had returned to Ninety-Six, sent messengers to discover them. But the messengers returned saying that the fugitives had not gone to the fort; the people there supposed them to be still among the Indians. Most of the red-skins came to believe that on that fearful night the whole family had been struck by lightning, and that wild beasts devoured their bodies.

Not all of them, however, entertained that view, and a party of the doubters finally set out to fully explore the mountain fastnesses in search of the vanished family. The searchers found their rude shelter, which their leader, the medicine man old Salue, contemptuously named "Stump House," and Stump-House Mountain was christened. Finally the explorers discovered Cateechee standing on the banks of the stream Tugaluyi (Tugaloo), and started in pursuit of her. The frightened mother, clasping her child, plunged into the stream and fled along its course, arrows whizzing about her head. Finally she reached a high cascade, and the pursuing Indians believed that certainly they had recovered their prey. But in desperation she leaped over the fall, and they were sure that they had seen her dashed into pieces on the stones below, so they turned back to the hollow tree to await the return of Francis.

But Cateechee had not been dashed to death. About ten feet below the fall there was a ledge, and on that she landed, and stepping behind the falling water was securely screened from view. At a little distance her husband had witnessed the whole episode. As soon as the Indians retired from the place, Francis by the help of leather thongs helped his wife to regain the bank, and together they climbed down the rocks so as to leave no trail, and waded down the shallow stream until they reached the bark boat which Francis had just completed. Into that they clambered, and floated down the river until next day when they came to the broad Savannah where they abandoned their frail bark, and traveling across country, rejoined their friends at Ninety-Six.

Issaqueena Falls still makes the leap which Issaqueena made with her little daughter in her arms.

Another Indian story told of this vicinity is that of Kiessa.

At Swansea Rock on the border of Anderson County there lived at the time of the Revolution a stalwart Indian said to have been almost seven feet tall. His nearest neighbor and closest friend was "Horseshoe Robinson." Between them was a love as strong as that between David and Jonathan. In the tent of Kiessa there dwelt with him his wife and their only child, a daughter whom they called Connesstee.

One day while Kiessa and Horseshoe were hunting in the forest, a band of Tories, cruel as the typical savage, entered the humble home seeking for their enemy Horseshoe Robinson, and willing because of their hatred of him to hurt his friends. Finding only women in the wigwam, they took them prisoners, stole everything of value, and burned all else, then went away towards King's Mountain to report their dirty trick.

Connesstee wore a robe ornamented with feathers from a pheasant's tail, and as she was carried away she often plucked a feather from her garment and threw it on the ground. These her keen-eyed father observed as soon as he discovered his loss, and he and his friend Horseshoe were soon in hot pursuit. On the sixth night when they stopped to rest, they saw lights at some distance, and after eating some of the food they carried, the two slipped forward in the dark and came to the foot of a high bluff, on the top of which was pitched a tent. Stealing softly to the place where the tent was just above them, Kiessa stood close to the rock, then Horseshoe, standing on his shoulders and carefully pulling himself by bushes, found that he was in the rear of Ferguson's tent. The people within, thinking themselves perfectly secure, talked freely of a bag of gold which had that day been received to pay the soldiers. Ferguson did not intend to pay them until he had first dislodged a camp of American soldiers not far from him, and he planned to make an attack upon them early next morning.

As he lay close to the tent Horseshoe Robinson saw a brown object protrude from beneath the edge, and examining it closely, found it to be the sleeve of Connesstee's feather trimmed robe. Rejoicing in what he had learned, the woodsman cut a thong from his own skin hunting shirt, and by its aid descended to carry the good news to Kiessa.

Watching for dawn, the two waited for their opportunity. Reveille sounded in the British camp and preparations were made for the troops to go forward. Suddenly above the noise of camp activities sounded the clear notes of a mocking bird, or so it seemed to the British soldiers. But Connesstee recognized her father's signal. As the sound of the soldiers' marching grew faint in the distance, Kiessa slipped beneath the rear flap of the tent, where lay his wife and daughter, bound with thongs. Severing their bonds, they were armed with hatchets, and when Robinson and the Indian man fell upon the guard, the two women attacked them from the rear, and every soldier who remained in the camp was slain. The invaders waited until they learned that Morgan had beaten his adversaries, then were fortunate enough to seize a two-horse wagon loaded with provisions and clothing, which, with the gold, they carried to their ruined home. The gold they buried between the two branches of the Saluda River, and so secure was the hiding place that they themselves could never find it again.

Horseshoe Robinson immediately returned to Marion's camp, and Kiessa moved for protection near to Keowee, and there was Connesstee wedded to a young Cherokee chief.

Almost in the old "General's Road" at Varennes, very near the home of the late Colonel J. W. Norris, is an Indian mound which is surrounded with rocks fixed on end, which have retained their position amid the various changes wrought by time.

There are several localities near Anderson which tradition names as Indian burial grounds; and it is said that as late as 1855 Indians came once a year to care for these ancient cemeteries.

Very early in the history of the country, enterprising tradesmen from the coast colonies penetrated far into the Indian wilds, trading worthless trinkets, fire arms and whiskey to the red men for hides, horns, baskets and pottery.

Closely following the trader came the cow driver in search of pasturage new for his cattle, and many cowpens, beside the one made famous by the chance of war, were established throughout the wild country. One step further placed the pioneer's cabin almost within sight of the Indian wigwam. From the seacoast, from Virginia, North Carolina and Pennsylvania came the frontier settler. Forests fell beneath his axe. Fields appeared where sombre woods had long held undisputed sway. On horseback and on foot they came, with an occasional heavy wheeled cart, the wheels being slices of some huge log with a hole made through the center. The carts were without springs. Roads there were none, and travelers required courage and endurance.

With increasing anger the Indians watched sullenly the encroachments of the whites, and disputed with them every foot of ground.

About fourteen miles from the city of Anderson in the neighborhood of old Calhoun, occurred in the early days a brutal Indian massacre of a white family.

HISTORY OF ANDERSON COUNTY

Their name is given variously as Smith, as Kemp, and as Callahan. There seems stronger evidence for the name Kemp than any of the others. At any rate, as Kemp they will figure in this narrative. Little is actually known about them. They may have been a part of the great Scotch-Irish migration which set in from more northern colonies towards the southwest in the middle of the eighteenth century. Tradition says they came from Virginia. Certainly they were people of some means for they brought with them slaves, the number unknown, though it is thought there were eight.

Mr. Kemp became friendly with some of the Indians who prowled about the country, entertained them in his home, and felt no fear of his red friends.

About the tragic fate of the family the late Judge J. P. Reed left in manuscript an interesting tale. How much is romance, and how much is history, at this distant day no one can determine. Judge Reed calls the name Callahan, but as he was writing a story, he most probably used fictitious names. He gives to the family a blooming young daughter and an adopted son, who as they grew up fell in love with each other, and were on the point of being married. He makes the family of the Catholic faith. Whether that is true, or whether as a story writer he had to find some way to get the father away as he would have use for him in the chase which followed, he at any rate sends him to Long Cane, the nearest settlement where the services of a Catholic priest could be obtained, to get the padre to return with him and perform the marriage ceremony for the young people. It was then that the Indians, instigated by a notorious Tory of the locality, whose name was Vaughn, surprised the family and killed all of them except one small negro boy who escaped in the dark and climbed a tree in the adjacent swamp, clasping to his breast a pet dog. The story of the little negro is said to be true; if the judge fabricated any of it, it was naturally the love story. The story of the boy has been handed down, and it was said that the Indians, knowing how many were in the family, missed the lad and spent several hours looking for him. The poor little fellow told when next day he reached Long Cane that sometimes the savages stopped under the very tree he had climbed, and that his little dog would bristle up as though he intended to growl, but never did, just cowered in the boy's arms in silence.

Mr. O. E. Horton, of Atlanta, tells the story as he heard it from his grandfather, Major Aaron Broyles, who knew the people, and lived as near them as any one did. He calls the people Kemp, says nothing of the boy and girl or the love story, says there were five in the family, and that the story of the little negro and his dog is true. The house was burned, the bodies mutilated and left lying where they fell. The sorrowing neighbors took them up and buried them just back of where the house stood. There a neighborhood graveyard afterwards grew up.

Embedded in the earth is a large flat stone which was probably the hearth stone of the ill-fated dwelling. The place was bought some years later by the grandfather of Georgia's war governor, Joe Brown, and it was long known as the old Brown place, though no other house has ever been built on the spot where Mr. Kemp's pioneer dwelling stood.

The Indians continued to give trouble for some years after the Revolutionary War. The final treaty between them and the state of South Carolina was negotiated by General Andrew Pickens. It took place beneath a red oak tree near Cherry's Crossing, which stood until just a few years ago, when it was blown down in a storm. The tree was known far and wide as "The Treaty Oak." The place is now marked with a large boulder.

The first step toward the acquisition of the South Carolina Piedmont section by the white race was a treaty made in 1730 by Sir Alexander Cumming, emissary of Governor Moore, for the colony of South Carolina, and for the Cherokee nation by its chief, Moytoy. Everlasting friendship was declared, and six warriors accompanied Sir Alexander to London in order to seal the compact by a personal interview with King George II.

It is told that the savages, wishing to make a good impression upon the court of Great Britain, adorned their heads with feathers, their necks with beads and their bodies with paint for their visit of state. It was with difficulty they were induced to add blankets. The Indians were received with great courtesy, and much attention was shown them in London. The friendship with England then cemented, lasted to the detriment of the American Colonies through the Revolution.

In 1755 Governor Glen wished to strengthen the alliance between the white settlers and the Indians, so he met about five hundred Cherokee warriors in their own country. From them he purchased land, and entered into a solemn treaty. The territory then acquired is now embraced in the counties of Edgefield, Abbeville, Laurens, Newberry, Union, Spartanburg, York, Chester, Fairfield and Richland. The line between Greenville and Spartanburg counties was about the boundary between South Carolina and the Cherokee Province.

Immediately the new lands were settled by white people, and it

HISTORY OF ANDERSON COUNTY

was a short time only before the more daring were pushing into the Cherokee country. The name, Ninety-Six District, was given to the newly acquired territory. Later territory gained from the Cherokees also became a part of Ninety-Six District, which was afterwards divided into Ninety-Six and Washington. Still later Washington was divided into Greenville and Pendleton, the latter named in honor of a popular Virginia judge of the time.

The divisions of the colony were first known as counties. Afterwards they were called districts, and in quite recent times became again counties.

All of what is now Anderson county belonged to the Cherokees until after the Revolutionary War, although probably before the war there were a number of white settlers located in the Indian territory.

CHAPTER II.

Formation of Anderson County and the Beginning of the City.

THE county seat of the new district of Pendleton, called by the same name, early became a popular summer resort of the low country people, and the little town of Pendleton was one of the most cultured and charming places in the South.

As immigration increased and people settled the forests, the huge district was found cumbrous, and another division became necessary. In 1828 Pendleton District disappeared, and was replaced by Anderson and Pickens, named in honor of two most distinguished and popular Revolutionary soldiers of the section, Colonel Robert Anderson and General Andrew Pickens. The commissioners to divide the county were J. C. Kilpatrick, Major Lewis and Thomas Garvin.

The town of Pendleton being too near the edge of the new district for the county seat, a new locality had to be chosen. Commissioners were appointed to select a site for the new town. They were James Harrison, Robert Norris, M. Gambrell, John C. Griffin and William Sherard.

The great highway running from the Cherokee country to Long Cane, a settlement in Abbeville county, was called "The General's Road," because it started near the home of General Pickens and was frequently traveled by him. On that road the new town was to be located, and placed about the middle of the district.

"White Hall" was a residence and store almost opposite the site of the Green home just above North Anderson. The old house under three fine trees still bears the name. The buildings of that earlier day stood close to the road, and either the dwelling or the adjacent store, or perhaps both, were whitewashed or painted, something unusual in that time and locality. One of the buildings had a cellar in which it was said a murdered man was once buried. Of course it was "haunted" or rather "hanted," and the children of that day scurried by the place with bated breath. The original buildings were blown away in a hurricane so severe that it carried into Spartanburg county a plank which had been built into the gable end of one of the houses, which had painted on it the name of the owner, which was Lipscomb.

White Hall was considered by some of the commissioners a suitable place for the new town. Others preferred a point about two miles further south, where the Orr Mill is now located. A Baptist church, Mt. Tabor, with its graveyard, was located there, and it was a popular gathering place.

Arguing the respective merits of the two sites the commissioners rode back and forth between them, until, becoming weary, they stopped at a backwoods bar which was about half way between the two. There they obtained stimulating refreshment, and watered their thirsty horses. The bar stood about where the Masonic Temple is now, and the spring from which they got water was very near the middle of the street between that place and Fleishman's store. Sitting around the door of the tavern discussing the matter on which they were engaged, all at once Mr. "Bobby" Norris got up, and walking some few feet away planted his heavy walking stick under a towering walnut tree, and exclaimed: "There shall be the southeast corner of the courthouse, and who says no, has got me to whip!" None of the gentlemen felt disposed to whip Mr. Norris, so on the spot of his selection stood the first courthouse, and those built subsequently have occupied almost the same place. The commissioners bought from Wm. Magee, Z. Chamblee, Manning Poole and H. Rice. The price paid was at the rate of $4.62½ per acre. One hundred and thirty acres were bought and fifty lots immediately sold for $8,145.00. The town was laid off by James Thompson, S. J. Hammond, J. E. Norris, Alexander Moorhead and L. L. Goode. A square for business was marked out, and on that same square much of Anderson's business is still transacted. Beyond, about three city blocks, they laid off four boundary streets, thinking they had given their embryo town plenty of room for growth. The contract for building the court house was given to Mr. Benjamin Denham, of the Brushy Creek section, and by him sublet to Mr. Robert Wilson, a brickmason of Greenville. Mr. Wilson moved his family to Anderson, and built a log house about where the Presbyterian manse is now; there he ran the first hotel in the place. Later he built on River street, where his family lived until recent years.

With Mr. Wilson when he came to Anderson was a son ten years old, Jeptha, who lived to become the oldest resident of the town of his time. He had seen Anderson in the making, and to his stories told to the younger generation is due much of the garnered lore of the community. Of the Wilson family so long identified with Anderson, Mrs. George Broyles alone remains now in the place.

The first courthouse was a square log building. Behind it was erected a high fence, which extended around and beyond the jail, which was located where Woolworth's Ten-Cent Store is now. Other space within the enclosure was occupied by stables, gardens, etc. The jail, also of logs, was a two-story structure. The sheriff lived on the first floor, and the prisoners were kept above.

The first court held in Anderson was on the third Monday in October, 1828. Hon. John S. Richardson presided; J. T. Lewis was clerk of the court, Theodore Gailliard foreman of the grand jury, John Reeves foreman of the petit jury No. 1, Walter C. Dickson foreman of jury No. 2. The first case tried was the State vs. William Eaton for assault and battery; verdict, guilty. Baylis J. Earle, later Judge Earle, was the solicitor.

Anderson used to punish her petty criminals by putting them in the pillory. One stood for years on the north side of the courthouse. Probably the last time that it was used was an occasion recollected by an old gentleman who died several years ago over ninety years of age. He said he remembered when he was a boy seeing a notorious drunkard and town nuisance pilloried. "Steve" mounted the platform with a grin, and after his head and hands were adjusted he called repeatedly to the jeering crowd below to throw him a "chaw o' backer." Before his release, however, he had become meek and quiet.

The first store in the new town stood on the extreme north end of the west side of the square, long known as "Brick Range." It was a general merchandise store owned by Mr. Samuel Earle, of "Evergreen," and managed by Mr. J. C. Griffin, who slept in the store. The building was a two-story wooden structure with a piazza all across the front. From the piazza the store was reached by several steps. Next in line was a one-story building occupied by Dr. Edmund Webb as a drug and book store, to which later was added the business of the postoffice. After that came the one-story printing office where Mr. J. P. Reed published Anderson's first newspaper. Next, the store, also one-story, kept by Cater and Rice. It stood about opposite the place occupied by the Confederate monument. Then came a gap of about twenty-five feet. On the south corner of the row stood another big two-story structure. It was also a general merchandise store kept by Mr. B. F. Mauldin, and later by his nephew who had been his clerk, Mr. Baylis F. Crayton. Horse racks in front of the stores, and horse blocks for the use of horseback riders in mounting and dismounting were indispensable adjuncts to every business house.

J. T. Lewis, the first clerk of the court, died February 11, 1833, while in office, and was succeeded by Mr. Van Lawhorn, who was also Anderson's second postmaster. The first was Macajah Webb.

He conducted the business of the postoffice in the courthouse. Mr. Van Lawhorn was succeeded as postmaster by Dr. Edmund Webb, and as clerk of the court by Mr. Elijah Webb, brothers. The postoffice and book store business remained in the same family for many years. Dr. Webb's son, the late T. J. Webb, was for a short time postmaster, and his wife was for a long time postmistress. Then Mrs. Webb's brother-in-law, the late Mr. George W. Fant, became postmaster. The Fant family has a commission issued to G. W. Fant in 1856 as postmaster. He had served before that time, but how long is uncertain. Mr. Fant was also commissioned postmaster by President Jefferson Davis of the Confederate States of America. After the war Mr. Fant, under radical rule, was ineligible to hold office, but his mother-in-law, Mrs. Williamston, was appointed postmistress and he continued to attend to the business. Until about sixteen years after the war between the states Mr. Fant continued the postoffice and book store business at the old stand of Dr. Edmund Webb. His successors in office have been Mrs. Grace Cochran, Mr. Charles Webb, Mr. W. F. Barr, Col. M. P. Tribble, Mr. W. W. Russell, Mr. John Cochran and Mr. Wm. Laughlin. Mr. Cochran held the office at the time of his death last fall. Mr. T. E. Howard is the present incumbent.

Mr. Elijah Webb was clerk of the court for nearly forty years. Since his death in 1865 the office has been filled by Captain John W. Daniels, whose wife was a daughter of Dr. Edmund Webb. He held the office for nineteen years. In 1884 he was succeeded by Colonel M. P. Tribble. His successor was Mr. John C. Watkins, who was succeeded by Mr. James Pearman, and he by Mr. John C. Taylor.

The first sheriff of Anderson county was G. E. Foster, who lived near Pendleton; his deputy was Perry McKinny, who practically ran the office. Then followed James McKinny, William Archer, A. N. McFall, John Martin, J. W. Guyton, J. D. M. Dobbins, J. B. McGee, William McGukin, James H. McConnell, William L. Bolt, M. B. Gaines, Nelson R. Green, W. B. King, Joseph M. H. Ashley, J. O. Sanders, Guerdon King, W. O. Marett and W. A. Clamp.

Judge Joseph N. Whitner represented Pendleton district in the state senate at the time of its division; and by the active interest taken in the measure, and his superintendence of details, he is understood to have been Anderson's chief sponsor, being regarded more than any other one person the founder of the place. Judge Whitner moved to Anderson in 1830. Out a little to the west of the new town lived a man named Zadoc Chamblee. His house, built of hewn logs and covered with oak boards, crowned a beautiful knoll. Judge Whitner bought the place, and used the strong log house as a nucleus for his own dwelling, which was considered a very fine mansion when completed. He weatherboarded over the logs, added rooms, piazzas and pillars, until the house assumed much its present appearance, only new and devoid of the age and ivy which now wraps it in a garment of living green. Mrs. Whitner, a flower lover, had the whole hill planted in roses, and named the place Rose Hill.

Before her marriage, Mrs. Whitner was Miss Elizabeth Harrison, of Andersonville.

On the Whitner place, which contained about nineteen acres, it is said a tree of every species known to grow in South Carolina was planted. Among others introduced into this section by Judge Whitner is the pecan.

Moses Chamblee, son of the original owner of Rose Hill, lived to be quite an old man; and he used to tell the younger people how in his boyhood he had often gone hunting on the site of the public square, and before breakfast had carried home a deer. Smaller game abounded, and on longer trips he often killed a bear.

A very early hotel stood on the lot now occupied by the G. F. Tolly residence. It is possible that Mr. Wilson lived there rather than across the street. However, from the first owner Dr. Edmund Webb purchased the place, and a part of the present house was erected by him. There his little daughter, Julia, was born. The little girl lived to see the village of her birth grow into a flourishing city. She was the late Mrs. J. W. Daniels. Her last home on the southwest corner of Church and McDuffie streets is one of the most attractive and popular places in Anderson. It is now the residence of her niece, Mrs. Julia von Hasseln. Across the street from Dr. Edmund Webb's residence, on the lot now occupied by the "Fowler Place," his brother, Mr. Elijah Webb, built a home, and there Mrs. Rebecca Hoyt, his daughter, was born—Anderson's first newspaper woman.

The next hotel was a more pretentious building. It stood on the corner of Benson and Main streets, now occupied by Evans Pharmacy No. 3. It was a long wooden building of two stories, running quite a distance down Main street. It had a long piazza in front, and there before the Benson House, the tri-weekly stage coach, running between Asheville and Augusta, was accustomed to stop with a flourish, heralded by every small boy in the place. The passengers alighted for dinner, and the horses, four in number, were changed. Among the best known stage drivers were Mr.

Moses Murphy and Mr. John Skelton, heroes in the envious eyes of the boys of the day.

The first owners of lots in the village of Anderson were J. P. Benson, Mr. McGill, Mr. Lipscomb, Samuel Maverick, K. Prince, Elias Earle, S. McQueen, J. Gray, D. Sloan, Micajah Webb, William Magee, W. S. Acker, Andrew McFall, J. Gilmore, Daniel Brown, J. Brown, Matthew Gambrell, Robert Wilson, J. N. Whitner, Christopher Orr, Mr. Mattison, G. E. W. Foster, D. H. Cochran, J. Rosamund, J. Thompson, R. F. Black, L. Barr, N. McCalister, W. Michiel, B. Durham, L. Goode, B. Duncan, D. Norris, J. Haney and J. Masters. They bought property at the first auction, Matthew Gambrell selling for the state, and buying several lots himself. The lots were laid off in half acres, and the town planned in squares.

The original grants on which the town of Anderson was built were made to William Turpin and Adam Crane Jones. Jones conveyed his to Bartholemew White, and Turpin conveyed his to Thomas Wadsworth, who bequeathed it to the Wadsworth School for the Poor in Laurens county. The school sold some of its inheritance, and leased some of it for ninety-nine years, thereby tying up and confusing titles very badly. The lease expired in the last years of the nineteenth century. Orr Mill is located on some of the Wadsworth property, and it is known to have extended as far as through the W. A. Chapman place on McDuffie street, and probably farther. It is said that at the time the lease expired, the late Mr. Robert Moorhead was the only living man who definitely knew the boundaries of the Wadsworth property; but he firmly declared that he would die before he would tell, and thereby disturb the security of innocent people in their homes.

Whatever Anderson may have become in recent years in the way of hotel accommodation, it was certainly well supplied in its early history. As just told, Mr. Robert Wilson operated the first inn of the new village. After him may have been one whose name has been lost who entertained travelers where the Old Tolly house now stands, or there may have been confusion as to where Mr. Wilson really lived in that neighborhood. Certainly there is a tradition that the Tolly house was originally a modest hotel. Soon Mr. H. Rice built the commodious hostelry later known as "The Benson House" on the southwest corner of the square and Main street. On the opposite side of South Main street, where the Bank of Anderson stands, Mr. Christopher Orr built a hotel, and operated it for years in connection with a general merchandise store, and the almost universal bar. Later Mr. Orr moved his hotel further down Benson street and built almost in the middle of the south side of the square. Some years later the house which he erected there was moved to South Manning street, where it is still standing, the home of Mrs. Julia Butler. It was the first, maybe the only house ever built in Anderson which had marble mantels, and it was one of the earliest if not the very first to indulge in the luxury of a basement. The basement rooms were used by Mr. Orr as office apartments.

On the site from which he had his dwelling moved, Mr. Orr built a new and for the time an elegant hotel. In 1876 the house, then become old and worn, was renovated, and in honor of the centennial year of the United States was named "The Centennial House."

On the site of the Plaza Hotel Mr. Daniel Brown kept a hotel known as "The Waverly House"; somebody in Anderson of that day appreciated Sir Walter. The hotel was a brick building of two stories, quite a handsome place when it was erected. A piazza ran across the whole front of the second story, and it was a favorite "loafing place." The hotel passed through many hands, until it disappeared to make room for a better successor.

In the great fire of 1845 both Mr. Benson's and Mr. Brown's hotels were burned. Both were rebuilt, and of course were better than before. Mr. Brown advertises that his new hotel on the west side of the square will contain 35 rooms. Mr. Benson superintended the making of the brick for his new hotel. It took about 530,000 brick. He advertises that now being ready for business he hopes for part of the favors, and states that he would endeavor to make his guests comfortable. He also gives his prices—Man per week, $3.50; man and horse per day, $1.25; man and horse per night, $1.00; single meal, 25 cents; lodging, 12 cents.

On October 20th, 1844, Mr. C. Orr advertises his town property for sale. He says: "The main building is situated on a two-acre lot adjoining the public square, fronting 54 feet on Main street, and 84 feet on Fifth street, containing twenty rooms and twelve fireplaces, handsomely finished, making it desirable as a commodious private or public boarding house. Immediately on the corner is a large store room well fitted, an excellent location for merchandising. Two law offices on Main street, kitchen, stables and carriage house, together with a small orchard of choice fruit trees, garden, etc."

In the late eighties was heard the wail, "no decent hotel in Anderson! Why doesn't somebody build a hotel! How can we expect traveling men to stop in Anderson if they can help it when we can offer them no better accommodations?" That old cry that most of us are familiar with.

HISTORY OF ANDERSON COUNTY

In 1887 Mr. Frank T. Wilhite got a company interested in the erection of a good hotel in Anderson. The old Waverly House was torn down and the new, elegant Chiquola took its place. It was finished in 1888 and on Tuesday, December 31, was formally dedicated with an imposing ball. The finance committee for the great occasion consisted of R. S. Ligon, B. F. Crayton, T. F. Hill, J. G. Cunningham and J. S. Fowler. Invitation committee: A. G. Means, Jr., Julian Bruce, Dr. S. M. Orr, F. T. Wilhite, R. S. Ligon, J. D. Maxwell. Banquet committee: B. W. Sperry, J. L. Mauldin, W. F. Cox. Committee of arrangements: F. T. Wilhite, J. L. Tribble, J. E. Peoples, W. B. Watson, W. W. Humphreys, J. A. Brock, J. J. Fretwell, J. D. Maxwell and W. G. Watson.

The afternoon train brought a large party of guests from Augusta, and people came from all the nearby towns. The newspaper write-up of the time says: "It was about 9 o'clock when the sweet strains of the Italian string band from Charlotte was heard, and in a short time twenty-five couples were on the floor anxious to 'trip the light fantastic.'

"Dr. S. M. Orr in his usual graceful style acted as floor manager, and the grand march opened with Mr. G. W. Evans and Miss Kate Marshall, of Abbeville, leading"—and so on and on, describing a very brilliant function. Other newspapers of the state congratulated Anderson on its beautiful, up-to-date hotel. It was said that there was no finer in the south.

Some of us remember when the poor Chiquola was abused and insulted in every possible way, very like some poor old people, it was outgrown, and had passed its useful days. B. W. Sperry was its first manager.

A few years ago it was freshened up, some changes made, and rechristened "The Plaza." Under that name it is still functioning, but its glory has departed.

On May 18th, 1925, Anderson's fine new modern hotel, The John C. Calhoun, was opened with a brilliant banquet.

CHAPTER III.

Some of the Pioneer People and Their Social Life.

ONE of the handsomest homes of Anderson's early days was that of Mr. Stephen McCully. Mr. McCully was an Irishman, and either he was brought up in a city, and his youthful eyes saw all elegant houses built directly on the street, and so he formed his idea of what was desirable, or he was brought up in the country, and to his country notions lawns, trees and yards were just ordinary things to be eschewed in building a real fine place. Whatever the reason, his house, an elegant one for the time, was built directly on the street. It stood just off the square. His former home was on what was long known as "McCully's corner," the place where Fant's drug store was located for years. And just back of it, fronting on Main street, was the new dwelling. A large two-story brick structure, it had a beautiful fan light over the front door, and the rooms were large and well adapted for entertaining.

Mr. McCully accumulated a good property for his time and locality. He owned a large section of the town on South Main street, and he donated to the city all of West Franklin street, opening up the street which, in the opinion of some people who know the history of the town, should have borne his name. A parallel street to Franklin is called McCully, but it is of less importance than Franklin. The site for the Johnson university was purchased from him, and he was a strong friend and advocate of the school.

Another of Anderson's noted citizens in the early days was Major Joseph Tyler Whitfield, lawyer and magistrate. A man of strong personality, Tyler Whitfield was quoted, and had amusing stories told about him long after death had removed him from among the living. His son, "Squire" John C. Whitfield, was also a person of distinctive qualities; his home stood where Mr. J. L. McGee's house is now. The old Whitfield home was rolled further down the street, and is now used as a boarding house. Squire Whitfield was a man who had many warm friends, some bitter enemies, but was never ignored. He had been born and brought up in this community. He knew all of the people who had made Anderson; knew all of their weaknesses and foibles, and had a keen intelligence which fully recognized all that he saw.

He wrote his recollections of persons and events, a history of early Anderson which doubtless contained much that can never be recovered now. But he said he did not dare to print it while he was alive, he would be mobbed. His partner in business at one time, Mr. E. A. Bell, said that he had seen the manuscript, and that it was racy. He laughed very much when he told about it. The squire left it to be published after his death, but his gentle daughter, Mrs. Ella Jones, had the manuscript destroyed. She felt that it would be unkind to publish it. However, it is a great pity that she did not have it edited, and in that way cut out the unnecessary and hurtful part, and preserve the history which he knew so fully, and which is entirely lost now.

Among the first dwellings in the place was that of Dan Cochran, a lame peddler of cheap jewelry. It stood where the jail is located. On his peddling trips old Dan Cochran used to ride a white mule. LeRoy Barr lived on the southwest corner of Church and Main streets.

Manning Poole owned a large tract of land which included the sites of Miss Varina Brown's residence, that of Mrs. B. F. Mauldin, the old Edwards Murray place, included all the land around Judge Cox's and Mr. E. P. Vandiver's residences; almost the whole of Anderson from the railroad cut to Greenville street, and from Fant street to the interurban railroad as it skirts the western portion of the city. The spring now known as Murray's spring was first called Poole's, then Harrison's before it became Murray's. It was always a popular rendezvous with the young people. Mr. Poole's home stood very near where that of Mrs. Mauldin is now.

The first sidewalk in Anderson was merely a smoothed down path at the side of the dirt road which has developed into Main street. It ran between the square and Greenville street on the east side of the road. It was the grand promenade of the young people, and on May Day, a popular holiday in the early times, there was a throng of pretty girls in pretty dresses marching on the sidewalk to the Benson house where there was always a May party. The only boy allowed in the parade was the one who marched at its head carrying the May pole. Arrived at the hotel there were recitations, speeches and the May pole dance, and the crowning of the May queen. The affair ended in a feast.

A two-plank bridge across a small gully was the first bridge in the town. It was just in front of the spot where Mrs. J. L. Tribble's residence now stands. There was no break where the railroad cut runs which was North Boundary street, and the cut was made twenty years later when the railroad was laid.

A great source of entertainment for the Anderson people in the 40s was horse racing. The track was somewhere near the Orr Mill site. A great ring it was, and the jockeys were little black boys fantastically garbed. Everybody attended the races, and people came from some distance for the event. Much money is said to have changed hands at those times.

Our forefathers took as much interest in debating societies as do high school pupils. Societies were formed of which the leading men of the town were members, taking an active part in the exercises. Public debates were held on every conceivable subject, political, social, religious, literary and nondescript. They were held on Friday evenings in the court house, and all the fashionable and unfashionable people attended. All men, however; women in those days were not expected to be heard in public; they went to listen to their sweethearts, brothers and even to their fathers. In fact, the older men so dominated the first society that the younger men formed another where they might have a chance.

However, even in those halcyon days, people got tired of what they had, and sought for some new entertainment.

About 1832 interest had lagged in the debating societies to such an extent that Mr. Peter Vandiver, a brilliant lawyer of the time, was appointed to discover if possible the cause of the loss of interest. His report is to the effect that he thought "perhaps the discussions have sometimes been too long; on the other hand auditors may sometimes have been so precocious and supersensitive as to take offense where none was intended." Also, "some of the members on each side had fallen into the habit of making no preparation, depending on others to study the subject, then when they were called upon to speak, consuming much time in apologies."

The society was reorganized Friday, December 20th, 1843, J. P. Reed in the chair. Officers were elected for two months. President, J. H. Creswell; vice-president, J. L. Mauldin; secretary and treasurer, J. L. Orr.

At one of its meetings the subject under discussion was "Should the interest on money be regulated by law?" Affirmative, Messrs. Peter Vandiver, Tyler Whitfield, J. P. Reed and Ibzen Rice. Negative, Messrs. Brownlee, J. L. Orr and J. N. Whitner. Decided by the president for the affirmative.

But the people of Anderson were not solely dependent upon their own efforts for entertainment. They seem to have been a serious-minded set and attended with interest lectures and debates that their descendants could not be driven into with whips.

Judge John Belton O'Neall was president of the State Temperance Society, and it was his influence and personality, probably, which made temperance societies so popular in his day. Anderson had one, all of the well known names of the time were found on its rolls.

In 1840 there was a Library Association formed. Peter Vandiver, chairman; Wesley Leverette, J. L. Orr, J. T. Whitfield and Jesse Norris, working members. How it was managed no one knows. Probably it was something like a reading club, where the members each bought a book, and passed it around. There have been numerous other library societies started in Anderson, all short-lived until the present, which was enabled to live by the generosity of Andrew Carnegie and Col. J. N. Brown.

In 1841 Anderson established a Bible Society. It met in the Baptist church, but was interdenominational, and its object was to supply Bibles to every person in the county who had none. Four battalions were formed to canvass the four sections of the county in order to find out where they should be placed. Application was made to the Bible Society of Charleston for 306 Bibles to begin with. That society lasted for thirty or more years.

On February 8, 1843, a lecture was given in the "Long Room" of the Benson House, which seems to have been the only hall of any kind in the town except the courthouse. The subject was "Animal Magnetism." The newspaper of the time says: "While his performance was not altogether satisfactory, he convinced his audience that there is something in animal magnetism."

Military companies abounded throughout the county, and there are in the early papers many calls for them to meet and drill. In 1843 John B. Wynne was captain of the Anderson Troop of Cavalry.

The Fourth of July was always celebrated before the war between the states with great festivities in Anderson. There is an account of the celebration of 1843 in the Benson Long Room. There was a grand feast, many toasts were given and responded to. At the height of the entertainment, the old stage driver, Moses Murphy, entered the room to look on at the fun. Catching sight of him, J. T. Richards proposed a toast to him, eulogizing him as a benefactor to the traveling public. The roar which greeted the toast was deafening, the old man was pushed forward to respond. He said he was no orator, but if "Captain Jack" would call for a few bottles of wine, he would see that they were paid for.

All of the debating and studying and speaking was not done in the town of Anderson. The county had its share. In Pendleton there had been all of the social activities for many years, but also in the new county there grew up various enterprises.

One of the earliest library associations formed in the county was

HISTORY OF ANDERSON COUNTY

at Calhoun. Wesley Leverette called a public meeting one Saturday in 1841 in the Academy building, and a library association was formed for the benefit of the school, and also for the use of the public. There was also a debating society at Calhoun called the Philological Society, K. Breazeale its secretary.

In the same neighborhood there was a Farmers' Society formed about 1845.

In July, 1845, "The New York Zoological Exhibition" showed in Anderson for one day only.

One of the landmark homes torn away just a few years ago stood where Mr. Clyde Stone's automobile show rooms are located. Originally a part of the Manning Poole property, it was bought by Mr. Wilson Van Lawhorn. A gin house stood on the lot. Mr. Van Lawhorn married Miss Archer, and as a wedding present her father built for the young couple a commodious house on Mr. Van Lawhorn's lot. The young people loved company and sport of every kind, and kept open house in the old time style. A lady who died in Anderson a few years ago, over ninety years old, said that the first dancing she ever saw was in the Van Lawhorn home. It consisted of the Virginia reel, cotillions and contra dances.

After the Van Lawhorns moved away, Mrs. Mahala Hubbard lived for a time in the house. While it was her residence her daughter married an Earle, and celebrated in the house a big and fashionable wedding.

In 1836 Samuel Cherry bought the place. Later it became the property of Dr. Cater, "the beloved physician" to many of the early Andersonians. After he moved, the Bensons owned it. Mrs. Benson, who before her marriage was Kitty Sloan, was a great lover of flowers, and had glorious gardens at both ends of the house. Mrs. Benson, as most people of the time did, accommodated boarders for the Johnson University. From that beginning she opened her house to others. She had already had the experience of helping her husband keep the Benson Hotel. During the war Mrs. Benson had boarding with her Miss Lillie Roper, of Charleston, and again was the old house the setting for a spectacular wedding when Miss Roper became the bride of Judge James Munro, a widower, and for a time one of Anderson's most prominent men. He came from the lower part of the state and bought land from Judge Whitner on which he built a house which is still standing, facing Monroe street on the western edge of the city. The street took its name from the judge, not from the president of the United States as people not knowing the history of the town suppose. And the name is spelled wrong.

HISTORY OF ANDERSON COUNTY

Judge Munro had two children when he came to Anderson, a son and a daughter. The daughter, "Miss Maggie," was a very aristocratic and exclusive young lady.

The son met with a tragic death soon after the Blue Ridge road was built from Pendleton to Anderson. An excursion was run, on which most of the young people went. The train had just crossed the creek near the Blue Ridge yards when the young man, who stood on the rear platform, was thrown from the train, and his head striking a rock, he was instantly killed.

The Munros left Anderson soon after the war between the states and went to live in Union.

Anderson's first doctors were Alexander Evans and A. P. Cater. For a time the two were in partnership, but later each practiced alone. Both were greatly beloved by their patients. Dr. Evans was a bachelor. They were what was called at that time "calomel doctors," that is, they gave medicine, usually at least tinctured with calomel. The other kind were "steam doctors," who "sweated" out an illness. Dr. Cater was a married man, and his family once lived in the old Van Lawhorn house.

Another interesting person who once boarded in the house was a Polish countess, banished from her native land in some political upheaval. She was first Madam Girard, later Mrs. Pinkind. In her youth she sang beautifully and was studying for the operatic stage, but from an illness she lost her voice, and spent the greater part of her life teaching music in Anderson and Pendleton. It is said that she was the first woman to play the violin on the stage in America, having taken part in a concert in New York, where she played on that instrument. Mrs. Pinkind went to Charleston, and from there, with the influx of low country people coming up for the summer, she landed in Pendleton, and from there came to Anderson.

Her children were Antoinette, known as "Nettie," and Anthony, known as "Tony." Miss Nettie Pinkind married Mr. Norton Hunter, of Pendleton.

A daughter of the Bensons, Mary, married first a Sloan, and afterwards a Sadler, and she became the owner of the house. There she lived for many years with her sons, Mr. Ed Sloan and Mr. John Sadler. Mr. D. P. Sloan is also her son.

Another popular home of early days was that of Colonel James Harrison. He lived first in the house purchased from Mr. Poole about where the Mauldin home stands; later his residence was where Judge Cox's house is now. In the Harrison family were several daughters, and his home was one of the gayest in the community.

Anderson seems to have existed very comfortably without policemen until 1840. By that time the town had grown to quite a little place, and there was mischief enough brewing for the citizens to need protection, so they elected Hugh McKinney the first policeman. The courthouse was the seat of the town government as well as that of the county. Where the city hall stands was a blacksmith shop, kept by Alfred Moore. Another blacksmith shop was located on the site of the Bleckley building.

The first child born in the town of Anderson was the late Dr. Ben Brown, of Williamston. He was the son of Daniel Brown and his first wife, Rhoda Acker. At the time of this son's birth Mr. Brown lived in the house built by Mr. McCully on the corner where Fant's drug store long stood. It was a two-story wooden structure with a long piazza across the front. In later years it was the tailor shop of Messrs. Clark and Smith, and still later the merchant tailor firm of J. R. and L. P. Smith.

Anderson's first furniture dealer was Ezekiel George, styled in that day cabinet maker. He married Miss Betty Poole. A few years after establishing his business in Anderson, Mr. George found that he needed an assistant, and he employed a young foreigner who was living in Greenville, George Frederick Tolly, who was born in Prussia November 7th, 1835, and emigrated to America with his parents in 1850. He learned his trade of cabinet maker in Baltimore and came to South Carolina about 1856, living for one year in Greenville. On May 24, 1859, Mr. Tolly married his employer's daughter, Miss Mary Jane George. For sixty years that couple were honored citizens of the growing city. The first seventeen years of their married life was spent in a little home on the site of Tolly's great store, and their furniture shop adjoined it. Then Mr. Tolly bought the Webb house, where the remainder of his life was passed. Mr. Tolly succeeded to the business of his father-in-law, and lived to see it develop into one of the largest furniture establishments in the state. Tolly's Furniture Store and Fant's Book Store are the oldest business houses in the town. They were started about the same time, and both grew out of previous businesses.

In writing the most modest history of any place it is always the men who are mentioned. But those quiet, useful women who remained in the homes and did well their part, are also largely responsible for the growth, prosperity and tone of a community; and while it is right to tell what "Mayor Tolly" was to Anderson, it is just as well to tell also something about "Mrs. Mayor Tolly." A strong, true woman; devoted member of the First Presbyterian Church. The kindest possible neighbor and a firm friend; she was a most useful woman in her day, and as she grew old, her kindly face and cordial smile were good to see. At the time of her death she left four children, thirteen grandchildren and five great grandchildren; truly she may be regarded as one of the founders of the city.

Mr. Tolly might be called Chronic Mayor of Anderson. He served two years as Intendant before the city was incorporated, and afterwards was mayor from 1884-87, 1890-97, 1900-02, when he retired, not running for the office any more. Mr. Tolly served in the Confederate army throughout the war in Company B, Fourth South Carolina Volunteer Regiment. He became greatly endeared to numbers of the soldiers whom he nursed back to health. His wonderful ability as a nurse for the sick and wounded became so well known that it was officially recognized, and he was often detailed to that duty; always to the delight of the sick soldiers.

Anderson's first jeweler, or watchmaker, was Mr. Samuel Owens. His shop was located in a building on South Main street, the east side between the square and Church street. It was known as "The Broyles Building." Mr. Owens married Miss Jane Robinson, of Pendleton. Mrs. Owens' mother, Mrs. Eliza Robinson, after her husband's death, came to Anderson, and on the corner of Church and McDuffie street, now occupied by the house of Mr. J. J. Fretwell, opened a boarding house for students of the Johnson Seminary and its later development, the Johnson University. Long after the school had passed away, Mrs. Robinson still kept a boarding house in the long, old fashioned house with a piazza across the front. She had a lovely flower garden at the end of the house away from McDuffie street.

Mr. and Mrs. Owens lived in a house which stood somewhat further back on the lot now occupied by the home of Mrs. Elizabeth Harrison on Evins Street. There for several years the young couple lived, and there were born to them three children, a son and two daughters. One unhappy afternoon the wife and mother, worn out with suffering from an aching tooth, took some sedative, and while she slept the house caught fire and she was burned to death. After the tragedy Mr. Owens took the children and went to Florida where he died. One of the daughters is still living in that state.

In the jewelry business succeeding Mr. Owens came Mr. W. K. Harris. Then the firm of Daniels and Reece. With them Mr.

John Hubbard learned the business, and the first shop that he opened for himself was in the building on South Main street once occupied by Mr. Owens.

Several years before the war between the states a young German, Frederick C. von Borstell, came to Anderson from Athens, Georgia, and opened a jewelry establishment. He prospered and after the war owned the building in which his shop was located, as well as several other store rooms. On the second floor was a comfortable apartment occupied by his family. He had married Miss Cassandra Hewitt, a music teacher in the Johnson University; and in her apartment on the west side of the square, Mrs Borstell gave music lessons for many years. Her daughters were Alice, who married J. D. Maxwell, and Christine, who married after leaving Anderson. The two sisters are now living in California. The block of stores and offices on the west side of the square known as the Maxwell building was once a part of the von Borstell estate. Mrs. Maxwell was a talented pianist, and for many years no musical affair in Anderson was conducted without her help.

An early settler who bequeathed his name to a section on the outskirts of the town was Robert Gordon. He owned the land on which the postoffice and library now stands. He also owned property where is located the home of the late Boyce Burriss, and it is that section which was long known as "Gordonville."

Mr. Lipscomb, one of the original buyers, lived for a time at Whitehall, and later built the house known as "the Old Towers House" on Whitner street. On a corner of that lot Dr. Alexander Evans, a famous physician of the early time, had a one-room office.

The handsome home of Mr. S. A. McCown, just east of the city, is built on land once owned by Mr. Samuel Brown, brother of Mr. Daniel Brown, and father of the late Colonel J. N. Brown, who was born about where the McCown garage now stands. Mr. Samuel Brown later moved to the Townville section.

One of the earliest homes in the village was located just north of the railroad cut. Built by a Mr. Drennan, it was bought, altered and greatly improved by B. F. Mauldin. After a few years spent in the mercantile business in Anderson Mr. Mauldin determined to move to Shady Grove at Calhoun; at the same time J. P. Reed, of Calhoun, determined to move to Anderson; consequently Mr. Mauldin sold his Anderson house to Mr. Reed who lived there when he first made Anderson his home. It was later bought by Mr. John B. Watson, and was long known as the old Watson place. It was a handsome house when it was built, and was almost surrounded by piazza, a long one wound around three sides of the house. A handsome flower garden stretched from the house to the street.

After a time Mr. Reed built the most artistic home that has ever been built in Anderson on South Main street; the house is gone, but a part of the beautiful shrubbery remains. He had a real English garden, and while Anderson has had many beautiful flower gardens, there has never been one quite as perfect as the old Reed garden at "Echo Hall."

Mr. Reed had a large family of daughters, and his house was not only a center of hospitality, but also of gayety. Mr. Reed himself often played the violin for dances at his home.

He brought from Calhoun the first newspaper to be published in the town. After a few years of newspaper work in the town he sold the paper, and devoted himself to the practice of law, in which he was very successful. He had a number of partners at different times, among them Judge Orr, Peter Vandiver, S. M. Wilkes, Colonel J. N. Brown and J. L. Orr, Jr.

He represented Anderson in the legislature and the senate. He was a member of the Secession Convention. If Mr. Tolly might be called the chronic mayor of Anderson, Colonel Reed might be called the chronic intendant. He served many terms in that capacity, and strenuously insisted upon people keeping their premises clean. In this day when everybody almost automatically keeps neat surroundings it is hard to realize that in those early days, with the exception of the few persons of culture and taste who had flower gardens and clean back yards, dirty premises, and, more especially, dirty streets, were the rule. Hogs roamed at will, and the notion of keeping them up, and attending to the out of doors part of one's home was rather resented by the hoi-polloi, but repeatedly in the newspapers there is a peremptory order from the intendant that the people keep their premises clean, shut hogs and cows in pens, and keep the streets in front of their dwellings in good condition.

Judge Reed was one of the most brilliant men Anderson ever produced. He started life handicapped, and overcame every obstacle. He attended Calhoun Accademy when Wesley Leverette was its teacher, and made good use of his opportunity. Finding privacy hard to obtain, the boy made use of a huge red oak, into which he used to climb in order to study in peace. The oak is still pointed out at old Calhoun.

When he came to Anderson he soon attained a position of eminence and influence. His fine taste expressed itself in all of the really good public buildings in the village of his time, for he was endowed by nature with artistic appreciation, and a talent for both music and painting which he transmitted to many of his descendants. In his youth he was a famous "fiddler." His eldest daughter, Mrs. Emilia Miller, had a remarkable voice. She taught music for a time at her alma mater, Johnson University. Her son, Reed Miller, attained a national reputation as a singer. Several of her other children also sang well.

Another of Judge Reed's daughters, Mrs. Cora Ligon, has for many years delighted Anderson people with her beautiful singing, and his grand daughter, Mrs. Helen Ligon, has a voice of unusual beauty and sweetness. Others of his children and grandchildren have been gifted in music and art. Most notable is Mrs. Lily Strickland Anderson, whose playing, even as a young girl, was remarkable, and who has become a composer of songs which are well known throughout the country. Mrs. Mamie Brown Mattison is an artist of no mean ability.

Colonel Reed was elected circuit judge of the first circuit, and went for a short time to live in Charleston.

The first intendant of Anderson is said by some people to have been Judge Whitner, by others, Dr. Edmund Webb. Certainly both of those men served at a very early date. When the big fire occurred in 1845 Mr. Reed was intendant, how long he had been in office, or whether that was his first term cannot be known, as the town records were in his office at the time, and were burned. In the fall of 1845, he was succeeded by Judge Whitner, who served until 1849, when Colonel Reed was again elected to the office which he filled until 1851 when Mr. B. F. Crayton succeeded him. In 1853 J. W. Harrison became intendant. In 1855 Colonel Reed was returned to the office and served until 1857 when Colonel John V. Moore was elected. In 1858 Joe Berry Sloan became intendant. In 1860 the office was filled by Samuel Wilkes, who was filling it when he went into the Confederate army in 1861. After his departure Dr. P. A. Wilhite acted intendant pro tem. until the time came for a new election when Colonel Reed was again called to the position. He filled the office then until 1866 when J. Scott Murray was elected. With him the records cease, because soon after the reconstruction period set in when no records were kept. During that time John Cochran was intendant, probably for the whole time, though it is possible that some others might have occupied the position at short intervals.

During the years between 1845 and 1856 many of Anderson's citizens served on the town council. Among them were Stephen McCully, repeatedly elected. W. B. Gibson served under various intendants, J. R. Smith, B. F. Crayton, Fleetwood Rice, A. M. Hol-

HISTORY OF ANDERSON COUNTY

land, S. M. Wilkes, A. L. Osborn. J. B. Clark, J. W. Harrison, William N. Fant, J. F. Wilson, S. A. Langston, B. F. Harlin, Lawson T. Arnold, Mr. Arnold also served several periods as intendant pro tem., Isham W. Taylor, J. E. England, Sylvester Bleckley, R. H. Hubbard, T. J. Webb, B. F. Brown, N. K. Sullivan, P. A. Cater, Thomas S. Crayton, C. C. Langston, P. A. Wilhite, E. W. Brown, A. B. Towers, J. A. Hoyt, W. H. Nardin, Fant, Whitner and White (no initials given).

A page of the old minute book neatly marked with a black border and inscribed in large beautifully formed letters is sacred to the memory of John Hunter Creswell, who died while a member of the council. It was written by Judge Reed, who was intendant at the time.

A. O. Norris was elected clerk of the town council in 1846 and served until 1856 when he was succeeded by Sylvester Bleckley who served until the reconstruction period.

Much of the business before those councils was appointing patrol companies to serve a month at a time. All of the men of the town were eligible for that duty, and captains were appointed with some thirty or forty men under them to patrol the village. In course of time the patrols became "Paterols" and accounts for the familiar couplet of long age, "Run Nigger, Run! ur de padero' ul git yer."

The most frequent petition made to the council is for a license to sell "spirituous liquors," and some of the persons applying would in later years have been mortified had they realized that there existed indisputable evidence that they once sold whiskey.

The cases tried before the council were mostly for drunkenness, though it is surprising how often some of the leading citizens are on trial for street fights. Several times the records tell of some man being brought before the body upon charge of drunkenness and disturbing the peace, and it continues—"he was suffered by the council to give leg bail for the present, which he did in a hurry." Some of them were tried and fined for "hollowing," also for "halloeing", moreover for speeding—some of the young bloods persistently "ran horses" through the town.

In 1882 Anderson was incorporated, and has since that time been governed by mayor and aldermen.

February 9, 1882, to August 21, 1882—Mayor Hon. W. H. Nardin: Alderman—J. F. Clinkscales, G. W. Fant, J. M. Payne, O. H. P. Fant.

August 21, 1882, to August 15, 1884—Mayor Hon. D. S.

[29]

HISTORY OF ANDERSON COUNTY

Maxwell: Aldermen—W. D. Brown, John E. Peoples, J. M. Smith, A. S. Stephens, S. M. Orr, R. L. Moorhead.

August 15, 1884, to August 15, 1886—Mayor Hon. G. F. Tolly: Aldermen—J. S. Fowler, B. F. Mauldin, Foster Fant, F. M. Murphy, J. L. Farmer, J. M. Payne.

August 15, 1886, to August 15, 1888—Mayor Hon. G. F. Tolly: Aldermen—J. L. McGee, J. M. Payne, Thos. F. Hill, C. F. Jones, Foster Fant, J. G. Cunningham.

August 15, 1888, to August 12, 1890—Mayor Hon. James L. Tribble: Aldermen—John M. Hubbard, John T. Baker, Frank T. Wilhite, W. W. Humphreys, G. Ernest Brown, Felix E. Watkins.

August 15, 1890, to August 14, 1892—Mayor Hon. G. F. Tolly; Aldermen—P. K. McCully, J. R. Vandiver, B. F. Moss, A. G. Means, A. C. Strickland, C. C. Langston.

August 16, 1892, to August 15, 1894—Mayor Hon. G. F. Tolly: Aldermen B. F. Moss, J. P. Duckett, A. C. Strickland, S. D. Brownlee, W. D. Brown.

August 15, 1894, to August 14, 1896—Mayor Hon. G. F. Tolly: Aldermen J. P. Duckett, Thos. F. Hill, J. M. Sullivan, R. E. Ligon, J. Reece Fant, W. R. Dillingham.

August 15, 1896, to August 14, 1898—Mayor Hon. G. F. Tolly: Aldermen W. R. Hubbard, J. T. Burriss, M. Kennedy, B. F. Wilson, J. M. Smith, T. D. Mullinax, J. M. Payne.

August 15, 1898, to August 15, 1900—Mayor Hon. John K. Hood: Aldermen: R. E. Ligon, C. S. Sullivan, W. F. Cox, G. W. Evans, F. G. Brown, J. M. Smith.

August 15, 1900, to August 15, 1902—Mayor Hon. G. F. Tolly: Aldermen: F. G. Brown, M. Kennedy, C. S. Sullivan, J. M. Patrick, H. C. Townsend, R. E. Ligon.

August 15, 1902, to August 15, 1904—Mayor Hon. J. M. Sullivan: Aldermen: J. L. Brissey, L. P. Smith, J. C. Harris, J. J. Norris, Lee G. Holleman, R. E. Ligon.

August 15, 1904, to August 15, 1906—Mayor Hon. J. M. Sullivan; Aldermen W. L. Brissey, W. H. Nardin, Jr., W. R. Osborne, O. B. VanWyck, C. W. Webb, Lee G. Holleman, R. E. Ligon.

August 15, 1906, to August 18, 1908—Mayor Hon. P. K. McCully, Sr.: Aldermen: J. E. Barton, W. R. Osborne, W. W. Robinson, C. E. Tolly, J. T. Pearson, R. E. Ligon.

August 18, 1908, to August 18, 1910—Mayor Hon. J. L. Sherard: Aldermen: T. S. Crayton, B. B. Bleckley, W. W. Robinson, C. E. Tolly, J. T. Pearson, W. C. Broadwell.

August, 18, 1910, to August 15, 1912—Mayor Hon. J. L. Sherard:

Aldermen: J. E. Barton, C. M. McClure, J. L. Hembree, C. E. Tolly, U. G. Salla, W. C. Broadwell.

August 15, 1912, to August 11, 1914—Mayor Hon. Lee G. Holleman; Aldermen: E. E. Elmore, C. M. McClure, C. F. Spearman, L. P. Fouche, W. F. Farmer, R. L. Carter.

August 11 1914, to August 8, 1916—Mayor Hon. J. H. Godfrey: Aldermen: J. E. Barton, Walter Dobbins, C. F. Spearman, J. H. Tate, R. R. King, R. L. Carter.

August 8, 1916, to August 7, 1918—Mayor, Hon. J. H. Godfrey: Aldermen: Walter Dobbins, C. F. Spearman, J. H. Tate, R. R. King, W. E. Atkinson, R. L. Carter.

August 7, 1918, to August 3, 1920—Mayor Hon. J. H. Godfrey: Aldermen: R. E. Burriss, Foster Fant, McDuffie Irwin, Levi N. Geer, J. T. Pearson, R. L. Carter.

August 3, 1920, to August 10, 1922—Mayor Hon. Foster Fant: Aldermen R. E. Burriss, J. D. Rast, J. Mack Beck, John S. Cromer, H. A. Powell, R. L. Carter.

August 10, 1922, to August 12, 1924—Mayor, Hon. W. A. Speer: Aldermen: G. E. Marchbanks, J. D. Rast, W. S. Divver, J. Reed Fowler, W. P. Drennan, J. Herman Dixon.

August 12, 1924, to August, 1926—Mayor Hon. Foster Fant: Alderman: R. E. Burris, W. T. Bailey, W. Harry McLeskey, J. Reed Fowler, W. P. Drennon, R. L. Carter.

August, 1926, to present time, 1928, Mayor, Hon. Foster Fant.

Another of the early beautiful and hospitable homes in the little village was that of Mr. Samuel Earle who later moved to his country home "Evergreen"; it was the colonial house on South Main street now the home of the Acker family. Mr. Earle built the house, and Mrs. Earle had there one of the most beautiful gardens of the time. Where Mrs. Chenault's house stands was a pond, and there aquatic plants were cultivated.

Mr. Daniel Brown in his later years built a home on South Main street which in his day was without the limits of the town. It was long known as "the old Wardlaw place," having been the inheritance of Mr. Brown's daughter, Mrs. C. C. Wardlaw. Like all of the homes of the well-to-do, prominent people of the time, it was surrounded by a fine garden. The old gabled house was attractive in its prime. A few years later it was remodeled and rolled some distance north of its former site and nearer to the street. There it stands today.

Sometime in those years preceding the war between the states, Dr. P. A. Wilhite built his home on South McDuffie street. Still a handsome residence.

CHAPTER IV.
THE CHURCHES.

PRESBYTERIAN.

FOR a time after reaching the wilderness the settlers had no churches. Like all new communities, those of the same faith met at each other's homes sometimes, to keep alive their own form of worship, and occasionally to hear an itinerant preacher. Often he stood in the door of the dwelling, addressing a congregation scattered about the cleared ground very often armed in preparation for an Indian raid.

Sometimes a rude arbor was erected under which the services were held. These traveling preachers came from North Carolina, Virginia, or even Pennsylvania; riding horseback and stopping in whatever homes they could reach at night. Occasionally, both man and beast spent the night under the stars.

The first church erected in what is now Anderson county, was of the Presbyterian faith. It was called Hopewell, later Hopewell Keowee, and located in the hamlet of Pendleton. It was built in 1785, a rude log structure without windows or means of heating; as were all of the early churches. Sometimes they had a great open place left at one end to admit light and air.

Hopewell congregation worshiped there until 1799, when they built a new house several miles from Pendleton. This structure was of rough native stone, some of it hauled from quite a distance. It soon became better known as "The Stone Church." It was there that General Pickens and General Robert Anderson worshiped, and is now universally called "The Old Stone Church." They with Major Dickson were its first elders, Mr. Simpson was its pastor, and all of them were Revolutionary soldiers. But with its removal from its first situation it passed out of Anderson county history. In its adjoining graveyard rest many of the leading men of the early days of South Carolina, and several soldiers of the Revolution.

In 1792 Rev. Thomas Reece was called to the pastorate of Hopewell and Carmel churches, which call he accepted. Carmel at that time consisted of about six families, and Hopewell of about forty. Dr. Reece wrote of them at the time: "The people who compose these two congregations are in general remarkable for the great simplicity of their manners, the plainness of their dress and their frugal manner of living. At the distance of two hundred and fifty miles from the capital they are strangers to luxury and refinement. Blest with a healthful climate, brought up in habits of labor and industry, and scarce of money, they are for the most part, clothed in homespun, nourished by the produce of their own farms, and happily appear to have neither taste nor inclination for high and expensive living. There is quite a degree of equality among them. By far the greater part are in what might be called the middle station in life. None are very rich, few slaves among them, and those are treated with kindness and humanity. They enjoy all that liberty which is compatible with their situation, and are exempted from that rigorous bondage to which their unhappy countrymen in the lower part of the state are subjected. These are all circumstances favorable to virtue and religion, and give ground to hope that they will flourish long here when they shall have been banished from those parts of the country where slavery, luxury and wealth have taken possession. As the country is in its infancy we have yet to expect that these congregations soon will become stronger, and in the course of a few years if peace continues, it is possible that each of them will be able to support a minister."

Dr. Reece was a man of learning who had ministered so much to the bodies as well as the souls of his congregation, that he attained a fair degree of excellence as a physician. A gentle, kindly man, he was greatly beloved by his parishioners. Dying in 1796 at the age of fifty-four years, he was the first person to be buried in the Old Stone Church yard. The degree D.D. was conferred on him by Princeton University.

In that old grave yard lie Andrew Pickens, "Printer John Miller" and several other distinguished men.

The site of the original Hopewell church is marked by a marble shaft.

In 1788 both a Presbyterian and a Baptist church were built in what is now Anderson county. The Presbyterian was "Brad-a-way," Broadaway, and finally Broadway, situated near the Abbeville line. Reverend Robert Hall was its first pastor, a man of education, as were all of the Presbyterian clergymen, and most of them were also teachers. The famous Moses Waddell was a Presbyterian minister. He had been taught by the Reverend Francis Cummins, who in his turn was a pupil of the renowned Dr. James Hall, who called his school "Clio's Nursery."

Robert Hall, Robert Mechlin and W. C. Davis were ordained in the old Bradaway church. The congregation was organized by Rev. Daniel T. Thatcher. In April, 1795, the church forwarded a request to Presbytery for the services of James Gilleland. The request was granted, and on the 20th of July a session of Presbytery was held for his ordination. At this meeting, however, a remonstrance signed by eleven or twelve persons was presented against his ordination on the ground that he had preached against slavery, and would continue to do so. Finally he consented to yield to the voice of Presbytery as to the voice of God, and submit to its council to be silent on that subject unless the consent of Presbytery could be obtained. At a meeting of the Synod of the Carolinas held at Morganton, N. C., November 3, 1796, Mr. Gilleland stated his conscientious difficulties in receiving the advice of the Presbytery of South Carolina which had enjoined on him silence on the subject of slavery, which injunction Mr. Gilleland declared to be in his opinion contrary to the counsel of God. After consideration the Synod concurred with the Presbytery, and advised Mr. Gilleland to content himself with using his utmost endeavor in private to open the way for emancipation. That intrepid preacher, however, could not reconcile his mind to a residence where slavery prevailed, and after a time he resigned his charge and went to Ohio. He was a southern man of Scotch-Irish ancestry, born in Lincoln county, N. C., October 28, 1769. Fitted for college by W. C. Davis, of South Carolina, and graduated from Dickenson College in 1792. Mr. Gilleland was a cheerful, social man, and even those who differed from him had a high regard for him, and perfect confidence in his high character.

The old Bradaway Church after several removals finally settled in Belton, and is today the Belton Presbyterian Church.

In 1789 Roberts Church was built, Rev. John Simpson, Princeton graduate, becoming its first pastor. It was first known as "Simpson's Meeting House." Later it acquired the name of Roberts, just how or why is not definitely known, though there is a tradition that it was so called in honor of a Revolutionary soldier. No one now living knows who he was, or why he was so honored.

Mr. Simpson was one of those traveling preachers who rode on horseback from Pennsylvania to South Carolina. He had been a soldier in the Revolution, and could fight as well as pray. To him the Presbyterian Church in South Carolina owed its first use of hymns as well as psalms in its worship. His innovation met with great opposition, but finally triumphed. The new tunes in Watts' Book of Psalms and Hymns met with even greater opposition than the words. The people of that faith had become accustomed to using what was known as "The twelve," among which were Old Hundredth, Meas, Isle of Wight, London, Bangor, etc. Some of the more conservative of the worshipers would leave the church when the new hymns were sung. Another great offence to them was the carrying of parts in the music. In their estimation the only pious way to sing was to use only the metrical version of the Psalms to the old tunes, and to have them lined out and sung in unison.

Mr. Simpson remained pastor of Roberts and Good Hope Churches until his death in 1808. He is buried in Roberts Church yard, and upon his tombstone is this inscription, "For more than forty years a preacher of the gospel in the Presbyterian Church. Mark the perfect man and behold the upright for the end of that man is peace," the text from which the Reverend Andrew Brown preached his funeral sermon.

A long line of splendid and useful men succeeded Mr. Simpson as pastor of those churches, among whom Reverend David Humphreys looms a giant. Mr. Humphreys took charge of them in 1821 at the munificent salary of three hundred dollars a year, and even that was not paid. Mr. Humphreys also taught school.

"Father Humphreys," as he was affectionately called, once sitting through a wearisome session of Presbytery when useless discussion and counter discussion had balled up the order of business until the moderator scarcely knew how to untangle the knot, rose to his feet and exclaimed: "Fiddle-faddle! fiddle-faddle! what's all this long talking about? Those of you who are in favor of the motion say aye! Those opposed no! There now, Mr. Moderator, it is all settled and you can go on with business."

Mr. Humphreys served Roberts and Good Hope Churches in all thirty-nine years, divided into two periods. An interval of nine years was spent as pastor of the Anderson Church.

There were a number of county churches of the Presbyterian faith before one was organized in the town. The people of the village worshiped at Roberts, Varennes and Midway.

Another early Presbyterian Church was Carmel, organized in 1787. Its first elders were Thomas Hamilton, John Hamilton, James Watson, John Watson, and Robert McCann. It was early associated with Hopewell from which it was distant but a few miles. The church was first known as Richmond, later mentioned as Twenty-Three Mile Church. It has been suggested that there may have been two churches of those names which united to form Carmel.

Before Anderson county was made Varennes Church and school were points of interest in Pendleton District. Very early in the history of the county Reverend Thomas Baird established an academy about where Mr. Jule Anderson's home is, and religious services were held in the school, the preacher standing on a platform, and the congregation seated on hewn logs to listen to him. In 1813 Reverend Richard Cater had a log house of worship erected near the school building. Mr. Cater preached at the new church once a month, giving the other Sundays to Broadaway, Good Hope and Roberts. The original elders were Mr. John Hillhouse, Mr. James Dobbins, Colonel Patrick Norris and Captain James Thompson.

Among its pastors the church has numbered Rev. David Humphreys, Rev. Joseph Hillhouse, Rev. William Carlisle, and Rev. William Harris. During this gentleman's term of service the church was taken down and removed three miles further south, on the same road to a site given by Mrs. James Thompson, Sr. That building was of hewn logs, and within its walls was a masterpiece of workmanship known as a sounding board, upon which was perched a beautiful wooden dove. The board was bell shaped, and by means of iron rods was suspended from the roof over the pulpit.

Rev. William McWhirter succeeded Mr. Harris, and following him came Rev. W. H. Singletary. About this time a Sunday school and Bible class was organized. The Rev. William Carlisle again became pastor of the church, and under his administration the location was again moved; John Wakefield and Theodore Trimmier together giving a site of seven and a half acres for the church and school. It was not far from Storeville. A substantial and creditable building was erected which is still used. Some of the ruling elders of the church have been Joshua Gailliard, Thomas Harris, Matthew Thompson, John Herron, Thomas Pennel, William A. Brownlee, James Thompson, A. E. Jackson, Samuel Webb, Henry L. McGill, W. G. Webb, D. P. McLin, and M. A. Thompson. The edifice was dedicated August, 1857, the sermon preached by Dr. Buist of Greenville. Other ministers present were Smith Gailliard, Robert Reid and William Carlisle. Mr. Carlisle remained pastor of Varennes Church until 1860 when he was succeeded by Rev. W. F. Pearson, who was employed by the Domestic Missionary Society of South Carolina. At the outbreak of the war, Mr. Pearson went with the army as chaplain. He was succeeded in the service of the church by Rev. D. X. LaFar, a refugee from Charleston. In 1866 Mr. Pearson resumed the charge which he held until 1870. He was followed by R. A. Fair, J. O. Linsey and H. C. Fennel.

The first stove for heating the church was bought in 1882. Old time religion was quite a bit warmer than the present variety, and our fathers, our mothers and their children, even to the baby, went to church every Sunday and some week days, sat through services that lasted from two to three hours, listened to their reverend pastor preach for an hour always, and sometimes longer, without any fire on the coldest day. But about the eighth decade of the nineteenth century, old Varennes was becoming very modern and up to date; following the stove came an organ, and in 1878 the building was renovated.

Other preachers served the church at various times, but Mr. Fennel and Mr. Pearson were repeatedly recalled to the charge. The beloved father in God, David Humphreys, preached his last sermon in Varennes church.

Seven being in the estimation of many Christians a mystic number, it is interesting to note its repeated occurrence in the history of this church. Built in 1814, removed three miles south in 1837, new building erected in 1857. Again renovated in 1907. Its grounds consist of seven acres.

Faithfully the Presbyterians of the growing village attended services at Varennes and Roberts churches for a number of years. But they found those Sabbath journeys rather wearying, and one afternoon in 1837 a group of Presbyterian ladies were gathered at the home of Judge Whitner, whether as a church society, or merely a social gathering history sayeth not, but they were there, and the need of a church of their own in the town was the topic of conversation. Judge Whitner became interested in the matter and offered to give them a lot if they would build on it a church. There was conceived the Anderson Presbyterian church. Women are always the most energetic church workers. And that group of ladies went to work with a will. Among them were Mrs. Kitty Benson, Mrs. Elizabeth Mauldin, lovingly known to the whole community as "Aunt Lizzie," Miss Sallie Cater, Mrs. Charles Prince and Mrs. Creswell.

The lot given by Judge Whitner was the same upon which the First Presbyterian church now stands, though at first it extended far beyond its present bounds. The Judge was not stingy in his giving. The first building erected was a small frame structure, which stood back of where the church now stands. It faced Tolly street. The dedication services were held on September 2, 1837. Rev. David Humphreys, Rev. William Carlisle, Rev. James Sewers, Rev. N. H. Harris, and Rev. Edwin Cater taking part. It had a membership of only thirteen persons to start with. Judge J. N. Whitner and Mr. J. P. Holt were its first elders; Rev. Edwin Cater, its first pastor. Mr. Cater served until 1839. In that year a new and more commodious church was erected, a frame building facing Whitner street, and further back than the present structure. The new house of worship was dedicated by Rev. A. W. Ross, of Pendleton, assisted by E. T. Buist, Rev. David Humphreys, and Rev. C. Marshall.

About 1878 the present brick building was erected, Rev. David E. Frierson being pastor. This was the first church in the town to have a separate room for the Sunday school; it was in the basement of the church. The adjoining graveyard was practically the town cemetery for many years. There was a graveyard surrounding the Baptist church also, but few except members of that faith, or persons closely connected with some of them, were buried there. The first grave to be made in the Presbyterian cemetery was that of a young lady, Miss Osborne, sister of the late Mr. Andrew Osborne.

By the time that the Anderson church was established, Watts' hymns were used entirely, but the music was altogether vocal. Mrs. Lizzie Mauldin was in the habit of raising the tunes. One Sunday the congregation was startled when a hymn was given out to hear in place of "Aunt Lizzie's" familiar voice, the notes of a melodeon issuing from the gallery at the back. Decorum was for once forgotten, and everybody "rubber-necked" around to see the source of the disturbance. It proved to be a young lady of the congregation, Miss Tocoa Glover, playing upon "an instrument," by many Christians of that day considered an auxiliary of the devil. Consternation prevailed; some liked the innovation, some did not. Fierce controversy was waged against organs by some of the churches and Christians until the nineteenth century was far advanced. Even Dr. W. B. Johnson, president of the Johnson University, and first president of the Southern Baptist convention, was a bitter opponent of organs and choirs.

The first Sunday school in Anderson was organized by Miss Sallie Cater, Mrs. Lizzie Mauldin and Mrs. Charles Prince. It was held on Sunday afternoons in the Presbyterian church, and young people of all denominations attended. Its first meeting was on February 1, 1842. Judge Whitner was its superintendent. It soon became so popular that it outgrew the church and moved across the street to the Presbyterian Seminary, where it occupied several rooms of the building.

Before a great while the other churches thought it worth while to recall their young people to their own allegiance, and Sunday schools became a part of every congregation.

Mr. A. B. Towers was superintendent of the Presbyterian Sunday school longer than any other one person, and it is probable that he held the position longer than any superintendent of any Sunday school in the town ever did.

Dr. Frierson was pastor of the Presbyterian church for a longer time than any other minister ever held any charge in Anderson. He was beloved by the whole town.

The salaries paid to the early ministers were meagre to begin with, and often the sum promised was not paid at all, or paid in produce. A watermelon left at the preacher's house was rarely a gift, its price was deducted by the donor from the preacher's salary. If by chance the poor preacher received something over what had been promised, he must either pay it back, or let it go on the next year's account. And that regardless of whether he had been paid in potatoes, and had raised sufficient potatoes for himself, and had no sugar at all. One minister of those early days who happened to be a Baptist, but the condition was true of all denominations, was paid for preaching once a month for two years at a church thirty miles from his home, by a pair of shoes, a vest, and an apron for his wife.

The traveling missionaries were supplied with necessities by the churches which they visited, but rarely given money. An old lady who was living in Anderson a few years ago, used to tell of such a visitor to her father's home. One day when her mother was ill, their old negro cook and laundress had planned a plain family dinner, which she put on early, and told the narrator, then a little girl, to watch while she went to the branch at some distance to wash the clothes.

After a while a young man rode up to the house and asked for the child's father, who was called from the field, and soon gave orders that "Aunt Margaret" should be summoned. The old woman came grumbling, and upon seeing the stranger's horse hitched to the rack said, " 'taint nothin' but po' white folks nohow, he ride such a skinny horse." The visitor proved to be a man distinguished throughout the south as a pulpit orator, Dr. B. M. Palmer, of New Orleans, then a theological student. The Anderson church had the honor of being served by Mr. Palmer on that trip through the country from July to September, 1841. As a part of the same incident the lady remembered her mother taking down some of her treasured "bought goods" brought from Charleston, and making of it garments for that same visiting theological student.

In 1900 the Presbyterian church divided and the new congregation formed the Central Church and erected a building on North

Main street. It was completed and opened for services with appropriate dedicatory exercises in 1902; Reverend Hugh Murchison, its first pastor.

The first Associate Reform Presbyterian Church in the county was Generostee, on Little Generostee Creek. The date of its organization is uncertain, but Reverend Robert Irwin, its first pastor, was installed in 1800, and in the beautiful custom of that early day, he remained with that congregation until his death in 1823. He was fifty-eight years old when he entered the ministry. Mr. Irwin had no children, and his farm of 250 acres, located near the church, by his will became the property of the congregation at the death of his wife; to be used as a home for the pastors of the church, the first parsonage in the county.

Mrs. Irwin lived thirty years after her husband's death, but her hospitable doors were opened so wide to the ministers, that her home almost fulfilled its destiny during her life time.

Mr. Irwin was succeeded by the Reverend Mr. Pressley, who had grown up under his preaching. Mr. Pressley also entered the ministry late, being forty years old when he began. Both of these men married late in life, and both lived to be very old. Neither left any children. One of them lived on one side of Generostee Creek, the other on the opposite. They were both pastors of but one church, and held long pastorates.

Shiloh was an early church of this faith, but little is known about it.

Concord, another A. R. P. Church, has a history dating back as far as 1796, and possibly earlier. Reverend Peter McMullin was its first pastor. The original building was of logs, and it served its people long and well. But the hand of time finally fell so heavily upon the ancient structure, that its congregation found it necessary for a time to hold services in the Midway Presbyterian church. In 1845 a new building was erected, the members of the congregation contributing the different parts, one sills, another flooring, another weather boarding until everything needful had been supplied. In 1900 the present building was erected.

In July, 1904, Dr. Pressley, Messrs. Robert Moorhead and Robert Stevenson were appointed by the superintendent of missions of the Second Presbytery to organize from Concord congregation a church in the city of Anderson. The old Concord church was sold to a Baptist congregation, but Mr. Robert Moorhead gave them the ground on which it stood. In its surrounding grave yard, and also one across the road, sleep some of the pioneers of the A. R. P. faith.

HISTORY OF ANDERSON COUNTY

In early times the A. R. Ps. were close communicants, and each church member was given a pewter coin which he had to show before he was allowed to take communion.

In 1810 the Presbyterian church in council assembled determined that a woman who had married her deceased sister's husband, should be debarred from communion. However, a man who had married a woman who had been unchaste, not knowing her character, and she after marriage having again fallen into the same sin, left her; but not having obtained a divorce, after a time married again, his first wife being still alive, asked to be received into that same church. After some discussion he was admitted, though "great care is recommended in such cases."

Baptist Churches.

Almost coeval with the Presbyterians in the county were the Baptists. Their first house of worship whose date is definitely known was Big Creek, about three miles from Williamston, erected in 1789. The Baptists of the Piedmont section have lovingly called that "the Mother of Churches," as many subsequent congregations sprang from it. Its first pastor was a grand old pioneer preacher from Virginia, Moses Holland.

The minutes of this church, which fortunately have been preserved, a thing rare among the early congregations, throws a most interesting light on the ideas and customs of those days. The people believed in, and practiced the scriptural injunction to settle all their affairs in council of the brethren. Negroes were received as members along with their masters' families, and in the church their right to be heard was equal to that of any other member. A negro woman belonging to Big Creek brought accusations of cruelty against her owners and the church spent two years trying to adjust the d i f f i c u l t y. The mistress was told that if she continued her mistreatment of her slave, she would be excluded from the fellowship of the congregation.

Even the beloved pastor, Mr. Holland, was not exempt from the strict dealings of the church. He had some business transaction with one of his members, which was most unsatisfactory to the minister, who did not hesitate to express his displeasure. The church failing to adjust the matter, declared Mr. Holland out of fellowship. For two years they had no pastor, though they continued to hold regular meetings, which Mr. Holland regularly attended. The quarrel was with Mr. Elijah Burnett over a matter involving five dollars. When the lower Pelzer dam was built there were discovered faint signs of an old chimney near the western end of the dam. That small pile of stones marked the place where stood Mr. Holland's dwelling. The river there was long known as "Holland's Ford." The road which leads to the power house used to be a public road. There is still a spring under the hill which furnished the family with water. Mr. Holland is buried in the Big Creek grave yard. His strong personality so impressed itself upon his community and the Baptist church of his day that the lapse of a hundred years has failed to obliterate it entirely.

The records of Big Creek tell interesting stories. Among cases excluded for drunkenness was sister N. A. A committee was appointed to go to brother H. and find out why he did not attend meetings. Brother W. reported his own case for getting drunk at tax paying, for which the church forgave him. Another brother was excluded for bringing home with him from Abbeville a stray hound, said dog not being his property. Sister E. was excluded for attending a shooting match and associating with bad company. A brother was excluded for attending an unlawful assembly and shooting for a prize. Another brother did not perform work according to promise, and charged too high for it. His work being examined by a committee and pronounced bad, he was excluded. One sister was excluded because she had been angry and said bad words, with other reports. She confessed her fault, denied reports, and was forgiven. A complaint was made by a brother against a sister for saying that two other women, blood sisters, were liars, and she could prove it. Having failed to substantiate the accusation, the brethren put on record that she had fallen under their censure until such time as she makes her accusation good. One brother applied for letters which he got, then told lies, ran away and left his debts unpaid. Sister E. applied for a letter of dismissal, and at the same time said she was not satisfied with the conduct of the church in turning out her husband; letters were refused. A favorite expression used in the minutes is "we disapprobate such conduct."

One of the negro members named Caesar was rather an unusual character. He was a preacher of considerable influence. He had been a slave who saved enough to buy his own freedom, and later bought his brother. The land just above the place where Rush and Vandiver's planing mill once stood, was owned by Caesar. He was buried in a field just in the rear of the old Williamston Female College buildings. In the records it is several times stated that "Brother Caesar made application to go about and exercise his gift." Sometimes his request was granted, sometimes refused. Caesar was once excluded from fellowship for persisting over the protest of the church in taking an additional wife. Later he was restored to fellowship, what befell wife No. 2 is not stated. He was admonished to preach "sound doctrine" on his preaching expeditions. Also he sometimes held services for the Big Creek congregation. Once "Brother Caesar" was up before the church for having knocked down with an axe a fellow servant.

A brother was declared out of fellowship for "voluntarily leaving us and joining the Methodist Society." A sister was excommunicated because she declared that she was "a Methodist indeed, and that she received more satisfaction with them than with us." She was excluded "To be numbered with us no more until she altered her principles."

One entry reads, "On the night of our next meeting we agree to go into washing each other's feet."

Moses Holland was pastor of that church for forty-one years, from 1788 to 1829. He was succeeded by Robert King (Uncle Bobby), 1830-1838. John Vandiver, 1838-1844. William P. Martin, 1848-1873.

During Mr. Martin's pastorate, a good brick church was erected. Big Creek is still an influential church in the county.

Until after the war of secession negroes belonged to all of the white churches, and some of the old time darkeys never became quite reconciled to the separation of the races. Many Anderson people remember "Old Uncle Henry Reed," a well known old colored gardener and handy man about town. He always told with pride that he joined the white Baptist church, and that Mr. Murray baptized him. He said to the last that he never liked any other church so well.

In 1843 Big Creek church was torn by dissension. An itinerant preacher from Tennessee named Edward Musgrove became a member of the church, and aspired to become its pastor. On one occasion, John Vandiver being already in the pulpit, Mr. Musgrove also entered it, and proceeded to conduct the services, Reverend Vandiver also doing the same. For a time pandemonium reigned. The two men entered into a bitter newspaper controversy, and in those days neither newspapers nor people were so polite as they are now, so the antagonists villified and scandalized each other in the coarsest and most violent way, until finally the editor or his readers got tired, and they were both shut off.

Mr. Musgrove was fiercely anti-missionary and anti-prohibitionist, both of which were virulent subjects of dispute at that time. Finally Musgrove became so offensive that he was forced to leave the state, although he was a very bright man, and must have had a great deal of magnetism, because he had some very warm friends and admirers.

Neal's Creek was the first offshoot from Big Creek. It was organized about the close of the eighteenth century. Its first pastor was "Uncle Bobby King," whose familiar soubriquet tells as much of his character and personality as a long description could. Typical of the Baptist ministers of his day, a strong earnest Christian, a gifted speaker, but a man of little or no education, for among primitive Baptists, education was regarded as a snare; he knew his Bible, and preached it as he understood it; reaching the unlettered people of those early times as a scholar could never have done.

Neal's Creek has been called "the mother of preachers." From that fold came William Magee, Sanford Vandiver, John Vandiver, Wiley Smith, Robert King, W. H. King, Mike McGee and J. K. Fant. As well as others.

About the time that Big Creek was organized, a church known as Shockley's Ferry was built near what is now Alford's Bridge. Its first pastor was James Chastain. Tradition has preserved of that missionary in the wilderness only his name, and the fact that he organized Shockley's Ferry and Mountain Creek churches.

The best remembered of Shockley Ferry pastors is Cooper Bennett. In the old days it was not Presbyterians alone who believed and taught the Calvinistic doctrine of election; that was likewise a tenet of the Baptist church, but one to which Mr. Bennett could not subscribe. A man of big loving heart, he believed and preached that Jesus Christ died for all mankind, and that any and all could and would be saved, if they chose to be. For such heresy he was excluded from the Saluda Association, and his church withdrew with him. He was its pastor for forty years. But as age laid its heavy hand upon him, his congregation scattered, and about 1826 the Shockley Ferry church ceased to exist. Mr. Bennett spent the last years of his life at the home of his son, near Greenville. When too feeble to stand to talk to a congregation, the gentle old pastor, confined to a chair, his silver hair falling upon his shoulders, liked to gather a few about him, and like St. John of old, talk about Christian love.

Dipping Branch Church, near the site of the old Shockley Ferry, bears in its name the history of the spot. The church in Anderson is indirectly an offshoot of Shockley Ferry.

As the old congregation disintegrated the remains were gathered up by William Magee, and Big Generostee was formed with Mr. Magee its pastor. He served that congregation for over thirty years. About 1860 the church became involved in a serious controversy which divided its members into hostile camps. One Saturday the congregation met and wrangled all day long, dispersing only as night fell, with the agreement to meet early the next day, Sunday though it would be, and renew the argument. When they arrived Sunday morning to their consternation they found that during the night their church building had been literally split in two, the roof and overhead timbers having fallen in. The phenomenon was taken as a warning from God that a house divided against itself shall not stand; so the quarrel was adjusted. However, the shock to the superstitious was too great, and the church in that locality never again flourished. In 1859 it was reorganized at Shockley Ferry, but the name Shiloh was given to the new place of worship.

When the nineteenth century was twenty years old, Pendleton District had become thickly settled, and there were numbers of people of the Baptist faith living between Shockley's Ferry and Big Creek churches to whom attending either meant quite a journey. James Burriss, a Scotch-Irishman, settled land along Generostee Creek; a devout man and a Baptist, he felt the burden of these sheep without a shepherd press upon his heart; and largely from Shockley Ferry members he established a congregation which gathered under a bush arbor near where Orr Mill is now located to hear him expound the scriptures. In 1821, with assistance of the mother church of which Mr. Burriss himself was a member, a log house replaced the bush arbor. Mt. Tabor was the name given to the new church. Reverend Sanford Vandiver became its pastor, and he served it until his death in 1841.

On a bright Sunday afternoon in the fall of 1917, Colonel J. N. Brown, a grandson of Mr. Vandiver, accompanied a party of interested people to the spot where that old church stood. He pointed out in the forgotten grave yard which remains hidden away in the woods near the busy mill, the graves of James Burriss and his wife, Susan Cage, marked only by rough stones of the field. At that site, located now by a great flat stone, which must have been the door stone of the old Mt. Tabor building, the venerable old gentleman stood with bared head, and told of the old days and the people of that elder time which hallowed the spot. The little memorial service was the outcome of a thought born in the heart of a woman, a great grand daughter of James Burriss, who wished to see the graves of her ancestors, and do honor to the memory of James Burriss and his wife, as much as the ancestors of her beloved First Baptist Church, as of her self. Knowledge of the gathering somehow became bruited about, and quite a number of people of various religious complexions, yet all Andersonians of long standing, were present. It was an impressive occasion, that impromptu meeting in the woods to do honor to people long dead who in their day had done what they could for their church and their community.

Those pioneer preachers were heroes, they lived hard and worked hard, and preached from strong conviction, without enough pay to feed the horses that carried them to the meetings. A lady who died a few years ago over ninety years old, said she remembered her mother telling how in her young days she used to see Reverend Jacob Burriss, a son of Mr. James Burriss, making his way from his home near the town to preach at Mountain Creek where he was pastor; walking, leading a horse upon which his wife sat holding a baby in her arms, with two children mounted behind her.

Mt. Tabor was the Baptist house of worship for the people of the village until 1834, when it was removed to the site of the First Baptist Church. The land was conveyed by Micajah Webb, a brother of Edmund and Elijah Webb, to Sanford Vandiver in trust for the church, and a frame building erected to the north of the present location, covering a part of what is the grave yard. The street now known as Church ran through where the building now stands. In 1853 a new brick church was to be erected, and Colonel J. P. Reed, who had a keen eye for a good effect and was endowed with artistic taste, procured permission from the town council to close the street, and place the church at its head, and there the Baptist Church stands today commanding the approach, and looking down the whole vista of the street. Reverend J. S. Murray was pastor when the brick building was erected.

Although the early Saluda Association was anti-missionary, all of the Baptist ministers were by no means of like opinion. In the 30s or 40s B. F. Mauldin, a lay preacher of that faith; Amaziah Rice, Sanford Vandiver and some others formed a missionary society which did much to change public opinion. Mr. Mauldin was in the habit of preaching wherever preaching was needed almost without salary. In the early 30s he came to Anderson and opened a mercantile establishment. Associated with him was his brother, J. L. Mauldin, and his nephew, B. F. Crayton, was his clerk. Later Mr. Mauldin's health failed and he sold the business to Mr. J. L. Mauldin and Mr. Crayton and moved to Calhoun. After going to the country he preached to four churches, one each Sunday in the month, driving about eighteen miles to reach them. Upon being asked once by his clerk, John C. Whitfield, later "Squire Whitfield", how much he got for his services, he replied—"Well, last year I got from the four of them, 98 dollars." The young man looked at him a moment, then said, "Well, you know your own business, but before I would work for them for such a sum, they might all die and go to hell."

The squire never thought much of either churches or preachers, although he was a descendent of George Whitfield. In his later years through the influence of his lovely wife he joined the Methodist Church. However, if all church members were as honest, true and genuinely kindly as he was, the churches would never be accused of harboring hypocrisy.

Governor Brown, of Georgia, joined the Baptist church at Shady Grove under Mr. Mauldin's preaching; and when he left that section of country was given by Mr. Mauldin a letter of introduction to a friend in Georgia, Dr. Lewis, a Baptist minister, but also a business man, who received the young man very kindly, befriending him whenever opportunity offered. Governor Brown never forgot a kindness shown him, and when he was governor, the position of United States senator from Georgia becoming vacant, Governor Brown appointed his old friend, Dr. Lewis, to fill the place.

Squire Whitfield had a fund of anecdotes, and loved a joke on his friends. There was one which he used to tell with relish about three of his friends, all members of the Baptist church, men of high standing and influence in the community. Their character and standing, however, did not save them in that puritanical age from being called before the church tribunal on the very grave and serious charge of fiddling and dancing. They were the Honorables J. P. Reed, Elijah Webb, and Daniel Brown. The charge was that Reed fiddled while the dignified deacons, Webb and Brown, tripped the light fantastic toe. When called to account, Mr. Reed answered, "Well, when I was young I was thought a pretty good fiddler, but that night I learned for certain that I was a damned good one, and am yet."

Mr. Webb being called, acknowledged his sin with penitence, and asked for forgiveness. Mr. Brown, when called, failed to respond and was found at the back of the church fast asleep. Squire Whitfield said: "Webb begged out of it, Reed swore out of it, and Brown snored out of it."

Amaziah Rice was a noted Baptist preacher of early times. He was born June 20, 1798, a son of Hezekiah and Polly Leftwich Rice, settlers in the district from Virginia. Mr. Rice began life as a clerk for his father and his uncle, Christopher Orr, at Craytonville. In his twenty-second year he married Miss Sallie Thompson. From this union there were nine children, eight of whom lived to be grown; three sons and five daughters.

In Mr. Rice's young days the state militia was a thing of great importance, it was especially good as a stepping stone to official position. Mr. Rice was elected colonel of the 4th South Carolina Regiment, and served several years. The title of colonel stuck to him through life, though later he became a minister of the Baptist Church. For six years he served the state in the legislature, from 1826 to 1832. It was at that time that he shared in the honor of granting a charter to the first railroad in America built for steam cars alone, the old South Carolina road.

Colonel Rice was a successful farmer and business man, and for over forty years prominent as a preacher, serving churches in Anderson and adjoining counties. It is said that he preached his first sermon in Georgia, and that he felt so ashamed of the effort, that for a long time he kept it a secret. He died July 31, 1878, and is buried in the old Rice family grave yard.

Salem Church, an arm of Shockley Ferry, was organized in 1798. Rocky River Church, first called Wilson's Creek, was organized in 1790. Mountain Creek in 1796. It, like Shockley Ferry, was probably organized by James Chastain. It was in that church that the Saluda Association was formed.

Barker's Creek church was organized in 1821. Reverend Arthur Williams was its first pastor. He served for nineteen years, and for all of that time nothing was ever said about paying their pastor a salary. Reverend D. W. Hiott served that congregation at four different times, and under his administration two of the four houses of worship of the congregation were built. The last, a handsome building, was dedicated Sunday, July 2nd, 1922.

The first church for negro people was St. Paul Baptist Church in the city. It was organized in 1865, Tabor Warren its first pastor. A plain frame building was erected, which, in 1893, gave way to the commodious brick structure that is now the house of worship for that congregation.

Those pioneer churches carefully guarded the tenets of their religion; heresy was not to be tolerated. Early in its annals the Saluda Association warns its churches against Thomas Rhodes, M. Smith, L. Johnson, N. R. Riplay, and a negro called Thomas Paul, otherwise Thomas Cook, all heretical preachers. Again in 1830 the churches are warned against the imposition of Jesse Denson.

The Baptist church has been a powerful factor in the history and development of the county. A large majority of the people are of that faith, and they have done much for the uplift of the community.

HISTORY OF ANDERSON COUNTY

METHODIST CHURCHES

The Methodist Church in America was formally organized in Baltimore in 1784. Immediately their circuit riders became familiar figures in every part of the new world. In upper South Carolina an army of these soldiers of the cross, commissioned and encouraged by Bishop Asbury, began a campaign for their church. That form of faith found a wonderful response among the people, who became Methodists by the hundred thousands.

Although the Baptist and Presbyterian communions preceded them in this section of the country, the Methodists soon gained a firm foothold. Their first church in the county was at Ebenezer, on Rocky River near the Abbeville line. The present building is the fourth on that spot. The first was about 1788 or 1789. Bishop Asbury himself preached to that pioneer congregation, and a tradition lingers of people traveling for miles, merely to see him pass along the road. There is in the present church a table on which Lorenzo Dow stood in order to see and be seen by the great congregation which thronged there to hear him preach.

From very early days there was a Sunday School in connection with Ebenezer Church. Not only was the Bible taught, but the pupils were instructed in the elements of the three Rs, and one of the earliest day schools in this part of the state was maintained among the people of that congregation. The first camp meetings in Anderson county were held at "Uncle Jerry's Spring," close to Ebenezer Church. One of the founders and organizers of this first Methodist Church was Mr. Elijah Brown, and the preachers on that circuit were always entertained at his house. They invariably made it possible to stop at "Brownville" on their trips, though a long, hard ride was necessary to accomplish it. Mr. Elijah Brown was a civil engineer, and assisted in laying off the town of Anderson.

Mr. Brown believed in education, and sent his older son to England to college. It was largely through his influence that a good school was maintained in his section; and from that neighborhood have come men who have been successful in the professional and business world.

In the early days of the nineteenth century camp meetings were a popular form of revivals, and they were held not alone by Methodists, but by Baptists and Presbyterians as well. The Methodist churches of Ruhamah and Providence were famous for their camp meetings. Those at Sandy Springs have made the most lasting impression on the community. In 1828 the Methodist congregation at that place bought from Sampson Pope fifteen acres of land for 45 dollars, the same upon which the Methodist Church now stands. It was at once neatly laid off in small lots contained in three rows surrounding a center square on which an arbor was erected. Fifty cents was paid for the privilege of putting up a tent on one of these lots, and after a time permanent shelters of wood were erected. In 1838 Edward Jefferson Britt hewed out the timber and built an arbor in which to hold the camp meetings. They continued until 1897. The present church was built in 1868, and a flourishing town has grown up around the old house of worship.

It was at Sandy Springs that Orr's Regiment of Rifles was organized July, 1861. And there for many years after the war was over the survivors held their annual reunions. With that regiment during the war was almost every man of the Sandy Springs neighborhood who could shoulder a gun.

The great Sandy Springs camp meetings began on the third Sunday in September, and continued about two weeks. Very many people became converted at these big revivals. There were four preaching hours every day and Mr. Satterfield, a Christian who felt that if he could neither preach nor pray, he could call the people to service, for many years sounded the trumpet which summoned the people to worship.

The first church of any denomination in the town of Anderson was Methodist. It stood about where the negro Presbyterian church is now. The land was bought by Whitfield Anthony, D. H. Calhoun and Isaac Hays, trustees for the church, from John and Mary Thompson. The congregation was small, but enthusiastic. Among the number was Anderson's first carpenter, Hugh Whittaker, who with his sons built the small log house, a labor of love. For several years it was the only house of worship within the bounds of the village. There were no windows, and no way of heating, but the people attended no matter what the weather. If the wind blew from the east they opened the south door for light, while if the wind or rain came from that direction, the east door was opened.

The description of that little church was furnished by the late Mr. T. J. Webb, who said that in his boyhood he had often been in the building, and that he knew personally the old carpenter Whittaker who did the work.

In 1843 that lot was sold to Mr. Baylis Crayton, and the present location on McDuffie street bought. There a neat frame building with windows on each side was erected, and painted white. The Reverend T. G. Herbert was its pastor during the war between the states. He came about every two weeks, Anderson being on his circuit. It was during his pastorate that the congregation built the first parsonage in the town. It was erected back of the church, and afterwards sold to the Lesser family, who have several times added to the original house, but the old parsonage is the nucleus of the Lesser home today.

In the early days there was a Sunday morning service for the white people, and one held on Sunday afternoons for negroes. Sometimes nurses took their charges with them to church, then, the white children were seated inside the communion railing whence they watched with interest the stately old butler who raised the hymns in a most fascinating way, marching up and down the aisles, and bending his body in time with the tune.

When a congregation gathered in the building, all of the women sat on one side of the center aisle or division, and all of the men on the other. When a boy became twelve or fourteen years old, he was promoted to the masculine side of the house. That custom was not peculiar to Methodist churches; it was the practice of all except the Episcopal and Roman Catholic. The custom is still observed in some rural sections.

In 1885 the frame building was replaced by a neat and commodious brick church, which the congregation hoped and believed would last for many years. But all the land beneath the building and for some distance around it is made earth; a great gulch once ran through there, and extended across Main street on down towarls the C. and W. C. railroad; and underground springs so undermined the foundations of the church, that in a little over twenty years it was pronounced unsafe, and the present handsome structure, with deeply laid foundations, is its successor.

Although the Methodist was the first church established in the town, it does not seem to have had a regular pastor for a long time. In an issue of The Highland Sentinel in 1844 a list of the Methodist ministers of the state and their appointments is given. No mention is made there of one sent to Anderson. Notice is given on March 9, 1844, that on the second Sabbath in March Reverend G. W. Moore will preach in the Methodist Church.

That servant of God died while on his knees at prayer in Providence Church. Mr. Moore was the father of Colonel John V. Moore, one of Anderson's best known citizens of ante-bellum days, and an honored Confederate soldier. A daughter of Reverend Mr. Moore was Mrs. de Fountain, named for her father, Georgia. She was at one time a well known writer on some of the big New York papers. Another of Mr. Moore's daughters was Mrs. Sallie Chapin, thirty years ago one of the most widely known W. C. T. U. lecturers in the state.

One of the oldest Methodist churches in the county is Asbury. Matthew Clark, a Revolutionary soldier, gave the ground on which it was built, and he and Mr. Goodrum were its leading members and largest contributors.

The Methodist Church at Starr is the old Bethsaida congregation removed to a new spot. Reverend James Hardy was the original promoter of that church, and he gave the ground on which it stood for many years. Mr. Hardy came to the section early in the nineteenth century, and his son, Richard Baxter Hardy, was born at the family homestead near the church in 1812. The old house is now occupied by the daughter of Rev. R. B. Hardy, Mrs. G. W. Hodges. Around the church there was in early times a great camp meeting ground, said by some people to have been the oldest in the state. The abandoned house of worship, surrounded by its ancient grave yard, stands desolate, a shade of the past.

In the southwestern part of the county, two miles from the Savannah River, stands another early Methodist Church, Ruhamah. It was organized in 1822, Mr. William Glenn giving the land upon which it was built. It was dedicated in 1836 by Reverend Levi Garrison, who also named it. The original building stood a little back of, and to the left of the site of the present one, which was erected in 1874. At that time Mr. John F. Glenn, son of the original donor, gave an additional half acre of land so that the cemetery might be enlarged. For some years camp meetings were held at Ruhamah also, but in 1849 conference determined that Providence was a more suitable place for those great gatherings, so the change was made.

A Methodist preacher of marked individuality who was once located in this county was Reverend James Dannally, of whom his friends had an inexhaustible fund of amusing stories to relate. He was a wooden-legged man, and familiarly called "Uncle Jimmy." With all his honest soul he hated pretense, and pretense masked in humility was no more acceptable to him than the blatant kind. It is told that in one of his churches there was a man very proud of his accumulations, and his well-kept surroundings, but who assumed a meek and humble attitude toward his treasured property, when speaking of it to others, basking in the denials of his allegations by his friends. When Mr. Dannally became his pastor he approached him one day and remarked: "Mr. Dannally, I am a very poor man, I have but little, and that very plain, but what I have I will gladly share with you; I want you to come and take dinner with me today." To his amazement, Mr. Dannally accepted his statement without protest, but declined his invitation, saying, "No, brother, I make it a rule never to impose on the poorest members of my flock; I will not take away from your family the pittance that they have." And never while he remained pastor of that church could he be induced to take a meal with that man, always treating him as though he believed him to be very poor. On one occasion during a revival meeting in one of his churches he had a young visiting minister assisting, and feeling ill, the old gentleman left the meeting to his helper and went to his nearby home to rest. The young theologue preached a "fetching" sermon, and when he called for penitents the rail was crowded. Highly pleased, and willing for the old pastor to see what he had done, the young man sent for him to come back and help pray with the mourners. Reluctantly Mr. Dannally responded to the summons. When he arrived, he looked over the line stretched around the rail, then turning to the preacher, said: "Bad haul, my young brother! Throw out your net again; I have been converting the same gang regularly at every camp meeting for the last ten years, and they are not worth trying to save. The last one of them will forget before the end of the week all about your prayers and be drinking, gambling and frolicking just the same." With that he turned his back and went home again.

He never hesitated to rebuke high or low, rich or poor. Once he was invited to preach in a fashionable Charleston church. There was in the building the usual gallery at the back for negroes. Upon rising in the pulpit Mr. Dannally cast his eyes over the congregation, then raised them to the gallery. After an impressive interval he said: "I was told when I was invited to preach in this great city, and to this gaudily arrayed congregation that they were a very refined people, and I must be careful what I said lest I offend their sensitive ears. From the number of mulattoes I see sitting in that gallery, I should judge that they are indeed refined, with the refinement of Sodom and Gomorrah." Then he proceeded to tell them what he thought they ought to hear.

He startled a congregation one Sunday as he stood in the pulpit by exclaiming: "There comes my wife with the bureau on her head." The poor lady, probably having worn one hat for ten years, had sold a bureau which she thought she could spare, and bought a "bonnet." Once having sharply reproved a party of young people who came to church and engaged in whispered conversation and much giggling, at the close of the service one of the young men accosted him and demanded an apology to the young ladies, or he said neither his clerical garments nor his wooden leg would prevent him from thrashing the old preacher. Mr. Dannally replied: "In my young days I used to be something of a scrapper. I drank and committed all manner of sins. In fact I lost my leg running a horse race on Sunday when half drunk. Now if some of the brethren will hold my coat I will give this young puppy such a thrashing as he has not had since his father used to take him out to the woodshed."

There was no fight, but naturally the young people never again went to hear Mr. Dannally preach.

But Uncle Jimmy met his match. In his old age he married a second wife. The lady was a maiden of uncertain age and temper, and the life of a poor preacher "got on her nerves," and she did not hesitate to express her opinion of it and of the preacher, too. Once Mr. Dannally is said to have gone to his church to begin a service, when he found his wife in the pulpit telling the congregation what an old hypocrite she had found him to be. The old man, unseen by the people, stood in the door a few minutes listening to her lurid pictures of him; then he turned and stole quietly away, leaving the field to her.

While Mr. Dannally preached often in Anderson county churches, his home was over the Abbeville line, near Lowndesville. He is buried in the old Smyrna grave yard, near the church to which he preached longest.

Near Pearl Spring, almost where the Piedmont Mills now stand, there was built in 1841 a church belonging to the denomination known as "Protestant Methodists." Its first pastor was Hendrix Arnold, a man whose memory was long revered. The next was Thomas Hutchins, who had formerly been connected with the conference of the M. E. Church before it added South to its name. The church was in existence until 1846 when it was discontinued, the building passing into the hands of the "Christian" denomination.

The Methodist Church, long known as "The Old Pickens Meeting House," was first a Presbyterian place of worship, the Pickens family being of that faith. But in the early days when there were practically no hotels, and the circuit rider penetrated into every part of the wilderness, Colonel Robert Pickens entertained in his home many of these peripatetic ministers, and his little daughter, Anne, became interested in their meetings, so much more lively than the dignified services to which she was accustomed.

After one of the Methodist revivals she asked permission of her parents to unite with the Methodist body. It was refused, and

Miss Anne was taken by her mother before a solemn assembly of Presbyterian divines to be lectured and instructed. The reverend gentlemen questioned the little maid in her mother's presence, and so drastic were their methods, that at the end of the ordeal the indignant mother turned to the child and said: "Now Anne, you may do as you please." Anne did as she pleased, and the whole family followed her. Then the church which Colonel Pickens had built on his place for Presbyterians, was turned over to the Methodists.

Changing their ministers every four years, if not oftener, no Methodist preacher has had the opportunity to impress himself on the community, as have the preachers of some other denominations who have remained for years a vital part of the life of the place. But among their laymen who have been an influence in the town have been such men as Dr. Nardin of blessed memory, Mr. "Charley" Jones, Mr. R. S. Hill, Mr. O. M. Heard and others, and such women as Mrs. Margaret Van Wyck, Mrs. Lucy Nardin, Mrs. Jones, and Anderson's loved librarian, Mrs. Sue Whitfield Geiger. All of these have passed on to other things, but there remain among us today, Mr. "Dick" Ligon, Mr. John Hubbard, another Dr. Nardin, Mr. John E. Wigginton, and others who are doing a great work for their church and their community.

Where the Elks' Club now stands there was twenty or more years ago a little church building erected by the Wesleyan Methodists. They worshiped there for several years, then sold the building to the A. R. P. congregation which was at that time moving from Concord into the city. They used the building for a year or two before they erected their present edifice across the street. The Wesleyan congregation has a church near Orr Mill.

THE EPISCOPAL CHURCH AND OTHER SMALL CONGREGATIONS.

Early in the nineteenth century Pendleton District, lying at the foot of the Blue Ridge Mountains, safe from Indians and protected by a growing population, appealed to the people of Charleston as an ideal place for a summer retreat from heat, sand flies and mosquitoes; and persons bearing such well known name as Ravenell, Pinckney, Huger, etc., built summer homes in Pendleton. Finding their great airy country homes very comfortable, and their surroundings agreeable, many of them remained permanently.

While the great wave of population coming in from the north was Presbyterian and Baptist, there were among it some members of the great English Church, and these meeting with fellow churchmen from Charleston, united to form a congregation of Episcopalians in Pendleton.

Among the churchmen from the north were those bearing the names Talliferro, Lewis, Shanklin, Harrison and others. True to their English traditions, no sooner had these people built homes than they turned their attention to establishing their church. About 1815 they organized a congregation; they elected church officers, and worshiped in what was then the Farmers' Hall, a building now owned by Mr. J. N. Bostic on the west side of the square. A young missionary named Delareaux, of Charleston, was sent by the Society for the Advancement of Christianity in South Carolina to serve the up-country congregation. He had charge of the mission from 1816-1818. Then steps were taken to erect a building. The material was hauled in ox carts from Augusta, and the building progressed slowly. The architect of that little chapel in the wilderness bore the auspicious name of Morningstar.

In 1822 the house was presented to council, and dedicated by Bishop Boone. Its first rector was Reverend Rodolphus Dickinson, then a missionary in Greenville. Mr. Dickinson was born in Massachusetts, a Harvard graduate, who set out to build tabernacles in the wilds. In eighteen months he traveled on horseback a thousand miles. Mr. Dickinson established not only the church in Pendleton, but also the one in Greenville. He was greatly opposed to slavery, and in 1826 preached an anti-slavery sermon which made for him some enemies; but his honesty and gentleness, his attainments and high Christian character, held many friends to him whose ideas were at variance with his own.

Like most people who are born in Massachusetts, Mr. Dickinson was a writer, and attained some note in his day, having published a number of books on a variety of subjects. He was a son of Thomas Wells Dickinson and Thankful Field. His father was a Revolutionary soldier of some note in his section of the country. His mother belonged to the family which has produced Cyrus Field, Samuel Field, the famous preacher; Eugene Field, the poet; Marshall Field, the merchant, and Thomas Jefferson.

Rodolphus Dickinson was born in 1786, graduated from Harvard in 1805, studied law and was admitted to the bar of old Hampshire in 1808. He was clerk of the court from 1811-1819. Being then ordained an Episcopal minister he came immediately to South Carolina. He was a Jeffersonian democrat, and once his party's candidate for congress. His published works show him to have been familiar with law, theology, history and general literature. His only son died in infancy, but two daughters lived to womanhood. He died in 1862, having returned to Massachusetts about 1835.

Mr. Dickinson was succeeded as rector in Pendleton by Reverend William S. Potter, who went to Greenville about 1848 and died there. After him came an interim when the church had no rector. Then the services of Andrew Cornish were secured. He served long and faithfully. Although the Episcopal churches never condemned the use of organs, for a long time the church in Pendleton had none, probably because they could not buy one. The tunes were raised by Dr. Dart, clerk, pronounced clark a la England. He sat in a short pew just under the high pulpit. Dr. Dart was better satisfied with his own performance than were his hearers. Mrs. John E. Calhoun, a very outspoken person, was vehement in her expressions of annoyance at the way he hissed with his tongue against his teeth, and failed to carry the tune as Mrs. Calhoun thought it ought to be carried. Finally an organ was purchased, and Mrs. Cornish was the first organist.

An old lady who was a little Methodist girl living in Pendleton ninety years ago used to tell of the profound impression made upon her when she went with her Episcopal grandmother to St. Paul Church. The beautiful red curtain surrounding the high pulpit, the reredos at the back, and above all the arch of gold letters around the chancel—"The Lord is in His Holy Temple! Let all the Earth keep silence before Him!" seemed to her childish imagination to open a glowing vista into another world.

In the church yard of St. Paul's lie some distinguished dead, among whom are General Barnard E. Bee, Reverend Jasper Adams, F. R. S.; Colonel Thomas Pinckney, Colonel Thomas Clemson, William Henry Trescott, Reverend Andrew Cornish, General Clement Stephens, Colonel J. B. E. Sloan, Dr. F. J. Pickens, and many others whose names adorn the annals of the state.

The first vestry of the church consisted of Colonel J. E. Calhoun, Dr. Hall, Warren R. Davis, Thomas Pinckney; wardens, Mr. Talliaferro and Mr. William Clarkson.

The only other Episcopal Church in the county is Grace Church, Anderson, which was organized some time in the 40s. A lot was bought, the same on which Grace Church now stands, and in 1860 a small, but pretty and "churchly" wooden building was erected. The congregation was at first composed almost entirely of women. Some of them were Mrs. Edward Morris, Mrs. Daniel Brown, Mrs. Elijah Webb, Misses Mary and Carrie Waller. The last four were sisters; their father, Mr. Waller, having come to Anderson in 1837. While he lived they had his assistance in holding their little band together, but he died Friday, June 7th, 1844, having met with the little congregation the previous Sunday. He was buried in the Presbyterian grave yard. Then women alone held the church together. They met at each other's homes, except when they could secure the services of some visiting clergyman, when Benson's Long Room was used.

After they succeeded in getting a church built they were at a loss for a man to attend to the financial affairs, and Mr. Daniel Brown, the Baptist husband of one of the number, filled the office of vestryman for Grace Church, and attended council meetings as its representative.

For a time just before the war, General, later Bishop Ellison Capers, who had come to Anderson to live, served the congregation as lay reader. Years later his son, the present Bishop W. T. Capers, of Texas, had as his first charge the same little church in which his distinguished father had served. Both of these men were greatly beloved, not only by Episcopalians, but by the whole community. Another much beloved and honored rector of the church was Reverend Thomas F. Gadsden, who served it for twenty-five years. Reverend R. C. Jeter, Chaplain of the First South Carolina Regiment, who died on the border in 1916, was rector of Grace Church for eight years.

Mrs. Webb, one of the founders, had two sons who loyally served the church as vestrymen and wardens all their lives. They were Charles W. Webb and Robert C. Webb. Besides Bishop Capers the church has had the good fortune to have two most excellent lay readers whose services when there has been no rector were inestimable. They were Mr. Ernest A. Bell, for forty years a devoted member, and for many years senior warden. Besides his services and his loyalty, Mr. Bell made most generous contributions towards the finances. The other was Mr. Robert C. Jenkins, son of General Micah Jenkins. who for ten or twelve years made Anderson his home.

Early in the present century a handsome brick building replaced the original frame church. The late Fred G. Brown was one of the building committee, and came to love the church so that at his death he left to it a generous bequest. In 1860 Mr. John Baker, of Charleston, placed in the new chapel a cabinet organ, the first ever brought to Anderson. Some twenty years later a small pipe organ was placed in the church, again the first in the city. Miss E. P. Morris was for years the organist. Miss Elizabeth Cornish, daughter of Rev. A. Cornish, also served Grace Church as organist for some time.

HISTORY OF ANDERSON COUNTY

The "Christian" Church made its appearance in the county in 1829. A log building was erected on Dooley's Ferry Road, and the name Antioch was given to the congregation. Mr. S. G. Earle was the leader. Having a minister very irregularly, he assembled the people and read a sermon to them, and often administered the communion. He also organized a Bible class which met every Sunday for study. They had no commentaries or other helps, and in place of attempting to construe scripture, their method was simply to memorize long extracts from the Bible and numbers of hymns. The star pupil of the school was a girl who had to work very hard, but as she sat at her loom she kept an open Bible beside her and memorized more of its contents than any one else in the congregation.

An early minister of this denomination was Mr. Moore, another was Mr. R. S. Sheshane, who lived at Mr. Earle's home, Evergreen, and in 1838 published there a church paper called The Morning Watch, which appeared monthly. It was probably the first religious publication in Anderson county.

Mr. Alexander Campbell and his father, Mr. Thomas Campbell, both preached once certainly, and perhaps oftener at Antioch. For years the church flourished, but after a time most of its members went to seek homes in the opening west, and the church dwindled away. In 1846 the Christian denomination gained possession of the old Pearl Springs Methodist Church building, and organized a church with William Roberts its pastor. He served until his death in 1852. Tradition hands down many interesting accounts of services held by him. After Mr. Roberts' death Mr. Lenderman served the congregation for several years. Before 1859, however, the church died entirely, and the building became a store house for wagons and farm tools.

A few persons of this faith lived in the town of Anderson and held occasional services until sometime early in the present century they erected a small frame church on Greenville street. But that, too, fell into disuse, and has been converted into an apartment house.

In 1861 two Roman Catholic families came to Anderson; they were those of Captain John McGrath, later one of Anderson's Confederate soldiers, and Mr. Mike Kennedy. These two families had services occasionally in one home or the other; at first it was not oftener than once, or at most twice a year, when a visiting priest came to look after the little flock. There were three brothers, all priests, to whom this mission was dear. Their name was O'Connell, and they were affectionately known to their parishioners as "Father

Joseph," "Father Lawrence" and "Doctor." As a few more families were added to the congregation, the services were held oftener. Father Felchia and Father Smith were the supplies.

The great hope and dream of the little band was realized when in 1881, a small plain church was erected, Captain McGrath and Mr. Kennedy attending to all the business, and the ladies working in every possible way to raise the money. The lot on McDuffie street was bought, and Reverend Father Woolahan was the first priest of the new church. The first couple to be married in it were Miss Annie McGrath, eldest daughter of Captain McGrath, and Mr. James O'Donnell. The first person buried in the church yard was the wife of Mr. Kennedy.

At the dedication of that church Bishop Lynch officiated, assisted by Reverend Harry Northrup, afterwards himself bishop; Reverend Claudian Northrup, Father Monahan, later Bishop of North Carolina, and Father Quigley.

In 1822 practically a new church replaced the old one. In the dedication of that church were two men who had assisted on the former occasion, Bishop Northrup and Bishop Monahan.

Among the many priests who have been in charge of the church in Anderson there have been two who especially impressed themselves upon the people of the town; one, Father Joseph Budds, whose kindly hands were often raised in blessings on Protestants as well as Catholics. The other, the genial Father Duff, whose pleasant manners and cordial fellowship made friends of all his acquaintances. He afterwards became one of the army chaplains in the world war, and his popularity followed him into the ranks.

For a few years there was a Congregational Church in the city, a split from the Central Presbyterian, under the Reverend Witherspoon Dodge, who was pastor of the Central Church. In consequence of some point of church doctrine, he left the church and a number of his flock went with him. A building was erected on the corner of McDuffie and Greenville streets. It lasted, however, but a few years; after Mr. Dodge took another pastorate the people mostly returned to one of the Presbyterian churches.

There was once a Quaker Church in the county. It was near the old Ebenezer Meeting House, but the congregation scattered long ago, and only an old grave yard remains to remind the people that once the gentle "Friends" formed a part of the population.

There has been one Lutheran Church in the county. It was in Fork Township, organized in 1876, Reverend Dr. Smeltzer its pastor. At that time the Lutheran College was located at Walhalla, and Dr. Smeltzer was its president. The membership of the church was never large, and after the removal of the college to Newberry the congregation dwindled away to such an extent that the building was finally sold to the Methodists who established a church there under the leadership of Reverend "Charley" Ligon. In its surrounding grave yard, however, sleep some of the Lutherans who once worshiped there. Among the leaders of the church were the Cromer family.

In 1869 there was organized in the county a Singing Convention, composed of members of churches of all denominations. It held its sessions with the Belton Churches. Reverend Willis Walker rode on horseback from his home in Virginia to assist in its organization. He preached on the first day of the meeting. Officers elected were: J. G. Douthit, president; L. W. Kay, vice-president; J. W. Eskew, secretary. Lessons in music were conducted by W. F. Anderson, of Providence; J. G. Sears, of Smith's Chapel; J. W. Winters, Shiloh; James Drennan, Concord; W. G. Smith, Slabtown; W. V. Vickery, Hart county, Georgia; musical lectures, Rev. Mr. Walker.

Delegates were sent to this convention from most of the churches of the county, and those who attended felt so greatly benefited that interest grew, and singing conventions have been popular ever since. They doubtless have been of great benefit to the music of the country churches.

Anderson has proved itself to have developed a missionary spirit since the early days when Saluda Association would scarcely admit to membership a believer in missions.

Many years ago the Presbyterians sent J. L. McBride to China. About 1889 Miss Della Wright, an Anderson girl, was sent by the Methodist church to China. In 1894 the Anderson Baptist Church sent Miss Mary Sullivan to the same country. The evening before her departure there were impressive ceremonies held in the church as a farewell demonstration to her. Ministers of other denominations took part in the exercises, and various Baptist churches of the county contributed to a purse for the young missionary. For a time the church had frequent letters from Miss Sullivan. The Baptists of the state had also in the field a young missionary, Mr. Royall, and the home people learned that Cupid is to be found in China as well as in America. The two young people were married, and after a time both left the Baptist Church and became Zionists.

One of the most interesting missionaries who went from Anderson was a negro woman, Georgia Ann Anderson. She was born before the war between the states, daughter of Washington Reeves, who was the property of Mr. Noah Reeves. After the war Wash-

HISTORY OF ANDERSON COUNTY

ington with his family moved to the Lick Skillet section of the county. Not a great distance from his home a white man with a wooden leg, named Spoon, taught a school for negroes, and Georgia Ann was one of his pupils. She was a very bright girl, always a great Sunday School worker, and a noted singer. She married Jim Anderson, and the two of them worked on Mr. William McFall's plantation for a time. In the year 1895 about 233 negroes sailed from Savannah, Ga., for Monrovia, in Africa, to establish a negro colony, and act as missionaries to their own people. Georgia and Jim were among them.

Arrived in Africa, Georgia established an industrial school for girls at Freetown, Sierra Leone. Jim died in Africa, and after eighteen years of work at her school, Georgia returned to America on a visit. One object of her trip was to induce other colored people to go to Africa and make homes. On her visit to Anderson she was asked to talk to the ladies of the First Baptist Church about her work. Her address was listened to by a large audience of interested women, and a contribution made by them to her school. In New York on her return trip to Africa she married another missionary.

In 1920 Dr. and Mrs. Sam Orr Pruitt went from the First Baptist Church as missionaries to China. They sailed on "The Princess of Japan," a vessel chartered to take missionaries to the Far East. For them, too, there were interesting farewell exercises held in the church.

The Methodist denomination has to its credit besides Miss Della Wright, Reverend and Mrs. Wolling, who left the Anderson Church to go to Brazil, where they labored for some years. There Mrs. Wolling died. On a visit home some few years later Mr. Wolling married again, and his second wife also became a missionary. Mr. John Mattison, of Honea Path, went to Brazil as a Methodist missionary. Mr. Claude Smith, of Belton, went from the same denomination to Brazil, as did Dr. and Mrs. John Lander, of Williamston. Mr. Newton was also a Methodist missionary from Anderson county, also Miss Smith. From the A. R. P. Church Mr. and Mrs. John Edwards went to Mexico, where they spent a number of years. Mrs. Edwards was an Anderson girl, Miss Amelia Brown, daughter of Mr. Elijah Brown, and before her marriage a favorite in society.

In 1898, John Davis, LL.D., an Episcopal minister of Hannibal, Mo., but who was born and grew up in Anderson, went to Tokyo as professor of Ecclesiastical History in Trinity College, a missionary enterprise of the American Episcopal Church. Mr. Davis was a very scholarly man, an acknowledged authority not only on Church

HISTORY OF ANDERSON COUNTY

History and Theology, but a botanist of rare attainments and wide reputation. He made a complete tour of the world and remained some time in the Holy Land. Some two or three years ago this gentle priest and scholar died in Anderson while spending the summer with his sisters.

From the Episcopal Church also has gone to foreign fields Miss Minnie Gadsden, daughter of Reverend Thomas Gadsden, so long rector of Grace Church. Miss Gadsden spent all of her girlhood in Anderson.

The Episcopal Church has in training for the missionary field Newton Heckle, who spent some years of his boyhood in Anderson, and even as a youth was an officer in the Church School, and a devoted church worker.

CHAPTER V.

THE REVOLUTIONARY WAR.

THERE was no Anderson at the time of the Revolutionary War, but many of the men and women who had borne part in that fight for American liberty, spent their last days in what is now Anderson county, and their dust mingles with its soil, so that Anderson may be said to have part in the Revolution.

First of all there is the name by which the town and county are known. It was that of a gallant soldier, Robert Anderson, who not only spent his last years in this community, but spent them to some purpose. He was a born leader of men, and one greatly honored by his fellow citizens. The town of Anderson was the second to have been named in his honor.

Robert Anderson was born in Virginia in 1741, the fifth child and second son of John and Jane Anderson, Scotch-Irish immigrants, who owned a comfortable farm in Augusta county about five miles from Staunton. Young Robert was baptized on the 15th day of November, 1741, by Reverend John Craig. He grew up living the ordinary life of a Virginia planter's son, receiving the average education of a Virginia gentleman; and became a surveyor by profession.

Among the neighbors of the Andersons was a family whose name was Thompson, having a daughter called Anne, whom Robert regarded as his "best girl," though he used no such undignified term in telling her about it, prattling instead of starry eyes, soul's ideal, and other such poetical things; and Anne listened with downcast eyes, believing in her young soul that Byron's laurels would wither should Robert Anderson choose to turn the brilliancy of his intellect to writing verse. But though young Anderson talked sentiment, he had an eye to business; and in pursuance of his profession he left his home, carrying a chain over trackless woods, bogs and marshes. In those days journeys took a long time, and such trips as young Anderson made required years. For two years he had been away, his destination was the new Cherokee country which had been opened up in South Carolina; and after so long with no word from him his friends believed that he must be dead.

To pretty Anne came other suitors, and at sixteen years of age there are few backward glances, life lies before. The girl consented to wed one of her admirers and though there may have been some tender moments of reminiscences given to the lover of her school days, the preparations went on.

Robert was not dead, however; he was only at the world's end, and it was impossible to send any word to those back home. Having seen few but Indian women, his heart beat true to the girl he left behind him. His task completed, he turned his face toward Virginia. Drawing nearer home the traveler began to meet some acquaintances, finally one who told him that Anne Thompson was going to be married. Setting spurs to his horse, young Robert galloped on.

The appointed day for the wedding dawned. A bevy of merry girls filled the Thompson home. Anne, surrounded by her bridesmaids, was in an upper room dressing for the ceremony, when looking out of a window she saw approaching a rider. Many times in the two years just passed the girl had looked out of her window, hoping to see that rider, but hope had grown faint and died. Could it be that at the last moment he was coming? She rather believed she had an hallucination. Yet steadily on he rode. Then the girl cried:

"By my soul! Yonder comes Robert Anderson, and I love his little finger better than I do the other man's whole body!"

Hastily she seized a shawl and throwing it over her head she sped away to meet the man she loved.

Young Lochinvar had come out of the west, and mounting his bride on the horse behind him, they rode away to seek for Eldorado. From that moment Anne Thompson is lost to history. She lived for twenty-five years longer, and left five children, one son, Robert, Jr., and four daughters, Anne, Elizabeth, Mary and Lydia; but of Anne herself there is never another word.

Robert Anderson married twice more, the second wife was Mrs. Maverick, a wealthy widow of Pendleton. One of Colonel Anderson's daughters liked her stepmother so much that she decided to have her also for a mother-in-law; Lydia Anderson married Samuel Maverick.

Colonel Anderson becoming again a widower, asked Mrs. Reece, widow of his former pastor, to marry him. The lady was coy, and stammered, "Oh! This is so sudden, I never thought of such a thing." To which the doughty old gentleman responded: "Oh, yes, you have. When Dr. Reece lived you used always to stop at my pew and ask about my family, but you never do that now, you have become quite shy of me." The lady capitulated and became the third Mrs. Anderson. He outlived that wife, too, and may have been looking out for her successor, when he, too, was overtaken by the rider on the white horse.

At the outbreak of the Revolutionary War Robert Anderson joined the volunteer army. At one time he was sergeant in the Fifth S. C. Regiment, later captain in the regiment commanded by his friend and neighbor, Andrew Pickens. That regiment met and defeated Boyd's Loyalists on their way to join Brown in Georgia. It also took part in the attack upon Stono under General Lincoln June 20th, 1715. When Lincoln was bottled up in Charleston this regiment was not with him; for some unknown reason it remained outside of the city, and did good work harassing the enemy. After the fall of Charleston, Pickens' Regiment did some skirmishing around Savannah, and Anderson was present at the conference which Williamston held with the partisan leaders at Ninety-Six. Most of the Americans refused to follow Williamston into North Carolina, because to do so would be to leave their families defenseless, and in good faith they gave their paroles to the British officers. Had the British kept their pledges history would probably have heard no more of Robert Anderson. But shamefully the Englishmen disregarded oaths and promises until human nature, unable longer to endure the outrages, the Americans took up arms again in desperation, fighting now with the fervor of despair, because they fought with a rope around their necks.

After the Battle of Cowpens, Pickens was made Brigadier General, and Anderson was promoted to colonel. It was Colonel Anderson's regiment that held the line between Augusta and Ninety-Six in the spring of 1781, and prevented Colonel Cruger of Ninety-Six from going to the assistance of Brown in Georgia. Later Anderson's regiment in union with the forces of "Light Horse" Harry Lee, captured Augusta, and by harrying the British, succeeded in keeping them from making any headway against the American forces. In the autumn of 1781 Governor Rutledge organized the militia in three classes, each class to serve two months in rotation, so that two-thirds could be relieved at one time. General Pickens had charge of one class, and Robert Anderson commanded a regiment under him.

At the Battle of Eutaw Anderson's regiment fought in the front line, though there they were defeated. Colonel Anderson took part in the Battle of Musgrove Mills. Much of the success of the great partisan fighter, Andrew Pickens, was due to the splendid work done by his sub-officer and warm friend, Robert Anderson.

After the war when the state of South Carolina wished to drive the Cherokees on, and get possession of their territory, Pickens and

Anderson were sent to do the job, and they carried it to a successful finish. The final treaty with the Indians was signed and delivered to General Pickens under a red oak tree near Cherry's Crossing, which stood for many years, but was finally blown down in a storm, and the spot is now marked by a large boulder.

Anderson took part in several other expeditions against the Indians as they retreated farther westward. The red men gave him the name, "Old Thunder Gusty," as his temper was equaled only by his courage.

After the war Colonel Anderson served several terms in the state legislature. But the greater part of his life was spent on his farm in that part of Pendleton District which was afterwards named in his honor.

General Anderson, for he attained that title in the state militia, was an elder in the Old Stone Church; a man of considerable wealth, although his father had remembered him in his will only to leave his "beloved son, Robert," the sum of ten pounds. It is probable that the father had given to this son his "portion" when he left the paternal home to set up for himself in a new country. General Anderson owned all of the land from Deep Creek to Andersonville, also land on Seneca River, Keowee River, Conneross Creek, Three and Twenty Creek, Six-Mile Mountain and in Pendleton. His estate at his death consisted of 2,100 acres. Of these 460 were bounty lands.

His will is rather unique. In it he makes minute provision for his slaves, and states that they shall never be sold from the place "unless they should turn out to be thieves, and unless they cannot be restrained by good treatment, friendly cautions and merciful use of the rod of correction. If by all these means they cannot be reclaimed, then it is my will that they should be sold." Disposing of two negroes which belonged to Mrs. Reece in her own right when he married her, he says: "These negroes and their increase are the legal right of myself and my heirs. But Mrs. Reece had children no better provided for than mine are, and whereas my own children are well enough off as to the things of this world if they make a prudent use of what they've got, if not they have too much already, therefore"—and so he bequeathed the two negroes to Mrs. Reece's son. In another place in his will he says apropos of these same negroes: "Whereas, I traded for Jeff, the husband of Hannah, at a considerable disadvantage on account of his great attachment to his wife and children, and although they have differed and are now apart, yet if they should compromise their differences and desire to be together, it is my will that Mr. Reece buy Jeff from Robert, or Robert buy Hannah and her two children from Mr. Reece." He closes with these words: "And now my blessed Redeemer do I with a lively faith lay hold of Thy meritorious death and sufferings, hoping to be washed clean by Thy precious blood from all my sins. In this hope I rest and wait Thy call."

In 1800 General Anderson was presidential elector on the ticket for Thomas Jefferson and Aaron Burr.

It is told of him that learning that one of his neighbors was ill and unable to attend to his farm, which, being a poor man without slaves, he worked himself, General Anderson rode over to the place a distance of ten miles, and performed the necessary labor upon his neighbor's fields.

When this good man died there had been a freshet, and it was found impossible to take his body to the Old Stone Church for interment, so he was buried temporarily on his plantation, there was no family burying ground there, he having always preferred the church yard, and where he was laid to await a more convenient season, his ashes rest today in a forgotten corner of an old field, for years without a stone to mark the place, but some few years ago Mrs. Lowry, who then owned the place, believing that there should be "names in the graves that should not be forgot," put a marker over his remains.

The descendants of Robert as nearly as can be ascertained are: 1st Anne, married Dr. William Hunter. Their children, Dr. John married Kitty Calhoun, moved to Alabama. William married Miss Clayton, Anne married John Smith and became lost in the great family of Smiths. Mary married Reverend David Humphreys, Andrew married———.

2nd Lydia married Samuel Maverick. Children, Elizabeth married Mr. Weyman; they had three children. Joseph married Emily Maxwell, lived in Pendleton, Samuel went to New York, Mary married Mr. Thompson of Memphis, Tenn., Lydia married William Van Wyck, children Samuel Maverick, Zemaly, William and Augustus.

Samuel Maverick Van Wyck married Margaret Broyles. Two sons, Samuel married Nina Harrison. They went to Atlanta where after a few years both died leaving a large family. Oze Van Wyck married Elizabeth Keith. Children, Lydia married Shuford, lives in Anderson, William Overman went West, Oze also went West, both married. Elizabeth married Zemp and lives in Sumter. Dr. Samuel M. Van Wyck was a surgeon in the Confederate army and was killed during the war. His young wife lived for sixty years longer, having become one of the oldest persons in the community, but to the end a vital part of the life of the town. An unusual and most interesting woman.

Zemaly married and lived in New York, William married a daughter of Professor Battle of the University of North Carolina. Augustus lived in New York for years, judge of the supreme court there, and in 1898 Democratic candidate for governor of New York. He was defeated by Theodore Roosevelt. He was the first mayor of Greater New York.

Another son of Lydia Anderson and Samuel Maverick was also Augustus. His father was at that time the richest man in South Carolina, but the dignified and aristocratic town of Pendleton was too slow for young Gus. He responded to the call of the wild and went to Texas, and that time truly "the wild and woolly west." It had not yet declared its independence of Mexico. The father used to send his son rough boxes containing seed, but buried in the seed was gold coin. In that day there was no other way of transmitting money but to send the actual cash. Young Maverick was to buy with it large tracts of land in the new country. He rapidly grew rich in his adopted home. He bought great quantities of stock and turned it loose to graze upon the plains. His cattle increased tremendously and soon the whole section of country was overrun with good cattle beearing no brand. Many of them were caught by anyone who chose to do so, and branded as he pleased; it became so common that any unclaimed domestic animal running free came to be called "a maverick," and the word has become a part of the English language. Some of Mr. Maverick's enemies, however, give a different version; they say that "Old Gus Maverick" was in the habit of catching any unbranded stock that happened to be running loose and put upon it his brand, and that was the way the term came into use.

Mr. Maverick, when attending court once in a town close to the Mexican border, was taken prisoner, carried into Mexico and made to work the highways with a ball and chain attached to his ankle. Waddy Thompson, at that time United States minister to Mexico, found him in that condition, and through his friendship with Santa Anna succeeded in procuring the release of the unfortunate man, and permission for him to return home.

It used to be told that when Thompson, who was a popular political speaker in South Carolina, was made minister to Mexico, one of his rustic admirers in Pendleton upon hearing of his appointment, remarked: "Well, I didn't know that Waddy was even a member of the church, but I bet he'll make a big preacher."

Other of General Anderson's descendants are living in the community, most of them bearing other names, as he had but one son and four daughters.

Several Revolutionary graves are known to be in the county. Andrew Liddell is buried in a family grave yard near Denver. The plantation was granted him after the Revolution. On his tombstone is the inscription: "A soldier of the Revolution." He was one of the first members of Roberts Church. His home was afterwards known as "The Reeves Place."

Elizabeth Anderson married a soldier of the Revolution, Robert Maxwell. They had two sons, Robert and John, and lived about where is now the town of Piedmont. General Maxwell, as he came to be in the state militia, was a member of the first Continental Congress. In 1798, as he was on his way to Pendleton, he was shot by a man disguised as an Indian. His son, John, married Elizabeth Hampton Earle, and settled on Seneca River; they had ten children. The other son, Robert, married Mary Prince Earle. They lived for a time at the old plantation where his parents had lived, but later moved to Pendleton. The brides were sisters, daughters of General Samuel Earle.

Robert Maxwell's widow, Elizabeth Anderson, married a second time, Mr. Caruth. They had one daughter, Louisa, who married James Gillam, of Greenwood.

Robert Anderson, Jr., married Maria Thomas, of Nassau. They had ten children. Their son, Robert the third, married a granddaughter of General Pickens. Their other children were: Edward Edmund, who became a Presbyterian preacher; Thomas, John, Julius, William, Henry, Anne, who married Joseph Harris; Caroline, who married Dr. Tervey Halsey, a Presbyterian preacher, professor in McCormick Theological Seminary, of Chicago. Martha married Samuel Pickens, a grandson of General Pickens.

A son of General Andrew Pickens was Robert. He served as lieutenant in the Revolutionary army under his father. The young man was married, and his home was a rude log cabin without windows. It stood not far from where the town of Pendleton afterwards grew up. Lieutenant Pickens was an object of especial hatred to some of his Tory neighbors who were on the alert to injure him. The young soldier's duties kept him away from home much of the time, but when possible he made flying visits to his family. On one of these occasions he was seen by some of his foes to enter his house, and then they thought they certainly had him captured. There was but one door, and about six men rushed upon that entrance, beating and demanding to be let in. Mrs. Pickens had seen them coming, and she had dropped the strong oak bar which did duty for a lock, into its socket. Then she hastily extinguished a fire which smouldered in the great fire place, and told her husband to climb out through the chimney while she held the attacking party as long as possible at the door. The scheme was successfully carried out, and the fire re-lighted before the valiant woman finally opened the door, at the same time assuring the Tories that her husband was not at home. They thought they knew better, and rushed in, expecting this time to capture their prey. Great was their perplexity when, after a thorough search of the cabin, they failed to find him.

This same Lieutenant Pickens had another narrow escape from his enemies. Once they were pursuing him through a woods, distinctly they saw him at intervals flying before them, and they thought they were rapidly overtaking him, when he disappeared as completely as though the earth had opened and swallowed him. Angrily they searched. Finally when they had convinced themselves that in some miraculous way he had really escaped, they gave up the hunt and returned home. Then Lieutenant Pickens emerged from beneath a hollow section of bark which, as he leaped over a fallen pine tree, had become loosened and as his foot slipped, detaching it, he fell on the opposite side of the fallen log from his pursuers, and the hollow bark turned over him, having the appearance of another fallen log. There he lay, safely concealed, while his foes passed over him.

Samuel Earle in 1776, at the age of sixteen, entered the Revolutionary army as an ensign. He remained in service until the war ended, and had risen to be captain. After the war he settled in Pendleton District, served the state in both legislature and Congress, and accumulated a good property.

Among the pioneer settlers in this section were two brothers-in-law, Samuel Dean and Harmon Cummin. They had married sisters, Misses James, and the two families came from Maryland some years after the war. Mr. Cummin had served as a soldier, but Mr. Dean had been rejected upon the ground of being more needed to keep the Indians in subjection. His home at that time was on the borders of civilization, and it was subject to terrible Indian ravages, which were so dreadful that the horror of them reconciled Mrs. Dean to leaving her mother so far away and removing to the new section of South Carolina. In her old age she used to tell her grandchildren about that long and trying trip. The family came in a cart whose wheels were sections of a big tree sawn out thicker in the center than on the edge, and a hole bored through for the support. Days and nights of slow moving through pathless forests, with the bitter consciousness of having left loved ones forever; not even letters passed in those days between South Carolina and Maryland. When the family first reached Pendleton District they were disappointed, but they settled on what is known as a Dean place, somewhere near Mountain Creek, and being free from Indian raids reconciled them to their new home. There they raised ten children, eight boys and two girls. Most of the family in later years went west, but one son, Moses Dean, remained and became one of the best known and most respected of Anderson's early citizens. Mr. A. A. Dean, beloved Confederate veteran of the county, was a son of Moses Dean. There is in the county a large Dean connection, and they have been useful and respected citizens.

The other immigrant from Maryland, Mr. Harmon Cummin, lived near Mountain Creek also. None of his descendants are in this county now. He was captured once by the British and held on a prison ship. Once he was struck on the head with a great iron key, and knocked senseless. He told many tales of the cruelty of the British to their prisoners. Before his death Mr. Cummin became bed-ridden. The doctor of all that section of country then was Dr. Thompson, father of the late Dr. Richard E. Thompson. On one occasion Dr. Thompson took his little son, Dick, with him to visit the sick man. When he entered the room he said: "Mr. Cummin, I have brought my little boy to see a real soldier of the Revolution." The old man raised himself up in bed and replied: "Well, here's one of 'em." The grave of the old soldier is lost now; it is thought probable that he was buried in the old Mountain Creek grave yard, but it is not certain, and no one living can locate his resting place. In the Dean section there is a spring still known as "The Cummin Spring."

There is a tradition that a Revolutionary soldier is buried at Cross Roads. Also a story is told about him. It is said that the Tories mashed off the fingers of one of his hands in an effort to make him tell where he had buried treasure. When they had finished their gruesome task he held out the other hand for them to work on if they were so disposed; but he would not open his lips. Not even his name is preserved.

It is believed that a Revolutionary soldier named La Far was buried on the Lon McGee farm, though his grave cannot be located.

A few years after the Revolutionary war Edward Vandiver came from Maryland and located not far from Neal's Creek Church. He had fought all through the war. He was away from his home so much that he became a stranger to his own children, and on one occasion when he found an opportunity to pay a visit to his family, the children hid under the bed because they feared he might be a Tory. He is buried in Neal's Creek grave yard.

Another Revolutionary soldier who spent his last years in this locality was Elisha Bennett. A neighbor of his named John Wornock was also a Revolutionary soldier. He lived on Pea Creek. Both of them are buried in an old grave yard not far from Carpenter's Mill on Broadaway Creek. A son of Mr. Bennett, Archibald, went to New Orleans where he became a millionaire wholesale merchant. He visited Anderson in 1872, and attended an association meeting at Neal's Creek. His elegant appearance made an impression on a young man who was present on that occasion that time has not effaced. While on that visit he had the old graves of his relatives in the grave yard just mentioned marked with neat tombstones to replace the rough rocks which had stood at the head and feet previously.

Thomas Dwyer, a Revolutionary soldier, is buried near Stauntonville.

A few years before the Revolutionary war seven brothers named Milford came from Ireland to America. It is said that they had paid their fare on a certain boat upon which they expected to sail, but she had taken aboard too many passengers for comfort, and the Milford brothers waited for the next vessel. It proved a fortunate thing for them, as the boat upon which they had intended to sail was lost at sea. The seven brothers fought through the war; afterwards they settled in Pendleton District, where they spent their lives and are buried in its soil. Their names were Joseph, Matthew, Henry, Robert, Thomas and John. One name has been lost. Once during the war Robert fell into the hands of Bloody Bill Cunningham, and saved himself from death by ready Irish wit, and a deviation from perfect truth.

Reverend John Simpson, first pastor of several of the early Presbyterian churches, was also a Revolutionary soldier. He and his wife, who was Miss Reamer, came from Delaware to South Carolina and settled first on Fishing Creek. While pastor there he headed a band of Revolutionists and defeated a Tory band at Beckhamsville and at Mobley's. The mortified loyalists determined to punish the fighting parson, and had planned to burn his church with him and his congregation in it at worship. They were, however, disappointed. The minister on the Friday preceding that Sunday, June 11th, 1780, had shouldered his musket and marched away under the command of Captain McClure, a youth who had grown up under his ministry. Finding no service in progress at the church, the Tories planned to go to his home and "burn the rascal out," but their design was overheard by some negroes who hastened to inform Mrs. Simpson of her danger. Hastily she gathered up her one set of silver teaspoons, a gift from her mother, and, with her children, concealed herself behind some bushes back of the house. From her vantage point she watched the miscreants rifle her house, taking everything of any value. They dragged her four feather beds into the yard where they cut them open. Such articles of clothing as they could use they appropriated, then set fire to the house. About to leave, they noticed an outbuilding which they had not yet examined. It proved to be Mr. Simpson's study, containing a valuable library. To that, too, they applied the torch and went on their way rejoicing. No sooner were they out of sight than Mrs. Simpson rushed into the burning study and succeeded in bringing out two apronsful of books, all she could save, and got some severe burns in securing those. The feather beds took fire, though the plucky dame managed to save feathers enough to make one bed. Neighbors soon arrived upon the scene and took charge of the poor woman, who was by that time ill. Four weeks later she became the mother of her fifth child. As soon as she was able she, with her five children and a young lady friend, Miss Neely, took residence in a small outhouse which had escaped the flames. Neither she nor her children owned a change of clothing. Getting possession of some cloth, she went to work to supply them. Scarcely was that done when another band of Tories descended upon them and took those away. Some of that band were wearing clothes which had belonged to her husband, and strutting before her, they demanded of her whether she did not think them better looking than Mr. Simpson, and telling her that one day they would bring her his head. She had some cattle which had escaped the first raid, which this crowd took, refusing her plea for just one cow to give milk for her children. They proceeded several miles with their spoil, when they penned the animals up for the night. Before morning two steers succeeded in making an opening through which the whole herd made its escape and returned home.

Mr. and Mrs. Simpson are both buried in Roberts Church yard.

There is a lonely grave on the side of the road near Townville. In it sleeps "Old Man Billy Day," a Revolutionary soldier who once lived in a cabin close by. He rests in that unhallowed place because he refused to be buried in the grave yard. He said the devil would go there to get Sam Brown, and might get him by mistake, so he gave strict orders that his grave should be out beside the road "because the devil wouldn't think of looking for anybody there."

HISTORY OF ANDERSON COUNTY

David Sadler is a Revolutionary soldier who lies in Roberts Church yard. He was one of the early settlers in the county, and died in 1848.

Peter Acker served in the Revolution under the Gen. Wade Hampton of that time.

Matthew Clark, a Revolutionary soldier, was founder of Asbury Church, where he is buried.

Among the earliest settlers who came to this section were three brothers, Irish, who had lived for a time in Virginia. They were Eliab, Samuel and William Moore. They built rude cabin homes in the wilderness, that of Samuel was very near what is now High Shoals.

Back in Ireland Samuel Moore left a dearly loved friend named Smith. After establishing himself in the new world, Mr. Moore wrote for his friend to bring his family and join him. Smith, with a wife and two children, started on the long journey, but while at sea Mr. Smith died and was buried beneath the waves. The widow continued the journey with her children, and after many trials they reached the home of her husband's friend, where they were warmly welcomed. There they made their home and proved a blessing to the family that took them in. Mrs. Moore was almost an invalid, and Mrs. Smith took on her strong shoulders the burden of the domestic work.

When the Revolutionary war came on the Moore brothers raised a company to join the partisan fighters; Samuel Moore became its colonel. The company, or more properly, regiment, was stationed near Ninety-Six, and "Bloody Bill Cunningham" was the foe they had to fight. News traveled slowly in that day, and the anxious ones at home knew little of what was transpiring on the battlefield. Also soldiers were poorly equipped. Mrs. Moore was distressed lest her husband might be suffering for good clothing, or even for food, and the intrepid widow who owed them so much undertook to carry to him whatever his wife wished to send. Over seventy miles of Tory-infested country the brave woman rode on horseback, taking to Colonel Moore home news and comforts.

Should not the Revolutionary ride of the Widow Smith be classed with those of Emily Geiger or Paul Revere? They carried war news, she bore only homely supplies and domestic news to a friend, but the risk she ran was just as great as theirs; she was instigated by love and gratitude, they by hatred of the enemy as much as by love of their country. After the war the Moores built for Mrs. Smith and her children a home near their own, and Mrs. Smith's descendants still live in the county.

Col. Moore was killed in the skirmish with Cunningham at Swansea's Ferry, and his brother, Eliab, assumed his command. The Moore family has been prominent in Anderson history since that day.

On the dividing line between Anderson and Oconee counties is an old grave. It lies half in each county; in it rests William Grant. He was a brave soldier of the Revolution, fought at Cowpens, Guilford Court House, Eutaw Springs, and several other places. After the war he took up land in the newly opened Cherokee country, and his home built on Conneross Creek, near its junction with the Seneca River, is standing on the road between Pendleton and Townville.

Mr. Grant was a Universalist in religion, and a Whig in politics. A staunch Union man during the nullification troubles. One day during the excitement caused by that political episode, a party of gentlemen, among whom were Col. Kilpatrick and some of the Harrisons of Harrisonburg, on the Seneca River, strong nullifiers, stopped at Mr. Grant's house. Conversation soon turned on politics; shortly argument waxed warm, the old soldier standing stoutly for the Union he had helped to form. One of the gentlemen banteringly accused him of having been a Tory. Immediately he announced his intention of applying for a pension, a thing he had always scorned to do. But he said if it required a pension to prove his loyalty, a pension he would have; and he got it.

Mr. Grant was a prosperous man, and something of a money lender. He was a rather rough old fellow, lived in a two-story cabin, went barefooted, and did pretty much as he pleased. He often sat on his little piazza with his bare feet propped on the banisters. A gentleman from Pendleton rode up to the house one day to talk to him about borrowing some money. The road at that time ran directly by the house and very close to it. The visitor found him in his favorite attitude on his porch. He rode up to the steps and stated his business. The old man did not change his position, merely wiggled his toes and replied: "Pay me what you owe me, then maybe you can get some more."

It was by his order that his grave was located. It was within unobstructed view of his home. He said when he arose, he wanted the first object his eyes encountered to be his own house, moreover he wanted to watch his wife sell corn to passing travelers. He used to say that when he died he was going to turn into a white horse.

The war records in Washington show that John Harris served during the war under Colonels Andrew Williamston, Andrew

Pickens, of South Carolina, Clark, of Georgia, McCall and Sampson Matthews, of Virginia. Under Captains Noble, McCall, Tucker and Johnson. He enlisted with his father at Little River, Abbeville county. Then he fought at Cowpens, was shot through the head at Savannah River. Drew a pension, No. 23234, December 9th, 1833. After the war he lived in Pendleton District, and married a daughter of General Andrew Pickens. Was a member of the state convention of 1790, was sheriff for a short term, and ordinary of Pendleton and Anderson District for about forty years. He practiced medicine and treated most of the prominent people of the district. He was a "Steam doctor."

Mr. Harris had come from Harrisburg, Pennsylvania, and partly in honor of his native place, and partly from his own name, he called his home at the confluence of Seneca River and Conneross Creek, Harrisburg. Popular with all classes, he was especially loved by children. His home was about two miles east of Townville, and he was buried on the plantation. His grave is marked.

His children were Andrew, Joseph P., Benjamin, Dr. Nathaniel and Eliza, who married a Mr. Burns.

Jehu Orr, a soldier of the Revolution, is buried in what used to be known as "The Rutledge Grave Yard," named for some of the earliest of its occupants.

Mr. Orr built a two story brick house about where Mr. Levi Martin now lives. His house had a cellar which was well stocked, and like all persons of that time, he kept open house, there were no country hotels, and travellers asked and received entertainment wherever night found them. On the evening of February 12th, 1827, a passing traveller named Uriah Sligh, stopped at the Orr home and asked for a night's shelter. He was received, and Mr. Orr brought out some of the contents of his cellar. The two proceeded to "make a night of it." But Sligh was one of those persons who became quarrelsome under the influence of stimulants. Mr. Orr may have been of the same temperament, at any rate a quarrel arose over a game of cards, and in the scuffle that followed, Sligh shot Orr. Until Mr. Martin tore down the old house a few years ago, there were plainly to be seen the marks made by the shots, one on the ceiling, the other on the wall beside the stair case. Mr. Orr lived until March 18th, 1827, when he died from the wound. Sligh was hanged for murder.

After fighting one's way through brier, brambles and tangled vines, over fences and through fields, the forgotten grave is found. Then when the overgrowth is torn away, the visitor reads with difficulty, the long and fond inscription. It gives a full history of the man and his war record, tells how dear he was to his own, how many were his friends, winds up with a long poem which assures the world that he will ever be remembered. When we are dead, we are very, very dead!

Mr. Jehu Orr married a daughter of "Squire McCann," of the Slabtown section. He was the father of one of Anderson's early merchants and hotel keepers, Mr. Christopher Orr, and grand father of Judge J. L. Orr, minister to Russia, just after the war of the 60s.

One of the original settlers in the county was Matthew Dickson, a Scotch-Irishman from County Tyrone, Ireland, who, in 1750, emigrated to Pennsylvania. He came to South Carolina with the influx of Scotch-Irish, that swept the Southern States just before the Revolution. At once Mr. Dickson took an active part with the patriots during the war, and later when the Cherokee country was opened, he moved to what is now Anderson county, and owned land on Six-and-Twenty Creek. He has many descendants in the county.

Another early settler and Revolutionary soldier was David Sloan, who with his wife, Susan, came to this section in 1784, and settled beside the canebrakes, on Seneca River. When they came to South Carolina, they had two children, twins, David and Susan. It is told that often during her husband's absence, Mrs. Sloan finding it necessary to take grain to the mill, some distance from her home, she put her children to sleep and hid them in the canebrake while she shouldered the sack of grain and did her errand, always returning in dread lest during her absence the Indians had raided the place and murdered the children. David Sloan was captain of a North Carolina company during the revolution.

"Horseshoe Robinson" was a Revolutionary soldier, and a character of note who lived in or near Pendleton. He was a blacksmith, and some people have thought that his trade gave him his soubriquet. Others believe that it was due to the fact that the river curved around his place in the shape of a horse shoe.

He was shrewd, and loved adventure. He was also gifted with an ability to tell about his adventures, in an interesting way. When years after the war, the novelist, Mr. J. P. Kennedy, visited Pendleton, he found talking to old Horseshoe a fascinating pastime, and on his return to his home, wrote the historical romance, "Horseshoe Robinson." Some friend read it to the old man, and asked what he thought of it, and whether the stories told about him, by Mr. Kennedy, were correct. He replied, "Well, I disremember about them women, but the rest of it is all so."

Late in life, Mr. Robinson followed his children to Alabama, where he died, and his grave is marked as the last resting place of "Horseshoe Robinson."

Many other Revolutionary soldiers settled in what later became Anderson county; but no records were kept, graves were unmarked, and the ruthless hand of time has obliterated all traces of many who did a good part in establishing American independence.

THE WAR OF 1812

A company went to this war from Anderson county; possibly there were more than one, and some soldiers, who belonged to other commands. Certainly S. G. Earle, of Evergreen, commanded one company. Mathias Staunton, of old Stauntonville, near Belton, was a soldier in the war of 1812. An ancestor of Mr. Asa Hall was also a soldier in that war. Probably there are a number of Anderson families who have records of an ancestor who served then.

CHAPTER VI.

NEWSPAPERS AND WRITERS.

THE first newspaper printed in Anderson county was *The Pendleton Messenger,* its publisher was "Printer John Miller," an Englishman who in his youth had been one of the printers who set the type for the famous "Letters of Junius." The paper was published before 1818, possibly several years before.

Pendleton had the first Farmers' Publication south of Baltimore. It was a small magazine, edited by Mr. George Seabrook, named *The Farmer and Planter.* In later years it was removed to Atlanta, and re-christened *The Southern Cultivator.*

On September 4th, 1840, at the country place of Calhoun, a newspaper was started by that brilliant young man, J. P. Reed. He called it *The Highland Sentinel,* and the wicked boys of the time immediately dubbed it *The Highland Moccasin.* So successful was the paper that in January, 1842, Mr. Reed moved it to the growing town, where under several names it survived for many years. After change of location it soon became *The Anderson Gazette.* The office was on the west side of the square, next to Dr. Webb's Drug and Book store.

An amusing story is told of the power of the press, in that early time. One day an old lady walked into the *Gazette* office and told the obliging editor that she wanted a Bible, saying she would wait while they printed it for her. She took a chair and pulled her knitting from her reticule. One of the printers stepped out of the back door of the office, and into the back door of the book store next door, and bought a Bible, with which he soon returned, handing it to the waiting lady. She was quite pleased, and praised their quick work, telling them that they "did not take so very long to print the whole book."

Local news was entirely too ignoble to appear in the dignified pages of a newspaper, in those early days. They were filled with the great doings of London, Paris, New York and Washington, and it was only two or three months old. An interesting item appears in *The Sentinel* for February 25th, 1842—the headlines very modest to our modern eyes. Marriage in High Life. "We see it stated in the papers that Caleb Cushing, a representative in Congress, lately led to the matrimonial altar a daughter of President Tyler. Another of the president's daughters, a few days since, was married to a Mr. Waller, of Williamsburg." Shades of Roosevelt! Was that all the papers could do for the marriage of a president's daughter in 1842?

An item which appears in *The Sentinel* for January 27th, 1843, is "A Talking Machine! A mechanician of a little town of Bohemia, has constructed an automaton which imitates perfectly the human voice, particularly soprano notes; it sings several different airs with the greatest accuracy; shades, runs and the chromatic scale, are all executed with surprising precision. The automaton in singing even pronounces certain words so as to be easily understood. The inventor hopes to arrive at such a point of perfection as to bring his machine to pronounce all the words of the best operas."

In 1846, there appears the statement—"Mr. Duncan McIver is now in our village, and will take off the countenance of all who may desire it, in an admirable manner. We have examined several of his pictures, and as regards both resemblance and finish, we consider them equal to any we have ever seen. We advise all who wish a perfect fac-simile of themselves, to call on Mr. McIver. He may be found at Benson Hotel, where he will exhibit specimens to all who wish to see them." The article was headed, Daguerrian Likenesses.

The Anderson people of 1860 must have been a reading people; the newspapers are full of advertisements of reading matter. Godey's Ladies' Book was the popular monthly magazine, and it was not so very different from women's magazines of the present day. One dollar would buy five popular novels—"The Merchant's Daughter, a beautiful novel, by Miss Eleanor Pickering; Cruikshanks' Omnibus, grotesquely illustrated; The Mosaic Workers of Venice, a beautiful tale from the French of Madame George Sand; Schillar's great romance, The Visionary; Romance and Reality and Other Tales, by T. S. Arthur, Esq., any persons sending us one dollar will receive the above choice novels, by mail. Address L. J. Galusha and Company, 42 West 4th street, Cincinnati, Ohio. Editors copying the above will be entitled to the books."

The public was by no means dependent upon firms so far away for interesting reading matter. J. P. Benson offers for sale, school books, standard novels, popular biographies, such as "Weems' Life of Marion," science, religion, politics, everything that a reader or a student could wish.

The last issue of *The Highland Sentinel* comes out October 13th, 1843. The plant was sold and J. L. Orr became the editor of the new *Anderson Gazette*. The first number of *The Gazette* appears Saturday, November 11th, R. F. Wyatt, publisher. Mr. Wyatt had come to Anderson when only sixteen years old, to work for Mr.

Reed on *The Highland Sentinel*. He and Mr. Archibald Todd were publishing *The Gazette* at the time of the big fire in 1845. Mr. Orr remained editor only a year; in the issue of November 20th, 1844, he takes leave. In his valedictory he thanks A. C. Norris for procuring for him the greatest number of subscribers.

Captain Archibald Todd succeeded Mr. Orr as editor. While he held the position the office was twice moved. The Todd family were for many years connected with the newspapers of the town.

The Gazette was published into the 50s, when it was overhauled, renovated and started out under a new name, that of *The Anderson Intelligencer*, which appeared for the first time on Tuesday, August 14th, 1860, James A. Hoyt and J. C. C. Featherston owners, publishers and editors. After a short time Mr. Featherston retired and J. A. Hoyt continued to be its editor until about 1877, when he left Anderson, going first to Columbia, then to Greenville, where he took charge of *The Baptist Courier*, and later became editor of *The Greenville Mountaineer*. It was on the *Courier* that Mrs. Hoyt, who had been Rebecca Webb, did her work, editing for years a department for young people.

Mr. Fleetwood Clinkscales became connected with *The Intelligencer*, soon after its first appearance, and continued on it for more than thirty years. C. C. Langston began to work on the paper under him, and later became its owner and editor.

There ought to be numerous delineations of the old time Anderson people, for there was always somebody "to take off their likenesses." In the first number of *The Intelligencer* is the advertisement—"To obtain a good ambrotype for a mere song, it is only necessary to pay a visit to Mr. John Milwee's gallery, where first rate pictures are taken at 50 cts. Milwee understands his business in all its branches, and is prepared to do work in that line. Entrance to his rooms, No. 2, Granite Row."

That first number of *The Intelligencer* states its reasons for existence, and its aims in life. It was a four-page, six-column newssheet, and on its first page says that it is an independent journal, devoted to politics, literature, news, morals, agriculture, and science. The first name on the list of subscribers was Colonel Eliot M. Keith. Some of the merchants whose names appear in the advertisements were: Sharpe and Watson, England and Bewley, D. A. Keasler, Sloan, Sullivan and Company, Sloan and Towers. Some of the law firms were Perrin and Creswell, Moore and Featherstone, Keith and Wilkes, John Peter Brown, and W. W. Humphreys. There were at least two dentists—J. T. Horne and R. M. Frost. Evans and Hubbard were druggists. Sloan and Towers advertise

HISTORY OF ANDERSON COUNTY

Kaolin crockery, made in Edgefield, and urge people to patronize southern manufacturers. Sloan and Sullivan call their place "Cheap Corner."

In looking over those old papers, the familiar name of Dr. B. A. Henry strikes one with surprise, as it is well known that the Dr. B. A. Henry of the present time is not a native of Anderson, having moved here some years ago from Lowndesville. The Dr. Henry of 1860 was not a resident of the place, but came over several times a week from Elberton; he seemed to practice here.

Anderson people of that day were not without amusement, travelling players frequently came for a week or more, and if their performance was too elaborate to be given in The Masonic Hall, for by that time one had been built, tents were set up large enough to accommodate the crowds, and with stages that could display the drama.

There was a paper called *The Southern Rights Advocate*, published in Anderson a few years before the war between the states. It was an anti-secessionist journal, owned by a company among whom were Col. Orr and Col. Reed. Coleman C. Puckett was its editor, the late Robert A. Thompson, of Walhalla, was foreman of the office.

An opposing journal called *The True Carolinian* was established with Colonel John V. Moore its editor. It, too, was owned by a company. The veteran newspaper man, Fleetwood Clinkscales, began his journalistic career by working on that paper. It was afterwards moved to Pendleton and to Hartwell, in 1876. John A. McGill and R. E. Belcher, with a mule and wagon, carried the outfit to its new home. In making the trip with the old time Smith handpress, and five cases of type, the wagon broke down at Holland's Store, and they spent the night in the store. In its new existence, the paper became *The Hartwell Sun*, which is still shining.

Mr. Puckett lived at Anderson for some years. He married a Miss Crawford, of the county, who taught painting, wax flower making, hair work, feather work, etc., all of which was very fashionable, and necessary for the girls of that time to know. Mrs. Jane Hubbard, mother of Miss Leonora and Miss Augusta Hubbard, present art teachers, taught all of that kind of work, and there are many specimens of the work done by her or her pupils, still to be found in the town.

The Pucketts had one child, Lester. Mr. Puckett went to Kansas, where he opened a newspaper office, which was on the second story of a building, and opened on a platform, having no railing. One dark night he stepped out on the platform, and going too far, fell and broke his neck. After Mr. Puckett's death, Mr. Ibzan Rice became editor of the paper. It was one of the first dollar papers in the county. In those days it was unusual to publish religious matter in secular papers. Mr. Rice introduced a religious column into his journal, but it proved to be unpopular, and was soon discontinued. On one occasion, there appeared an editorial in *The Southern Rights Advocate* that so pleased Congressman Orr that he stepped into the office and handing the editor twenty dollars, with a list of names, asked to have the paper sent to those people for one year. The next issue comes out with quite a brag about having added twenty new subscribers to its list the previous Saturday. The paper finally merged with *The Gazette*, which was then called *The Gazette-Advocate*.

Archibald Todd, once editor of *The Gazette*, was one of the first mail clerks on G. and C. road. In 1860, he was stricken with paralysis in Belton, and brought home where he died in a few days.

Frank Norris was at one time editor of *The Gazette*, and he and Ibzan Rice, editor of *The Advocate*, once came very near fighting a duel over the burning question of secession, on which their respective journals represented opposite views.

In 1848 Mr. Thomas H. Russell, father of the late D. H. Russell, purchased an interest in *The Gazette*, at that time owned and edited by Mr. Todd. The office then was about where Reed's Music House stood so long; it was later moved to the Todd lot, almost opposite to The Central Presbyterian Church. Mr. Russell edited the paper for eight years, during which time he moved the office to where the Bank of Anderson now stands. Later he discontinued to edit the paper, though he still owned it. In 1859, he sold to Harrison, Norris and Company. The printing office remained where he had located it, until the new "Granite Row" was completed, then the newspaper occupied an office very near the center of the row.

In the early part of the seventh decade of the nineteenth century, Mr. Edwards B. Murray edited a paper in Anderson called *The Conservator*. His office in Granite row was burned in 1874. In 1875 *The Conservator* united with *The Intelligencer*, Hoyt and Murray, joint editors.

In the 70s Mr. Preston Earle established a weekly in Anderson, which he named *The Anderson Journal*. After a few years he sold to Messrs. Summer and Robert Todd, sons of Mr. Archibald Todd. They ran the paper until sometime in the early 90s, when both of them left Anderson, and *The Journal* was discontinued.

The People's Advocate started in 1890, as a Farmers' Alliance paper, Pierce Brown, publisher. Later *The Advocate* became the weekly edition of *The Daily Mail*, which made its first appearance Friday morning, October 6th, 1899, a little four-page, six-column paper, but a "real truly" daily. Its editors have been G. Cullen Sullivan, D. H. Russell, A. M. Carpenter and William Banks. Finally Mr. Brown, owner and publisher, assumed also the duties of editor. After a few years as a morning paper, it changed to afternoon.

About 1913 *The Intelligencer*, which since 1860 had existed as a weekly, was converted into a morning paper, Mr. William Banks becoming its first editor. *The Daily Intelligencer* was a first class paper, but having started under too great an expense, it ran for several years under difficulties, and finally about 1917, stopped publication, much to the regret of the people of the community, as *The Intelligencer* had been the chief paper of the town for over fifty years. Mell Glenn was its last editor.

About 1916 or '17, Victor B. Cheshire, at one time editor of the weekly *Intelligencer*, established a new weekly, *The Tribune*, later The *Anderson Daily Tribune*, a morning paper whose specialty was "pep." One feature of *The Tribune* which had also been a feature of *The Intelligencer* when Mr. Cheshire was its editor, was "Letters of an Old Country Lady," which touched a responsive chord in every heart, they were so wise, so kindly, so plain, and touched with the hand of experience, the vital things of life. The author was Mr. Cheshire's mother.

In 1923 Wilton E. Hall, former editor of *The Tribune*, and once state editor of *The Greenville News*, made a new venture in the newspaper world, establishing another morning paper in Anderson, *The Independent*, which after a time absorbed *The Tribune*. This paper speaks for itself, having attained the largest circulation of any paper ever published in Anderson. It is *The Independent* which sponsors this book of Anderson county reminiscences and gleanings.

About 1915 the Methodist Church in South Carolina selected Anderson as the place to publish their church paper, *The Southern Christian Advocate*. Reverend Mr. Kirkland, originally of old Barnwell District, was its editor, and when in 1918 the church decided to establish a permanent home for its publication in Columbia the removal of Dr. Kirkland and *The Southern Christian Advocate* was a distinct loss to the city of Anderson.

In 1914 J. Homer Oulla, who had for several years conducted a printing establishment in the town, undertook the ambitious enterprise of establishing a literary magazine. Its name was *The Piedmont Magazine*, and it was designed especially to exploit the Piedmont section of the state. The publication never received the support that it deserved, and which the originator expected. After an existence of about two years it was discontinued. Some of the people who wrote for it were: Mr. J. B. Lewis, Hon. Julius Boggs, Mr. L. E. Norryce, who was also associate editor; Mrs. Belle Mahon Pickle, Miss Augusta Hubbard, Mrs. Rebecca Lee, of Piedmont, and others.

Mr. Oulla gave to Anderson its first up-to-date printing office, complete with ruling and binding machinery, linotype composition and a complete rubber stamp outfit in connection.

Some two or three years ago The Rotary Club of the city determined to bring out a publication devoted to its own affairs. It selected for a name that of a by-gone paper of the town, *The Anderson Gazette*. It is a bright little sheet, and has for its editor Mr. John E. Wigginton. That gentleman is also the editor of a most attractive little magazine issued by the Methodist Church, it is called *Church Work,* and is solely an organ of St. John's Church and Sunday school.

The various schools of Anderson have had publications of their own, beginning away back in the 50s with *La Bas Bleu* of the Johnson Female University. There was *The Seminary Leaflet* of the Anderson Female Seminary in the 80s. *The P. M. I. Journal* of the Patrick Military Institute, in the 90s, and lastly *The Orion* of the Anderson College for Women, in this third decade of the twentieth century. All of these have been creditable publications, and have helped prepare writers for a larger field.

Dr. Luther Rice Burriss once published a paper in Anderson called *Baptist Refreshments.* He was born in 1840, eight miles southwest of Anderson, and moved to Mississippi before the war between the states. He was both a preacher and a teacher. Later he moved to Texas where he died.

In 1914 a paper, *The Comian,* a Y. M. C. A. publication, was being printed in the town especially for the benefit of the mills.

The Morning Watch, published on Mr. Earle's plantation, "Evergreen," was the first religious periodical in the county.

In the 90s Mr. John E. Wigginton, then a youth, published on a little hand press, a little four-page, four-column paper called *The Brushy Creek Banner*. It gave the news of the Brushy Creek section, and showed what the boy could and would do, when trained by time and experience.

HISTORY OF ANDERSON COUNTY

In 1894 B. F. Brown, Jr., published in Anderson a magazine named *The Columbian*.

There have always been writers who expressed their thoughts and opinions in the newspapers. However, back in the 40s they deemed it immodest to appear over their own signatures, consequently, who some of the early correspondents were cannot now be known. The papers, like the oratory of that time, were grandiloquent. They expressed their lurid views in Johnsonian English, and gave happenings all over the world except at home, local affairs were too puny to obstruct the great wave of world intelligence which they must help disseminate. Persons having something to say through the medium of newspapers, signed most frequent Latin names; if they knew no Latin, or preferred "a language understanded of the people," they signed themselves "Constant Reader," "Old Batchelor," "Friend," and scores of other pseudonymns.

Among writers which Anderson has produced is Thadeus Horton, brilliant young journalist who was born and grew to manhood in Williamston. He began when a boy, writing for home papers. At the time of his death in 1899, he was a valued member of the staff of *The New York Times*. At the age of twenty-three, Mr. Horton was appointed by the governor to represent South Carolina at the Commercial and Industrial convention in Paris; and his letters to the *News and Courier* and *The New York Herald* at that time established his reputation, and opened large opportunities for him. He died just when life promised him a brilliant future in his chosen work. Since his death his wife has become well known as a magazine writer.

Henry Trescott, of Pendleton, was the author of several books and numerous poems. His lines on the Confederate monument in Columbia have been greatly admired. Miss Katherine Trescott, of Pendleton, is also the author of numerous stories and poems. J. Adger Mullally handles the English language in a masterly manner. He is gifted as a speaker as well as a writer of both prose and verse. Colonel R. W. Simpson, of Pendleton, published a History of Pendleton District. While Colonel Simpson lived in Pendleton, he practiced law in Anderson, coming to the city every day. The great John C. Calhoun, author of books and pamphlets on government and statescraft, though he lived just outside of Anderson county, had his law office in Pendleton.

John G. Clinkscales, for many years a resident of Spartanburg, being connected with Wofford College, was born and grew to manhood in Anderson county. He was once County Superintendent of Education. He has written several novels, and contributed to many periodicals. His two books, "The Dark Corner" and "When Zach Went to College," well represent the Anderson county of his boyhood.

John Stevenson, for years a successful journalist in New York City, was Anderson bred.

J. Augustus Sullivan, under the name of "Nathan Beeswax", was making a wide reputation as a delineator of humorous character and native, uncultured wisdom when cut short by death at twenty-seven years of age.

J. L. Orr, both father and son of the same name, were prominent politicians of the section, and wrote political pamphlets and newspaper articles.

The late J. L. Tribble was a fluent writer, and his magazine and newspaper articles always attracted attention. Colonel Joseph Newton Brown wrote as he spoke, carefully, consequently his historical articles, which were largely on Confederate matters, are considered particularly accurate and trustworthy. His daughter, Miss Varina Brown, has written a biography of her father, which not only gives in an interesting way the life of that good citizen of the county, but also gives a most accurate and carefully studied account of some of the battles in which her father participated, especially those of Gettysburg, and Spottsylvania.

Julius E. Boggs, who died while practicing law in Anderson, was a graceful writer. He had been for years editor of *The Pickens Sentinel*, and he wrote for a number of papers and magazines. Mr. Boggs was one of the last students of the famous old Thalian Academy, and was a man of liberal education. He was the first president of the Pickens Railway, and for a time a member of the legislature. A fluent speaker, a great raconteur, and always fine company.

Among modern novelists and story writers, Anderson's own school superintendent, Dr. E. C. McCants, has no superior. Mr. J. L. Sherard is also a gifted writer, especially in the difficult field of writing for children. Mrs. Reid Sherard, who was Miss Mabel Brown, of Belton, is winning a place in the literary world by her brilliant short stories. She has won several international prizes for the best story submitted out of many thousand. Miss Eloise Dean, of Atlanta, is also becoming widely known by her stories. She was born in Anderson county, a member of the old Dean family. The Messrs. Horton, of Atlanta, also contribute to magazines and big newspapers, and Mr. M. C. Horton has published one novel, "Joan of the Everglades." The brothers are lawyers, and were born and grew to manhood in Anderson. A son of Mr. O. A. Horton is showing literary promise also.

General Lewis M. Ayer wrote for religious and agricultural magazines, and published one book, a religious one. Before the War between the States General Ayer was a political writer of some note. He also wrote some poetry, and one of his poems at least is a gem, "The Christian's Prayer." His daughter, Verna Ayer Akerberg, has written some graceful poetry. She is an artist and mosaic worker, and has spent most of her life abroad.

Victor I. Masters, another Anderson county writer, was born four miles southwest of Anderson. He attended numerous country schools until in his fourteenth year, when he began his real education under Professor Ligon, in Anderson. He entered Furman University where he graduated with A. M. degree in 1889. Mr. Masters has attained distinction as a Baptist preacher, and a writer chiefly on religious subjects. His first appearance in print was when attending Mr. Ligon's school under Professor J. G. Clinkscales, who was teaching in the school at the time. He wrote an article which his teacher thought worthy of publication in the Educational Department of *The Intelligencer*. The die was cast, and the boy became from that moment a potential writer. At Furman he was elected first editor of the college magazine, *The Philosophian*. At the Southern Baptist Theological Seminary he was one of the editors of the Seminary magazine, and Seminary correspondent for *The Baptist Courier*. Thus Mr. Masters was already known as a writer when he entered into his work as a minister. He has always been selected for editorial work of some kind. He has been Baptist Press Associate editor of *The Religious Herald* in Richmond, Va., and finally editorial secretary of the Home Mission Board in Atlanta. The name of that position has been c h a n g e d to superintendent of publicity. He is the author of several books, among which are: "Home Mission Work," "Baptist Home Missions," "Baptist Missions in the South," "Country Church in the South," "The Call of the South," and numerous tracts and pamphlets, and many articles for various Baptist publications.

Many of the preachers who have served the Anderson churches have written for church papers, and some of them have published volumes of sermons. Dr. D. E. Frierson was one of the most profound thinkers and scholarly writers who have ever lived in Anderson.

The two daughters of Reverend George Moore, Mrs. de Fontaine and Mrs. Chapin, were both writers of recognized ability.

Mrs. Teresa Strickland, youngest daughter of Judge J. P. Reed, published one novel and wrote many poems and other articles. A poem that she wrote about the old Reed home, "Echo Hall," is particularly beautiful. Her daughter, Mrs. Lily Strickland Anderson, is a writer as well as a musician.

The two sisters, Kate and Lizzie Cornish, wrote poems which breathe the fragrance of forgotten years. They contributed to large northern papers, writing under the names "Kil" and "Brad Courtland." Mrs. Luta Bewley Sullivan writes poetry of a peculiarly ethereal quality, and composes music which is of the same kind.

Samuel Derieux, whose death a few years ago cut short a most promising literary career, was once a teacher in the Anderson schools. Mrs. W. W. Russell, whose home was Anderson for many years, was a newspaper correspondent, and wrote for *The Sunny South*, *The Youth's Companion*, and several other well-known publications.

Mrs. Carrie McCully Patrick is a newspaper woman of ability, she has served on the Anderson papers for a number of years, and also as correspondent for other publications.

Other women who have done good work on the newspapers of the city are Mrs. Lucia Taylor Hudgens, Mrs. Jennie Kramer Gilmer, Mrs. Blanche Johnson, Mrs. Viola Pearman McDougal and Mrs. Peggy Blanton Smith.

Mrs. Elizabeth Hammond Bleckley had the pen of a ready writer. She published one volume of essays, and had another about ready for the press when felled by the hand of disease.

Dr. Milledge L. Bonham, Jr., has brought out several books of an historical and biographical nature. Having occupied the chair of history in several leading universities, he is thoroughly conversant with the subject upon which he writes. His father, Judge M. L. Bonham, is as fluent with his pen as with his tongue. For years he has been the speaker whom Anderson has always put forward when wishing to do a particularly good thing, and his writings display the same grace and charm that has made his addresses popular.

M. B. Camak, once teacher in the Anderson schools, writes poetry that promises a future for him as a writer of verse.

There are probably a number of other writers who were born in Anderson, or who at some time made Anderson their home. Also there are possibly some now in the schools and colleges who shall, in the days to come, reflect literary credit upon the county.

CHAPTER VII.

Some of the Early Industries.

THERE were in the early days of the nineteenth century various kinds of craftsmen in Pendleton and Anderson Districts. There was little machinery. In almost every home there stood a spinning wheel, and girls early learned to use it. In the village goods could be bought from the stores, but nothing in the way of women's and girls' clothing could be found ready made, therefore every woman had to become a seamstress, even though she might be able to have her "best dress" made by "a mantua maker," for such was the imposing name for a dress maker.

In the early forties, there was a great movement in Anderson county towards silk manufacture. Mulberry trees were planted, and silk cocoons bought by the hundred. Some people were quite successful, and many were the silk dresses worn in Anderson, made from home manufactured material. There must be some of those gowns still in existence, and such a garment would be a most interesting exhibit at the Antique and Curio Booth at the County Fair. At that time, and for many years later, a married lady to be well and properly dressed, must have a black silk, no other color, black, and that black silk dress had to last for ten or twelve years. It was turned and returned, made over again and again, and when first made the dressmaker was expected to cut it up as little as possible, leaving big pieces, so that when it was remodeled the "breadths" would adapt themselves readily to the remaking.

Until the dawn of "The New Era," some forty years ago, women worked outside of the home, or for pay as seldom as possible, and when driven by hard necessity to support the family, or help an inefficient or delicate husband to do so, there were few businesses open to them. Teaching, sewing and before the time of cheap and abundant "store cloth," weaving and spinning were feminine employments which sometimes brought in a little money. Those who had to support their children, went to work as best they could. On October 30, 1846, there appears in *The Highland Sentinel* this advertisement: "Margaret Vandiver, wife of Ibzan Vandiver, a farmer residing in Anderson District, South Carolina, hereby gives notice that from and after the 30th day of November next, she intends to become a Sole Trader and carry on the business of spinning and weaving." And on February 7, 1846, appears this notice, "I do hereby give notice to the public that I shall, within thirty days from the publication of this notice, avail myself of the provisions of Act of Legislature, regulating the mode under which married women become sole traders. In accordance with the act of the Legislature, I will hereafter carry on the business as sole trader in the capacity of tailoress and vendor, and avail myself of all advantages belonging to such sole trader under the acts of the General Assembly, in such cases made and provided." Signed Matilda Ann Barr, wife of LeRoy Barr, who is a house carpenter.

Whether the acts of the legislature permitting these and other married women to become "sole traders" meant that they should be allowed to pursue their daily labors unmolested by their respective husbands, retaining for their own use the money they might make, the record sayeth not.

There was at one time some rice raised in Anderson county. It was cleaned on the banks of a stream by a contrivance called a "Lazy Joe," which was a kind of mortar and pestle arrangement worked by the running of the water, which threshed out the rice. However, rice culture so far up the state was not found profitable, and was soon abandoned. Also the flooding of the fields was thought to make malaria.

Mr. Long, grandfather of Mr. J. J. Major, was a manufacturer of spinning wheels, both the large and the small kind; the former used for cotton and the smaller for flax, which was raised extensively in the country, as was also wool, sheep being found on almost every farm. Mr. Long could make a wheel a day, and when he had made a number, he used to load up a wagon with them, and travel over the upper section of the state selling them.

In those days a furniture dealer was a cabinet maker, often making with his own hands the furniture which he sold, and good and durable furniture it was. The woods were full of fine hardwood trees, and some artistic and beautiful furniture was manufactured in the shops, and in such little furniture factories as flourished at Rock Mills, where all the work was done by hand.

Many of the people owned their own spoon molds, and made spoons for the use of their families. Some of those old molds have been exhibited at county fairs in recent years. In the blacksmith shops many iron farm and household tools were fashioned over the forge.

While in the town, glass lamps filled with kerosene oil were used for lights, in the country districts, candles long held sway, and the candles were made on the farms in molds. Those for ordinary use were made of tallow, but for great occasions there were beautiful wax candles in lovely old silver or brass candlesticks, or sometimes branching candelabra. Mrs. Carrie McCully, in her young housekeeping days, was the proud possessor of the first lamp in the town. It was brought to her by her husband on his return from a visit to Charleston.

The first woman merchant in town was Miss Charlotte Daniels. She was companion or housekeeper for Mrs. J. L. Orr, who recognizing her business ability, urged her to open a "Ladies' Store" which she finally did, and made a success of it. She had associated with her two old friends and neighbors, Misses Lizzie and Sallie Williams, and after the death of Miss Daniels, those ladies, with their sisters, continued the business for many years.

The first girl clerk in a store kept by a man was Miss Helen Cater. She proved her fitness for a business career by becoming the highest paid woman clerk in the town when it came to have many girls and women in the stores.

In the early times, before the invention of the cotton gin, the money crop was tobacco. It was hauled to Charleston or to Hamburg in great hogsheads which had a long pole thrust through the center to which shafts were attached, and mules, oxen or horses dragged it. The driver sat on one animal, and on the other loaded his camping outfit, for he usually had to stop in the woods at night, and cook his own food. Arrived at the market, if the tobacco was in good condition he was paid, and then he had a list of things to buy, the most necessary being salt. Coffee, "store cloth" and a few such things that could not be made or raised on the plantation were the articles wished for and greatly prized by the family at home.

Military companies were formed all over the state, and the old muster grounds where they met for practice were located in many places about the various counties. These meetings and drilling were perhaps work of a kind, but they were also means of great enjoyment to the members.

Another source of pleasure to the men was their Masonic Lodge. There was one in Pendleton before Anderson was formed, and it was not long before one was established in the new town. Mr. John Wynn and Mr. Joseph Taylor were active in its formation. The lodge rooms were in the second story of one of the buildings on the west side of the square.

The mystery of the Masons appealed strongly to a party of little girls around twelve years old, and they begged Mr. Wynn to let them see the fearsome place. He took them up the stairs and let them look into a room which had in the center of its floor an old style black wooden coffin, one which narrowed toward both ends. Shaking with excitement and awe, the girls crept inside the door, and their conductor stepped softly out, pulling it shut after him. The girls tried to be plucky and laugh, but their mirth was rather hysterical. They were completely cured of their curiosity about Masons.

Sometime in the fifties, the Masons erected a building and it contained a large hall, which was henceforth used for plays, lectures and other entertainments. It was the only play house Anderson had, and as the town grew became very inadequate. In the early eighties the Masonic lodge tore down the old building and put up a new one on the same spot. It contained Anderson's "opera house," believed when it was erected to be ample for years to come. The new Masonic temple was dedicated with great ceremonies. Dr. R. F. Divver, grand master, in charge. All of the talent of the town was enlisted in that day's festivities, and a bevy of girls in pretty dresses added to its gay appearance. The laying of its corner stone had also been the occasion of a grand celebration. The final touches were put on the stone by four little girls, Emily Divver, Anna Humphreys, Eunice Hill and Mamie Andrews, using a silver trowel which had been used in laying the corner stone of the de Kalb monument in Camden.

In the course of time that opera house and Masonic temple also became obsolete, and in 1914 a handsome new theater building was erected on Whitner street, and soon after the Masons renovated their building, greatly improving and beautifying it for their own use.

The people of the community have always found plenty of work and plenty of play to keep them normal and fit for life.

After the war between the states conditions changed and great manufactories took the place of the former hand and home work. Those businesses must have a chapter to themselves.

CHAPTER VIII.

IN SCHOOLROOM WALLS.

SECTION I—THE COUNTY.

THERE were schools in Old Pendleton before Anderson came into existence. In 1811 the Circulating Library of Pendleton was incorporated by the legislature. In 1825 the library was incorporated as The Pendleton Male Academy, and a brick building was erected on land which had been granted to the library. In 1835 the brick building was converted into a dwelling for the teacher, and a large frame structure was put up for the school. Both of these buildings remain and are now used for public schools.

In 1834 a manual labor school for boys was organized under the direction of the noted teacher, J. L. Kennedy. Soon after the new venture got well under way, an epidemic of typhoid fever broke out among the students, and in that day nothing was known about polluted water, so the inference was that the work in the hot sun was too severe for the boys, and the manual labor school was discontinued.

In 1827 an academy for girls was opened. The building used had been the county jail. There girls were jailed, for a girls' boarding school of long ago differed from a jail only in having its prisoners young and innocent maidens, who no matter how closely they were confined or restricted, were yet hopeful, happy girls looking forward to life, in place of hopeless, miserable criminals.

Two of the teachers of that school were sisters, Misses Bates from Massachusetts. After the lapse of seventy-five years, one of the former pupils, then over ninety years old, told with a touch of the horror inspired at the time, of a visit made by those honored teachers to her parents' home in Anderson, and of how Miss Bates asked to be taken to visit some of the negroes on the place, as she wished to become acquainted with them at close range.

There was in the village also a primary school taught by Miss Mary Hunter, which the little boys and girls attended until they grew old enough to enter the two academies.

Pupils attended these institutions of learning brought in all kinds of conveyances, buggies, sulkeys, carriages, carryalls, and even wagons. Many rode horseback. When there were both boys and girls to go to school from one house, the boys drove their sisters to the female academy first, then went on to their own, where the horses were kept and cared for until time to go home, which was well into the late afternoon, for school in those days lasted from early in the morning until the shades of evening were growing very long. The boys would drive with many a flourish up to the door of the girls' school, where a bewildering group of maidens were always waiting to be called for, and many were the sidelong glances cast by bashful boys at some other fellow's sister, while their own were climbing unassisted to their seats.

At old Calhoun, some ten or twelve miles northeast of Anderson, sometime in the first quarter of the nineteenth century Wesley Leverette opened an academy which became rather noted in its day. It was to this school that an ambitious youth named Joe Brown went from his home in Pickens county, close to the Georgia line. He may have been returning to his native heath, for the ill-fated Kemp place near the site of the academy had been for some time the property of his father, though he built no house on it.

The boy Joe Brown was 19 years old when he drove a pair of oxen from his home and sold them to Dr. Aaron Broyles, with whom he boarded while he attended the Calhoun Academy. Wesley Leverette, however, was not his instructor; Mr. Pleasant Jordan was the teacher when Governor Brown attended the school. The boy had to work in order to obtain an education, and he would attend school one term, then teach a term, until he finished his course. He divided his time between two Anderson schools, the Calhoun Academy and a school taught by an old Irishman named Breckenridge, located somewhere near the site of the Julius H. Anderson home. When attending the latter school the boy boarded with Dr. John McFall. However, if Mr. Leverette was not teaching the Calhoun Academy when Joe Brown was a student there, the boy went to him somewhere, for Mr. Leverette was often heard to say that Joe Brown and Peter Vandiver were the brightest boys he ever taught, so it is possible that he attended Calhoun Academy under two different teachers.

Mr. Leverette was an orator as well as a teacher, and was called on to speak on most public occasions. It is told that once he was summoned to appear in some case being tried in the court house; the old man looked around on the judge and the lawyers, among whom were Judge J. P. Reed, Hon. J. L. Orr, Mr. Peter Vandiver and several other prominent men of the time, and remarked: "I have thrashed the judge, the solicitor and the lawyers on both sides of this case, besides several other men present. I guess this court has no terrors for me."

Mr. Leverette finally moved to Williamston where he was teaching a flourishing school for boys at the time of his death. He is buried in Big Creek Church yard, and his grave is marked by a monument erected by his former pupils.

Stephen Leverette, brother of Wesley, and often his assistant in teaching, never married. He became a minister of the Christian denomination. Like his brother, he was a thorough scholar, and a nephew, the late Mr. J. B. Leverette, who in his youth lived with that uncle, in his own old age used to tell about the old gentleman reading his Greek testament aloud, translating as he went, and the nephew was expected to follow with the King James version, and when the uncle differed from the English Bible, the boy was expected to note the difference and ask the reason.

The parents of these two teachers were Stephen and Margaret Leverette, who came from Virginia and settled first in Newberry, afterwards going for a time to Augusta, and later to Pendleton District, where they bought land and made their home in the lower part of the district close by Wilson's Creek, near what is now Carswell Institute. It was there that Wesley, the youngest of a large family, was born and grew to manhood.

The "Old Field" schools of those early days were as uncomfortable as it was possible to make them. Built of logs, sometimes with great open chinks through which the winter winds found easy access. The teacher sat at one end, where there was a big fire place, until after some years a stove was placed in the middle of the room. The pupils occupied rude benches made of split logs with legs fitted to them, and without backs. The older pupils were often allowed to go outside and study under the trees. Around some of the more pretentious schools there were rude huts built where young men students lived and kept sort of bachelor's hall from Monday to Saturday. Such was the school of that old Irishman, "Uncle Billy Breckenridge," who was a teacher for seventy years. He is buried in Ebenezer grave yard.

The "Blue Back Speller" was the child's first textbook, and he continued to study it until he was almost grown. The poor little tots had to sit all day on the split log benches and swing their feet, as they could not reach the floor with them. The children studied aloud, usually at the top of their voices; the country people gave such schools the appropriate name of "a blab school." On one side of the room a long plank was fastened to the wall, slanting downwards. Just after dinner all of the younger children had to sit there and learn to write. They had home made copy books of foolscap paper, and "teacher" would set each one a copy. The wise sayings of Poor Richard, or a text from the Bible were the favorite sentences set for the children to write.

There were no lead pencils in those early days. The older boys used to make pencils for the school by securing cane and cutting it off in joints which were hollow in the center. Then they would melt lead and pour it in, let it harden and sharpen it—behold your lead pencil. Pens were made of quills, and the making of a good pen was quite an accomplishment.

An interesting school of early days was Pearl Spring, which stood about where the Piedmont Mill is now. It was built in 1837, a log house with its big chimney at one end. Its first teacher was Robert Moore. Some later teachers were Spencer Moore, Richard Murphy, Charles Murphy, and there were others.

One of the customs of the time was to "turn out the teacher" at the close of the term. Two of these occasions at Pearl Spring School were long remembered, and told with relish by old men who in their boyhood days had taken part in the frolic. The first was when Mr. Spencer Moore was teacher. An old gentleman long in his grave, Mr. Asbury Spearman, used to tell about it. He was one of the boys. The understanding was that if on the last school day the students could succeed in keeping the teacher out of the building he should treat them, but if he should succeed in making an entrance, the boys had to stand treat. In those days "treat" meant whiskey, cheap and strong.

Before day on the appointed date, some of the boys in the dark before dawn, stole upon the silent building. They formed a cordon around the house so close to each other that not even a dog could have passed the ring unseen. Also there were groups stationed at strategic points to rally at need. Soon there were many spectators on the outskirts, drawn by curiosity to see the outcome. Several hours passed but no schoolmaster appeared. He was suspected of lurking near, watching his chance, but where no one could guess.

After a while Squire W. A. Williams from White Plains drove up in his carriage, accompanied by a gentleman and two young ladies. They alighted and went into the school house, and the boys showed them every courtesy. Many young men who were not on duty crowded into the building to see the girls. After some pleasant chat among the young people, one of the ladies suddenly arose and, striking an attitude, exclaimed in most unfeminine tones: "Why didn't you keep the schoolmaster from coming in?"

The boys were dumfounded and crestfallen, acknowledging themselves defeated. The triumphant teacher, however, produced

HISTORY OF ANDERSON COUNTY

a jug from the carriage and the refreshment went round, restoring good humor; and a day of fun and frolic set in.

The second incident was during the administration of Mr. Richard Murphy, some years later. This time, instead of waiting for day, some of the boys spent the night in the school house. One of them had a rifle with him. They built a fire in the huge fire place, and whiled away the hours as best they could.

Mr. Murphy, thinking to be in good time, in company with a friend, made his appearance an hour or two before sunrise. Of course he could see while still some distance away that the students held the citadel.

It was still dark and the two conspirators, Mr. Murphy and his friend, procured a pumpkin, made a "scare face," putting a lighted candle inside; then one of them covering his body as best he could, put the thing on his head and marched to the school house, relying on the superstitious terror of the boys making them take the frightful object for a "hant," and running away. The lads, however, didn't scare as easily as the teacher thought they would; he who held the gun put a bullet through the grinning "hant," and the retreat was not on the part of the boys.

Every effort the teacher made was frustrated. At last the friend put on the master's hat and coat, and mounting a horse, rode away. The ruse succeeded. The students, thinking the teacher had given up, rushed out to see him ride away, and the unguarded fortress was taken by the enemy. A neighbor interested in the fun furnished peach brandy and the merriment was fast and furious.

The Pearl Spring School antedated the church by some years.

In 1848 a log school house was erected near Tugaloo Creek and a school established which was taught by Manning Belcher, a Massachusetts man. It was literally an "Old Field School," having been erected on the edge of an old field which became the school play grounds. The children of that day were not weighted with books. The Blue Back Speller constituting their whole course until they were ready to be promoted to the New Testament Class, and be presented with a copy of the multiplication table drawn on a thick piece of paper or cardboard, soon to be followed by Smiley's Arithmetic. Then their troubles really began.

Sometimes the children were not required to buy arithmetic books; their lessons were given out by the teacher, written down by the student, and after all of the problems and the context were corrected and approved they were carefully copied in as fine a hand as the pupil could produce in a book made of foolscap paper sewed together and bound with stout home made jeans, a whole arithmetic written out by hand.

Old Field School as it was, the teacher, Mr. Belcher, was a fine scholar, and after the right amount of arithmetic, English grammar and geography, he taught such of his pupils as were willing to learn them Latin and Greek.

What is now known as "Sunset Forest," or "Fretwell's Spring," was once called "Crystal Springs," and years ago there was a school there. Two of its teachers were Hiram Bolt and William Eskew.

Cool Springs School was in the Hall settlement. One of its teachers was Mr. Samuel Wakefield. A report of a school exhibition held there in 1860 says: "The examinations would have done credit to a college class." Those school exhibitions consisted not only of speeches and recitations by the students, but the best orators of the time were invited to make addresses. The exercises usually closed with a picnic dinner.

In 1851 Mr. William Haynie taught school at Cold Water Branch, just south of the city. His sister, Sarah, afterwards Mrs. Edward Vandiver, was also a teacher. She was the mother of Messrs. David S. and Edward P. Vandiver, of Anderson.

Mr. P. S. Mahaffey, who died near Townville in 1920 at the age of 88 years, once taught the Sourwood Spring Academy, just west of Anderson. Later he taught at Brown's Old Muster Ground in the Fork. He was one of the most successful teachers of his day. His son, Mr. L. M. Mahaffey, is Anderson's efficient County Superintendent of Education. Formerly a successful teacher himself.

In the year 1848 a school was taught in a small log house which stood within half a mile of the present White Rock Academy. The teacher was Waddell Hillhouse, who afterwards became a soldier in the Confederate Army and was killed on the field of the First Battle of Manassas the day after the fight by the explosion of a shell carelessly handled. Succeeding Mr. Hillhouse as a teacher of the school was Mr. Robert H. Harrison, a young man from Georgia, who later became a Methodist preacher, and was murdered in Edgefield while at prayer with his family.

About the time that Mr. Harrison was teaching the school there was a great educational awakening in that section of the county, largely due to his influence. A more central location was selected for the school and a better house built. It was a frame structure, twenty by thirty-six feet, ceiled, lighted with glass windows, and heated by chimneys at each end with big fire places. The cost of the building was borne chiefly by Joseph R. Shelor, Cleveland Marett, Morgan Harbin and Thomas R. Shelor, all of whom were men of means, and who always manifested great interest in everything pertaining to the school. In 1887 that house was burned; Mr. William A. Sheldon was the teacher at the time. He continued the school without interruption, using a nearby building until the school house could be replaced.

In the fall of 1891 a handsome two-story structure was erected on the site of the burned building; the idea was to use the second story for a neighborhood assembly hall. Mr. John W. Shelor was chairman of the building committee, and he was for years chairman of the board of trustees.

Reverend C. H. Speer, of Franklin, Ga., was the first teacher chosen for the new academy, about 1850. He taught the school for about five years, and raised it to a high position, attracting students from various parts of the state. The closing exercises became famous and were attended by people from miles around.

Mr. Speer was an example of what one can accomplish who will. He never attended school until he was about grown; and so awkward and ill at ease was he among the small children that he felt almost in despair, and tempted to give up the struggle. But his teacher encouraged him and induced him to continue; and with his kindly help the ambitious youth soon passed two or three classes, and by the end of his first year was with boys almost his own age.

Those early difficulties made Mr. Speer an unusually sympathetic and consequently a very successful teacher. He took up the work early, and often in the first years found himself only about a day's march ahead of his students. He became a Methodist preacher and was noted for his fine singing voice. After teaching at White Rock for about five years he went elsewhere, but the people of the community requested his return. He went back, and for four years longer taught the school with all of his former success. He died while teaching that school and was buried in a nearby church yard.

Following him as a teacher came Robert Pulliam, who taught only one year, leaving to enter the Confederate Army. Then came H. M. Burton who, unlike Mr. Speer, was a more successful preacher than teacher. He, too, rests in South Union grave yard, near the scene of his former labors. The next two teachers, Elijah Keese and Miss Eliza Bibb, had been pupils of Mr. Speer. After that came several who served only a year each, then the school got Miss Fannie Dumas, of Georgia. She had among her pupils some young men, formerly soldiers in the Confederate Army. They did not over-awe that stringent teacher, however, and some of them said they greatly preferred to face the Yankee army than "Miss Fannie when she was mad."

Mr. S. P. Stribbling, for several years School Commissioner of Oconee County, taught this school very successfully, as did also Reverend W. W. Leathers. W. A. Dickson, well-known teacher and newspaper writer of Townville, was in charge of White Rock Academy for a time.

Among the soldiers of the Confederacy were a number of former White Rock students. Three of them, Park McJukin, Sam Bibb and Nat Harbin, were killed. Some of the other students became prominent in various lines in after life. Theodore Caskin, a pupil at some time in the fifties, became vice-president of a large insurance company in New York at a salary of $30,000.00 a year. Dr. John McJukin was a prominent physician. N. L. Davis succeeded in politics, Joseph W. Shelor in law and newspaper work. Many others have been useful and successful in various lines of work.

"Anderson High School," at Orange Grove, on the Pendleton road, in 1866 was taught by Major Ben Sloan, who was succeeded by J. B. Hillhouse and Ellison Capers, distinguished general in the Confederate Army, and later an Episcopal minister, for years rector of Christ Church, Greenville, finally becoming the beloved bishop of the diocese of South Carolina. Major Sloan afterwards became president of the University of South Carolina.

White Plains School, so called on account of the white sand about it, was organized soon after the War Between the States. The building was of pine logs hewn from the surrounding forest. It was one room, about 19 by 20 feet, lined with split oak boards. The seats were pine slabs with sweet gum pegs driven in the ends for legs. The chimney at one end was of sticks and clay, and the room was only about seven feet high. In the winter when a fire was made in the fire place the teacher and most of the big boys were kept busy bringing water from the nearby spring to drench the stick chimney in order to keep it from catching fire and burning up the place. There was but one small window in the house, but light, air and cold came in through the cracks. The window was in the back of the house. It consisted of two logs sawed away, leaving an opening about eighteen inches wide. There was no glass and the shutter was a piece of plank.

Some of the teachers of the school were J. R. Guyton, Dr. G. N. Richardson, Reverend Jesse Vermillian, William Cason, J. B. Spearman, J. B. Harris, Reverend and Mrs. P. J. Vermillian, Miss Jennie Shirley, John Majors, Robert Gentry, William Strickland, Mr. and Miss Burns, Miss Bessie Miller, Miss Minnie Simpson, Miss Minnie

Webb, Miss Sallie Wright, D. C. Colson, Miss Louise Mahaffey, R. E. L. Smith, Miss Alma Garnet, Miss Mamie Rogers, Miss Mae Wigginton, R. E. Pennell, Miss Ruth Hays, Miss Elizabeth Allgood, Miss Helen Arnold, Miss Lillian Holtzclaw and M. L. Mahaffey. Since these notes were collected, there have been other good teachers of the school which is now occupying its third building, a handsome and comfortable one, which stands about one mile west of the original site, and employs four teachers.

One of the most famous schools of the early time was Thalian Academy, near Slabtown. An old Revolutionary soldier, an elder in Carmel Church, was the instigator. His earnest interest in the community caused him to issue a call to the citizens in the year 1832 which resulted in the formulation of plans for the school. Reverend John Leland Kennedy was chosen for its teacher. He was a wonderful instructor, and soon the fame of the institution spread abroad. The people living near erected cabins, sometimes three or four to a farm, in order to accommodate the students who came from a distance. Some of the most distinguished men of the state were pupils of Mr. Kennedy at Thalian Academy. A. Ross Kennedy, a son of the teacher, married the eldest sister of President Wilson.

There was a good sized school building, and across the road from it stood a row of small buildings, almost huts, which were used by the older boys as study rooms. In summer, however, the shade of the trees gave them pleasant outdoor studies, which they freely used, sitting in split bottomed chairs about a spreading oak. When the hour for a recitation came, Mr. Kennedy stepped to the door and in tones which emulated a megaphone, called: "Caesar," "Virgil" or "Horace," and the students of that class responded. At the close of the recitation the youths returned to their former places, anl other classes were called.

The younger students were kept seated in the building and taught by Mr. J. B. Hillhouse. School in those days opened at eight o'clock and held until five. There were two hours for dinner when teachers and pupils ate their meals from tin pails or from baskets which they brought every morning. There were also two short recesses, one in the forenoon, the other in the afternoon.

Mr. Kennedy did not approve the custom of locking out the schoolmaster. It was tried once only at Thalian Academy, and every participant, big and little, was punished. It was never again attempted. The school was broken up by the War of the 60s, most of its students shouldered arms and marched away. Many never returned, and those who did were never boys again.

In the cemetery of Carmel Church is a stone which marks the grave of John L. Kennedy, erected by his former pupils.

William Hamilton, son of the old soldier who started the action which resulted in Thalian Academy, was also a gifted teacher. He taught at Slabtown, at Ebenezer, and at Moffattsville. The Moffattsville Academy was a school of high type, and turned out some good citizens. In 1870 there was a picnic at the school which was long remembered as a great gala occasion. General Ellison Capers was orator of the day, the Anderson band furnished music, and there was formed a branch of "The Survivors Association," forerunner of the Association of Confederate Veterans. That was while Mr. Hamilton was its teacher. He is buried in an old grave yard of an ancient church not far from where the academy stood. The school was named for a distinguished A. R. P. minister, Dr. Moffatt.

One of the old county schools was at Providence. Mr. Lewis W. Gentry had charge of it in 1867. Among his pupils were boys and girls bearing the names: Whitaker, Anderson, Skelton, McLees, Williford, Norris, Manning, Garrison, Shearer, McLeskey, Dobbins, Bowie, Hembree, Barrett, Richardson, Cleveland, Simpson, Crow, Martin, Rice, Latham and Ledbetter. There were others besides at various times, but this list comes from a diary kept by Mr. Gentry in 1867, and preserved in his family. The schools furnished three preachers to the Presbyterian and three to the Methodist churches. John, Hugh and James McLees were Presbyterian ministers, and J. F. Anderson, W. H. and Robert Whittaker were Methodists.

In Brushy Creek there was a fine school before the War Between the States, its first teacher was J. N. Bramlett. He was followed by Joshua Smith, T. Strawther Reeves, Major Wales Smith, and others.

One of the earliest schools in the county was at Lick Skillet, taught by Mr. Huff.

In January in 1866 a mixed school opened at Williamston under Mr. R. W. Todd, assisted by his daughter, Miss Mettie Todd. Greek, algebra, geometry, chemistry, English grammar, geography, mental, moral and natural philosophy, rhetoric and English composition, history, reading, writing and music lessons were included in the curriculum. The trustees were D. L. Donald, J. J. Acker, Dr. John Wilson, C. E. Horton and H. O. Herrick.

Mrs. Gregory kept a school in Pendleton in 1819, "Southern Hall Female Academy."

Mr. R. Willis Todd taught school in Belton at one time. It was a primary school. Mr. Todd was more indulgent and gentler than the majority of schoolmasters of his day. He gave little children a fine start, and was liked by his pupils.

Old Mr. Breckenridge's first school was Poplar Springs. He produced the finest spellers of any teacher of his time. A plan adopted by teachers who had slow pupils, was to cut the page with the alphabet in all its phases from the book, paste it on a paddle and paddle the child with his own lesson page when he thought proper.

Colonel Robert McCann was one of the earliest teachers in the county. He taught in the Slabtown section.

Thomas D. Baird established and conducted Old Varennes Academy on the Generostee road about one mile west of High Shoals. It is not known when the school was started, but it was there in 1814, when the church was built. A few of the many pupils who attended that old school were Major Thompson, Colonel Norris, Colonel Eliab Moore, Jr., and Dr. O. R. Broyles.

There have long been good schools at and near Townville. The late W. A. Dickson was a gifted teacher as well as a forceful newspaper writer. He taught in that section of the county for many years. His sister-in-law, Miss Mattie McCarley, has done a great work as a teacher among the young people of Townville for a long time. Mr. P. A. Mahaffey was also an honored teacher in Townville in days long past. More recently Miss Fannie Broyles, whose tragic death in an automobile accident a few years ago brought sorrow to hearts, was a loved teacher of Townville.

The Townville public school has a most beautiful grove of water oaks in front of it, and a row running for some distance on each side of the road. The lovely trees are a monument to Miss Mattie McCarley, who induced the trustees to have them set out when she was teaching the school. The play grounds, which are ample, are at the side and the back of the building. The school grounds and those of both the Presbyterian and Methodist churches run together, and all being beautified, make a lovely park that no ambitious "city council" can encroach upon to destroy the trees for the benefit of speeders.

There has been for many years a school about one mile from Mountain Creek Church. It, too, bears the name, Mountain Creek. The first building was of logs, and stood just back of where the church is located. It was there in 1852, and probably for some years earlier. David Junkin taught there 1862-3. It also had at one time a teacher, Captain Glenn, one Weston Hayes. From 1864 to 1866 the teacher was Colonel W. S. Shaw. After the war Colonel Shaw taught a negro school and became very unpopular with the white people of the section. Between 1862 and 1865

Anderson Durham taught the school. In 1867 Miss Elmira Burriss (Mrs. Stevenson); 1868, B. Crayton Snipes; 1869, T. D. Erwin. Some later teachers have been Reuben Burriss, Pearl Thompson (Mrs. Kyle Shirley), Bertha Burriss, Roy Masters, May Fant, Vashti George, Miss Julia Burriss (Mrs. Laurence Burriss), Miss Lizzie Osborne, Miss Maggie Daniels (Mrs. McCown), Miss Bettie Earle, Mr. Carlisle, Charles McPhail, Clarence Elgin, Miss May Russell, Miss Zella Campbell (Mrs. Walter Anderson), Miss Lena Campbell (Mrs. Gambrell), Miss Alice Davis (Mrs. C. O. Burriss), Miss Eddie Davis, Miss Hattie Smith (Mrs. Minter), Miss Lillie Grant, Miss Maggie Tribble, Miss Louise Anderson, Mrs. McPhail, Miss Lucile Findley, Miss Toccoa Burriss (Mrs. Arthur Gatlin). Some of the former pupils of this school are Dr. Harrison Pruitt, Dr. Olga Pruitt, Reverend Victor I. Masters, Reverend R. H. Burriss, Reverend John Shaw, and many others who have "made good."

A school known as Three and Twenty was built on land five times deeded to a Robert Pickens. The first was the Colonel who escaped from the Tories by climbing out of the chimney. In 1886 R. W. Pickens, of the fifth generation, was teaching the school.

At Flat Rock School Berry Long was once the teacher.

There is at Lebanon one of the best schools in the county.

There was once in Varennes Township a school called The Armstrong Academy.

Carswell Institute, though later than many of the county schools, deserves a prominent place in the list. The school was organized and the building erected January, 1876. There was a board of trustees, but the owners and teachers were the Carswell brothers, graduates of Mercer University, with their sister, Georgia, who taught music and art. They were E. R. Carswell, Jr., and L. Carswell.

This was from the first an institution of high standing. It opened on the first Monday in February, 1876. There were three departments, primary, intermediate and academic. Many young people who could not have college advantages received there not only a good education, but also acquired accomplishments.

In 1882 Reverend Hugh McLees made an address at Carmel Church on industrial education. Among his audience was a lady, Mrs. Eleanor J. Walker, who was so impressed that, being a woman of means, she determined to do something for education. She accordingly deeded to a body of fifteen trustees one hundred and thirty acres of land, upon which should be built a college to be known as The Walker-McElmoyle College. As provided for in the original constitution an effort was made to raise an endowment fund, but that failed, so the constitution was changed, making it possible to have the institution chartered as a graded school. Good buildings were erected, and Miss Olivia Newton was for a long time the efficient principal of the school. Miss McElmoyle, a sister of Mrs. Walker, was joint donor of the land. In one of her advertisements Miss Newton says that the school might be called "Triumvirate," as it had three teachers, herself, Mr. Julius R. Newton and Professor John Rives; three seasons, winter, spring and summer; three grades, primary, common school and high school; and three prices, six, eight and ten cents per day, respectively.

Williamston early became an educational center. When the town was laid off two lots were reserved for a male and a female high school. The one for boys was from the first successful. Among its teachers was Wesley Leverette, who conducted a boarding school which was patronized from all over the state. Mr. Leverette died while teaching that school.

Other teachers were William Garrison, J. M. Walker, Mr. Smith, Mr. Kennedy, Townsend Carlisle, Mr. Whitfield, Mr. Muller, Mr. Pickle, Mr. Merriweather, Mr. Brown, Mr. Hardin, Mr. Blacock, Mr. McSwain, Watson Grady, Mr. Gaines, Mr. Goodgion and probably others. The school finally passed into the hands of a stock company and continued to flourish.

The school for girls, however, languished from the first and finally died.

In 1871 the South Carolina Methodist Conference sent Reverend Samuel Lander to take charge of the Williamston church. Mr. Lander, when he got there, found that the church expected a bachelor, and that there were no accommodations for his family. Brought face to face with a meagre prospect for support, the minister consulted with his presiding elder and with his sanction opened a school for girls. He rented the little vacant hotel building across the road from the spring park, and in February, 1872, The Williamston Female College started on its brilliant career. So successful was the new school that Dr. Lander was released from the duties of a pastor in order that he might give his whole time to teaching, which the church was wise enough to see was his God-given talent. The college became popular, and Dr. Lander turned out some of the best educated women of the state. A short time before his death he requested that the Methodist Church of South Carolina take over the school, which it did, removing it to Greenwood, where, as Lander College, it continues to do good work.

Early in the history of the county there was a school founded at Generostee. Dr. Chalmers Priestly was one of its teachers.

HISTORY OF ANDERSON COUNTY

During the war and just after it, Mrs. Anderson, wife and widow of Major William Anderson, taught a school for children at her home about half way between Belton and Anderson. Later Mrs. Anderson married Mr. B. B. Breazeale, who, in addition to the affection he manifested toward her as his own wife, seemed also never to forget that she was the widow of his deeply honored major, and to treat her with the respect he thought due that exalted position.

Mrs. Breazeale used to tell of her difficulties in teaching children accustomed to the "blab school" method to study quietly. Her daughter, Miss Maggie Anderson, was for several years one of the best known of the county teachers.

There were free schools in Anderson District in the forties. In one number of *The Anderson Gazette* Mr. Christopher Orr, secretary and treasurer (of what, not stated), advertises for all teachers of free schools in the district to call and receive the money due them.

Irving Gregg, a cripple, taught the school at Evergreen. He was considered a fine scholar, though a strict disciplinarian who believed in the liberal use of the rod.

In 1866 there was a school in Belton known as the Belton Academy. Captain George Dean, of the State Military Academy, was its head teacher. He was assisted by Mrs. Samuel Brown.

The closing exercises in 1866 were held in the Presbyterian Church. After the speaking and music were over, there was a dance at the McGee Hotel.

In 1870 W. H. Haynie was school commissioner for Anderson county. He divided the county into school districts coincident with its townships. A committee consisting of chairman and secretary was appointed in each district to conduct an election of three school trustees in each district. The town of Anderson was to constitute a separate district. He advertises having blanks for teachers to fill out. Was also ready to receive their accounts for services rendered during the year beginning November 1st, 1867, ending October 31st, 1868. Persons who desired to teach under the free and common school system were invited to meet the county board of examiners on April 9th at the court house to stand examinations and get certificates of qualification.

There is an amusing story told about the famous old teacher, "Uncle Billy Breckenridge." Being an Irishman, he was a social soul, and he was not in favor of prohibition. On one occasion while court was in session the old gentleman came into town to see what was going on, and he had partaken too freely of refreshments. He strolled into the court room and taking a seat far back began to converse with those around him and became somewhat hilarious. L. J. Orr was the presiding judge, and he becoming annoyed by the noise and disorder, instructed the sheriff to arrest the offender, whom he had not identified, and lock him up in jail.

Mr. Breckenridge could not believe that his ears had not deceived him. He rose in his seat and exclaimed: "Arrest ME! Why, Lawrence, you can't put me in jail! I've tanned you and most of the court. You can't put me in jail!"

The judge smiled and said: "Why, no, Mr. Breckenridge, I guess I can't, but please keep better order back in that corner, and when court adjourns, go home and spend the night with me. We'll talk over old times."

When things settled down the old man was heard to mutter to himself: "Put me in jail? I knew Lawrence couldn't put me in jail."

There is a story told of Judge Orr's youth in connection with another of Anderson's judges.

When J. L. Orr was a boy he clerked in his father's store, and one day another boy about his own age approached him and said: "Lawrence, if you're not going to school next term can't you let me have your spelling book?"

Young Orr knew that money was scarce with the other lad and he agreed to sell him his blue back speller cheap. The boy was J. P. Reed. In later life the two agreed to form a partnership in law, and they tossed coins to see whose name should be first in the firm name. Reed won, and the firm was Reed and Orr. Some years after Judge Orr was dead Colonel Reed formed a law partnership with his son, J. L. Orr, Jr., and this time his age and experience, and the youth of his partner, made the name inevitably Reed and Orr.

CHAPTER IX.

IN SCHOOL ROOM WALLS.

SECTION II—THE TOWN.

ANDERSON has been the scene of many and varied schools. Any person in the village, town or city who remained without education was without excuse. And some of the finest teachers that the state or the South has known, exercised their talents upon the youth of this community.

The first school known to have existed in the village of Anderson was in operation in 1832; how much earlier is not known. It was located on what is now West Market street where Brown's Lumber Plant has long stood. Its teacher was Mr. Templeton, who came from Laurens. He taught both boys and girls of all ages; and ninety-six years ago boys and girls were very like what boys and girls are in 1928.

Among Mr. Templeton's pupils was a little maid whose name was Teresa Brown; she was the daughter of Mr. Daniel Brown, who had so great a part in forming the new town of Anderson.

Most of the pupils took their dinner to school in tin pails, for the sessions were long. The small Teresa carried her mid-day meal to school in a dainty basket, which was the admiration of all her schoolmates, and the envy of some. One day the pretty basket disappeared, and no amount of searching could find it, until when tired of the prank, a small urchin stepped to the great fireplace which occupied the whole end of the building, and pretended to find the lost basket which was suspended in the wide mouthed chimney, of course covered with soot.

A dunce cap often adorned the brows of some of Mr. Templeton's pupils, and even in old age a feeling of horror sweeps over those former pupils when they recall the ignominy. The boys of the school took turns in bringing brush and wood to burn in the great chimney. Water they brought from a spring behind the school at the foot of a long hill which extended about to where Mrs. G. N. Broyles now lives on West River street.

Mr. Templeton was succeeded in that school by Rev. J. L. Kennedy, a Presbyterian preacher from about Slabtown, who made a name throughout the state and beyond as a gifted teacher. While in charge of the school Mr. Kennedy lived in an adjoining house.

The next school in the village, of which there is any tradition, was located near Mt. Tabor Church. Its teacher was John Stevenson.

In 1835 the Presbyterians opened an academy on the corner of West Whitner and Towers streets, across from the church. A large two-story wooden building was erected. It was a mixed school and its first teachers were Wesley and Stephen Leverette, and Ebenezer Pressley. Later the school was divided, the Leverette brothers taking the boys and opening a school for them on what is now the Van Wyck lot. The school house was a two-room brick structure which is the nucleus around which the handsome Van Wyck house is built. Mr. James Brownlee, a graduate of the University of Georgia, once taught that school.

A new two-story brick building was erected for the girls on the old site, Mr. Pressley remaining in charge. His assistants were Mrs. McElroy, Mr. John V. Moore, Miss McQueen and Professor Morse. The first German who ever came to Anderson to live was a Mr. Miller, who taught music in that school. The name Presbyterian Female Seminary was given to the school, and it made a reputation as an excellent institution of learning. Girls from all parts of South Carolina, and from several other states were among its students. All of the fashionable branches were taught. The girls boarded in the homes of the village. Mrs. McElroy has left a fragrant memory as a teacher and trainer of young ladies.

About the year 1855 Mr. M. P. Wilhite, father of the late Dr. P. A. Wilhite and grandfather of the late Dr. J. O. Wilhite, taught a school for boys and girls in a brick school house which stood near where the St. Paul Baptist Church for colored people now stands—the same which Mr. Samuel Crawford taught in later years, first a school for white children, then after the war a school for negro children. Mr. Wilhite was a graduate of the Georgia State University, and moved to Anderson from Athens with his son when he began his long and prosperous career as a physician in the town.

One of Mr. Wilhite's pupils remembered him best as carrying a curious and keen whip rolled up in his pocket. Among the boys who were his pupils were Captain P. K. McCully, General C. A. Reed, and L. P. Smith. Mr. Wilhite did not live in Anderson very long, he returned to Georgia where he attained a very great age, almost reaching the centennial of his birth.

In 1848 some of the prominent men of the town, among whom were Mr. Daniel Brown, Colonel J. P. Reed, and Mr. Stephen McCully, determined that Anderson needed a larger and better equipped school for girls. The Baptists, who were numerous and wealthy, were induced to adopt the institution, and Reverend William Bullion Johnson was made its president. Originally it was an eight-roomed brick building which stood on the spot now occupied by the Baptist parsonage. Mrs. Mary E. Daniel, a lady from Maine, was probably the favorite teacher. Mr. J. S. Murray was principal and taught Latin and Greek if any of the girls wished to learn those branches. William Wagstaff, an Englishman, taught music. Later Mr. James Bacon, of Edgefield, also taught music in the school, as did Miss Emilia Reed, who may have been a pupil teacher, or may have graduated from the institution before she became a teacher. Mr. Wagstaff had been a soldier at the Battle of Waterloo. The institution prospered beyond the most sanguine expectations of its promoters, and in its fifth year Dr. Johnson delivered an address in which he set forth the superiority of the university system of education, and put the question, "If the university system be the better one for boys and young men, why should it not be for girls and young women?" The trustees gave the subject serious thought, and resolved to raise their seminary to a university. An application was accordingly made to the legislature in December, 1852, for a charter, and the next year the Johnson University commenced its existence with an able faculty. In five years the institution numbered six hundred students. Dr. Johnson was made chancellor, Reverend J. S. Murray president, and Mrs. Mary E. Daniel principal. A new building was erected on University Hill, almost where Mrs. C. S. Sullivan's house now stands. It was a two story structure with projecting wings on both sides, the whole surmounted by a cupola. The dormitories were in a great three story brick house on one side. That house was burned in 1883, or 1884. The University Sanitarium now occupies the site.

Some of the teachers of that famous old school besides those already mentioned were Mrs. Claudia Murray, who both as Miss Edwards and as Mrs. Murray belonged to the faculty; two aunts of Mrs. Daniel, also from Maine, Misses Charlotte and Phoebe Paine. Miss Charlotte kept at hand a cat-o'-nine-tails, and did not hesitate to use it, though her pupils were grown young women. The narrator of these old time things, with a real school girl laugh of glee, recalled an occasion on which Miss Charlotte caught her class with one accord peeping into their books during recitation. Her ire arose, and the cat-o-nine-tales arose also. Fiercely, the angry lady lunged forward to strike the offenders, when her wig fell off, and her naked head was shamelessly exposed to view. In her wild clutch for her vanishing hair, the weapon fell unheeded on the floor, and the wicked girls smothered their mirth as best they could.

Other teachers were: Miss Cote, Miss Elizabeth Edwards, Miss

Cynthia Fisher, Reverend William E. Walters, Miss Klute, Miss Mary Judson, who lived until just a few years ago, a teacher, even in her old age, in the Greenville Woman's College; Professor Hall, Miss Mary Waller, Miss Carrie Waller, Miss Rosa Waller, who married Mr. Elijah Webb; Miss Carrie Edwards, and a northern lady, Miss Haughton, who tested the validity of the lax South Carolina marriage laws of that time. A young man of the town fell in love with her, but for some unknown reason, found it inexpedient for them to be publicly married, so he gave her a written contract of marriage, perhaps the only one ever given in the state. She remained in Anderson for some time longer, then returned to her distant home, where very soon after a son was born to her. She bore her husband's name, and her son was also known by it; but naturally, there was always in the minds of many people some doubt as to the validity of her marriage. Her husband's love did not stand the test of separation, for he never went for her, nor asked her to return to him. After her son was a grown man, he went to Anderson to claim a share in his father's property, the father being then dead; and to clear his own and his mother's name. The case was tried in the South Carolina courts, and the young man won his cause.

Another music teacher in the Johnson University was Miss Cassandra Hewett, who married the jeweler, F. C. von Borstel, and as Mrs. Borstel, taught music in Anderson for years. She was the mother and the teacher of the accomplished musician, Mrs. Alice Maxwell.

Miss Sarah Overby and Miss Mary Trowbridge taught singing and painting.

This able corps of teachers made a lasting impression on the community, and were honored and respected. Mrs. Mary E. Daniel must have been a very remarkable woman, and a teacher of great ability. One of her pupils who lived to be well on towards ninety, said once, when talking about her alma mater, that though, at that time almost seventy years had passed since her school days, she never looked at a beautiful sunset that the memory of Mrs. Daniel did not come to her mind, because one day that honored teacher, surrounded by a group of her young pupils, said to them—"Girls, look at that magnificent sky, there is nothing in all this world more beautiful than that painting from the hand of God himself. We have been closely associated here in our school life, and have learned to love each other well; when you, my pupils, go forth into the world, we may never meet again, but I want you always to remember me; so I ask you whenever in the future you gaze upon the wonderful pageant of the setting sun, send back a thought to your school girl days, and then remember me."

Mrs. Daniel had been under the sod for more than sixty years, but the women whom she had trained, were even then in their own old age, noting and pointing out to others the true, the good and the beautiful, and raising the standard of thinking. They too have passed on now, but who can say how far Mrs. Daniel's influence still extends itself in this little city at the foot hills?

A northern woman, Mrs. Daniel married a southern man, a native of Spartanburg, where she taught before going to Anderson. But her married life lasted but six weeks; then death removed her husband, and forced her back into the work marked out for her to do. She is buried in the Baptist grave yard.

Dr. Johnson lived in the house at the head of Manning street, long the home of the Misses Morris. When he died in 1862, his casket, preceded by the students of the University, walking two and two, was carried from his house to the Baptist Church, where funeral services were conducted by Reverend J. S. Murray. Dr. Johnson, too, sleeps his dreamless sleep in the shadows of the church he loved so well. For many years his grave was unmarked by any memorial stone, but was conspicuous on account of its being built over with a high brick arch, which was completely covered with ivy. In 1910 the Baptists of the state placed a stone over his grave, he having been the first president of the Southern Baptist convention.

When Dr. Johnson entered a school room every student rose to her feet and remained standing in perfect silence until he was seated. To be questioned by the chancellor struck terror to a girl's soul.

Dr. Johnson's death and the ever thickening war cloud caused the school to close and it was never reopened.

One of the old time teachers in Anderson was Reverend D. X. LaFar, a Presbyterian minister, and for a time pastor of the Anderson Church. He taught a mixed school on the south west corner of Earle and Main streets, where Evans Brothers drug store now stands.

On May Day, 1865, Mr. LaFar took not only his pupils, but a great party of the Anderson young people to Silver Brook, then well in the country, and not used for a cemetery, for a picnic, and a May party. The queen chosen for that tragic May Day was Miss Lillie Hubbard, better known to some people still living in Anderson, as Mrs. W. F. Barr. The sky was bright, and the revellers were happy. The May Day exercises were just over and the picnic dinner was spread, Dr. LaFar cutting with greatest care a pie of "real mincemeat" brought by one of the pupils, saying that there must be as many pieces as possible of such a dainty, when there was raised a fearful cry; a messenger sent from town, riding with frantic haste into the picnic party exclaiming—"Get home! Get home! The Yankees are coming, they are nearly here!" Who got the mince pie no one ever knew.

The presence of the Yankees in the town made little difference to the school children, after the first excitement was over. Some of Mr. LaFar's students remember watching from their school room windows, the soldiers drill on Main street.

There was another school picnic party on that first day of May, 1865. Miss Harbour was teaching a school for children, in the house on the southeast corner of River and Manning streets, long the home of Mrs. John Bleckley. Her pupils were having a picnic on Rocky River near Bailey's Bridge. More fortunate, they had finished their exercises and were almost through dinner when the alarm was given them. Miss Janie Pruitt was Queen of that May Party; she has been for years Mrs. Crowther.

In 1861 Mr. Thomas P. Hall, like Miss Harbour, a refugee from Charleston, opened a school for boys in a room in the north end of one of the old Johnson Female University dormitories, he afterwards taught in a room on Brick Range, and still later in his home where he accommodated a few boarders. He lived where Judge Cox's house now stands. Mr. Hall was a graduate of West Point, and during the first years of the war organized his students into a military company, which later went to the front and did active service in the Confederate army. Mr. Hall was a Baptist preacher, and for a time when the church had no pastor he preached for the Anderson congregation. After the war he went to New Orleans. One of his former students tells of the school being dismissed one day, that the pupils might go to see a negro hanged. The hanging ground at that time was out North Main street near the old Bell home.

During the war and just after, Charleston gave the up-country some of its best teachers. Persons of education and attainments "refugeed" towards the mountains, and found a demand for their services in the schools. Among the finest was Mr. Edward R. Miles, who came to Anderson about two years before the end of the war, and lived first in the house on the corner of River and Manning streets where Miss Harbour later had her school. Then he occupied a house which stood where the Felix Watkins home is now. There being no high school in the town, Mr. Miles, a man of great learning, was asked by some of the residents to teach young men. He consented, and opened a school in the old Johnson University building; later when the Confederate treasury was brought to Anderson and was housed in that building, he removed his school to his home.

After Brown's raiders came through looking for Jefferson Davis and Confederate gold, and the money was spirited away, Mr. Miles took his school back to its original location. The number of his pupils was limited to thirty at $100 each per term. His assistants were his brother, Reverend James Miles, who lived with him, and taught higher mathematics, and his brother-in-law, Mr. Henry Perinneau.

One of his former pupils says of him: "I could write a eulogy on Mr. Miles as a teacher, a gentleman and a Christian. I learned more under him than any teacher I ever had. He was firm and stern, but always just, and had the happy faculty of being able to impart his knowledge to his pupils."

After the war Mr. Miles moved to Abbeville where he taught for a short time, and then entered the ministry. He was for many years an honored and beloved Episcopal clergyman. Among the Anderson men who were his pupils were two sons of Dr. Holland, one of Anderson's citizens of former days, two Sloans, one Broyles, J. Lawrence Orr, Jr., and Mr. R. E. Belcher. There were others, but after the lapse of years those are all of the names that one of the former pupils could recall.

During the early years of the war there was a large school for boys and girls taught by Mr. Samuel Crawford, somewhere near the St. Paul church for colored people. Many of Anderson's most substantial citizens of fifteen or twenty years ago were taught by Mr. Crawford. After Northern capital made it more remunerative to teach the negroes than the white children, Mr. Crawford taught a negro school, probably the first for colored children ever organized in the town. It was in the same building that he had used for white children during the war.

Just after the war Reverend John S. Pressley taught a school for a time in a two-room brick building which stood to one side of the old Sharpe residence where Judge Cox's house now stands. Later in conjunction with Mr. Joseph M. Adams, a graduate of the Citadel, Mr. Pressley taught a Military Academy where Mr. Crawford had taught, and also at the Sharpe place.

Some years before the war there was a school taught by Mr. McKiller, in a little brick building which stood where the Greeley Institute was so long located on South McDuffie street, now the site of Mr. Aubrey Marshall's residence. Mr. McKiller married Miss Gussie Jeffers, daughter of Mr. H. L. Jeffers, a Charleston man who built for a summer home the house now occupied by Mrs. J. P. Sullivan, near Mr. McKeller's school, so it seems that Cupid got in some work along with readin', writin' and 'rithmetic, laboriously acquired at that place.

Miss Sue Opie taught school before the war in a small house which stood on the lot of Mr. Elijah W. Brown, more recently the residence of Mrs. Corrie Watson.

About that time or a little later, Colonel E. M. Rucker induced Captain Anthony, of Washington, Ga., to come to Anderson and open a high class school. Captain Anthony was a man of attainments, and he taught some of the men and women who have been factors in the life of the community. His first school was taught on the lot where the Presbyterian Female Seminary had been; later he taught in a small building which had been erected for a doctor's office on the northwest corner of the large lot bounded by McDuffie, Church, Market and Manning streets, later The Anderson Female Seminary under General Lewis M. Ayer. A filling station now occupies the spot where Captain Anthony's school house stood.

About 1866 there was an effort made by Northern philanthropists to buy the Johnson Female University buildings in order to use it as a school for the "freedmen." Some of the leading men of the town, learning of the plan, speedily organized and arranged to have the buildings serve for a boys' school, and Professor W. J. Ligon, who had been conducting a successful school in Pendleton, was urged to move to Anderson and take charge of the proposed institution. To that school and its justly famous teacher practically all of the men who grew up in Anderson in the twenty years following the war owed their education. There were many of his pupils who never went to college, or had any scholastic training except what they received from him, who easily held their own among college bred men, and whose knowledge of Latin and mathematics surpassed that of students graduated from more pretentious institutions. The school bore the name "Carolina Collegiate Institute," and had among its students some of the leading business men of the state, and many of Mr. Ligon's pupils rose to high position elsewhere. Not long before his death the old teacher received a letter from one of his former students, then a judge on the supreme bench of California, who wrote: "All that I am I owe to you."

In 1874 the school opened it doors to girls, who were received as students for about six years, then again excluded. Mr. Ligon better understood boys, and according to the traditions of his time he had a most effective way of handling them. Some of his assistants at various times were Reverend Mr. Round, Major Pink Reed, Mrs. Claudia R. Murray, Dr. D. E. Frierson, General L. M. Ayer, Miss Janie Frierson, Miss Vic Hammond, Mrs. Margaret Van Wyck, Mr. William S. Ligon, his son; Mr. Marcus Burriss, Mr. Laughlin, a Scotchman, who taught French and German; Miss Lewis, Mrs. Jane Hubbard, Dr. Emil Wahl, and others.

About 1866 Mr. Ligon associated with him Mr. Henry Reed, and the school added a military feature. In 1889 Mr. Ligon dissolved partnership with Mr. Reed, and removed his school to a nearby wooden building which was afterwards made into a dwelling. There he taught two years while the old University buildings were occupied by a military school under the management of General Kemper and Mr. Reed. But as long as Mr. Ligon taught a boys' school in Anderson there was no room for another, and the new Military Academy was soon abandoned; after which Mr. Ligon again occupied the former building, where he continued his chosen work until struck with paralysis. He died in 1891, and is buried in Silver Brook Cemetery, his being the first adult grave to have been made there.

Though a citizen of Anderson for more than thirty years, and highly respected by everybody, Mr. Ligon never sought public office. Once he was urged to run for state superintendent of education, but like a wise man he consulted his wife before making a decision, and she emphatically negatived the proposition. Once he was persuaded to come out for county superintendent of education, and attended one campaign meeting. Being called on for a speech, he immediately withdrew from the race, saying that speech making was not in his line of business, and he preferred attending to a business which he understood.

Although born in Virginia, Mr. Ligon came early to South Carolina. He graduated from the University of South Carolina in the class of 1848. There were sixty-four graduates and Mr. Ligon used to say that of the number there were only five who never became distinguished men. He modestly counted himself among the five, but who, in studying the history of the state, and especially the history of Anderson, can fail to realize that William J. Ligon was a great man. His influence is far reaching, and for the uplifting of the community. More than any other one man who has lived in the town except Mr. Wesley Leverette has Mr. Ligon influenced the community, for he trained, educated and directed the men who shaped the destiny of Anderson for fifty years.

HISTORY OF ANDERSON COUNTY

While Mr. Ligon was teaching the boys and young men of the town there was a superb woman whose impress upon the girls and the little boys was just as great. Mrs. Claudia R. Murray came to Anderson in her youth when Miss Claudia Edwards, to teach in the Johnson Seminary. After that school was closed by the war Mrs. Murray taught in the old Christopher Orr hotel building on the south side of the square, which was also her home. Later the family and the school moved to the place long known as the "Old Murray Place" on the corner of North Main and Greenville streets, where she had one of the most beautiful old fashioned flower gardens the town has ever boasted, and she was generous with her flowers. Few people, and no child or young girl ever went to Mrs. Murray's house for any purpose, that as they were leaving the dear lady did not say, "Would you like some flowers?" Then taking her shears she went about from bush to bush cutting an armful for the eager visitor. Mrs. Murray was assisted in her school by her lovely sisters, Misses Agnes and Jeffie Edwards. Sweet, gracious, dignified women they were, all of the large family of Edwards sisters, and their influence on the womanhood of Anderson was inestimable.

In 1881 General Lewis M. Ayer, of Barnwell, opened a school for girls known as The Anderson Female Seminary. This was a chartered institution empowered by the state to confer degrees. Endowed by nature in a prominent degree with a faculty for teaching, General Ayer succeeded in impressing himself indelibly upon his pupils; and today many of the best educated and most cultured women in South Carolina acknowledge their indebtedness to him. Among his former pupils is often heard the expression: "That reminds me of something General Ayer used to tell us." The president of Vassar College after receiving a pupil prepared by General Ayer wrote him that Vassar would receive pupils from The Anderson Female Seminary without examination.

General Ayer taught in a building just back of his dwelling, which was also the dormitory for the boarding pupils. Among General Ayer's teachers were Miss Bessie Bagby, whom he used to call his "first lieutenant." She is well known to many people as Mrs. J. T. Rice, of Belton; Miss Mary Bagby, now Mrs. Haynes, of Virginia; Miss Annie Belle Hall, now Mrs. McCrary, of Florida; Mrs. Margaret Van Wyck, long one of Anderson's most honored citizens; Mrs. Genevieve Spinner; Miss Sarah Atkinson, of Pennsylvania; Miss Florence Fleet, of Virginia; Mrs. Tabb, of Virginia; Miss Clara Hauck, of New York; Mrs. Rembert, of Georgia; Miss Julia Gray, of Mobile; Miss Lula Ayers, later Dr. Lula Rockwell, an osteopathic physician of Asheville (A son of this lady achieved distinction, and lost his life in the aviation service during the Great

War); Miss Lizzie Baldwin, of Virginia; Miss Whaley, from near Charleston, and Dr. Emil Wahl, of Germany. Assistant teachers, Miss Eva Nardin, now Mrs. J. D. Simpson, of Toccoa, Ga.; Miss Maggie Simpson, now Mrs. W. W. Watkins, of Clemson; Miss Marie Louise Ayer, now Mrs. J. R. Vandiver, and Mr. Hartwell M. Ayer, late of Florence, S. C.; art teachers, Miss Susan Wilson, and Miss Blanche Goodman, now Mrs. C. H. Silliman, of New York; music teachers, Mrs. L. M. Ayer, Miss Rimmer, of Vienna, and Miss Verna Ayer, now Mrs. Knut Akerberg, of Florence, Italy.

The Anderson Female Seminary existed only about seven years, having an average attendance of about two hundred pupils each session. Its students were given an opportunity to learn all of the branches taught in an up to date Southern College. Then years pressing too heavily upon its president, he threw off the great responsibility of a girls' school, and in his last years taught only two hours a day in the Patrick Military Institute. He was as successful with boys as with girls, and many of the men who were his pupils regard his memory with veneration, and think they learned more when in his classes than at any other period of their lives.

General Ayer died in 1895, and rests in Silver Brook Cemetery; but his influence is still felt in the community which he made his home.

In 1889 Colonel John B. Patrick, who for years had conducted a flourishing military school in Greenville, was induced to remove the institution to Anderson, and in conjunction with Mr. Ligon to occupy the old Johnson University buildings. The Patrick Military Institution became one of the best schools the town ever had. The board of trustees consisted of General W. W. Humphreys, president; J. J. Baker, secretary and treasurer; D. S. Maxwell, J. E. Breazeale, John B. Watson, J. B. Lewis, W. G. Watson, W. F. Barr, J. W. Daniels, G. W. Fant, R. F. Divver, J. L. Tribble and S. Bleckley.

Colonel John B. Patrick was president of the school and instructor in mathematics; Captain John M. Patrick taught French and German, military science and tactics, and gave instruction in a business course; Professor Ligon, Latin and Greek; Reverend A. A. Marshall, Mental and Moral Philosophy; First Lieutenant J. H. Noland, English History; Second Lieutenant Thomas W. Gary, assistant in Mathematics and Modern Languages; General Lewis M. Ayer, Mental and Political Science; Dr. W. H. Nardin, Hygiene; Dr. S. M. Orr, Physiology; Lieutenant A. G. Miller, English and History; J. L. Tribble, Jurisprudence; J. F. McElwee, Belles-Lettres and History; R. S. Patrick, Assistant Instructor in

Mathematics and English; Reverend Charles Manley, Mental and Moral Science; W. H. Nardin, Jr., Chemistry and Hygiene; B. O. Powell, Assistant Mathematics and English; R. D. Epps, Belles-Lettres, History, Military Science and Tactics; Nardin and Orr, Surgeons.

In the roster of P. M. I. appears names from every county in South Carolina, and a number from other states. The fame of the school extended far, and when one morning in early fall the summons came to its honored president to come up higher, there was widespread grief; Dr. Judson, of Furman University, expressed the sentiment felt by hundreds of Colonel Patrick's former pupils when he wrote: "Many men in South Carolina can say, 'For what I am, for my sense of justice, right and honor, I am greatly indebted to the influence of Colonel John B. Patrick on my early life.'"

From 1890 to 1892 there was again a school in the old Sharpe place, this time it occupied the dwelling; it was known as The Anderson Female College, and Reverend A. A. Marshall, pastor of the Baptist church, was its president. His teachers were Miss Margaret Evans, Miss Lois Watson, Miss Varina Brown and Miss Lucille Nardin, all former pupils of General Ayer.

One of the schools which existed for a longer time and trained a greater number of young Andersonians, except those taught by Mr. Leverette, Mr. Ligon and Mrs. Murray, was "The Home School," taught by Miss Leonora C. Hubbard. Both boys and girls were her pupils and her excellence as a teacher has long been established. The school was in existence for thirteen years, and grew from one assistant, Miss Augusta V. Hubbard, to a complete faculty for all modern high school work. The first building occupied was a house on South Main Street, owned by J. M. Payne. Later Miss Hubbard built a commodious house on Evins street next to her mother's residence. Some of her assistants were Miss Minnie Wilson, sister of Mrs. George Broyles, who died young; Miss Minnie Gadsden, French teacher; Miss Ellen Gordon, who came to be one of the best known of the public school teachers (she died several years ago); Miss Anna Brown, who is still employed in teaching Anderson young people; Miss Carrie Seel, now Mrs. J. M. Bell, and whose son was one of the teachers in the Boys' High School several years ago; Miss Eugenia Benson, now Mrs. D. P. McBrayer; Miss Virginia Evans, now Mrs. Hammond of California, was music teacher, as was also Miss Lizzie Cornish, who died several years ago. Dr. S. M. Orr was lecturer on Physiology.

Miss Hubbard's school was the first organization in the town to plan and work for a monument to the Anderson Confederate dead, and that earnest teacher never ceased her efforts until the monument stood on the public square. This school also revived the custom, fallen into disuse, of the observance of Memorial Day. All colleges in South Carolina, and The Peabody Normal College of Nashville, Tennessee, received graduates from this school into their junior classes without examination.

After the public schools were established "Miss Nora" held for many years the important position of First Grade teacher, starting on the path of knowledge the little children, to whom it is so important to give a good start. After that she taught drawing in the schools, and later held the position of librarian in the Girls' High School.

For years after Mrs. Murray ceased to teach, her sisters, Misses Edwards, continued a school for small children in her home, and their influence was a benediction to every child fortunate enough to have come under their instruction.

In 1878 there was a school taught by Miss Sallie Robinson, afterwards Mrs. Shanklin, of Pendleton, in the home of her sister, Mrs. "Bettie" Moore, widow of Colonel John V. Moore. The residence stood where the Girls' High school is now located. Miss Robinson had to assist her Miss Jane Wade. The name was "The Southern Home School."

During the war, and for years after, there were a number of small schools of which the names of the teachers and the locations of the schools is all that time has preserved. Among them was one taught in the Presbyterian Sessions House by Miss Emma East. She also taught for a time where Judge Cox's house now stands. Miss Maggie Munro also taught in the Presbyterian Sessions House. Miss Amanda Drennan taught on Orr Street about where Mr. Hatcher's house now stands. Miss Ella Gaines, later Mrs. Hudgens, of Honea Path, and mother of Captain W. A. Hudgens, who laid down his life in France, once taught school in Anderson in the home of her sister, Mrs. J. C. Whitfield, on South Main Street. Mrs. Whitfield, too, was a teacher, and her school was located on the lot long occupied by the home of the late Dr. W. H. Nardin, Sr. Miss Della Keys, now Mrs. Thompson, taught for a time in a double-roomed brick building on the corner of Towers and Whitner Streets, the location of the ancient Presbyterian Seminary. J. H. Creswell once conducted a school for lawyers in Anderson. Mrs. J. E. Hubbard for many years taught all kinds of fancy work, hair, feather, wax, as well as water-color painting and drawing. There was also for a short time a Mrs. Pickett, who taught the same kind of work in the second story of a wooden building on the site of the first store in Anderson. She may have taught in the original building; at any rate, the house in which was located her studio was said to have been moved from the Savannah River to that spot.

Mrs. Corrie Watson, when a young lady, taught school in Anderson, as did Miss Janie Frierson and Miss Emma Osborne. Mrs. Bacot taught for a time in the old Johnson University. Miss Kittie Burriss, afterwards Mrs. Thomas R. Ayer, of Macon, Ga., taught a school for small children, first in the two-story brick house so often used for a school which stood on the Sharpe or Cox lot. Later she taught in a room of her mother's house, which was the same in which Mrs. Van Wyck now lives. One of her pupils was little Hartwell Ayer, son of General L. M. Ayer, and he so loved his teacher that he told her one day that his brother, Tom, was coming to see the family, and he wanted her to be Brother Tom's sweetheart. Whether she looked with favorable eyes upon "Brother Tom" as a result of the little boy's suggestion, she would never say, but certainly, for more than forty years, she was his adored sweetheart.

Miss Emmie Tew taught a Parish School for several years in a house erected for the purpose by Reverend T. F. Gadsden, on the end of Grace Church lot which was afterwards sold to Mr. J. H. McConnell, and where his residence now stands.

Miss Elizabeth P. Morris taught school in her home at the head of Manning Street. She also had a large music class. Miss Kate Cornish taught a school for small children for a time, and Miss Lizzie Cornish taught music for many years. Mrs. Von Borstel taught a school for children in her home over her husband's jewelry store for a short time. She taught music as long as she lived. Miss Rosa Webb taught children in her mother's home on South Main Street. She was long known and loved as Mrs. C. F. Jones. Miss Pet Allen, later Mrs. S. M. Orr, taught a school for children in a brick building on South Main Street just next to Mrs. Webb's residence. Mrs. Grace Cochran taught a school for children in her home on South Main Street, long used as a boarding house. Mrs. McSmith taught a class in music and art in a building on Brick Range.

In the early nineties Miss Margaret Evans opened a High School for Girls, first in her home on West Franklin Street, later in a house which she had erected next to her father's residence on North McDuffie Street. Her assistants were Miss Lucille Nardin, later Mrs. S. C. Baker; Miss Leila Russell, Miss Olive Brown, now Mrs. H. G. Anderson; Miss Elise Mauldin, now Mrs. J. M. Paget; Miss Carrie Pearman and Miss Virginia Evans, later Mrs. Hammond, who was long one of Anderson's best known music teachers, as well as organist of the First Baptist Church.

Mrs. Jane Sayre taught a school for small children in her home which, during the life of her brother, Reverend T. F. Gadsden, was in the Episcopal Rectory. Later she taught in the building erected by Mr. Gadsden for Miss Tew's Parish School. Mrs. Sayre's impression on her pupils may be illustrated by conversation overheard between one of her pupils, an eight year-old boy, who is now Dr. W. H. Nardin, and a small friend of his who has been long in his grave, concerning their school experiences. Little "Waller," telling of his teacher and her methods, said: "I tell you she is a well-born Christian." The listener being of a military turn of mind, and greatly impressed by Mrs. Sayre's religious teachings, replied: "Yes, sir, she's a solid military Christian."

Mrs. Bessie Taylor for a time taught school in her home on Earle Street. Miss Nellie Brown taught many of the Anderson men and women in their not very distant childhood. Mrs. Ernest Moorer, who, as Miss Emily Divver, had been a teacher in the public schools, taught a few children in her home on Orr Street.

Mr. G. H. Geiger, for several years, taught a school for boys in the building erected by the Wesleyan Methodist on the site of the Elks' Club. Later he used the house across the street, built by Miss Margaret Evans for her school. Some of Mr. Geiger's boys upon leaving his tutorage took a very high stand in the schools and colleges which they attended.

Miss Mary McCoy, of Charleston, now Mrs. Earle Watson, came to Anderson to teach a kindergarten, which was conducted in the home of Judge Cox, his children being her first pupils. Miss McCoy later conducted a kindergarten in the Anderson Mill School, and after that was for some years a teacher in the City schools.

Miss Lucille Nardin for a time conducted a school in her father's house, and later in a room of General Ayer's former Anderson Female Seminary building. Mr. W. F. Moncrief taught a private school for a time while he was waiting for the first graded school building to be finished; he, too, used the room which Miss Nardin had occupied in the old Seminary after she vacated it, saying that it was much better for his purpose than the one he had.

In 1910 Professor Watkins moved to Anderson from Honea Path and taught a school for boys in the building built by General Ayer for his school rooms, and which had been used for years as a residence. Mr. Watkins lived in the house as well as taught in it.

In 1913 Dr. Frazier, pastor of the First Presbyterian Church, opened The Frazier Academy, a preparatory school for boys. His assistants were Mr. B. M. Parks, Mr. Sam Anderson and Professor Banks. It was conducted in the annex of the church. Later it became the Harbin School, and still later was united with a business school opened in the old Whitner house by a Professor Evans. Soon after that it was discontinued entirely.

In January, 1896, the public school with its system of grades was established in Anderson. Judge G. E. Prince, who was then a lawyer at the Anderson bar, was the prime factor in the establishment of the system. Not without great opposition was the measure carried through. Mr. D. H. Russell, at that time editor of *The Daily Mail*, arrayed himself on the side of Mr. Prince and the education of the masses, and after hard fighting were the people of the community brought to realize their obligation to the next generation.

There was at first but one building, that on West Market Street, and great was the protest that arose against the "useless expenditure of the people's money" in the erection of so large a building. In 1928 there are thirteen buildings, several of them have been enlarged more than once, and still the cry is constantly going up for more room.

The first superintendent was W. F. Moncrief, who had been a professor at Clemson when he was invited to take charge of the Anderson "Graded School." The first teachers were Miss Leonora C. Hubbard, Miss Margaret Evans, Mrs. S. C. Baker, Miss May Russell, Mr. Adkins, Miss Fannie Watkins, Miss Stokes. The school opened with three hundred and eighty students, which was regarded an overwhelming number, and a complete vindication of those who had contended the need of a public school. In 1898, after two years' service, Professor Moncrief resigned, and was succeeded by Professor T. C. Walton, originally a Georgia man who came from Florida to take a position. Mr. Walton remained at the head of the school until 1907, nine years, and under his administration two new buildings were erected, and the force of teachers greatly increased. Then Mr. Walton accepted the position of president of a Girls' College in Lexington, Ky., and Mr. E. C. McCants was his successor, and is still holding the position. Under Dr. McCants the school system has grown enormously; it now embraces all of the outlying mill districts, has thirteen buildings and 179 teachers; two handsome high school buildings, one for boys and the other for girls, belong to the system. Both of those buildings, when first erected, were burned a short time after but were immediately rebuilt. In 1928 there was an enrollment of 5,896 students.

There have been hundreds of teachers in the schools since the public school was organized, and many young men and women have obtained there all the education that they have received, and have found themselves well equipped for the battle of life. Dr. McCants ranks now among the teachers who have served the Anderson people longest, and has assisted in the making of a large number of useful citizens.

While it is impossible to mention the teachers who have assisted in making the public schools the force that they are, yet among the number is one who has done such a splendid work, and been such an uplifting force in the community, that her name should appear. That teacher is Mrs. Lottie Crosby Estes, who, both before her marriage and after, has been first a teacher then principal of the Glenn Street School, whose pupils come from three mill districts. While very many of those children come from good homes and have been carefully trained, there are numbers of others who have had no home training, and to them Mrs. Estes has been a wonderful friend.

In 1910 a campaign was started to raise funds for a college in Anderson. Interest was aroused, and one hundred thousand dollars was subscribed, and the money, with a most desirable lot, was offered to the Baptist State Convention, asking it, as the wealthiest and largest Christian body in the section, to take under its auspices the projected college. The proposition was accepted, and a board of trustees elected. This board consisted of J. J. Fretwell, R. S. Ligon, C. S. Sullivan, W. H. Hunt, W. A. Watson, L. M. Roper, W. B. Wilbur, J. L. Bristow, J. N. Brown, J. K. Durst, W. E. Thayer, C. C. Brown, S. C. Mitchell, H. H. Watkins and M. M. Mattison.

Three handsome buildings were erected, and Mr. C. S. Sullivan built a home for the president in keeping with the others. The school opened September 18th, 1912, with Dr. J. A. Chambliss its first president. His faculty was composed of J. K. Breeden, Dean and Teacher of History; Miss Mary Seymour Abbott, Lady Principal and Teacher of Modern Languages; Dr. Charles Fisher, Director of Music; Mrs. Grace Cater Divver, Matron; Miss Hazel Park, Domestic Science; Miss Ada Culner, English; Miss Lucy Riser, Mathematics; Mrs. R. C. Fisher, Piano; Miss Ellie Hudson, Piano; Miss Sara Stranathan, Voice; Miss Lula B. Jones, Art; Miss Robbie Wakefield, Expression and Physical Culture; Dr. Olga V. Pruitt, College Physician and Teacher of Physiology and Hygiene; Mrs. J. K. Breeden, teacher in charge of the Preparatory Department; Miss Helen F. Hunter, Ancient Languages; Miss Lillian Duggan, Natural Sciences.

Dr. Chambliss undertook the duties of president of the college with the understanding that he should be released as soon as the trustees could find a suitable man for the position. Since his term of service Dr. James P. Kinard, Mr. John E. Vines and Dr. John E. White have served as presidents of the college. The position is now filled by Miss Denmark.

Such have been the educational advantages of Anderson county and city. A noble body of men and women have served to uplift the youth and prepare them for good citizenship, and to them is largely due the fact that Anderson is an enlightened and progressive community.

In the chapel of Anderson college hang two memorial tablets to teachers of former times. The older is weather-stained and timeworn. It was originally erected in the chapel of Johnson University, not a great while after the death of the beloved principal of that school, Mrs. Mary E. Daniel, in honor to her memory by the pupils of the institution. After the old school buildings passed through so many phases, the tablet was thrown out, and the late Mrs. Elizabeth Bleckley, seeing it lying neglected in a trash-heap, took it and placed it on Mrs. Daniel's grave. She had been one of the girls who erected the tablet. For a number of years it remained where Mrs. Bleckley had laid it. Then another of the girls who had been a student under Mrs. Daniel and had helped to raise the memorial to her honor, seeing it lying exposed to wind and weather, appealed to women of a later generation, those who had been pupils of General Ayer, to retrieve the dishonored memorial to a teacher and a woman, who, in her day, had been such a power for good in the community. She was Mrs. Rebecca Hoyt, and her younger friends, impressed by her earnestness, asked and received permission to place the stone in the new college for women which the twentieth century had established in Anderson. After placing the memorial to Mrs. Daniel, whom they had never seen, they resolved to place one to their own loved teacher, General Ayer, and gaining permission it, too, was placed to grace the schoolroom walls.

The Girls' High School some years ago established memorials to two of Anderson's former teachers of a different nature. They named their two literary societies Ayer and Ligon, thus keeping before the minds of the students the memory of two of the most influential teachers of former times.

An Anderson-born woman, who was once a pupil of General Ayer, dying without children, and having a considerable property, left a large bequest to be used for the education of girls. The Horton brothers, of Atlanta, themselves Anderson-born and bred, are trustees of the fund. Anderson College was not in existence when Mrs. Frances Clementine Tucker, in her girlhood Clemmie Garrison, made her will, consequently it does not appear in the list of those selected by her for her beneficiaries. They are: Lander College, Piedmont College, of Demorest, Ga.; Young Harris College, Young Harris, Ga.; Martha Berry School, and the Georgia Normal and Industrial School, of Athens, Ga.

Mrs. Tucker was the adopted daughter of Henry Garrison and her girlhood home stood on the corner of South Main and Church streets. Mrs. Tucker's body lies in a mausoleum in Silver Brook Cemetery.

A school in the town which existed sometime just after 1895 or 1896, was somewhere in what is known as the "Bleckley Annex," and was taught by Mr. Lee. It was for boys of from 15 to 18 years of age.

The negroes of the town have had good schools. After Mr. Crawford, a school was established for them by the Horace Greeley Fund. A property was purchased on McDuffie street, and among other teachers which officiated there was Captain Parker, a Charleston man, reduced by the war to doing what he could for a living. Later negro teachers took charge, among them M. H. Gassaway and his wife, Caroline. For a number of years these negroes did good work for the people of their race. For some reason they, after a time, left the Greeley Institute on McDuffie street, and built a wooden building, which was never fully completed, on Thomas street. After the graded school system was adopted, they became the first of its teachers. An industrial feature was always prominently stressed in their school, and their pupils, both boys and girls, did some fine work. On several occasions Caroline Gassaway had her girls prepare a dinner, to which she invited the white people who had manifested any interest in the school, the city superintendent, and some of the ministers. They always served a superb dinner, well prepared. The needlework of the girls was also fine, and the manual work of the boys showed up well.

After some years, Gassaway had his head completely turned by a negro preacher who came to take charge of one of the churches, and it became necessary to ask him to leave the community, and to the credit of the negroes, they were the first to ask him to leave.

Mary Earle, widow of Anderson's first negro physician, was a woman of good education and right ideas. She taught in the schools for years. There have been other negro teachers who deserve credit for the good work they are doing among their own people. There are three negro schools belonging to the Public School System, and they have never been neglected by the school superintendent, who really has at heart the best interest of his colored students as he has of the children of his friends. In 1928 the enrollment in the schools for colored children was 1,251, with 37 teachers. Two of the schools for these children are grammar schools, one is a high school, all good buildings.

CHAPTER X.

SOME OF THE EARLY CITIZENS AND HOMES.

THE MEXICAN WAR, THE BIG FIRE AND OLD REFORMER.

ONE of Anderson County's earliest families was that of Alexander Moorhead. In fact, Mr. Moorhead came before the county did. He built, in 1813, the quaint little house out several miles north of Anderson which his son, Mr. Robert Moorhead, occupied until his death several years ago. The house is probably still standing.

There is an interesting story told of the origin of the name. It is said that long, long ago there lived in Scotland, in the same neighborhood, two men of the same name, John Muir. One lived on the top of a hill, and became known as John Muir, at the hill or "heed," and the other as John Muir, on the bray face. It chanced that a bull in the neighborhood became mad and the men of the community, armed with anything that could be carried as a weapon, went out to slay the beast. John Muir, of the "heed," armed himself with a pitchfork, and was fortunate enough to kill the bull, whose head he carried home in triumph. That doughty deed, added to the "heed" already used in connection with his name, finally fixed it as Muirhead, which in process of time became Moorhead.

The Anderson Moorheads lived first in Union District. The head of the family was another John. He, during the Revolutionary War, was loyal to Britain. His two sons, however, fought in the army of the patriots. Alexander Moorhead was a little boy at the time of the war with England, and he used to tell about seeing the "Red Coats" pass his father's house, and running to hide in a fence corner until they were out of sight.

He was one of the first white men to settle in this section of the country. His house was built of logs, the interstices filled with small brick made to fit the place they were to occupy. A few years before his death Mr. Robert Moorhead was over-persuaded to cover the front and sides of his house with weatherboarding, but the original logs are still there, and at the back may be seen.

In 1814 Mr. Alexander Moorhead was elected captain of a military company composed of men of Pendleton district, and living in what afterwards became Anderson, which went into Georgia to fight Indians. The company spent six months on that business.

The people of this vicinity lived largely on sweet potatoes in that early time, and Mr. Alexander Moorhead sold probably the greater part of the potatoes sold. Even to people who raised their own potatoes he sold those needed for seed. He also sold large quantities of tobacco.

A little distance back of the Moorhead house is a quaint old Dutch oven of brick. It has a large cavity for baking and a small one for fire.

The Moorhead place was originally owned by an Irishman named Loflin. He lived in a log cabin. In 1704 Mr. Moorhead, then a young man, came from Union and bought the property. At once he went to work to make a crop, and after it was made and gathered, he returned to Union and got his parents to come and live with him. The youth was only twenty years old at the time. With the parents came also a young sister, who was married to a Mr. Lewis, grandfather of Mr. J. B. Lewis. The present house was not built at the time. The family occupied the cabin of Mr. Loflin, and in the low loft the bride dressed for the wedding. The original house is still standing, an outbuilding of the farm, and the dingy loft is to be seen. The bride may not have been tall; if she was, she dressed bent over.

Alexander also soon married, and it was for his young wife he built the present house, a two-story structure with a large living room and an ell containing two other rooms—quite a pretentious house when it was erected. Mr. Moorhead and his wife are buried in Concord church yard, not far from their home place.

To the west of the city of Anderson is still standing a well-known house yet called by many people "the old Keys Place." The first owner of the name was Peter Keys, born in Ireland in 1761. He, too, came before the county did. It is said that his house had the first glass windows ever seen in the community, and that people drove out of their way in order to pass the place and see the innovation. He also built the first vault for the dead. It is still to be seen, a brick structure some distance from the house, once in the heart of the cool forest, now almost beside the public road. In the vault rest the bodies of Mr. Keys and his wife, several of their children and grandchildren, and other relatives; in all, about eighteen people. The vault is walled up and sealed now. There is no way of getting into it other than to tear it down.

The streets of the town, as well as the country roads in the early days, were kept in traveling condition by contracting with the lowest bidder for the job, who then put his slaves, if he had any, at the task, or, owning none, hired hands. The work consisted in cutting down weeds, filling holes and smoothing off the surface.

Even as late as 1860 the roads in Anderson county were mere trails, or plantation ways. There were few public highways, and those few wretchedly kept. Most travel was done by means of horses, or on foot. Horseback riding was easier than vehicle traveling, and it was a common sight to see a man riding with his wife or daughter mounted behind him. The very stylish people used a pillion for the women to sit on, but among ordinary folks they just climbed up on the horse's bare back and hung to the man in front.

There were stage routes established by the middle of the nineteenth century between important towns, and they ran, when practicable, through smaller places. Coaches were very heavy and not infrequently stuck in the mud of some almost impassable road, and the men passengers, and most of them were men—women seldom went far from home—had to get out and help pry them out. On "the cold Saturday" in 1833 the only way that the stage coach could move at all was by the driver carrying an axe with which he cut away ice-laden tree branches which blocked his progress. Meantime the passengers, if any, who were rash enough to travel on that dreadful day, sat inside the coach and narrowly escaped actual freezing.

Anderson's first carpenter, Hugh Whittaker, lived somewhere back of the west side of the square. Close around the new town were many settlers. David Anderson lived where Mrs. Frank Johnson's house now stands, quite a little distance out of town it was in his day, and he used to haul wood in to sell. A noble line of old pear trees planted by the Andersons is still standing at the side of the present house.

Some other of the original names in the county were Breazeale, Gambrell, Kay, Major, Erskine, Shirley, Long, Roseman, Wellborn, Broyles, Reed, and many others.

It is said that Mr. Enoch Reed, an uncle of Judge J. P. Reed, went from South Carolina in the fall of 1818 to Indiana, because of the very severe drought that visited Pendleton. Mr. Grief Horton and Mr. Enoch Reed, neighbors, ran three or four ploughs each, and made between them only about sixty bushels of corn. Mr. Horton bought Mr. Reed's corn, and that, with what oats and other provender he made, enabled him to pull through until the next year. Mr. Reed, or Reid, for the name was spelled both ways, left that section of country. It seems probable that he was the ancestor of Whitelaw Reid, the stateman who not many years ago was United States minister to England. There is a tradition in the Whitelaw Reid family that their ancestor moved to Indiana from

South Carolina when Indiana was a part of the almost unexplored west.

Anderson took great interest in the war with Mexico. It sent some soldiers to the army, and the people at home got greatly excited over war news. An account has been preserved of how the town celebrated the news of a victory.

Messrs. Reed and Orr were the leading lawyers at the time, and on that particular evening the brilliant appearance of their office, which stood on Brick Range, rather more than half way towards its northern end, attracted a crowd around its doors to find out the meaning of the illumination. Colonel Orr was absent from the town, but Colonel Reed, with his usual eye for good effect, had arranged the decorations. The front of the office was largely glass, great windows and a big light in the door affording ample space for lights. At a short distance in front of the door a beautiful transparency was elevated with appropriate devices and mottoes in honor of "Our Gallant Army and the illustrious and patriotic generals who led them on to victory," which of course explained to those who had not heard the news the occasion of the display. Upon the front of the transparency next to the public square appeared in bold relief, seemingly in letters of gold, the device: "General Taylor, the hero of four battles in one year—the People's Man." Upon the left, in similar characters, was "General Scott, Lundy's Lane, Vera Cruz and Cerro Gordo, Monuments to his fame," and upon the right, "Colonel Butler and the Palmetto Regiment." The perusal of these devices sufficed to arouse the patriotic enthusiasm of the crowd, which was manifested by vociferous cheering. Bonfires were kindled on the square, and amid shouts a procession was bearing at its head the transparency. It marched around the square and along the principal streets of the village, returning about eleven o'clock to the point from which it started.

Calling for speeches, the crowd was addressed from the steps of the office by Colonel Reed, Mr. Peter Vandiver and Mr. John V. Moore.

On April 9, 1845, there was a high wind blowing over the little town, and about midnight the sleeping people were aroused by the cry, "Fire!" The store of Mr. Earle, on the corner of the one business street in the place, the place now occupied by Efird's department store, was in flames. Mr. Griffin, the manager of the store, slept in it, and he awoke to find the building full of smoke. It was with difficulty that he fought his way into the air. The wind spread the fire rapidly, and the "bucket brigade," a double line from the fire to the wells which stood on each side of the court house, passing full buckets on one side and empty ones on the other, handing them to fire fighters, could make no headway against the flames. The whole row of buildings was destroyed.

Mr. Crayton's store, which stood on the extreme end from where the fire started, caught last, of course, and he had time to get his goods out. They were piled on the square about where the Confederate Monument stands, and the next day were taken into the courthouse, where he continued to do business for quite a while. He was still occupying the courthouse when the time came for the spring term of court. Judge Johnson was to preside. When he reached Anderson and learned of the situation, he refused to allow Mr. Crayton's business to be disturbed, and conducted the whole court from the piazza of the Orr Hotel.

But the printing office, where Mr. Reed was publishing *The Highland Sentinel*, was not so fortunate. It was burned with all its contents, among which was the book in which had been kept the minutes of the town council from its very beginning. Mr. Reed was intendant at the time, and the meetings were held in his office, and the book kept there.

The fire burned the whole west side of the square, then jumped the street and caught the Benson Hotel. However, there had been time to prepare for it; the building was covered with wet blankets, which were kept saturated, and there the fire was checked. On that night the little children of Mr. Crayton were staying with their grandparents, Mr. and Mrs. Benson. They were awakened and sent out to Rose Hill, then well out of town. The fierce wind carried burning timbers as far as Judge Whitner's lawn, and the woods, as far out as the Quattlebaum place, were set on fire. Sheds erected over vats on Mr. Osborne's tan yard on Whitner creek were burned.

Never has Anderson had such a fire, and although there are few people now living who remember that dreadful night, yet it is to Anderson still "The Big Fire."

In 1845 Anderson built a market house. It stood about where Penny's store is now, and a high fence was built all back of the courthouse, enclosing all of the east side of the square. The only way to reach the market was through the courthouse. People had to go before day to get meat, and the rule was "first come, first served." Late comers got poor cuts, or did without.

The little old cannon, now known as "Old Reformer," was brought to Anderson in the early days from Fort Ninety-Six, and its joyful note was heard on all public occasions. Governor Mc-

HISTORY OF ANDERSON COUNTY

Duffie used to come to Anderson often to review the militia, and at those times the cannon spoke.

Just when it came to the county is uncertain, as is its previous history. Certainly before 1850 it belonged to an artillery company which was organized by the people living in the sections now known as Deans and Starr. The muster ground was at Howard's Old Field, about one mile east of the present town of Starr. The uniform of that company was copperas trousers and blue coats. The company was in existence in 1832; how much earlier is not known. The little cannon was the object around which they rallied, the detonations of which aroused enthusiasm, and fanned to greater fervor the flame of patriotism which burned in the breasts of the gallant boys.

That company was succeeded by one consisting of 102 men, commanded by Major Thomas Dean; their uniform was black jackets and white trousers. The cannon was their only field piece, and dear to their hearts. They built a house on the muster grounds for its safe keeping, and at all general musters it was brought out and put into service. Its reverberations continued to thrill men until the great struggle of the 60s; after that it was made to lend its voice, which is said to be remarkably powerful, to more than one celebration of Confederate victories. After the defeat of the South the cannon, like its people, sank into despondent silence until 1876, when again its joyful note was heard shouting, as did the people, "Hurrah For Hampton."

Major John B. Moore conceived the idea of rescuing the old cannon from oblivion, and Mr. "Pink" Reed went after it. He found it half covered with dirt out in an old field and brought it to the town. Colonel Hoyt, then editor of *The Intelligencer,* named it "Old Reformer."

The cannon is of English make, brass, and was probably used during the Revolution, though there is no authentic account of it at that time, yet there is a tradition that it was used by both British and Americans. It is said to have been transported to Anderson county in 1814 by a man named Hanks, believed by many people to have been the father of Nancy Hanks, who afterwards married Thomas Lincoln, and became the mother of Abraham Lincoln. All that story, however, is pure tradition, and lacks confirmation.

The old brass field piece weighs 600 pounds, and was touched off with a fuse instead of the lanyard of later days. Its fine carriage rotted away more than a hundred years ago. During the war, there being no iron in the county, and no money to buy implements, the iron from the old support was used to make ploughshares.

There is a tradition that the cannon was borrowed in December, 1860, from the old muster grounds, and that its voice blazoned the news that the Ordinance of Secession had been signed, after which it was returned to its former place until sixteen years should pass. After the Hampton campaign, it was again forgotten and neglected. For a long time it lay, again half buried in the earth out near the freight depot, and thirty or more years ago the late W. R. Hubbard rescued it, and placed it on his lawn. There it remained until about 1905 or 1906, when Mrs. J. L. McGee, then regent of Cateechee Chapter, Daughters of the American Revolution, interested her chapter in procuring the historic piece and having it placed in a conspicuous position on North Main street, just about opposite to the Central Presbyterian Church. There it stood for several years, until an automobile-crazy city council, after having cut down all of the trees in the street, turned its attention to the little cannon, deciding that it was in the way of speeders, and took it down. Then it disappeared from sight and memory, until Mayor Foster Fant, during his first term, had it mounted and placed in its present position.

CHAPTER XI.

SOME OF THE FOREFATHERS.

ONE of the earliest families in the country was that of Peter Acker. The founder of the family in America was William Acker, who came from Germany about 1750, having started with three sons, one of whom was lost overboard on the voyage. The two left were William, Jr., and Peter. They settled in New Jersey, not a great distance from Philadelphia. Of the elder, William, Jr., nothing is known by the southern branch; it is supposed that he lived, died and left descendants in New Jersey.

The other son, Peter, with his wife, Jane Southerland, moved to Fair Field, South Carolina. He, too, may have descendants in New Jersey, as Jane Southerland was his second wife. He may have left older children in the Northern State.

Peter was a soldier in the Revolutionary War. He must have settled on the public domain in Fair Field, for no record can be found of his owning property there. In 1790 he moved to Pendleton District, buying many acres on Saluda River, near Shady Grove. Peter Acker died about 1815.

The father of Mrs. Peter Acker, Alexander Southerland, came to America under peculiar circumstances. He was a student at the University of Edinborough, and with a party of college boys one day boarded a vessel to see the sights. The ship sailed away with them, and upon reaching Boston the students were sold to pay their passage. Southerland must have liked the new country; at any rate, he remained and later married Mrs. Betsey Williams.

The children of Peter Acker and Jane Southerland were William, who married Miss Clement, Joseph, who married Ruth Alexander, Peter married Susannah Halbert, Alexander married Orma Burton, Mary married James Grace, Nancy married John McDavid, Elizabeth married James Taylor, Susan married Sanford Vandiver, Amos married Ruth Halbert.

The children of William and Clement were: Mahala married Welborn Keaton, Peter married Miss Stevenson, Rhoda married Daniel Brown, William married Miss White, John married Miss Harper, Dearborn married Miss Cox, Amos married Miss Davis.

From Rhoda Acker and Daniel Brown are descended the family of the late Dr. Ben Brown, of Williamston; the late Elijah Brown, of Anderson; the late Samuel Brown, of Anderson, and others, a numerous connection many of of whom have been in the past, and are now useful and prominent citizens of the community.

The children of Peter, Jr., and Susannah Halbert were Halbert, who married Elizabeth Garrison; Frances married William Hammond, Alexander married Mourning Garrison, William V. died young, Elizabeth married William Mattison, Mary married Joel Townsend, Teresa married Allen McDavid, Lucinda married Jesse McGee, Peter Newton married first Miss Shumate, second Miss Garris, third Mrs. Caldwell; Joel Milton moved to Mississippi where he became a judge, and was the founder of a wealthy and prominent family in that state; Joshua S. married Matilda Williams. From their sons, Peter and Amos, are descended most of the South Carolina Ackers.

Susannah Halbert, wife of Peter Acker, Jr., was the daughter of William Halbert and Elizabeth Hill. William's father, Joel Halbert, came from Wales and settled in Virginia. Whom he married is unknown, a Virginia girl certainly, as tradition makes this William Halbert eighth in descent from Pocahontas, and also related to the Randolphs of Virginia. William was born in Virginia. In 1768 he married Elizabeth Hill and in 1786 they moved to Pendleton, settling on the Saluda River. William Halbert died in 1808, leaving to his wife and to each of his children 200 acres of land and several negroes. He was a staunch Whig, and served in the army of Virginia. After coming to South Carolina he became a man of prominence in his community; served as justice of the peace for many years. He was about five feet nine inches in height, of stout build, and had a red beard. His children were Joel, Martha, John, Enos, Arthur, James, Susannah, Frances, William Joshua, Elizabeth, Mary and Lucinda. Most of these children moved west, and today there are thousands of Halberts in Mississippi, Indiana, and other western states, but in South Carolina there is not one of the name. Joel married Mary Lindsey and went to Indiana in 1819. His daughter, Sarah, married Moses Welborn, of Anderson county. Another, Ruth, married Amos Acker, youngest son of Peter, Sr., and Jane Southerland. This couple lived at Williamston. One of their sons, "Squire" R. V. Acker, was living just a few years ago. They have many descendants who are valuable citizens, among them Mrs. D. H. Russell and her children.

Martha Halbert married John Gresham, and from them was descended Governor Joe Brown, of Georgia.

John Halbert married Margaret Harper and moved to Mississippi. Professor Harper, of Clemson College, is descended from them. Enos married Lucy Garner and went to Tennessee; James married Fanny Pepper and went to Missouri, Susannah married Peter Acker, Frances married Charles Garrison; they remained in South Carolina. Arthur married Elizabeth Cobb.

William Halbert, Jr., married Betty Brown and went to Alabama. Elizabeth married William Berry and went to Mississippi, Mary married John Sherrell and went to Missouri, Lucinda married David Berry and went to Mississippi.

The children of Alexander Acker, son of Peter, Sr., and Orma Burton, were George, Cecil, Mary, Elizabeth and Peter Wilson, Mary married Mr. Grace; they had a son, Baylis. Nancy Acker, daughter of Peter, Sr., married John McDavid; they were the parents of Lucinda, Richmond and five other children.

Susan Acker and her husband, Sanford Vandiver, were the parents of Helena, Peter, James, Emmaline and Hezekiah. Helena married Samuel Brown and lived in Townville; their children were: John Peter married Julia Reed, Joseph Newton married Elizabeth Bruce, Milton married Emma Farmer, Emma married Mr. Feaster, Samuel F. married Mollie Lewis; he died in a short time and his widow married Colonel C. S. Mattison, Sanford married first Maggie Longshore, second Ella Smith.

The youngest son of Peter, Sr., and Jane Southerland was Amos, who married Ruth Halbert. Their children were Mary, who married Humphrey Williams; she died and he married her sister, Elizabeth; then he died and his widow married Alfred Reed. Martha married James D. Smith, Halbert married Mary Marsh, Alfred S. married first Miss Martin, second Miss O'Rea; Joseph married Nancy Sitton, Elihu H. never married, Teresa married James Reece, Sallie married Jackson Surratt, Richmond V. married Delia Roper, Susan died young.

The Acker-Halbert reunion in Anderson takes place at Shady Grove Church, where the early members of the families worshiped, many of them being buried in the adjacent grave yard.

Another old Anderson county family is the Milford. Seven Irish brothers of the name came to South Carolina before the Revolution and served through the war. Thomas stopped first in North Carolina where he married Miss Jamison, later he, too, joined his brothers in South Carolina. They settled in what is now Abbeville county. Rebecca, a daughter of Thomas, married a son of John Milford, whose name was also John. One of their sons was C. S. Milford, born in Anderson county, where his parents made their home. In 1852 they went to Pickens, settling where the town of Westminster afterward grew up. Mr. Milford bought two hundred acres of land from J. D. Kay at two dollars per acre.

C. S. Milford married Miriam Addis December 1st, 1853. They were the parents of six children, Samuel Marshall, later of Kansas City; John Thomas died young, Clayton Jones went to Lavonia, Ga.; Eliza Jane married W. F. Wooten, of Corner Township; Albert Calloway, of Anderson county, Charles Arlington, of Abbeville. Mr. Milford bought three hundred acres at one dollar an acre from Robert Steele, state senator from Pickens district, and with his bride went to live on it. He became a soldier of the Confederacy.

In 1779 Thomas Martin and his wife, Hester Roundtree, left Martinsville, Va., and came to South Carolina. They had several little children, and creeping slowly forward in heavy carts, it was a long journey. In those pioneering days when night fell parties traveling the same way would often camp together for mutual protection. All provisions had to be transported with them, save what game they could kill on the road, and an occasional purchase made of the few farmers whose homes they passed.

At the beginning of the trip Mr. Martin promised to give two dollars and a half to such of the children as should make the whole journey without crying. Mr. Martin's children appreciated to the full the generous offer, and valiantly they strove to win the reward. But they were very little, the journey was very long, and they encountered many hardships, including winter weather; and children have always had nerves, though our forefathers scouted such attributes for small people. One by one the little folks succumbed to trials and miseries, until all but Jacob, the eldest, had lost the coveted prize. That little lad wanted $2.50 very much indeed. It was a big sum of money, and probably he had never in his life had so much of his own. Not a tear had fallen from his bright eyes, and the journey was almost over. One day toward the very end Jacob was seated high upon the stack of domestic goods, and the heavy wagon was creaking, grumbling, and painfully rolling along over the dreadful roads, mere trails through the woods, the trees hanging low over the path. Passing under one of the sweeping branches, whoever held the reins that day reached out and pushed up the swinging limb. It could not have been the father, for fathers remember their little ones, and that driver forgot the boy perched aloft; as he let go the branch it swung back, striking the lad severely about the face and head, and poor little Jacob, startled and frightened by the sudden stinging pain, as a little boy could not help doing, lost his coveted prize.

The family settled in what is now Williamston township, a mile or two east of where Piercetown is located. Big Creek church was their place of worship. There were nine children in the family who grew up. What education they got was from small country schools in their vicinity.

In later years William, a son of these early settlers, gave the site of Beaver Dam Baptist Church, and was prominently connected with it for many years.

The children of Thomas and Hester Martin were Jacob, who married his cousin, Cathrine Martin, from Edgefield. The mother of Cathrine Martin was a Rowan. The second son of Thomas and Hester was William, who married Elizabeth Duckworth, then came Charity, who married Ezekiel Murphy. James L. Orr, Sr., once said of Mrs. Charity Murphy that she was a wonderfully bright old lady. When she was over seventy years of age, he had occasion to see and hear her examined as a witness in a property case which involved twenty or thirty thousand dollars. Mrs. Murphy, though her educational advantages had been limited, showed a brilliant mind. She was catechised for four hours, lawyers bandying words over her; some of them in their usual style making every effort to confuse the witness, or to trap her into making contradictory statements. But their attempts were futile; she answered clearly and intelligently through the whole time. She told what real estate, live stock, and all other property involved had sold for so accurately that when it was over and her statements were compared with written records the difference between the two did not amount to so much as one dollar.

The next child of Thomas and Hester was Mary, called Polly, who married Thomas Welborn. Then came Abram, who married Ruth Duckworth; Frances, or "Frankie," married Baylis Watkins, Elizabeth married James Wilbanks, James married Mary Gregg, of Newberry, and Chesley married Annie Duckworth. These couples all settled in Anderson county, except the Wilbankses; and from them are descended many of the people of the county.

A daughter of Charity Murphy married a Mr. Richardson, and they were the parents of the late Matthias and A. N. Richardson, of the Lebanon section. The family furnished a number of soldiers to the Confederacy.

When the Reverend John Simpson came to Pendleton his eldest daughter, Jane, was eight years old. When she grew up she married and returned to the Fishing Creek section from whence she had come. One of the sons, Dr. James Simpson, married a daughter of Colonel John Bratton, another married a daughter of Colonel Pickens, one daughter married Colonel Moffatt, a Revolutionary soldier, from whom Moffattsville took its name; two of the daughters married into the Sadler family, which along with the Simpsons had moved from York to Pendleton.

Jane's first husband was James Neely. They had one son, John, who died a young man, though he had married, and left several children. Jane's husband, James Neely, died after a few years, and she married John Boyd.

Other children of Reverend John Simpson remained near the old Pendleton section of the country. The late Mrs. R. F. Divver was a descendant of that pioneer preacher, and the Simpsons have added much to Anderson county. Mrs. Emmie Cathcart and Mrs. Lila Sullivan are also descendants of the family.

The original McFall in this community was John, born at Craig's Head, Antrim, Ireland. Having quarreled with his stepmother, he ran away to sea, landing at Charleston, S. C., in 1784, when he was about sixteen years old. He went to work and became a good business man, owning quite a comfortable property.

Early in the history of Anderson county Mr. McFall became one of its citizens. He possessed a number of slaves and a good plantation near Neal's Creek Church. He married the daughter of another early settler in the community, Miss Mary Norris. Mr. McFall was a proud, rather haughty man, generous and hospitable, and always immaculately dressed, wearing a snowy shirt adorned with ruffles, sometimes lace-trimmed. He was proud of his ancestry, and claimed descent from Mary Queen of Scots.

Mr. McFall left three sons, John, Andrew and Samuel. He and his wife are buried in the Neal's Creek cemetery. Their descendants are among our best people. Those of the name are well known; there are some, however, who bear other names, among them Mr. John McFall Hubbard and Miss Nora Hubbard, to both of whom one collecting Anderson county data has to make frequent appeals, as they know much and remember well.

The name Clinkscales is found everywhere in the Piedmont section, and especially does the family seem to belong to Anderson county. Professor John G. Clinkscales, of Wofford, a scholar and writer of ability, is an Anderson county man. Mr. Fleetwood Clinkscales was for more than fifty years a newspaper man in the town. A youth in 1854, he began as a compositor apprentice in the office of *The Southern Rights Advocate*. When *The Anderson Intelligencer* was founded in 1860, Mr. Clinkscales became associated with it. He remained with the same paper until advancing age forced him to retire from active work. Dr. Clinkscales and Mrs. E. W. Masters are members of the family well known to Anderson people.

HISTORY OF ANDERSON COUNTY

One of the very first families in the town was that of Robert Wilson. He was a son of William Wilson and his wife, who had been Jane Cunningham. She died in Anderson at the home of one of her children in 1834. Robert had a brother named William. Robert's wife was named Sarah Norton.

The family consisted of three sons and two daughters, all members of Anderson's first "younger set." One son, Joseph, went to Alabama soon after he grew up, and from a few letters written to him by members of the family in Anderson, which have miraculously escaped destruction, brief glimpses may be caught of that far away Anderson; also by reading those simple family letters written when railroad trains and mail service were few and poor, one can understand how near kindred came to lose each other so completely as many of them did long ago.

When Joseph went away, it was merely an experiment, He was trying the western country. His brother, Jeptha, made him a visit, and in a letter written to Joseph soon after his return to Anderson, Jeptha tells him that he told their parents that he thought the reason Joseph did not return with him was that he was going to be married out there. Then there are letters from the mother telling the absent boy that she misses him, and hopes he will soon make them a visit. If he gets married he must be sure to bring his wife to see the home people. In one of her letters to her son, Sarah Wilson tells him of the marriages of a number of his young friends, and as those couples became ancestors of many Anderson people of the present time, the old news is still interesting. Berry Lewis has married Matilda Poole, Gillison Harris weds Matilda Smith, Thomas George marries Matilda Wilson—Matilda seems to have been a popular name—Haynes Whitaker to Maria Drennan, Robert Whitaker to a Georgia lady whose name Mrs. Wilson does not seem to know, Peter Byrum and Mary Ann Drennan, William Archer to Harriet Norris, James McDonald to Elvira Pickens, Baker Gentry to Betsy Moorhead, James Gordon to Miss — (that name is undecipherable), Jesse Smith to Betsey Clark. Since those young couples were married three generations of their descendants have grown up, their grandchildren are the grandparents of the present young people.

In 1837 Jeptha Wilson writes his brother, "I now take the opportunity to inform you that I got home safely, and came in six days and a half." He does not mention the means of transportation. Further he says, "I do want you to come home, for we are in high prosperity. There is more money in the county than I ever saw, every one is able to pay his debts, except those who do not want to do so."

A sister of Jeptha Wilson, named Elizabeth, married first a Mr. Overby. Little is said of him, or of the marriage. The indications are, however, that it was not a happy one, and Mr. Overby seems to have left the country without taking his wife with him. Later he seems to have died and Elizabeth marries Mr. Jackson.

The first letter of the series was written by the mother in 1834. She tells Joseph that his grandmother and grandfather Wilson have died. She says: "Your sister is going to be married December 11th, and we want you to come home at that time, if you can." That sister was Elvira, who married Marshall Stensel. In several subsequent letters both Elvira and Marshall are mentioned, and several times their children are written about as being fine interesting little people. The most of the letters are written by Jeptha, though there are several from the mother, who always urges the faraway son to come home on a visit. In one written many years after the first, she says: "If you could come to see us just once I would try to be satisfied." Both the mother and the sister Elizabeth ask the number of Joseph's children and their names. Joseph seems never to have returned, and the family left at home never saw his wife nor any of his children.

The youngest member of the Wilson family was a boy called Tandy, who was a little fellow when his brother Joseph went away, and his brother Jeptha was almost like a father to him. A spoiled youngster he must have been, the pet and pride of all of the older brothers and sisters, as well as the Benjamin of his parents. In some of the earlier letters Jeptha tells Joseph: "Tandy is eighteen years old, and nearly as large as I am, and as lazy as ever." Again he says: "Tandy is a good workman when you can get him down to it, but he likes better to frolic." Again: "Tandy has been laid up, and has done nothing for four months, with something like white swelling in his shoulder. He is on the mend now. He is as large as I am and a tolerable good workman." Another time he says that he sent Tandy to school in Pendleton, but that he would rather dance than study. Then after a long while comes another letter in which Jeptha says: "For fear you did not get a letter concerning the death of our brother, Tandy W. Wilson, which I wrote you last summer I will state the facts again: Tandy volunteered in the company of volunteers that went to Mexico from this district. He fought through all the battles until they took the city of Mexico. After they had been there some time, they went out of the city to take up the body of Colonel Butler of their regiment. On returning to the city, three young men from Charleston got behind the main body and were killed by the guerrillas. When the roll was called on the return of the regiment to the city, Tandy and the others were missing. The company of cavalry that belonged to the regiment was ordered out to search for them, and foud them near the road, shot, and their throats cut. They were buried with the honors of war where their bodies were found. This is all I could ever learn about Tandy."

In one letter the mother says: "Elvira thinks hard of you, that you never write to her, for she thinks more of you than any of her brothers. I have a good many things to talk to you about, and tell you about my troubles in this world. I cannot express my feelings at this time, for I write with tears in my eyes. I never expect to see you again unless you think enough of me to come to see me. I have a great desire to see your wife and children. If you would only come to see me one time I would try to be satisfied."

Joseph seems to have a tenderness in his heart for Elvira, for the mother says in one letter: "Elvira wants you to bring her namesake to see her."

It was not only real distance that separated families in those hard days; members of the clan living much closer together saw each other at long intervals. In one letter to Joseph the mother, in telling about the family, says: "I have not seen your sister Elizabeth in about five years; she never comes to see me, but the children come sometime." At that time the Wilson family seems to have been living in Due West, where they spent several years, and Mrs. Wilson, in writing of her home and her neighbors, unconsciously gives a good idea of herself. She says: "We live in a very religious place. The neighbors are friendly and kind, they are like sisters and mothers to me. Let me go where I will, I find friends." In telling about the family the mother writes: "Your grandmother Norton is still living at the old place. Your uncle Robert Emberson is living with her (married her daughter). Your aunt Betsy Wilkerson lives on the same plantation."

In 1862 Jeptha writes: "I have not heard from you in three years until this spring. I met with a man in Charleston that said he lived in the adjoining county. He told me you were still living. Uncle Jep still lives in Greenville (Jeptha Norton); his son William lives in this place, and is getting rich carrying on a merchant tailor business." The old Grandmother Norton was still living with her daughter and son-in-law. "Sister Elizabeth and Bill Jackson live where the old Mt. Tabor church road turns out of the General's Road. M. M. Stansel and Elvira live in a mile and a half of this place. They have four boys and two girls." They seem to have moved later to Calhoun.

HISTORY OF ANDERSON COUNTY

The last letter is written in 1862. Jeptha says that his father died at his home December 21, 1861, in his eighty-third year. Their mother had gone to live with Elvira at Calhoun. He says further: "I have rented a farm from one of my brothers-in-law in the army, that is, my wife's brothers. There is not a single man in this country who is thought anything of who is not in the army."

The war ended the letters. Joseph seems to have treasured these missives from his old home, and as age increased their interest, his descendants in Alabama still preserve them. They are few, but extend over a period of twenty-eight years. They present a simple picture of life as Anderson people were living it in those days.

Mr. Jeptha Wilson lived to be the oldest man in Anderson, and the one who had resided in the place the longest time. His memory was always good, and it is to incidents related by him to younger people, and remembered by them, that much of Anderson's early history has been preserved.

One of the oldest and most numerous families in the county is that of Burriss, spelled in several different ways, but all of the same blood. The first of the name to come to Anderson county was Joshua, born in Virginia in 1724. He moved to South Carolina in 1776. His wife was Sarah Chamblee, and they lived not far from where Gluck Mill is now located. They were the parents of seven children, all of whom settled on land given them by their father on Generostee Creek. The names of Joshua Burriss' children with the names of the men and women they married are: Elisha married Margaret Greelee; Elizabeth, born 1768, married Asa Castleberry in 1796; James, born 1776, married Susan Cain in 1794; John, born 1776, married Elizabeth Davis in 1796; Mary, born 1778, married Lewis Chamblee in 1798; Thomas, born 1782, married Jane Davis in 1800; Nancy, born 1794, married Silas Massey in 1812. All of these couples left descendants who have intermarried with most of the old families of the community. Many of them have moved away, and in 1906 records had been collected of living people at that time of 1,313 descendants of the original Burriss family; they were then scattered over eleven states, and the work had been only begun. Since that year much has been added to the family history.

Joshua Burriss became a man of wealth. On his arrival in what is now Anderson County, he bought land from James McCarley, and the deed bears the date October 4th, 1795. At one time Joshua Burriss owned as much land as constitutes a township now. His possessions embrace parts of what is now Centerville, Rock

Mills, Savannah and Varennes townships. In settling his sons, Mr. Burriss had a method all his own. He placed them up and down Generostee Creek according to their ages. Elisha, the oldest, was placed farthest north, on what was long known as the "Old Byrum Place," now the Anderson Country Club. The next was James, whose home stood near where the Orr Mill is now. He and his wife are buried in the old Mt. Tabor grave yard. John's land was about where the "Old Watson home" is now, the place which belonged to the late Manley Watson. Thomas's land was near Old Rock Mills, and he is buried in an ancient grave yard at that place. His daughters were differently placed. One of them, Mary Chamblee, owned the old Whitner place, which Judge Whitner bought from Moses Chamblee, probably her son.

The original Burriss in this community spelled his name Boroughs, but his sons spelled it Burriss, and in the next generation there were three brothers who spelled it in three different ways. Burriss has, however, come to be the general way of writing the name.

The Burriss family soon began to own slaves as well as real estate. Among those belonging to Mr. Jacob Burriss was a native African who always insisted upon using a rock for a pillow.

Among the many who have borne the name, William Burriss stands high. He was a son of the pioneer Baptist preacher, Jacob Burriss, who must have been a grandson of the original Joshua. Modest, quiet, unassuming, he yet rose to a prominent and dignified position solely by his sterling character. In a eulogy of him at the time of his death, the late W. W. Keys, editor of *The Baptist Courier*, whose wife was a relative of Mr. Burriss, said of him in the words of Byron: "Though modest, on his unembarrassed brow nature had written gentleman." His home was not on the public road; it stood about half a mile back on the farm, shut from view by woods sequestered and quiet, a stately building surrounded by luxuriant vegetation, and a plantation well managed and thoroughly worked.

Mr. Burriss married Sarah Moorhead. His family were loyal and prominent members of Salem Church for many years. Mr. Burriss served that church as deacon and treasurer for an ordinary lifetime.

While William Burriss attended strictly to his own affairs, he was not indifferent to the just demands of his community. Always ready to cooperate in any enterprise that was for the public good. He never sought office of any kind, but was well informed on public affairs. A fine type of citizen, and one who has left an impression on the community in which he passed his life.

Three of his sons became citizens of the town of Anderson, and each showed many of his father's characteristics—gentleness, modesty and kindness being very pronounced in all of them. They were the three brothers, all dead now—Marcus, Rufus and Boyce Burriss.

Another of the builder families of Anderson is that of Broyles. The pioneer in this section was Aaron, who settled somewhere not far from the old Calhoun section, and married Fannie Reed, daughter of another early settler. They began life with love, courage and industry, their only assets. Their first home was a log cabin with a dirt floor. Mr. Broyles was of German descent, and Mrs. Broyles of French Huguenot blood. While their children were still small, they had begun to accumulate a good share of worldly goods, and they gave their boys and girls what educational advantages the section offered. Their sons were John T., born in 1806; Oze, Cain and Abel. The youngest died when a boy. Cain and Oze lost their lives during the War Between the States.

The eldest, John T., had quite a number of adventures. In 1817 he accompanied a relative to Fort Hawkins, which stood where the city of Macon, Ga., is now located. They drove cattle which the owner sold to the government for the soldiers stationed there. When a little older he accompanied his father to Hamburg, S. C., then a flourishing trade center.

Mr. Broyles raised a quantity of tobacco, which was the staple crop of this section in the early times. Young John rode one of the animals which drew the hogshead and his father rode the other, their camping outfit packed between them as best they could.

As a youth Major John Broyles was well acquainted with John C. Calhoun, then a rising young lawyer. He attended Calhoun Academy at the same time that his cousin Joe Brown was a student there. Later John Broyles was sent to Tusculum College in Greenville, Tennessee, where he studied under Reverend Samuel Doark, the father of Presbyterianism in Tennessee. At that time there were a number of South Carolina students in the institution, among them Francis Pickens and John Hammond, both afterwards Governors of South Carolina. Pickens was the room-mate of young Broyles. John graduated with honors at Tusculum, and after bidding an affectionate farewell to Father Doark, he returned to Anderson district, where in 1829 he married Miss Clorinda Hammond, daughter of Dudley Hammond, a wealthy planter of the district. The young couple went to housekeeping in what was at the time a fine residence, the gift of the bride's father.

In 1832 came troublous times in South Carolina; the tariff

bill passed by Congress enraged the planters, and the State declared the act null and void. A conflict was feared, and Governor George McDuffie called a meeting of the people of Anderson district in the summer of 1832 to be held at Varennes. There the governor made an appeal for volunteers to support the commonwealth against the Federal encroachments.

John T. Broyles was the first man to offer his service. He did it amid general cheering, and Governor McDuffie made him a Major of infantry on the spot.

In 1834 he served as a member of the South Carolina legislature. In 1847 Major Broyles moved to Tennessee. In 1856 he returned to Anderson, and was again elected to the legislature.

At the outbreak of the War Between the States Major Broyles was not permitted to enlist in the army on account of his age, but his sons served until the surrender.

In 1862 Major Broyles went to Dalton, Ga., and in 1864 he went with other refugees to Marshallville, Ga., returning in 1866 to Chickamauga, where he lived until 1895. He died at the age of ninety-three years.

Like many members of his family, he was musical, and at one time played the violin well. He also wrote a number of pamphlets, chiefly of a political nature, though he had fine literary taste also.

Major Broyles was the father of seven children, five boys and two girls. Two sons died in infancy. Those who grew up were Edward, who died in Chattanooga in 1898; Dudley Hammond, killed in the war; Dr. Julius J. died in Chattanooga in 1898; Claudia, who is Mrs. Renan, of Chattanooga, Tenn., and Mrs. Clark, of Rome, Ga.

Mrs. Renan visited Anderson in 1920, and though then an old lady, her music and her vivacity made a deep impression on all who had the pleasure of meeting her. She played the piano in a way that few people, old or young, can approach.

Dr. Oze Broyles spent his life in Anderson. His home was the house on South Main street built by Mr. Samuel G. Earle, now occupied by the Acker family. He not only spent his life there, but remained for a number of years after his death. He was buried on the south-east corner of the lot, and a circle of cedar trees cut the haunted looking section off from the rest of the place. His wife had him buried there where she could spend a great part of her time near him, expecting at her death that the body should be removed and both of them interred in a cemetery. But when she died her son, Captain Augustus Taliaferro Broyles, a bachelor who had lived alone with his aged mother for many years, wished to keep her near him, and he buried her beside his father in the corner of the home lot. There very often one in passing the place could see the eccentric old man sitting on a bench beside his parents' graves. When he died, quite old, all of the bodies were taken to Silver Brook Cemetery, and now the weird spot has become a part of Mrs. Chenault's beautiful lawn, and the dense shadows have passed away.

Captain Broyles was the eldest child of his parents, Dr. Oze R. Broyles and Sarah Ann Taliaferro. The boy Augustus attended the Pendleton Male Academy. In 1848 he graduated from the South Carolina University. He studied law in the office of General J. W. Harrison, and was later taken into partnership with his instructor. He was a diligent student, and his legal opinions were always highly respected, and seldom found to be erroneous. By many he was accredited with being the best informed lawyer of his time in his section of the state. He wrote some valuable legal pamphlets, and at his death had in manuscript many commentaries on abstruse points of law. He was engaged in revising those papers when death fell upon him.

Captain Broyles served several times in the legislature; but while he always took an active interest in things pertaining to his county, he had no political ambition, and preferred to spend his time in the pursuit of his profession. When the War Between the States came on, Augustus Broyles, then a young man, was elected captain of one of the companies formed in the county, and he served in Virginia until forced to resign on account of disease, which caused him great suffering during all the rest of his long life.

Captain Broyles, like all persons of force, or great individuality, had some peculiarities, probably many of them inherited from a line of forceful ancestors. At times he was abrupt in the expression of his opinions, but withal he was very tenderhearted and sympathetic, particularly with old people and children.

Captain Broyles was well read, and a fluent and interesting talker, when he chose to take the trouble to converse. He had opinions, and the courage of his convictions under all circumstances. In all the relations of life he was honest and straight. Having never married, the chief love of his life seems to have been given to his mother, and for years the two of them dwelt hidden from the world by the dense cedars that shrouded their homes. Mrs. Broyles had flowers, too, but the outstanding characteristic of the place were the cedars. Planted when Anderson was an infant by Mr. Earle, they had grown very large and thick, and they suited the

HISTORY OF ANDERSON COUNTY

feelings and taste of the two lonely old people who lived behind them. The cedars, like those who loved them, have gone now.

After the death of Mrs. Broyles, the family of Captain Broyles' brother, Mr. John T. Broyles, went to live with him. Mr. John Broyles married Miss Bettie Hibbard, and their children were the chief interest of Captain Broyles' declining years; especially was this true of the only daughter, Zoe, whom he called "Dudie"; though at the time of her birth he insisted upon hanging crepe on the door; he wanted no girls about him.

Another son of Dr. Oze Broyles was Dr. Robert Broyles. He removed with his family from Anderson many years ago.

The late Mrs. Margaret VanWyck was a daughter of Dr. Oze Broyles, and a sister of "Mr. Gus." Mrs. VanWyck in her early days must have been a beautiful woman; certainly in her old age she was lovely, and her manners were as lovely as her face. Enthusiastic in everything that interested her, she was a great teacher. Her husband, Dr. Samuel Maverick VanWyck, was killed during the war, leaving her with three little children, two boys and one girl. The little daughter soon followed her father to the grave, carrying a part of the mother's heart with her. Towards little girls Mrs. Van Wyck was always most tender.

The young widow took up life as well as she could, and worked for her boys. They were Samuel M. VanWyck, who married Nina Harrison, and Oze, who married Bessie Keith. Mrs. VanWyck taught school in Anderson for many years, and impressed her vivid personality on many of the women who have in later years carried a portion of the responsibility of making Anderson a worthwhile town. Of the Methodist Church she was a most loyal and enthusiastic member. Mrs. VanWyck lived to be very old, and almost blind, but her cheerfulness, enthusiasm and interest in life never failed.

The other daughter of Dr. Oze Broyles married a Mr. Williams and went to Tennessee years ago. For a long time her daughters used to come to Anderson on visits, and with their beautiful music delighted all who heard them. The elder, Maggie, died young; the other, Marie, is living and singing for the pleasure of other people in Tennessee.

A brother of Dr. Oze Broyles, and son of Major Aaron Broyles, was Major Cain Broyles. He lived at old Stauntonville, one of the early settlements in Anderson district, which was located a few miles east of where Belton now stands. Major Cain Broyles left several children. Perhaps the one best known to Anderson people was Major A. R. Broyles, better known as "Witt" Broyles.

HISTORY OF ANDERSON COUNTY

Born at his father's home he grew up on the farm. In 1845 he married Miss Martha Brown, daughter of Dr. George Brown, the founder and sponsor of Belton. Major Broyles purchased the old Sloan Ferry plantation in "the Fork," and was a prominent planter of that section for years. He was the father of three attractive daughters. They were Mary, Lula and Clara. Miss Mary Broyles married Mr. Frank Crayton, and it is only recently that she has passed over to join the majority of her people who have gone before. Mr. Crayton is still among the best loved and most respected citizens of the town.

Miss Lula Broyles married Mr. John Baker, and for years their home was in Anderson, where they had many friends. Mr. and Mrs. Baker were an unusually handsome couple. Many Anderson people remember them and their children well. Bob, Eva, George and Helen were the young people, and Eva was a very lovely girl. She married Basil Manley Gawthmey and went to Richmond to live. The son Robert married Minnie Smith, of Anderson, who is to be remembered among Anderson's literary people, having written many successful stories. George Baker became a Baptist minister. Helen, a baby when the family left Anderson, became the head of a girls' college in Richmond. Mrs. Baker died a few years ago, and is buried at Silver Brook.

The youngest daughter, Clara, married first Mr. Hewett, of Bamberg, afterwards Mr. McCauley. She died young and left two children, May, who died about the time she was grown, and "Witt," well known in Anderson as a musician. Miss Clara Broyles was an unusually lovely woman, in face as well as in character.

The late George Broyles, who married Emma Wilson, daughter of Jeptha Wilson, was a nephew of Major Witt Broyles.

Colonel Bayliss Crayton, who lived to be Anderson's oldest citizen both in the years of his life and the years of his residence, came to the place when it was a very new little village, in 1838, to clerk for his uncle, B. F. Mauldin. In 1841 Mr. Mauldin retired and Mr. Crayton succeeded to the business. He moved from Mr. Mauldin's location on Brick Range, and occupied several places at different times. His last and most pretentious mercantile establishment was situated on the corner of Benson and Main streets, long occupied by the Bank of Anderson. The main floor of the store was approached by a short double flight of horse-shoe shaped stairs just within the street door, and it was there that Anderson women from before the war until about 1882 bought their finery.

Mr. Crayton was born in Greenville in 1820, but it is with Anderson County that his name is associated. He at one time represented the county in the Legislature, and in 1878 he was elected State Senator from Anderson and served four years. He was chairman of the first board of County Commissioners, provided for in the constitution of 1868. Colonel J. W. Norris and Colonel W. S. Pickens were the other members, and they managed the affairs of the county in an able and satisfactory manner, especially in regard to the Alms House, or "County Home," as Anderson prefers to call it.

Mr. Crayton was a warm advocate of the stock law which agitated the state greatly in the seventies and early eighties, by which stock were required to be fenced in. Before that time stock roamed at will, and the farmers had to keep all of their fields fenced to protect their crops. After the adoption of that law all of the old time unsightly rail or "snake" fences disappeared, and the country lay open.

Mr. Crayton engaged in farming on an extensive scale. He was the most progressive farmer of his day, and introduced many new methods into the community. He kept fine blooded stock, and the fairs, which were the delight of the people in the seventies, were the result of his efforts, and did much to awaken interest in good stock. The fair grounds were located where Mr. A. G. Means and Mr. J. M. Paget now live. There was a huge building wtih an open gallery on the second story, and the things displayed therein were a feast to the eye, and a stimulus to the imagination. Without there were places for the live stock and a race track. Some of the little people of those far off days grew up and saw great world fairs at New Orleans, Atlanta, Chicago and St. Louis, but not one of them appeared as wonderful, as marvelous, as had those old Anderson fairs of their childhood. Just as neither St. Paul's Cathedral, St. Peter's, nor Cologne were to those same childish eyes grown old finer or more impressive than was the old Johnson Female University buildings which were the first big brick public buildings those little eyes had ever seen, just as to the same not a skyscraper in New York City approaches half so near to Heaven as did the beautiful tapering spire of the old dignified rectangular Anderson Baptist Church.

In 1868 Mr. Crayton organized in the county an Agricultural and Mechanical Society which did much for the farmers of the section. Some years after the war, finding the labor of the free negroes unsatisfactory, Mr. Crayton was instrumental in bringing to the county a number of German laborers. He employed many of them himself, and induced some other progressive farmers to use them. The Germans proved good citizens. Most of them soon became independent farmers, and some of the best planters of the county are their descendants.

The workers were known as "Mr. Crayton's Germans," and as long as the original emigrants lived they preserved toward him a most kindly feeling, considering him their special protector. In his mercantile business Mr. Crayton employed first and last a great number of young men, and his interest in them, and friendly counsel helped many of them to attain a higher goal than some of them had contemplated.

When life insurance first began to be practiced in Anderson Mr. Crayton applied to a company to be insured, and was rejected on account of physical fragility. In his old age the old man used to chuckle and tell how he had outlived the doctor who examined him, the agent from whom he solicited papers, the very company itself. He was Anderson's first banker, lending money in connection with his mercantile business before the war. It was not until 1872 that a bank was organized in the town, and Mr. Crayton was one of its directors. Its president was Colonel J. N. Brown, Mr. J. A. Brock, cashier, and Mr. Frank B. Mauldin, assistant cashier. It was located on Brick Range, and was called The Anderson National Bank.

At the beginning of the War Between the States Mr. Crayton closed his store and joined Orr's Regiment. He was appointed quartermaster of the regiment, but later had to resign on account of ill health. He was appointed by President Davis state's depository at Anderson, and handled for the government large amounts of money and bonds. In 1862 he was elected to the legislature and re-elected in 1864. In 1865 he went to Greenville to attend a called meeting of the legislature, which was prevented from meeting in Columbia by Stoneman's invasion. Mr. Crayton's interests were, however, agricultural, mercantile and civic rather than political.

He was in his prime a figure of great force and distinction, not only in the county, but throughout the state and to some extent throughout the South. He was for many years president of the State Agricultural Association, and had many honors and distinctions conferred upon him.

He lived to be almost ninety years old, retaining his faculties to the end. He married Miss Evelyn Benson sometime in the forties, and an old number of either *The Highland Sentinel*, or *The Anderson Gazette*, thanks the young couple for the gift of a delicious cake sent after the wedding to the printers. The marriage supper took place in the Benson Hotel, kept by the bride's parents. Mrs. Crayton, too, lived to be very old. The couple were the parents of three children who grew up; they were Samuel, who married Miss Sallie Nevitt; Frank, who married Miss Mary Broyles, and Kate, who married Mr. Sloan Maxwell.

The McGee family, which is now scattered over Greenwood, Greenville, Abbeville, Anderson and Oconee counties, are descended from John McGee and his wife, a Miss Sims, who came to the section in 1772 from Rockingham, N. C. They settled on a plantation where the manufacturing plant of Ware Shoals now stands. The trip was made to that place by horseback, Mrs. McGee riding while her husband walked, carrying on his back all their earthly possessions. They bought from the government on credit several hundred acres of land in what is now Greenwood county, paying $1.40 an acre for it. To them were born five sons, William, Burrell, Abner, John and Mike. The William McGee, or Magee, from whom some of the land on which the town of Anderson was located, was their son, a well known Baptist preacher of the early days. The beloved Reverend Mike McGee, who lived to be an old man, and died just a few years ago, was the son of William.

Another pioneer was William Staunton. His wife was Katie Richardson. They came from Virginia, and settled not far from where the town of Belton grew up. Mr. Staunton was a wealthy man for his day, and in a community of log houses he erected a three-story mansion. His name was given to the locality which became Stauntonville.

Matthias Staunton, possibly their son, was a soldier in the war of 1812.

Some of the other men who lived in that section were William Holland, Allen Johnson, Reuben Phillips and George Turner.

There is a spot of some interest half way between Belton and Williamston, three miles from Calhoun, and three from Cooley's Bridge. It is at the intersection of the Calhoun, Anderson, Williamston and Belton roads; the old muster ground. There elections were held. About 1855 Berry Lewis ran a store there. It also boasted a tailor shop, run by Mr. Jesse Smith, afterwards one of Anderson's best known merchant tailors, or men's clothiers. A whipping post stood at the place for the correction of both black and white. Big Creek was the church and burial ground of the community.

Muster grounds were at various convenient places in the early days, because every man between the ages of eighteen and forty-five belonged by law to the militia, and were compelled to undergo some military training. That also accounts for the frequency of military titles among the earlier people.

Stephen McCully, an Irishman, came in the early times and settled first at Whitehall, where he manufactured shoes for the surrounding territory. Later he became one of Anderson's leading merchants, a public spirited man, and a wealthy one for his time. He donated the ground on which Johnson Female University was built.

In 1829 there was born in the Calhoun settlement a baby boy who was destined to play a part in the history of the little town which had been started in the woods the year before he was born. He was George W. Fant, eldest son of William Fant. In his childhood his parents moved to Garvin township, near Pendleton, where he grew up. At about twenty years of age he located in Anderson and worked on the *Gazette* when Todd and Russell were its publishers. In 1856 Mr. Fant was appointed postmaster, which position he held until 1880. He married Miss Myra Williamston, and T. J. Webb married her sister Elizabeth. Dr. Webb was postmaster and also book seller, and his business passed first into the hands of his son, T. J. Webb, and from him to his brother-in-law, G. W. Fant. The book store of Fant and Son is still Anderson's chief source of literature; other book stores have come and gone in the years that have elapsed since Mr. Fant first began to sell books to the Anderson people, but that one remains, still in the hands of the same family. That and Tolly's furniture establishment are the two oldest business houses in the place. Mr. George W. Fant was the father of Anderson's Mayor, Foster Fant. His other children were the late Rufus Fant, Theo Fant, the late Ben Fant, Walter Fant, of Texas; Neb Fant, of Walhalla; Mrs. Belle Fant Acker and Mrs. Lillie Fant Grant, of Oklahoma.

John Brown, of the Neal's Creek section, had two sons who became foremost citizens of the county; they were Daniel and Samuel Brown. The name of Daniel Brown is found often in connection with most of the early Anderson enterprises. He located in the town, and took at once a leading position. He built the first brick house in the town. It was later destroyed by fire, and his books and accounts were saved by the courage and coolheadedness of a young son. The first discussion of the proposed Johnson Female Seminary was in his house. It was he who was instrumental in securing the services of the fine teachers, Mrs. Daniel and the Misses Payne.

Before 1860, McDuffie was a rather short street. It started at Earle street and ran to Mr. Daniel Brown's home place, Sunnyside, which was a suburban residence standing on many acres, and blocked the street about where the Boys' High School and other buildings in that vicinity stand. Mr. Brown opened the street through his property on the Shockley Ferry Road, which was about at the Fulwer Watson place. The street had been named for Governor McDuffie, who was a great favorite in Anderson, but there was a movement started then to change the name to Brown Street. It, however, was not carried out, and while Mr. Brown deserves to be remembered and honored, still it is rather fortunate that the street retains its name. It is a distinctive name, and one which attracts favorable attention. Some years ago the Episcopal Church held its diocesan convention in Anderson, and the Reverend John Johnson, rector of St. Philip's Church in Charleston, and distinguished for his services in the Charleston Harbor during the war, was entertained in a home on McDuffie Street. He was struck with the name, and remarked that he believed that to be the only street in the state which honored Governor George McDuffie by being called for him.

In 1876, when the State redeemed itself from radical rule, Mr. Brown was too feeble to leave his home, but a crowd of his old friends came for him in a carriage, and bore him to the polls to cast his last vote for Hampton and reform. He lived until after the election, and news was brought to him of Hampton's election. He made no immediate reply, but feebly smiled, and in a few minutes said: "I will sleep now," and turning away fell into the sleep that knows no waking.

He had five sons in the Confederate army. His eldest, J. J. Brown, was killed with his colonel, John V. Moore, in one of the first battles around Richmond. His youngest son, Nardin Brown, member of Company C, under Captain Prue Benson, was killed at Second Manassas, and lived long enough after he was wounded to send his mother a message. He asked one of his comrades to tell her that he was doing his duty, and that he died happy.

Mr. Brown's second wife was Eleanor St. Clair (Waller) Nardin, a widow when he married her, and mother of Anderson's dearly loved Dr. Waller H. Nardin, Sr.

Mr. Samuel Brown, brother of Mr. Daniel Brown, did not live in the town. For a time he resided a little distance out, where the McCown home is now on the Belton road. It was there that his son, Joseph Newton, was born. Later Mr. Brown moved to Townville and he became identified with that community, though his son, J. N. Brown, was to become Anderson's wealthiest citizen. Mr. Samuel Brown married Helena Vandiver, daughter of Reverend

Sanford Vandiver, the first pastor of the Anderson Baptist Church. Young Newton Brown attended school under Wesley Leverette. In 1855 the young man decided to go to Laurens to live. He engaged in merchandising in that place for two years, then entered the law office of Colonel J. H. Irby and began the study of law. He was admitted to the bar in 1858, and became a partner of Colonel Irby. That partnership was dissolved by the death of Colonel Irby in 1860. Then the four years of war intervened, and after the war he married Miss Lizzie Bruce, of Townville, and they made Anderson their home. Colonel Brown has stood very high in the legal profession and in the financial affairs of Anderson for many years. He accumulated the largest property that any one has ever made in the town.

He has been prominent in the Baptist Church all of his life, and has left the greater part of his property to be used for missionary work after the death of his only child, Miss Varina D. Brown.

The Anderson Library received a generous donation at his hands; he gave the lot upon which it was built, and the sum of ten thousand dollars to be invested, and the income used in the upkeep of the library and the purchase of books.

Another of the early settlers in the county was Captain James Thomson. He was one of the commissioners who laid off the town. Captain Thomson's home was on Beaver Creek, near Rocky River. He was the grandfather of Dr. M. A. Thomson.

Among the pioneers was Edward Vandiver, who came from Maryland just after the Revolutionary War. He was born in that State in 1748, and served in the Revolutionary War. He was once a soldier under Captain Andrew Thomas; also he served under Captain Amandus Leslie, and his colonels were Winnie and Easterland. He fought in the battle of Eutaw Spring, and drew a pension from South Carolina. In 1782 he was serving under Colonel Brestling at Four Hole Bridge. He died at his home near Neal's Creek Church in 1837, and is buried in that church yard. Edward Vandiver was the father of twenty children, all boys but two. He was twice married, first to Helena Turley, and second to Catherine Poole. He had seven sons who were Baptist preachers, the most distinguished of whom was Sanford Vandiver.

Another pioneer of the county was David Sadler, also a Revolutionary soldier. He died in 1848 and is buried in Roberts church yard, having been a faithful member of that church. His wife was Miss Eliza Bratton, of York County.

Other families which made their appearance in Anderson with

the first tide of emigration are those of Breazeale, Gambrill, Kay, Major, Erskine, Shirley, Long, Roseman, Wellborn, John Goodwyn, to whom public lands had been granted, and who signs his name in a coppper plate hand; Field Farrar, also one to whom public land had been granted (he was sheriff of Ninety-Six district in 1780); Henry Stevens, professor of music; Louis D. Martin, another land grantee in 1789; Thomas Jones, and Betty, his wife, sell land on First creek, a branch of Rocky river. The grant had been made in 1785 to Betty Wilkison, probably some enterprising woman, who had taken up land and was doing something for herself until she fell under the spell of Thomas Jones, and marrying him, lost land as well as liberty and name. Anderson Lee has a grant of land on Hen Coop creek; James Shirley on Rocky River; William Wheeler on the south side of Saluda River, dated October 3rd, 1785. In December, 1798, John Mauldin has a grant of land on "Government Creek," a branch of "Great Rocky Creek." Among early settlers on Six and Twenty Creek appear the names of Jonathan Clark, David Clark, Bolin Clark, George Forbes, John McMakin, Hugh McVay, and James Long. In various other parts of the district appear the names of James Highshaw, William Duncan, Emerial Felton, John Fields, Colonel Richard Lewis, William Walker, Benjamin Dickson, John McAlister, Edward Morgan, Solomon Geer and Thomas Harrison. Most of these men take out brands for their cattle. Duncan Cameron and Mary, his wife, sell land granted them on One Mile creek. John Caruthers, Martha Lemon and Robert Lemon, her son, William Holleman, Justice of the Peace John Miles, James Moreland, on Rocky River; Harry Pearson on Six and Twenty; Joseph Woodall, Joshua Hill, William Hammond, James Martin, Samuel Taylor, "Jon" Winn, Robert Tate has a grant on Seneca river in 1784 (he spells it "Senekaw"); John Hugner, John Postelle, William Lowery, Isaac Titworth, James Crowder, David Brag, Samuel Caldwell, James Hamilton, and Benjamin Farmer.

In 1791 the records begin to be made in Pendleton county, Washington district, not Ninety-Six, as formerly. These good people in place of making oath on the Holy Bible, made their oaths on "The Holy Evangelist," no Hebrew scripture for them to swear by.

Some of the business men of the days preceding the War Between the States were John P. Benson and Joel J. Cunningham, Baylis F. and Thomas S. Crayton, Elias Earle, Alexander Evans and John C. Griffin, Fleetwood Rice and John R. Towers, Alexander B. and Joel J. Towers, Daniel Brown, Stephen McCully, Jesse R. Smith, Asbury M. Holland, J. N. Pendleton, Enoch B. Benson and Son,

John S. Lawton, John C. and Henry C. Cherry, John and Thomas J. Sloan, John Hastie and Co. These were all of the village in the year 1849.

This list was furnished, along with a list of all of the merchants of the county, by an Anderson lawyer of the time to a New York business man who wrote asking him for confidential information about the merchants. He was a shrewd man, and his opinion and comments on the business men of his time are worth reading, as they tell the reader what kind of people formed the county. The lawyer is very frank and very full in his information, tells the ages of the men, whether married or single, number of children and approximates the value of each man's property. Often he says, "Is good for more than he will promise," tells whether he buys and sells for cash or credit, whether his credit is good. Sometimes he says some man has married a rich widow, and can use her property, which he will to his advantage. Of one he says he is extravagant, hasn't much sense, but is full of high notions—"If he is worth any property I don't know it." Of one he says: "He hasn't much sense, but he knows it; is cautious and will not venture much." Of another he says: "He hasn't much education, but is a fine business man, and 'a perfect shaver as you ever saw.' He owns town lots worth $5,000, has land in the vicinity worth $--000, has $2,000 or $3,000 in stocks, and bank, and about 40 slaves; he merchandises and farms, buys and sells on credit, owes money at home, but pays promptly. His father is a rich man, very old, and when he dies will come in for a good share. If he should visit North those who sell him much will earn all the profit they make."

Seven or eight or ten thousand dollars was wealth, and forty negroes a great number; most of them owned two or three slaves. Only one man is quoted as having a hundred, and lands worth $20,000, and a capital of $100,000.

He winds up his account by writing: "Above you have a pretty full account of all the merchants of any importance in the district. It may strike you that my account of our merchants is rather a eulogy, I could not, however, say less and tell the truth. I feel certain that I am under the mark oftener than over it."

CHAPTER XII.

ANDERSONVILLE AND SOME EARLY SETTLERS.

AT the head waters of the Savannah, where the Tugaloo and Seneca Rivers meet, once stood a flourishing town. Now the beautiful site is given over to bats and owls except when some camping or picnic party revive for a brief moment youth and life on the deserted spot.

Andersonville was founded in 1801, twenty-six years before Anderson was laid off. An act of the legislature of that time created the town on land owned by Colonel Elias Earle, one of the pioneer settlers of upper South Carolina. General Robert Anderson, General Samuel Earle and Colonel Elias Earle were appointed to lay it off, and it was named for General Anderson.

Colonel Elias Earle had been an officer in the War for Independence, and afterwards a member of Congress. He sold some lots in the new town, but retained the greater part for himself; later he sold a half interest to his son-in-law, James Harrison. With his interest added to his wife's share in her father's estate, Mr. Harrison became the second owner of Andersonville, and the place is still owned by the Harrison family. Only the old Harrison dwelling, the second house built for the family residence, remains to mark the spot, and it is fast falling to decay.

Mr. Harrison carried on a large mercantile business and amassed a fortune. Later he took as partners Colonel F. E. Harrison and Mr. John B. Wynne. Colonel F. E. Harrison and Mr. Claudius Earle succeeded this firm as "Harrison and Earle." There were in the town a flour and grist mill, a cotton gin, an iron foundry, and a flourishing academy for young ladies. The town also supported a small cotton factory and a wool factory, and housed the operatives of both mills; there were tailor shop, shoe shop and livery stable in the place, and quite a number of residents. Andersonville was the cotton market for the whole of what is now called the Piedmont Section of the State, and a large area of Georgia; its trade with Hamburg and Augusta was brisk, during the days when river navigation was the means of carrying freight.

After the War Between the States there was a factory established in Andersonville for making yarn from cotton seed. It was probably the only one of its kind ever operated in the South.

In 1840 a great freshet swept away the cotton and wool mills and the cotton gin. They were rebuilt, a second time carried away by the rampant waters of 1852, and never erected again. Andersonville had then entered upon its decline. The building of the Columbia and Greenville railroad was a death blow to the river town. Colonel Frank E. Harrison, the owner at the time, did all in his power to uphold the place; he even tried to get a railroad through it, and one was actually surveyed, but never built. The grim monster war was stalking the South, and the town fell its prey even before its actual horrors were realized.

Colonel Frank Harrison had married a daughter of the former owner, Colonel James Harrison, and so inherited the village. He was the father of a large family, and his beautiful home on the tongue of land lying between the Seneca and Tugaloo rivers as they come together, was for years the scene of gayety and hospitality; now it stands "a ragged beggar sunning," tenanted by rats and owls; but about it lingers the fragrance of other days, and it is a favorite summer camping place for young people fortunate enough to have permission to use it.

After the death and decay of old Andersonville, it probably had its most distinguished visitor. On July 24, 1889, Henry Grady attended a political picnic held there, and made one of his brilliant speeches.

Of the old buildings, beside the Harrison residence, little remains. The forest is dense, the birds and wild animals are free and unafraid. On Beaver Dam Creek stands the rock foundation of one of the mills, a lone sentinel guarding ancient memories—that is all that is left of Andersonville.

John Earle, one of the founders of the family in South Carolina, was born in Westmoreland county, Virginia, June 5, 1737. He was a son of Major Samuel Earle and Anna Sorrel Earle, his first wife, and a brother of Colonel Elias Earle, another founder, and a Revolutionary soldier. John Earle emigrated from Virginia to the region lying on the boundary line between North and South Carolina in 1773, and the same year built Earle's Fort, a place of rendezvous and protection for white people during Indian raids; it also served as a refuge for Whigs during the Revolution. The combat of Earle's Fort, N. C., was fought during the revolution upon the lands of John Earle's brother, Baylis Earle. The greater part of John Earle's service during the war was rendered as a commander of partisan forces. On April 16, 1757, John Earle married Thomasina Prince, daughter of John and Mary Prince, of Frederick county, Virginia. John Earle was captain in Brigadier-General Bougette's expedition in Ohio in 1764 and was complimented by the Virginia House of Burgesses in acknowledgment of his merit and extraordinary service rendered the colony. Colonel Earle was a great grandson of John Earle, who came from Dorset county, England, in 1652, and received a grant of land consisting of 1,000 acres, for the transportation of thirty-two persons to Virginia. John Earle was the father of General John Baylis Earle, who entered the Revolutionary Army at sixteen years of age. He was later adjutant and inspector-general of South Carolina for eight terms of two years each, and represented his district in Congress from 1803 to 1807.

Some miles across country from Andersonville stands another old Earle home, "Evergreen." It was built by Samuel Girard Earle, who was born at Centerville, May 1, 1789, and was educated at the South Carolina College. He served as captain of a company in the war of 1812. His sister, Sarah, was the wife of James Harrison, of Andersonville. Mr. Earle married Elizabeth Hampton Harrison, a niece of his brother-in-law, and they lived four years at Andersonville in a house that stood at the fork of the road, just after crossing the Seneca River. While living there they became the parents of two little boys, Elias John and Adolphus. The latter died in infancy and is buried at Andersonville.

About 1828 Mr. Earle bought the plantation which he named "Evergreen" from Samuel Smith. It had a dwelling on it which stood near the spring, a brick house originally, which had been enlarged by the addition of a second story of wood. It was in that house that their son, Julius Richard, was born in 1829. Later they built the present residence which Mrs. Earle named "Evergreen." She was very fond of flowers and her gardens were famous. In the front yard she set out thirty-two cedar trees which were kept trimmed up so that they grew tall, and it was their perpetual green that suggested the name given the place. The Earles must have been partial to cedar trees, as it was they who planted the row that stood until after the death of Mr. "Gus" Broyles on the outer edge of the flower garden of his home, which was the house now the residence of Mr. H. H. Acker's family on South Main street, at one time having been the Earle home.

There grew up about "Evergreen" a complete village. There was on it a wheat and corn mill, a post office, a cotton gin, a general store, a drug store kept by Dr. Glover, a blacksmith shop, a school, a printing office, besides the usual blacksmith and carpenter shops to be found on every farm. The store did a flourishing business. Mr. Earle's partner was Mr. Lewis, father of Mr. J. B. Lewis, of Belton, and it was while located there that Mr. Lewis married Miss Sarah Gregg, and lived near. At their home was the first well in that part of the country, and it was quite a curiosity.

After Mr. Earle's death, his eldest living son, Elias John, bought the place and moved there in 1852, and his mother and five brothers lived with him. He married Miss Amanda Hammond on April 18, 1850. They lived at a place some little distance from the "Evergreen" home until after his father's death, and he called it "Hardscrabble," because he said it was so hard to make a living there.

During the War Between the States Mr. Earle collected "tax in kind," ground grain for the army, gave out rations to wives, widows and orphans of soldiers, and had a shoe shop for making soldier shoes. Sometimes his mill ground all night. One of his millers, a slave named Thomas Jefferson, was living in 1923, over ninety years of age. Mr. Earle died February 22, 1897, and for several years his family remained at the "Evergreen" home, but later sold it to Mr. J. J. Fretwell, who sold it to a negro, Andy Martin, who at once cut down the ancient cedars and sold them for telephone posts.

The old house has gone greatly to decay, but like a forlorn and poverty-stricken aristocrat, still looks to the manor born. The walls surrounding the place are smothered in tangled rose vines, and venerable trees droop over gardens and lawn. The front rooms are large and airy, and in the room known in the far-off days as "the parlor," there is a unique mantel piece. Made of some hard wood, it was painted a mottled grey, and while wet liberally sprinkled with shining pieces of mica. There is a mica, and also an amethyst mine, on the old Earle property, and very pretty amethysts have been picked up about the place.

The first mimosa tree ever brought to this section was planted by Mr. Samuel G. Earle on the "Evergreen" plantation. It stood beside the front steps. The seeds were given Mr. Earle by Malcolm McPherson, a Scotchman, who lived near and who was an enthusiastic botanist. Mr. McPherson also introduced poppies and currants in this part of the world. He possibly brought them from California, as he traveled all over the United States on horseback for his health, going to the extreme West, the North, and into Mexico.

Although "Evergreen" was never a town, it was a busy and populous plantation, containing within itself ample means and industries to maintain life and culture, excluded from the rest of the world. Its school, taught by Irving Gregg, was an academy of high standing, including Latin, Greek and higher mathematics in its curriculum. Young men came from a distance to become pupils, and boarded with Mr. Earle and neighboring families. Mr. Gregg married Miss Earp. Her family lived about a mile from "Evergreen." One of its members, probably her father, saw at Andersonville in the Harrison home the first piano ever brought to the county, and being greatly impressed with it, after carefully studying the instrument, returned home and built one for his own family, which is said to have been quite a successful instrument.

In that neighborhood, but nearer the McPherson than the Earle home, once lived a mysterious character named Coosey. He was a silent, unsocial man, making no visits and receiving none. He dwelt in a log cabin alone, and in that day of slave labor, did all of his own work, even his laundry. Every once in a while people passing had their curiosity aroused by the sight of a woman's garments hanging on the clothes line to dry. However, if any ever had the temerity to ask the old man how they came to be there, that person was snubbed, and tried no more questions, for none ever learned whether romance lay hidden in that rough old home, or whether the queer old customer took delight in arousing curiosity just to foil it.

In that day a man's observance or non-observance of Sunday, or as it was almost universally called in the rural districts, "the Sabbath," meaning, however, the first and not the seventh day of the week, was the business of the community; and one who dared to desecrate the day by performing any unnecessary labor was summarily ejected, as the people of today would eject a Bolshevik or a Nihilist. Mr. Coosey lived so to himself that he may never have known when Sunday came. At any rate he outraged the proprieties by ploughing on "the Sabbath," and remonstrated with by his neighbors, in the obscurity of one night he "folded his tent like the Arabs, and as silently stole away." Where he went, or who he was, none ever knew.

On the road between "Evergreen" and Anderson lived a man named Alec McClinton, a wagon maker. His house was on the summit of a hill, and he said he established himself there because the road, being hilly and ungraded in both directions, travelers going and coming would very likely need repairs by the time they reached his place, so he was prepared for them. Wagons, carriages, buggies, or any other kind of vehicle he could mend; also he made coffins, and most of the old-time residents of that section sleep their last sleep in beds of his manufacture. There were many walnut trees in the country, and not only coffins, but much of the locally made furniture was of solid black walnut.

The Lewis home mentioned was the nucleus of another promising settlement now gone to decay.

Major Lewis had come from Pendleton to manage the largest merchant mill in the district, established by himself and Mr. Maverick in partnership. The settlement received the name Rock Mills, on account of the solid rock foundation of the buildings. A miniature village grew up, and had every prospect of becoming a town. There was a furniture factory, a store, a wagon shop and other industries, as well as homes for all of the people employed in these places. Of the old village nothing remains. Mr. John Wright owns the old Lewis home, and on the foundation of the original rock mill has built another, which does good business.

Colonel Elias Earle, son of Samuel and Anna Sorrel Earle, was born in Virginia, but emigrated at an early day to South Carolina. In 1782 he married Miss Frances Whitten Robinson, and for a time they lived at Three Forks of the Saluda River in Greenville county, but later he emigrated to Pendleton district and bought several thousand acres of land on the Seneca and Tugaloo Rivers, extending to Three-and-Twenty and Six-and-Twenty creeks, which he named Centerville, probably hoping that it would become a center of business and population. Colonel Earle served his district for five terms in the United States Congress. While in Washington he induced the government to permit him to manufacture guns for the use of the army, proving to them that there was iron on his land in South Carolina by making some guns from it, and taking them to Washington for inspection. The contract was given him, and he made some of the guns used in the war of 1812. The enterprise, however, did not prove to be a success, and was abandoned. The remains of the old gun factory may be seen on Six-and-Twenty creek.

Assisting in the gun-making was a young man named Daniel Tillinghast. The youth may have been deeply interested in his business, but it did not prevent his being also interested in Mr. Earle's pretty daughter, Franky (Frances Wilton), as they were married and became the ancestors of some of the leading people of the county.

Mr. Earle's children, besides Frances, were Samuel Girard, Elias, John Baylis, Robinson M., Elizabeth, Nancy and Sarah.

Mr. Earle built a fine house at Central, which became a center of hospitality.

Samuel Earle in 1776, at the age of sixteen, entered the Revolutionary army as ensign. He remained to the close of the war, having attained the rank of captain. He held various offices under the state government, and was chosen to represent his district in Congress as successor to General Pickens. At the close of his term he retired to his plantation and engaged in agriculture, steadfastly refusing the solicitations of his friends again to enter politics. He accumulated what for his day was a large fortune, and died in 1883, seventy-three years old. His wife, whom he married at sixteen, was a daughter of James Harrison, a family related to that which has given the country two presidents. Her mother was Elizabeth Hampton, of the noted South Carolina family.

Their son, Baylis John Earle, was endowed with intellect of the highest order, and graduated in 1811 at the age of sixteen from the South Carolina College at the head of a very large class. He entered the legal profession and became a judge.

John Maxwell, grandson of Robert Anderson, married Elizabeth Earle; his brother, Robert, married her cousin, Mary Prince Earle.

John Baylis Earle, son of John and Thomasina Earle, was born on Pacolet River in Rutherford county, N. C., October 23, 1766. He was called General from having been adjutant and inspector-general of the State of North Carolina. He entered the war of the Revolution when a boy as a drummer, and later served as a soldier to the end. He was twice married. His first wife was Sarah Taylor, whom he married September 11, 1791. His second wife, whom he married December 17, 1816, was Anna Douglass, widow of Archibald Douglass.

Mr. Earle once lived near Fort Hill, now Clemson; also at Pendleton, and afterwards, for many years, and until his death, at Silver Glade in Anderson county. He died January 5, 1836, and was buried on his plantation. He was the father of eleven children, Nellie, John, Hannah, Eliza, Carolina, Samuel Sydney, Baylis Wood, Joseph Taylor, Sarah Anne, Mary, Paul, his first wife's children. His second wife had but one, Georgia W.

The old Cross Roads place was originally owned by a man named Anderson. He sold to Mr. Elias Earle. Mrs. Anderson would never sign her dower; Mr. Earle offered Mr. Anderson a pair of horses and a carriage to get Mrs. Anderson (her name was Tennie) to sign the dower, but she never would consent to do it. The Anderson family went west, leaving the dower unsigned.

Harriet Earle, daughter of Samuel Earle, married Elias Earle. One of their sons was Wilton Robinson Earle, who at the age of twenty-three was fatally wounded at the first battle of Manassas. Honorable Preston Earle, Miss Fannie Earle, Mrs. Miriam Earle Lee, Mrs. Mary Earle Sloan were others of their children. There may have been others.

Some other children of Samuel Earle were James Hampton, 1799-1829; Morgan Priestly, 1804-1850; Edward Hampton, 1820-1849.

There was a postoffice at Beaver Dam named Tokoheno, pronounced Tokena; it was kept by Elias Earle. At the old Beaver Dam place his son, Preston, spent his life. He married Nettie Harrison, daughter of Colonel F. E. Harrison, of Andersonville.

One of the best known and most highly respected among the early citizens of the county was Amaziah Rice, born in the Neal's

Creek community June 20, 1798. He received an academic education which included a limited knowledge of the classics. He was colonel of the old fourth regiment. From 1826 to 1832 he represented his district in the General Assembly of South Carolina, and had the honor of voting for the charter of the South Carolina railroad, the first built in the State, and the first built in the United States solely for the use of steam engines, for a time the longest railroad in the world.

In later life he became a Baptist minister, was ordained at Neal's Creek Church May 27, 1837, by a presbytery composed of Elders A. Williams, C. Gant, Matthew Gambrell, Sanford Vandiver, Paul Vandiver and William McGee. He was the second pastor of the Anderson Baptist Church.

In 1832 John Vandiver was ordained at Neal's Creek church. The first little log building erected for that church was on land owned by John Vandiver, about 1803.

Another early family in Anderson county was that of King. The founder of the family in America was Robert, who emigrated from Ireland in 1770. He stopped first in Maryland, then came south over the old Post Road or great southern trail over which countless travelers migrated in the pioneer days seeking homes. This road traversed Pennsylvania, Virginia, North Carolina and South Carolina, over very much the route now followed by the great National Highway.

Mr. King stopped first on Broadmouth creek, a few miles from where Belton afterwards grew up. But learning of the massacre of the Kemp family not long before very near where he contemplated making his home, he moved a few miles further south. The land he settled is still in the possession of the King family.

His eldest son, Peter, was born on ship board as he was making his passage over in 1770. He was the progenitor of the Kings of Hopewell township. He is buried at Neal's Creek church, after living about one hundred years. Robert, the pioneer, fought in the Revolutionary war. His family consisted of twenty-one children. His son, Robert King, known widely in his life time as "Uncle Bobby," was a Baptist preacher of influence throughout his life.

An interesting story is told of another Anderson man of long ago. He was Walter M. Gibson, and lived near Sandy Springs. He was an adventurer, and it is said was once prime minister of the Sandwich Islands. Being banished during a revolution, he went to one of the South Sea islands, where he always claimed he was made King, but after a time was banished from there, too. Later he was imprisoned by the Dutch for attempting to instigate a revolution in Java. He said that he managed to escape, and found his way to America, finally drifting up country until he reached Pendleton district, and there he settled down to spend the remainder of his days in peace and quiet. He must at least have been a convincing talker.

John Thompson and his wife, Mary Hale, were among the first citizens of the new district of Anderson. Their home was not far from Silver Brook, then quite a distance in the country. The name of the plantation was "Oak Grove." There lived with them for many years their widowed daughter who had married Dr. William Calhoun Norris, Sr., who died young, leaving her with four children. John Thompson and his wife, Mary Hale, are buried in the cemetery of the First Presbyterian church. There also sleep their daughter, Elvira Thompson Norris, and her husband, William C.

The parents of Dr. W. C. Norris were Patrick Norris, a colonel in the Revolutionary army, and Rachel Calhoun. Among their many descendants in the county are Mrs. Flora Overman, Mrs. Bessie VanWyck and her children, and the children of Mr. William A. Chapman.

There is a rather gruesome story told of an old place which many years ago was somewhere on the General's Road. There was an inn kept by a brother and two sisters whose name was Moore. They were strays in the community, belonging to no other Moore family that has ever lived in the county.

It was a wooden building and had near it an old style well. It was said that in the days when there was little traveling, that sometimes persons stopped at the Moore Inn and were never seen or heard of again.

The two women were named Rachel and Leah. It is said that on one occasion Leah was tried in court for some suspected crime, and that the lady spit in the face of the presiding judge. They had some arrangement by which they could cut baggage off of a coach, and after they moved away, which they did when the county got too hot to hold them, there were numbers of bones found in the old well.

The house finally fell to decay, as nobody would live there, and it was popularly believed to be haunted.

CHAPTER XIII.

WATERS AND GRAVEYARDS.

THE waters of the world are its life. In the early days the waterways were the highways, and they were of the greatest importance. The springs and branches made the land inhabitable, hence they, too, were of value.

The Savannah River, which divides South Carolina from Georgia, also divides Anderson county from Hart county. It is a great stream, and in primitive times was the highway of traffic. Naturally there were all the crossings possible, people always wishing to make the shortest cut. One of the earliest was Shockley's Ferry, which played a large part in the history of the county; later it became known as Brown's Ferry, and as such achieved tragic notoriety.

The celebrated Shockley apple first made its appearance within 100 yards of the old ferry, which must have been named from some early settler close beside the stream. The old Baptist Church, which was located there in the earliest time, did not stand the test of years as did some of its contemporaries elsewhere.

At the time of the War Between the States the ferryman at the old place was named Brown, and the ferry was then called Brown's Ferry.

Just after the war, when feeling was bitter, there was stationed in Anderson a Yankee Garrison. Among its members were boys too young to have served in the army during the war; probably the eagerness of their age for adventure was the prime cause of their belonging to the army then, and they doubtless failed to find the adventure for which they sought, and would gladly have been at home.

One sad day three homesick, lonely lads in blue were ordered by their captain to go to Brown's Ferry, about fourteen miles away, and guard a lot of cotton which he had been told was there awaiting an opportunity of being floated down the river to Augusta for sale. The cotton belonged to Mr. Crawford Keys. The soldiers were to prevent its being removed, as all cotton was confiscated by the United States Government.

During the night of their vigil, armed men—none ever knew the number—rode out to the ferry and brutally murdered the guard. Who did the deed, no one ever knew. Crawford Keys, Elisha Byrum, Gaines Stowers and Robert Keys were arrested, tried and condemned to be hanged at Castle Pinckney. However, as the evidence against them was doubtful, the sentence was commuted to life imprisonment at Dry Tortugas. After some months they were pardoned by President Johnson. They were condemned on the evidence of Ferryman Brown. The sympathy of the community was entirely with the convicted men, and Anderson county became a dangerous place for Mr. William Penn Brown, who left, making his home elsewhere for forty-five years; then, drawn back to the scene of the tragedy, he returned, and lived on a little farm on the Georgia side of the river, just at the ferry, until in 1913, at the age of eighty-five years he killed himself, perhaps in remorse. The secret of the death of the boys has never been revealed. Their bodies were brought to Anderson and interred in the Presbyterian grave yard, where their dust remained for over thirty years. There was in Anderson one tender-hearted woman who, for all that time, remembered those lonely graves and took care of them. She was the veteran teacher, Miss Leonora C. Hubbard. When, in 1905, the bodies were taken up and carried to the Federal Cemetery in Atlanta, Miss Nora received the official thanks of the legislature of Maine for her humane and womanly conduct.

In 1917, William Pierce, ferryman at the beautiful, but ill-fated ferry, was brutally murdered, not for plunder nor robbery, not for anything that he had done, but because he knew too much about the nefarious traffic of a band of rum-runners who used the ferry in their business. At his death, Mr. Alford, his employer, took up his work and also offered a reward of $1,000 for the apprehension of his murderer. His poor old father added $300.00 to the sum.

South Carolina and Georgia had long discussed the advisability of a bridge at that place, but could never come to any agreement. Finally Mr. A. N. Alford, of Hartwell, single-handed, accomplished what the two great counties had failed to do. In 1916 he made a contract with Austin Brothers, bridge builders; they undertook the work and it was completed in the fall of 1917. For several years it was operated as a toll bridge, and the father of the murdered ferryman was given the job of toll taker. The scenery on both sides of the river at this point is beautiful and impressive.

There are a number of other ferries across Savannah River, but Brown's is the most famous and the most tragic. It is to be hoped that with the coming of the bridge, the ancient spirit of evil which haunted the place has been exorcised.

In November, 1841, Hiram Cooley gives notice that he will apply to the next legislature for a renewal of charter to a toll bridge over Saluda River in his own name, for the bridge at Pierce's

Ford heretofore known as Poore's bridge, for fourteen years with the usual privileges.

There was in the early part of the nineteenth century a smooth crossing called "The Shallow Ford" over the Seneca River, about three hundred yards below the site of the bridge now known as Earle's Bridge. Another account mentions the ferry as being at the place of the bridge, and says that it was probably established a little later than 1830; goes on to say: "The probabilities are that the ferry was never chartered, as there is no mention of it in the act of the General Assembly." The first mention of the ferry calls it "McDaniel's Ferry." Mr. McDaniel lived about half a mile east of the river, and the public road ran just beside his place, joining the present road at the branch near the river. Mr. McDaniel had a number of sons, and one of them became the father of Governor McDaniel, of Georgia.

The next owner of the ferry was Andy Shearer, who sold it in 1844 to Thomas Griffin. He kept the place for a few years, then deeded it back to the Shearer heirs, who were several maiden sisters who tended the ferry themselves in all kinds of weather.

In the year 1854 Reverend David Simmons, Messrs. Daniel and Samuel Brown, and perhaps others, formed a company and erected an open bridge at the ferry, supported by immense hewn logs. People made great fun of it, calling it "the corn stalk bridge." It stood, perhaps, a year, when it was swept away by the rising river.

A few years later the property passed into the hands of Baylis Earle, who, in 1860, built a substantial covered bridge over the ferry, resting on three stone piers. It stood about eighteen feet above the water. They were the work of John McGrath, of Anderson. The heaviest strain this bridge ever had from freshets was in January, 1865, when the water washed some eighteen inches up its weatherboarded sides. The same freshet washed away Cherry's bridge farther up the river, the wreckage passing under Earle's bridge before the water had quite reached it.

Anderson County bought Earle's bridge about 1876, and made it free to travel. In 1893 the old structure was torn away, the piers raised to twenty-one feet in height, and a splendid steel bridge built at a cost of about $6,000. That bridge was swept away by the flood of 1902, which ruined Portman Dam.

There are two creeks which have been landmarks in Anderson history—Big and Little Generostee. The name is of Indian origin, and unless Dr. Daniel has in the last six years discovered it, the meaning is lost. He, however, had some years ago a hope of finding the meaning of the word.

HISTORY OF ANDERSON COUNTY

Big Creek, Deep Creek, Broadaway Creek are all self-explanatory. Hen Coop Creek is more mysterious. Naturally the name has given rise to many more or less silly stories which attempt to explain its origin. Mr. Mike McGee, who was born and raised beside the stream, and who had a taste for historical research, could give no reason for the name. He said that his mother had remarked that when she came there to live, nobody could give a reason for the peculiar name. Mr. McGee said that long ago there used to be numbers of wild turkeys trapped in that locality, and he felt sure that in some way the name commemorated an unusual catch of turkey hens. If that were not the explanation, he could give none.

Saluda, Seneca, Savannah are all Indian names.

There was a ford in the county in early times named for a woman, Esther's Ford on the Generostee, named for Esther Watson, daughter of the planter on whose land the ford stood. There are rocks yet to be seen which indicate the hearth of the old homestead.

There are springs in Anderson County which perpetuate the names of men or families of importance, old homesteads or picturesque localities. There is one which bears the name of a faithful black man who served his mistress as best he could. It is the "Uncle Ben Spring," and is located on the old Jacob Burriss place three miles north of Anderson.

Long ago an old lady whose children had married and scattered, feeling the weight of years upon her, left the home that she could no longer manage, and set out in her carriage for the house of her daughter, Mrs. Jacob Burriss, with whom she wished to spend her remaining days. Trains and trolleys there were none, and the dame made the journey in her coach driven by her sable coachman, Ben, who for years had been her faithful servitor. The other servants could be scattered around among the children and grandchildren, but this one old man had too long been her stay and prop for her to part with him. Where "Mistis" went to live there, too, went Uncle Ben with carriage and horses. "How else ole Miss gwine git 'bout? Ain't I done driv her all dese yers? Fink ole Miss gwin let no young nigger drive her bout? Huh!!"

In those days springs were the most frequent source of water supply to country houses, and there was on this place one bold and beautiful. A home was built for Uncle Ben close beside the spring, and his proud task was to keep it clean and in good condition, hence it came to be called Uncle Ben's Spring, and Uncle Ben's Spring it is to this day, though now it is equipped with a modern hydraulic ram which pumps pure spring water into the spotless hygienic dairy, managed by Mr. Thomas Eskew, a descendant of that dame of other days. But careful as Mr. Eskew is to keep his water supply pure for his herd of cows, he is not more careful, nor does he take more pride in his up-to-date machinery, than Uncle Ben did for his beautiful spring in the green glade of long ago.

Keys' Spring, at the old Keys place west of Anderson, has been the scene of many a jollification. Fretwell's Spring at his beautiful home, Sunset Forest, was long known as Crystal Spring, and both in the old time, and now, it is and has been a popular resort.

Jolly's Spring, formerly a popular picnic ground, is now a carp pond.

Hurricane creek has borne the name ever since white men have been in the country, nobody knows how it originated. The William Otwell land grant of 1,000 acres, entered in 1792, was on "Hurricane Creek." It has known some hurricane weather, especially was this true in 1865 and again in 1884.

On June 16th, 1843, a letter appears in *The Highland Sentinel* telling of a mineral spring discovered on the edge of the village, which the editor thought might turn out to be of great medicinal value and attract many visitors to the place, provided a big hotel should be built near it. That must have been the spring in the southeastern part of the town, over near Thomas street, which was long known as "Miss Teresa Brown's Spring," and which the old lady always maintained had remarkable powers.

Whatever Anderson is now, in the early days it was not a dry town. Besides the Poole or Murray Spring, always a popular resort for young people, there was a spring on South Main street about where Mrs. Lizzelle Clinkscales lives. There was a large pond where Mrs. Chenault's house is, there was a spring just back of the Carolina National Bank, and its waters may still be seen trickling down the walls of the railroad cut. There was also a spring where Mr. J. L. E. Jones and the Misses Bohannon's shops are on McDuffie street. There was a spring right in the center of Benson street between Fleischman's corner and the Bleckley building. Before the street was paved, there were often traces of it in the dirt street which ran over its ancient site. There were others, probably many others, Anderson was decidedly not dry.

Among the many creeks of the county are Goldin's Eighteen Mile, known as "the 18," Three-and-Twenty, Six-and-Twenty, Snow, Conneross, Great Rocky, Brushy Mountain, Golden Grove, Cain's, Georges, and there must once have been a Neal's creek somewhere near the church of that name. The spring probably bears some other name now, and all tradition of the name Neal in that locality has vanished.

On the J. S. Fowler place a few miles west of the city is a beautiful bold spring in a lovely piece of woods, a sort of natural amphitheater is said to surround the place. From the natural grouping of the surrounding hills, says one familiar with the locality, it would be possible by the addition of a stand alone, to permit a speaker to address with the greatest ease 5,000 persons seated upon the grass. Though half a mile from his home, the spring supplies Mr. Fowler's house with water forced by hydraulic ram.

No place is fit for human habitation unless it is well watered, hence the interest in springs and rivers and creeks, they must accompany the homes of people. There is another necessity near to human habitations, and that is a place to bury the dead; a place to live and a place for a grave must go together. Our ancestors lived closer to their dead than we do, every farm had its family graveyard in the first days, then followed community cemeteries. The traveler along the highways may not realize that often the clump of trees which he admires at a little distance from the road conceals one of those old burying grounds. If the traveler happens to be of an investigating turn of mind, and dismounts, turning aside to see what is hidden by the trees, he is sometimes startled at being confronted with grave stones, often moulded and broken.

Such a graveyard lies on the road from Anderson to Carpenter's Mill, a clump of trees across a cotton field. When the thicket is penetrated one finds four neat head stones bearing the name Bennett. Elisha Bennett died September 30th, 1833, age 66 years; Sarah Bennett died November 27th, 1828, age 54 years; Egloe Bennett died March, 1828, age 18 years; Mitchell Bennett died January 20th, 1827, age 10 years. Perfect strangers to the intruder, yet there speaks the sorrows of a long past day—a father and mother and two sons. The little boy died in January, 1827, his eighteen-year-old brother in March, 1828, and the mother unable to bear the double loss, follows them the next November. The father lingers on a few years, and probably they were sad years, then he, too, is gone. There was some one left, however, who did not forget. Those stones are distinctly modern, they have been put there in recent years. Lying on the ground not far from the graves, is a rough native rock, still bearing signs of having been inscribed, and "age 66 years" is still decipherable. Other graves there are in this old burying ground, but the rough boulders at their heads, if they ever bore any inscription, show no remains of it now. Sometimes there is not even the rude headstone, only a sunken place in the ground tells that once a human body was placed there. The Bennetts were early settlers, the name occurs every once in a while in the study of the county history, and after years, one accidentally stumbles on the fact that a member of the family went to New Orleans and got rich, and visited Anderson along in the 80s, that of course, was when he put up the stones in memory of his parents and his brothers. It is believed that one of the other graves may be that of a Revolutionary soldier, father of the Elisha Bennett whose grave is marked.

In the old Sally Reed burying ground near Calhoun, lie the unfortunate Kemp family. The most pretentious graves in that cemetery are those of the Harkness family. One tall handsome shaft on a substantial pedestal has fallen flat, the pedestal is turned over, and the shaft is half buried in the earth. The sinking of the grave caused the overthrow. There are several other graves inside the rock fence which enclosed that family plot, most of the stones are badly broken and defaced. It is told that one of the graves was broken open by a sacrilegious hunter who was chasing an opossum. There are several Telford graves in very good condition. About one hundred and fifty graves have been counted in the cemetery, locating them either by the depressions, or by the rough pieces of rock which marked so many early resting places of Anderson county dead. A stream runs through the cemetery, and on one side of it is a great mysterious looking cave. The whole place is wild and overgrown, a forgotten spot, and all who sleep there are forgotten too.

In the old McPherson graveyard are some time-stained graves, those having stones bear the names, Elizabeth McPherson, wife of William McPherson, daughter of John and Sarah Gillilan, born April 12, 1766, died May 30th, 1818; William McPherson, son of William and Phoebe McPherson, born October 4th, 1758, died August 8th, 1832; Mary Gunnin, daughter of William and Elizabeth McPherson, born November 8th, 1792, died September 30th, 1839; Cyrus Gunnin, son of James and Mary Gunnin, born July 10th, 1822, died January 28th, 1845. Besides the graves that are marked, there are others having only boulders, and any rude inscription that might once have been scratched on the stone has long since disappeared.

The Haney Muster Ground was on the Generostee Road, several miles below Anderson. Not far from that muster ground, at a bend in the road, the unsuspecting traveler of today rolls over the ancient resting place of an old time "bad negro." He killed a young lady, sister of Mr. Dudley Howard, who lived in that section of the country. She was walking alone, and he struck her on the head with a pine knot. Needless to say he speedily paid the penalty of his act, and was buried where the crime was committed.

Further out from town on the Emmerson Bridge Road neighborhood, on Drake land, is an old graveyard, originally it was known as the Rutledge Graveyard, because it was laid off on the immense plantation of a man named Rutledge who moved to this section of the country before the Revolutionary war, taking up government lands, owning hundreds of acres, and having for his part of the world, a large number of slaves. He built a two-story house, a rarity in that day, on a knoll several hundred yards from where the graveyard was located.

Mr. Rutledge was one of the prominent men of his time, greatly looked up to by his neighbors. On his place was a beautiful spring bubbling out of the side of the hill. A pipe was fastened in the spring carrying water to the foot of the hill where it was caught in troughs, and there was the family laundry. The locality has been known as "the Wash Place" by the successive people who have owned it, for all have used it for that purpose.

Mr. Rutledge had three daughters; one, Anne, married James Emmerson, another married Zacheriah Hall, and the other married John Martin for whom Martin Township was named.

James Emmerson, his wife and one son are buried in the old cemetery. There are two graves there marked by the rough native stones, but some care has been taken to shape them, and the names and dates are chiseled on them. One is Arch Gillison, age 64, who died in March, 1792. The inscription is almost illegible now, but by careful peering and using the fingers as the blind do, it may be deciphered. The other is Jane Gillison, died November 2, 1796, age 32. Whether she was his wife or his daughter is not stated. It is known where a Gillison house once stood in the neighborhood, but there are none of the name or kindred in the county now, and practically nothing is known as to who they were, or why they are buried in the Rutledge graveyard.

Mr. Rutledge in his old age married a widow, known as "Aunt Armand Kay," they left Anderson and went to Georgia, both leaving children in this section. It may be that the children objected so strenuously to the old couple marrying, that they went away on that account. However, if that were the case, the children were justified; the old couple after a few years together separated, each retiring to its own family.

When Mr. Rutledge settled the home in Anderson county he

planted two cedar trees in his yard, and some years before the War Between the States, the trees which had grown very large were cut down. The house was moved on the opposite side of the graveyard, and is now occupied by the Keaton family.

The most interesting grave in the cemetery is that of Jehu Orr who was murdered.

The graveyards surrounding the old churches are interesting. The graves are in much better state of preservation than those in family or private cemeteries. Bare, unbeautified, but usually fairly clean and easily accessible. There are interesting names on all the old tombstones in those early church yards, but it is the old family burying grounds that somehow tell the life story of the dust that they are holding in their hearts.

On one of the roads between Anderson and Belton there gleams a tombstone beside the road.

Seventy odd years ago there was a doctor who lived near where the town of Piedmont has grown up. He had one little daughter, and several sons. The little girl loved people, she liked to see them moving about, and she constantly played beside the public road, until her little figure became familiar to the people who often passed that way, and they called her "the girl who plays by the side of the road." In 1859 the child died, and they buried her where she had loved to play, beside the public road. And there today, protected by a little fence and marked by a stone, sleeps the girl who played by the side of the road. A few days after her death her family, the Howells, went to Texas.

In the spring of the year 1835, a poor, almost destitute looking stranger walked into Mr. J. P. Reed's printing office in Calhoun, and asked for work. Mr. Reed liked his appearance in spite of his poverty, and employed him. Mr. Reed said of him: "The man gave his name as Seth Catlin, and claimed to be from Richmond, Va. He performed his duties with promptness, diligence and skill. He sought no companionship with his fellow-workers, nor did any one intrude upon him, for there was a sadness and dignity about the man which commanded respect."

When Mr. Reed brought his paper to the town the stranger came with him. But very soon after the move was made the lonely alien developed typhoid fever and died. When the attending physician told him that he must die, he sent no message, spoke of no relative, but he placed in Mr. Reed's hands a bundle of manuscripts, some of which were poems of rare beauty, all signed Seth Catlin; but whether that was a pen name, or his own, none ever knew. No one ever made inquiry about him, and when he was laid to rest in the Presbyterian graveyard, he passed completely out of the life. An unknown poet, lying among strangers, in a strange place.

In Broadaway township is an old forgotten graveyard, few graves are marked except by the usual rough boulder, but there is one with a tombstone bearing the inscription: "Here lies the body of Mary Smith, a heroine of the American Revolution, who died August 17th, 1829, aged 78 years." Who she was none seem to know. Could she have been the Mrs. Smith who carried messages and comfort to Colonel Eliab Moore during the Revolutionary war? Another grave has a tomb stone marked John George, Esq., died November 4th, 1827, aged 78 years.

There are countless other graveyards on old farms, and in forgotten corners. There the "rude forefathers of the hamlet sleep." Forgotten people in forgotten graves, yet they made our county, they gave us our civilization. Well, we, too, shall follow them and other "bards shall walk these dells."

Near the old Evergreen home used to be two lonely graves close beside the public road, which the children of Mr. Elias John Earle took great pleasure in tending seventy odd years ago. They often laid wild flowers, or sometimes blossoms, from their mother's garden on the little mounds, marked by rude stones of the field at head and feet.

They were the graves of two little children, who away back in the days of the western gold craze, started with their parents to seek the place where gold was to be had for the gathering. Traveling in wagons, they camped at night, and that family made one of their camps close to the Earle home. While in camp they killed a hog, and allowed their little children to eat as much of the fresh pork as they liked; naturally they got sick, and nothing could counteract the pernicious diet. The little travelers went on a longer journey than was planned, and their small bodies were laid away beside the public road. How often in the years that followed, that mother's heart must have turned back to those lonely little graves by the wayside. Time has probably obliterated every trace of them now. But the mother's heart is at rest too, somewhere in the golden west.

Near High Shoals is the old family burying ground of the Moore family. There the Revolutionary patriot Eliab Moore rests, and about him are many of his descendants.

CHAPTER XIV.

RAILROADS.

IN the late forties, railroads began to occupy the attention of the people of the Piedmont section. A line was projected from Columbia toward the mountains, and the burning question was where should be its terminal. A newspaper item of November 20th, 1847, signed "O," says: "The contest has ended and the road located on the west side of Saluda, with every probability that Anderson will be the terminal, as Greenville has in a pet dissolved her connection with the enterprise. The majority was 950 in favor of our route. Columbia, Charleston, most of Newberry, Abbeville and Anderson voting for this route."

Anderson people rested content, they were sure they had the railroad; was it not officially known as "the A. and C. R. R.?" But other people were at work, Greenville repented of its pet, and worked untiringly until the plans were changed, and the road is now and ever shall be the Greenville and Columbia railroad. An Anderson man was, however, elected president, Mr. Daniel Brown. The main line was built in 1853, and a year or two later a branch was run from Belton to Anderson to connect with the Blue Ridge, which had begun running from Anderson to Pendleton, and later to Walhalla, its ultimate aim being Knoxville, Tenn. The whole line was surveyed, and partly graded and tunneled; the old tunnel at Walhalla is a mute witness to the blasted hopes of its promoters.

When the first railroad in Anderson was in condition to run cars, the people were wild in their enthusiasm. The little engine drawing the first train, which consisted of the engine and a funny, stuffy, poor little combination passenger and baggage coach, was named in honor of Governor McDuffie, who was popular with Anderson people. The engineer was Smith Bass, a graduate of the Citadel Academy. The first depot agent was E. C. Rice, who served about six years, when he went to Texas in the fall of 1859. Mr. Rice was a son of Fleetwood Rice, who was a brother of Reverend Amaziah Rice, an honored Baptist preacher of early times.

When "George McDuffie" first steamed into Anderson, the whole populace was out to greet him, and they made the welkin ring with cheers and huzzas.

As the world has progressed and the people have traveled and mixed with the rushing tide, great have been the complaints of our little railroad, which has always given us the best service possible for the money we have put into it, and which has gallantly kept us in touch with the big world. Those who complain of inadequate service, and say Anderson is cut off from the rest of the country should regard what the grandmothers and fathers of the little town thought a tremendous stride toward cosmopolitanism. On August 4th, 1860, the *Intelligencer* carries a schedule of the Blue Ridge road. "Cars leave Pendleton on Mondays, Wednesdays and Fridays at 15 minutes before 4 o'clock a. m.; on Tuesdays, Thursdays and Saturdays at 1 o'clock p. m. Leave Anderson on Mondays, Wednesdays and Fridays immediately after the cars leave for Belton; Tuesdays, Thursdays and Saturdays on the arrival of the cars from Belton." The time of the arrival from Belton is left to the imagination. But there was no danger of the people not knowing, what those small engines lacked in size they made up in noise, and came in with unspeakable screeching. The first cars run from Belton were flat cars with planks on supports, stretched across for seats.

In 1856 the cut running through the town just north of the square, and now bridged on the east side by the railroad station, was made for the Blue Ridge. There were strong advocates for having the road enter the town almost exactly as the Piedmont and Northern does now; but the majority thought that too far out, they wanted their road right through the town and they got it. The three railroad bridges across the cut made excellent places from which to see the wonderful cars, and for a long time they were lined with spectators when the train passed under. Even as recently as the early 80's the boys of the town were to be seen hanging over the balustrade when the cars came in or went out.

Where the cut was excavated used to be a street. As usual, the work was given to the man making the most advantageous bid for it. In this case Mr. Crawford Keys got the contract, and being a wealthy man with a number of slaves, he easily accomplished the job.

For many years Anderson boasted the highest railroad trestle in the whole country, some people claimed in the world. However that may have been, certainly it was a trestle of great and unusual height, and it spanned Six and Twenty Creek.

After a few years of running the ten mile branch of the C. and G. from Belton to Anderson as a separate road to connect with the Blue Ridge, the two little roads united. Judge Belton O'Neal was greatly interested in the C. and G. road, and being a very religious man, he was instrumental in having incorporated into the charter a clause forbidding the trains on that road from running on Sunday. The restriction passed over to the Blue Ridge, and

HISTORY OF ANDERSON COUNTY

until sometime in the late 80's, no sound of puffing engine or rushing train broke the Sabbath stillness of the village at the foot of the mountains.

In the days prior to the great war between the North and the South, there was projected another railroad. Savannah Valley was the pretty name selected for it and Mr. Daniel Brown was also greatly interested in that scheme. Its chief sponsor, however, was Mr. Stephen McCully. For a long time the new road was the chief topic of conversation and its advocates not only talked but liberally subscribed to it. Anderson was to be one terminal, Augusta the other. But the war scourge, in its career of ruin, demolished the chances of the road.

Some sixteen or seventeen years after the war was over, the project was revived. Most of the early promoters were dead, but Colonel Latimer, of Lowndsville, became its chief advocate, and worked up much interest in the enterprise. However, he did not live to see the road completed. Still his work went on. Mr. McCully, then a very old man, was living, and to him was given the pleasure of throwing the first shovel of earth when the road bed was started. On its completion in 1885, two of his granddaughters, little girls then, threw the last with a silver shovel bought for the occasion. They were Carrie McCully (Mrs. Carrie McC. Patrick) and Anna Humphreys (Mrs. Anna Weston). The old grandfather was dead, and he was thus honored in the attention paid his granddaughters.

From the amount of clamor made over the completion of that road one might think that it was going to make Anderson a city of national importance. There were meetings and speeches and banquets and dances, and rejoicings of every possible kind, not only in Anderson, but in every hamlet on the route and at the last a tremendous affair in Augusta to which about half of the Anderson people went. Mr. Tolly was Mayor of Anderson at the time, and the boys who loved to "rag" him, used to maintain that when at the big banquet in Augusta he was called on for a speech, he said that he had not expected to make a speech, and that he was altogether unprepared but that he always responded to the call of duty. Whereupon he took from his pocket about thirty pages of typewritten matter. The crowd saw the joke and cheered Anderson's mayor to the echo.

The Piedmont and Northern electric line was projected in the early twentieth century. The first spur of the road ran from Anderson to Belton. The cars used to run from the square in Anderson to the door of the hotel in Belton, and a favorite pleasure trip for Anderson peaple was to go over to Belton and take supper, when the hotel was kept by Mr. and Mrs. H. M. Geer. And a noble supper they always got.

The Anderson railroads have had very few accidents. The most tragic one occurred on Saturday morning, June 17th, 1876. A little before daylight the courthouse bell began to ring furiously, people sprang from their beds and rushed to the windows to see where the fire might be, for in that day of "the bucket brigade," when a fire occurred every able-bodied man in town was expected to lend a hand in fighting the flames.

From his home no man could see the glow of conflagration, and hurriedly they made their way to the square to find out what was the matter. Not fire at that time, but a fearful railroad accident outside of the town. A messenger, William Holmes, had just arrived breathless from his run, bringing news that Broadaway trestle had fallen, plunging the train and all on board to instant death.

The afternoon before, Friday, the passenger train from Belton had come in at its usual time, and in addition to its usual equipment there was attached a private coach belonging to Mr. G. W. Williams, a wealthy Charleston merchant, and occupied by his family who, with some friends, were en route for their summer home in Georgia. The party consisted of thirteen people. They expected to go to Seneca, where the coach was to be attached to the Southern, or, as it was called at that time, the Air Line train. On reaching Anderson, Conductor LaFoy learned that there was a break on the Blue Ridge road about seven miles above the town, and he received instructions to go and ascertain the extent of the damage. Returning to Anderson a little before dark, Mr. LaFoy reported the condition so serious that it was not possible to continue the journey in that direction. There had been very heavy and continuous rains for some time, and the whole road bed was greatly weakened. Colonel Dodamead, satisfied that the Williams party could not reach Seneca by that route, sent a messenger with the intelligence to Mr. Williams, and asked whether he wished to have his car taken to Greenville that night, where it could make the desired connection. Mr. Williams replied that he should like to have such arrangements made as soon as possible. Conductor LaFoy was then instructed to take the party to Belton where another engine would meet him and take them on to Greenville. Colonel Dodamead expressly ordered the railroad men, however, to remain in Belton the night.

Accordingly Mr. LaFoy left Anderson with the private car about eight o'clock. Besides the Williams party, the persons on the train were N. W. LaFoy, conductor; M. J. Wilson, engineer; Jefferson Kitsinger, baggage master; Allen Johnson, negro fireman, and Henry

Thomson, negro wood-passer. The Blue Ridge engines of that day burned wood. The mail agent, Mr. Thomas Sullivan, was in the act of getting on the train when, for some unknown reason, he was requested to remain in Anderson that night and consented to do so. The engine and baggage car, with Mr. Williams' coach, formed the train.

On reaching Broadaway creek, four miles from Anderson, the train was halted and an examination made of the trestle, after which the train passed safely over, reaching Belton in good time. After turning the coach over to the waiting engineer, the train crew then disregarded the orders they had received to remain in Belton for the night. Some of them had made engagements in Anderson for the evening, which they were anxious to keep, and the fated train left Belton at nine-thirty; it consisted now of only the engine and baggage car. Mr. Wilson and the negroes were on the engine, Mr. LaFoy and Mr. Kitsinger were alone in the baggage car. The train proceeded slowly and carefully, as was testified by the watches of the conductor and engineer; that of Mr. Wilson stopped at ten o'clock, and that of Mr. LaFoy at 10:08. Henry Thomson, the negro wood-passer, was the only one of that crew who lived to tell what transpired; he said that the brakes were put on the engine and the car, and just as the awful plunge was made, the brakes were whistled off. The train had just fairly gotten on the trestle when the structure crumbled. It was eighty-one feet high and into that fearful chasm the train dropped. The tender went down first, and the engine turned a complete somersault, the car was splintered upon the fallen timbers; all except the negro, Henry Thomson, were instantly killed.

The tremendous crash awakened every person living in the vicinity, and soon every man was on the spot. The darkness, however, prevented those who had congregated from giving any assistance to the poor negro who was the only one who needed any, and those people who heard his dreadful groans could never forget them. About sunrise he was rescued and taken to a nearby house; Doctors Sharpe, McFall and Scudday attended him. Henry was able to tell the story, but lived only until about four o'clock the following afternoon.

It was necessary to overturn the engine before the bodies of Engineer Wilson and Allen Johnson could be recovered. They were fearfully mangled. It was Sunday before the machinery necessary for the handling of the wreck, and consequently for the recovery of the bodies, could be obtained. Mr. LaFoy and Mr. Kitsinger were found farther down the stream.

Mr. Kitsinger was a native of Abbeville county and had been in the employment of the Columbia and Greenville road for about twenty years. He came to the Anderson branch about 1862, after his discharge from military service. About a year before the accident he had left the railroad, and it was only about six weeks before the catastrophe that he had returned to it.

Mr. LaFoy had been on the Anderson branch about ten years, and for efficient service had been several times promoted. He had been placed in charge of the train as conductor about eighteen months previously. All of the men were married and left families.

The Broadaway trestle had for sometime been considered unsafe and the severe rains completed its debacle.

When the Air Line Road was projected in the decade following the war it, too, was scheduled to pass through Anderson and again the people were too sure of their road. The route had been determined upon, but Colonel Easley, who lived some miles above Greenville, never rested until he had secured influence and subscriptions enough to divert the line from the projected Air Line into one of the crookedest on the map, but it passed through Colonel Easley's property, made the town of Easley, and went on through Greenville.

When the Blue Ridge was begun with such high hopes, there was a great big brick roundhouse with a fascinating turntable in it, located somewhere behind where the P. and N. station is now, and after the war, when all hopes of completing the road were abandoned, it became the beloved play house of the small boys. There stood in it for years an old forgotten engine, which once had been known as "Fort Hill," and it afforded more real joy to the youngsters than any of them have ever experienced in later life.

The boys of fifty years ago had fun of various kinds. One great stunt was to slide down the railroad cut; that it dyed their garments a brilliant red from the clay sides of the gully, was to them a matter of little moment. They, and generations which have succeeded them, learned to swim in the "wash hole" in Rocky river, a little below where the concrete bridge crosses the stream. They fought mud battles, arrayed in the uniforms in which they were born, under the culvert which stood back of the old Osborne place, somewhere over toward the Anderson Mills locality. They slid astride and backwards down the iron railing of the old courthouse steps. They rode on the sweep of the mill which ground bark at Osborne's Tan Yard on Whitner's creek, which was then Tan Yard creek, and one of the old-time boys speaks in terms of affection of the little blue mule which used to pull that sweep and says he also remembers a most interesting monkey that lived in Judge Reed's back yard. A little girl of that old time remembers a lovely deer which lived in Mr. C. A. Reed's back yard in the days of long ago.

One of Anderson's most valued citizens gained for himself the soubriquet of "Black Diamond Jim" from his strenuous efforts in the last years of the ninteenth century to renew interest in pushing the Blue Ridge Road over the mountains, rechristening it the Black Diamond Road. He was the brilliant lawyer, James L. Tribble.

One of the widest known and best loved railroad men of Anderson was Captain "Billy" Smith, long a conductor on the Blue Ridge, then on the C. and G. His well known calls at the various stations always brought a smile. "Bel-TON, not Williams-TON; don't forget your umbrellas, packages and babies;" "Williams-TON, where you get a good drink that won't make you drunk," and so on for every station that he passed.

Captain "Billy" served the Southern railroad fifty-four years. During the war he transported between forty and fifty thousand soldiers. He used to tell with pride of having helped once to guard the Confederate treasury when it was in transit, to join Jefferson Davis on his retreat toward Mississippi. The boxes of gold, paper and other valuables had to remain over night at Alston, and Captain Smith was anxious about it. He, with others, kept watch over it until it passed from the hands of the train people to wagons to be taken to Abbeville. It was then that it got lost.

Captain Smith had charge of the train on that unhappy day when young Calvin Crozier was taken from the cars at Newberry and murdered by negro troops from Massachusetts.

It is told of Captain Smith that on one occasion soon after the war Colonel Orr, who was a director of the road, boarded the train at Columbia, en route for his home in Anderson, and that in violation of the railroad regulations he had some articles strapped to his trunk. Captain Smith saw the trunk before the train started and notified Colonel Orr that he must separate the baggage and pay fifty cents for the transportation of the extra articles. The colonel made some joking rejoinder and took his seat in the train, thinking of course his trunk was safely in the baggage car. When he reached Anderson he found that Captain Smith had left it in Columbia. After that, when Colonel Orr rode on Captain "Billy's" train, he observed the rules of the road.

Captain Smith lived for many years in Walhalla, but had made Anderson his home for quite a while before his death, which took place in Anderson.

Captain John R. Anderson was one of the more recent superintendents of the Blue Ridge Road. His greatest ambition was to bring his road up to the highest standard. He had worked up from a clerk in the freight office in Belton in 1885, then brakeman and fireman, and on from one position to the next, until in 1889 he became conductor on the C. and G., and in 1894 took charge of the Blue Ridge Road. He materially improved the service, removing the small, inadequate coaches which had served for so long, and putting on as good day coaches as any road in the state ran. He died very suddenly about 1912 or 1913, and was succeeded by Mr. William Archer. It has been during Mr. Archer's administration that Anderson for the first time had Pullman trains passing through town, making the run from Atlanta to Columbia.

CHAPTER XV.

TOWNSHIPS.

CENTERVILLE.

TOWNSHIPS are not indigenous to the South. In early times the divisions were parishes and counties, later called districts and still later restored to counties. Townships were a reconstruction measure.

An act to organize townships and define their powers and privileges was introduced in the senate by D. T. Corbin and duly became a law in 1868. It was but a copy of a statute of some northern state, presumably of Vermont, as Corbin had come to South Carolina from that State. The act (of sixty-nine sections) embodies a most elaborate scheme to township government. Every township was made a body corporate, and provision made for township meetings, each to be presided over by a moderator. Every town (township) was required to choose a town club, three selectmen, one or more surveyors of highways and one constable. The selectmen were to be overseers of the poor, registrars in town elections, general supervisors of the affairs of the township and the auditors of its accounts. They were charged with repairs and maintenance of highways, and might levy taxes therefor.

The surveyors, in addition to duties as such, were the "warners" to call out the road working gangs, and to those officers the selectmen were to depute their work. The pay of the selectmen was fixed at $1.50 a day, of the club the same.

This law was soon found to be utterly impracticable to conditions in South Carolina, and it was summarily repealed by the act of January 19th, 1870. The manifest object of the measure was to create a multitude of offices to be filled by negroes and carpetbaggers, for they would have control of every township meeting.

However, Anderson was fortunate in having appointed as commissioners to lay off her townships, Hon. B. F. Crayton, Colonel W. S. Pickens and Colonel J. W. Norris. Mr. William Sanford Hall was employed as deputy surveyor to survey the county and mark the townships. Mr. Hall divided the county into sixteen subdivisions and made a map showing each township as now constituted except that Anderson was made a township for school purposes only, and was numbered 17, the boundaries being the town limits of one mile in each direction from the court house as a center. The names of the townships were suggested by Mr. Hall and adopted by the board.

The city is now in Centerville township, and very near the Broadaway line. Centerville township was named from an ancient settlement, which once promised to become a village. The hamlet was almost in the center of the district of Anderson and Colonel Elias Earle, its owner, hoped that it would become the center of activity in the newly settled section of the state. Colonel Earle was a Virginian, and for services rendered during the Revolution received a grant of land in the newly opened Cherokee country.

He built a home a short distance from the road now running between Anderson and Townville, on the dividing ridge between Deep creek and Seneca river, something over three miles from where Portman Dam now stands. The main body of the house as originally built was standing a few years ago, and may be still. Colonel Earle began the development of the shoals of Six-and-Twenty creek at a point about eight miles northwest of the spot where the town of Anderson was afterward located. It was then that he gave his home the name of Centerville.

A merchant mill was one of the first things erected in the new settlement. That was a mill which not only ground the wheat and corn, but kept the products on hand for sale. There was also erected a saw mill, a blacksmith shop and a postoffice or, rather, a postoffice was established at Centerville. It was probably located in some building already used for business purposes, as separate postoffice buildings were erected only in large towns. There was a general store at the place, and it was probably there that the postoffice was located. Colonel Earle was postmaster.

The remains of Earle's gun factory were long visible about Six-and-Twenty creek, but the freshet of 1908 which caused a tremendous overflow of the creek, washed away most of the ancient rubbish. It also, however, uncovered some great hammers and shafting which had been buried from sight for almost one hundred years. The hammers weighed from two to three pounds and were operated by water. The charcoal used in the smelting was obtained from the nearby hills and until recent years piles of cinders showing where coal kilns had been burned were scattered about the old fields and pine woods around. Until a very few years ago there was in the locality a large body of pine woods generally known as the "coaling ground."

Another industry established at Centerville by Colonel Earle was the raising of silk worms and the manufacture of silk.

A few years ago there remained remnants of a race which conveyed water from Six-and-Twenty creek to a tan yard which was located between where the Anderson road now runs and Salem creek near where it empties into Six-and-Twenty.

Centerville remained the property of the Earles until sometime in the 60s when it was sold by John Baylis Earle to Haynes Whitaker. Since that time it has passed through many hands.

Immediately above the Earle grant was a large body of land given by the government to Andrew Liddell, also a Revolutionary soldier, who lived for many years on the tract, a good, industrious citizen. He gave off parts of his property to his children as they grew up. There are a number of his descendants still in the county, though none of the name. The old soldier is buried in an old family graveyard, now surrounded by fields, located about half a mile from the public road.

VARENNES.

The township lying south of Anderson was named from old Varennes church. It had been a sort of social center for many years, having been one of the earliest churches and schools in the section.

The word Varennes is French and means waste land. How the school, for it preceded the church, came to be called by so unpromising a name can only be conjectured. French Huguenots settled Abbeville county and town, and named it from their old home in France. It is probable that this section lying north of the little town was at first inhabited by Indians, and came to be known to the white people as the waste land—Varennes. When the tongue became Anglicized, the meaning of the word was lost, but it was a pretty word, sounded well, and so came to be given to the school and church, and also to a sort of trading post which grew up there; then when a township was to be named, why there was the pretty name ready to be bestowed upon it.

The word long ago lost its French pronunciation, though it retained its original spelling, and the Americans by degrees pronounced it according to the rules of their own tongue.

The town of Starr in Varennes township was named for one of the officers of the C. and W. C. railroad which passed through the place.

One of the leading citizens of Varennes township was Colonel C. S. Mattison, who had long been colonel in the old militia service of the Fourth Regiment, and when the state called for volunteers in 1861 he entered the army as lieutenant colonel of the Fourth, which became famous. When that regiment expired he was elected colonel of the Fourth Battalion in which the reorganization resulted.

At the battle of Seven Pines he was wounded in the chest and received an honorable discharge from the army. No braver soldier went from Anderson, and after he was disabled for active service there was no call of the Confederacy, nor any way in which he could assist the South, to which he failed to respond. After the war he was three times elected to the state legislature and finally declined to run for the position again.

Colonel Mattison was a man of fine practical judgment and in every way worthy of the confidence of his community. A man of large means for his time and locality, he was always generous. Just and upright himself, he never entertained suspicions of others. His home was ever open to his friends and his hospitality was gladly accepted and eagerly sought by many.

Colonel Jesse Norris was another of the prominent citizens of the township and a man of large means, highly respected by all who knew him. A devoted member for many years of the First Presbyterian church in Anderson. He had no sons but was the father of three daughters, Mrs. Will Simpson, of Anderson; Mrs. Jule Anderson and Mrs. Thompson.

A well-known character in Varennes was Dr. Dick Thompson. He was the son of Dr. Addison Thompson, of Savannah township, and grew up in that section.

BROADAWAY.

Named from the brawling little stream of that resounding name.

In May, 1784, Governor Benjamin Guerard granted to Eliab Moore a tract of land of 640 acres situated on Broadaway creek, bounded by "vacant land." In February, 1783, Thomas Buford received a grant of 640 acres, also on Broadaway creek. Buford's Mill was the first built on Broadaway, one of the earliest in the county. It is believed to be the same mill which has been successively known as Brown's, Townsend's, Carpenter's and now Burriss', a favorite picnic spot for the people of the town, also a place often used for big political speakings. One of the especially beautiful localities of the county.

In 1783 John Wardlaw, son of Hugh Wardlaw, of Abbeville, also got a grant on the same creek. William Lesley had a tract of land adjoining Buford's. Most of the public land thereabout was taken up before 1790. James Wardlaw, a nephew of Captain Hugh Wardlaw, was likewise one of the early settlers in the locality.

Names of other pioneer settlers, most of whom came in the first years of the nineteenth century, were William Nevitt, Albert Carpenter, Davis Geer, William Holmes, the noted constable, court caller and church builder; John C. Horton, magistrate and surveyor; Captain John Holland, Edward Vandiver, Strother Kay, James Major, a wealthy man for the time, a mill owner and possessor of a number of slaves; Jesse Kay, Jack Reeves, Erskine, Telford, Todd, McFall, Smith, Anderson, Rice.

One of the wealthiest among those early settlers was John Brown, merchant, planter and mill owner. He was a native of Maryland, and settled first in Abbeville. He moved to Pendleton district, Broadaway neighborhood, in 1817. He settled a little east of Buford's Mill. It is said he came to own nearly all of the land from Rocky river to Neal's creek, and more in other sections. He was the father of Daniel Brown, who was so prominent in the early days of the town of Anderson, and Samuel Brown, the founder of Townville, and grandfather of Colonel J. N. Brown, of Anderson. He and his wife are buried in the Presbyterian graveyard in the town.

Much of the land in Anderson county was granted to soldiers of the Revolution after the General Assembly of South Carolina passed an act in March, 1784, authorizing such recognition of their services. The wording of the old deeds is quaint. In some of them the tracts were described as "being vacant land in Ninety-Six district, above the ancient boundary line," and the grant is made "for being a soldier in the continental line."

Colonel Eliab Moore was a state senator from Ninety-Six district. He was the first colonel of the old Fourth Regiment, famous in the county. His son, Eliab, Jr., was also colonel of the same regiment. It used to muster in the long ago at Varennes and figured in all real big county occasions.

Colonel Eliab Moore, Jr., married Nancy, a daughter of John Brown, sister of Daniel and Samuel Brown.

Silas Risener was neighborhood blacksmith. Dick Kitsinger made spinning wheels. Nearby lived James and Samuel McCoy. They had a sister, Polly, who married a man named Mayfield before the family left Virginia. He deserted her, and she came to her brothers who were too poor to keep her. Destitute, she appealed to Rev. Wm. McGee, pastor of Neal's Creek church. He took her into his home and his family were blessed in the loving service she rendered them. "Granny" Mayfield took entire charge of a baby boy who arrived in the McGee home about the time that she did, his mother being too delicate to do much for her baby. He lived to become the beloved preacher, Reverend Mike McGee, pastor and friend for very many years to a large number of Anderson county people, a man of sterling character, a brave Confederate soldier and withal gentle and lovable as a child.

Other early people of that section were Adam Todd, district surveyor, father of Archibald Todd, who was one of Anderson's early newspaper men; Ephriam Mitchell, a cabinet maker—a few of the pieces of furniture made by him are still in use in the county; Jonathan Lovelace, long forgotten in the locality in which he once lived; Burrell McGee, Michael McGee, Captain Billy Cox. Burrell McGee was the father of G. W. McGee, for many years the popular proprietor of the Belton Hotel. His brother, Michael McGee, was the grandfather of Mr. J. L. McGee, one of Anderson's best known citizens of the present time.

In the fork of Hencoop and Cherokee creeks is a stately old residence built by Chester Kingsley, who came to the section in the early part of the nineteenth century from the far-away northeast. With him were two other men, Martin Trowbridge and a Mr. Barney. They were all cabinet makers. Mr. Kingsley married Miss Broyles, of Calhoun. They both died young and in a short time of each other, leaving two orphan children, one of whom was the well known and popular wife of Mr. Clifton A. Reed, of Anderson. Mr. and Mrs. Kingsley were first buried in the old Gurley burying ground near their home, but afterwards removed to Shady Grove cemetery.

Others were Alfred Carpenter, who married a Miss Brown, and Elijah Major, who married Miss Wardlaw. The Carpenters were the parents of eleven children who all died of tuberculosis just as they were grown up.

Neal's Creek Baptist and Broadaway Presbyterian churches were the places of worship for most of these people.

The old stage road between Knoxville and Augusta ran through this settlement. There was a relay house about every seventeen miles where the horses were changed and passengers could for a few moments stretch their cramped limbs. One such house was in that old neighborhood, kept by Riley John Shirley. Before the coach was in sight the horn could be heard sounding a blast to warn the hostler to have the horses ready; when the great coach and four drew up the harness was loosened in a twinkling and four other horses without any leading took their place at the whippletree. In a very few minutes they were fastened up and the coach was ready to proceed on its way. The coach carried seven passengers, six inside, and one out with the driver. The fare was ten cents a mile. There was a rack for baggage at the back and the mail bag was carried at the driver's feet.

BELTON.

The town of Belton gave its name to the township and it was

named in honor of Judge John Belton O'Neal. He was the first president and an ardent promoter of the C. and G. railroad and Belton is a child of the road, having come into existence as a station and junction of that railway. Miss Josephine Brown, daughter of Dr. George Brown, suggested the name for the new town.

When it became certain that the road would be built and pass through that section of country lots were laid off and sold at public auction. Several acres, including what is now the public square, were given in perpetuity to the railroad company and a school house lot was conveyed in trust to the town for educational purposes. The land belonged to Dr. George Brown, a physician with a large practice all through the section. Soon he and his son-in-law, Major (Witt) Broyles began the erection of a hotel. Mattison Gambrell became its manager. In 1855 the hotel was bought by G. W. McGee, who greatly improved and enlarged it and for many years ran a successful and popular house.

G. W. McGee, G. W. Taylor and A. J. Stringer were among Belton's earliest residents, and they lived in the town until they seemed to become an integral part of it. Among the earliest homes built were those of Colonel William Smith, Alexander Stevens and Thomas Cater. The original country home of Dr. George Brown stood almost where the residence of Carroll Brown is now located.

Tragedy as well as success attended the development of the infant town. One of the hopeful new settlers was Ephriam Mayfield. Trusting in the boom predicted for the place he ventured too deeply in its promised results, and losing everything that he owned in despair killed himself in a woods adjoining his home.

The railroad was completed in 1853, and when in that year the first train, in charge of Conductor Feaster, rolled into the station the whole population, white, black and yellow, turned out to see the train come in. Two months later the branch to Anderson was completed to Broadaway trestle.

The first school in Belton was taught by W. Carroll Brown, a nephew of Dr. George Brown, under whom the young man studied medicine while teaching. Dr. Carroll Brown subsequently became one of the wealthiest and most prominent citizens of the community.

The first Belton boy to be sent to college was Judge W. F. Cox. He attended Furman University. Upon his graduation he taught school eight years. Judge Cox became mayor of Belton when he was only twenty-one years of age, and at the same time was made magistrate through the influence of Colonel J. A. Hoyt. In 1887 he became probate judge in Anderson, which place he had adopted as his home.

Belton has given Anderson a number of valuable citizens. The town is fortunate in the number of cultured and talented people who call it home.

The first church in Belton was the Presbyterian, the old Broadaway church removed to a new location. Among the earlier members of that congregation were George Harvey, William Telford, Thomas Erskine, Thomas Cox, Thomas Anderson, Robert Smith and Green Taylor.

The limits of the new town were one-half mile in every direction from the railroad station. Supervisor Chamberlain, of the C. and G. road, was the first intendant of the town.

Mr. William Holmes gave the land on which the first Baptist Church was built. It stood near the cemetery. Belton feels that it is still indebted to the Reverend Charles Manley who, while president of Furman University, yet found time to be the pastor of the Baptist Church in the little town from 1880 to 1895, and whose influence was all for the highest type of man and womanhood.

Asbury C. Latimer, of Belton, was for many years Congressman from the third district. He was prominent in the Farmers' Alliance movement, and was one of the leaders in establishing a large and prosperous Farmers' Alliance store in Anderson, which was under the able management of Mr. R. S. Hill.

PENDLETON.

Pendleton township of course received its name from the village of Pendleton, which is the oldest and most historic part of Anderson County. Pendleton was old when Anderson was born.

In 1790, a tract of land was purchased from Isaac Lynch, a carpenter who had taken up government lands in the newly opened Cherokee country. His grant is dated July 2, 1787. Lynch was uneducated, and made his mark in place of writing his name when he sold the tract of woods, which was laid off into a town, and named in honor of Judge Pendleton, a noted Virginia jurist of early times.

The commissioners for the town were Andrew Pickens, John Miller, John Wilson, Benjamin Cleveland, William Halbert, Henry Clark, John Moffatt and Robert Anderson, "justices of the peace for Pendleton County," or their successors in office received in trust "all that plantation or tract of land containing 685 acres, to be the same more or less, lying and being in the District of Ninety-Six and county aforesaid, on the branches of Eighteen-Mile Creek, and Three-and-Twenty-Mile Creek," etc., continued in redundant phrases—for the sum of five shillings current money of the said state, to him in hand well and truly paid by the said (commissioners again named), etc., year 1787. Witnesses: Henry Burch and Joseph Box, Thomas Pinckney, esquire, Governor and commander-in-chief in and over the State. Recorded in Grant Book YYYY in the secretary's office in the said state.

The men buying were called "squires" and the men selling "yeomen." The five shillings seems to have been paid at once as a guarantee of the future payment of twenty-five pounds on April 9, 1790. In enumerating what went with the land when sold, the old deed reads: "Gardens, orchards, fences, ways, wells, watercourses, easements, profits, commodities, advantages, emoluments, hereditaments, and appurtenances whatsoever to the said plantation or tract of land." It also says: "Yielding and paying therefor unto the said Isaac Lynch, or his executor or administrator, the rent of one barley corn on the last day of the said term if the same shall be lawfully demanded."

In many old deeds one barley corn, one pepper corn, or one ear of corn was to be paid if demanded at the end of the first year of possession if the property was not fully paid for.

The land thus acquired was laid off into lots and streets, all numbered. The first courthouse of logs was built on a small stream known as "Tanyard Branch." It stood near the site of the culvert of the Blue Ridge railroad, the spot at which the stage road which ran from Pendleton to Old Pickens crossed the track.

The first court held in Pendleton was on April 2, 1790. It was held by Magistrates Robert Anderson, John Wilson and William Halbert; Samuel Lofton was the first sheriff.

Among interesting people who settled in Pendleton, was "Printer John Miller," a man who had worked in the printing office in London which published the famous "Letters of Junius," which created much excitement in England when they appeared. Possibly Mr. Miller could have named the writer, but as he never did the probabilities are that he did not know. If he did know, he would have had a stronger guard over his tongue that any man possesses today, to have kept the secret away off in the wilderness of North America, when the whole world was agog to know who the writer might be.

Mr. Miller published the first newspaper in the up-country, and there was no other in America published so far west at that time. It was first known as *Miller's Weekly Messenger*, later becoming *The Pendleton Messenger*. Mr. Miller's successor as editor was Dr. F. W. Semmes, who sold it in 1849 to Burt & Thompson. They continued to publish it for a number of years.

A later newspaper published in Pendleton was *The Farmer and Planter*, Major George Seaborn is editor and publisher. Mr. Miller was the first clerk of the court for Pendleton District.

Early in its career Pendleton boasted a jockey club; the people of the district were noted for their fine horses, and the annual races were fashionable, and long anticipated events.

Some of the other original settlers in Pendleton were John Harris, William McCaleb, William Steele, Calhouns, Earles, Harrisons, Taliaferros, Lewises, Adamses, Maxwells, Seaborns, Symmeses, Kilpatricks, Rosses, Lattas, Shanklins, Dicksons, Sloans, Smiths, Taylors, VanWycks, Whitners, Reeces, Cherrys, Hunters, Clemsons, Millers, Gilmans, Sittons, and Burtses. Most of these early settlers were emigrants from Virginia, Pennsylvania, and colonies farther north. They were Scotch-Irish for the most part, and with them came churches and schools.

Wealthy families from the coast or "low-country" were also attracted to the mountain regions, as the district was considered then, and while most of them came only for the summer months, many were so pleased with the beautiful hill country that they remained, and their names, too, have become part of the history of this section. Such were the Pinckneys, Elliotts, Bees, Stevenses, Cheveses, Haskels, Turners, Jenningses, Porchers, Norths, Adgers, Campbells, Wilsons, Trescotts, Cuthberts, Gibbeses, Stuarts, and Hugers.

In 1808 the Legislature passed an act authorizing and directing the commissioners appointed to sell lots into which the tract of land purchased from Isaac Lynch had been divided, to turn over all the money in their hands to certain persons therein named for the purpose of establishing a circulating library. By the same authority other moneys and lands were added to the library fund. In 1811 the circulating library was incorporated, and authority was given to the corporation to buy and sell land, and all the remainder of the Lynch tract unsold was by said act vested in the said corporation. The circulating library continued in operation until 1825, when by act of the Legislature the library was incorporated as the Pendleton Male Academy.

In 1815 the men of Pendleton organized a Farmers' Society, which is still in existence. There were few such societies prior to the one in Pendleton. Pennsylvania had one, so did Charleston and Georgetown. Pendleton is justly proud of this ancient and honorable institution. The original officers of the society were James

C. Griffith, president; Josiah Gailliard, vice-president; Robert Anderson, secretary and treasurer; Joseph V. Shanklin, corresponding secretary, and the list of members contains the names of all of the prominent men of the section.

In 1828 the Farmers' Society bought the old courthouse and the new one which had been commenced when the district was divided into Anderson and Pickens. With the material of the old one they completed the new building, which still stands in the center of the business square, and is still the Farmers' Hall. In 1830 the Society had as its president John C. Calhoun. Colonel Clemson, his son-in-law, also served the Society as its president. While Fort Hill, Mr. Calhoun's plantation, was just outside of the limits of Anderson district, he may yet be considered one of the county men, as his law office was in Pendleton and he transacted most of his business in that town.

No clanging iron tongue from belfry heights marks time for ancient Pendleton. Only the noiseless shadow cast by the pointer of a sundial tells how the hours are flying; just as it has told the same story to generations of Pendleton people, who, like shadows themselves, have passed across the village life and disappeared forever. The sundial was the gift of Colonel Huger long ago when Pendleton was young.

The Dickinson Hotel, which may be still standing—it certainly was a very few years ago—is over one hundred years old. There are, or were, two cedars standing in its yard around which tradition has woven a love story. It was said that long ago handsome young Dr. Cater fell in love with pretty Miss Postelle, who lived at the fine hotel. Laughingly one day Miss Postelle planted two young cedar trees, naming them for Dr. Cater and herself; if they lived their sponsor would unite in the holy bonds of matrimony with the waiting doctor; if the trees died—why, she might not. The cedars flourished like their prototypes of Lebanon and have for many years outlived the laughing girl who planted them. The name of one of Anderson's greatly respected citizens tells the rest of their story. They were the grand, or possibly the great-grandparents of Mr. Postelle Cater.

In later years there was a popular hotel in Pendleton known as "The Old Tom Cherry Hotel." In its long room the young people danced and gave charades and tableaux, and frolicked as young people always have and will. A popular landlord of one of Pendleton's hotels was "Mine Host Billy Hubbard." The landlord of those old hostelries was always an important figure in the social life of the town.

HISTORY OF ANDERSON COUNTY

The natural beauties of Pendleton so impressed a visiting Englishman, Lord Lother, that he built a house on the highest point in the town, intending to return often to the pretty little village hidden among the South Carolina foot-hills. The house is now known as "The Trescott Place."

In 1822 Samuel Cherry, Enoch B. Benson and Joseph Shanklin were appointed street commissioners for Pendleton. Ordinarily every male citizen was liable for road work, but later those who preferred might pay 50 cents for each day he was expected to work, which was fixed at twelve days a year. The commissioners were responsible for the roads for one mile beyond the town, and for the bridge over Eighteen-Mile Creek. They were elected by those liable for road work.

In 1798 Pendleton district was allowed representation in the Legislature. In 1811 an act was passed establishing free schools in every district, a certain number of school commissioners to be elected in every district. Pendleton district had thirteen, an unusually large number.

The inhabitants of Old Pendleton were a reading and cultured people. In 1818, one William Anderson advertises some of the volumes in his book store. First is a long list of medical books. Then an equally long list of theological books. Only eight historical volumes, and among them is included a work on natural history. But then follows a long list of miscellanies showing what the people read. It begins with Shakespeare, includes Blackstone's Commentaries, Homer's Iliad, Cook's Voyages, several of Scott's novels, and the works of several standard English poets, several biographies and books of letters.

There was a Bible Society in Pendleton very early, Joseph Grisham was its secretary.

In one issue of the paper the munificent sum of six cents is offered as a reward for a runaway apprentice, a boy named William Heaton; the man offering the reward was William Gaston.

John S. Lewis, postmaster in Pendleton in 1818, advertises a long list of uncalled for letters, which he says will be kept for three months, then sent to the dead letter office. William Cleveland advertises a new flat at his ferry on the Tugaloo River, 14 feet long, between 9 and 10 feet wide, "the nearest and best way from Pendleton courthouse to Carnesville, Ga." Sounds quite modern. James Chapman advertises a wool-carding machine just brought from Pennsylvania, which he has set up to card wool into rolls for spinning or for hatters.

In 1902 Dr. W. K. Sharpe, at Pendleton, owned a trunk which

he bought at a sale when he was a boy. It was shallow and oval, topped with raw-hide, made of poplar and native pine three-fourths of an inch in thickness. W. A. Dickson, of Townville, owned just such a trunk, except that his has hair on the rawhide cover. Both trunks were lined with copies of the old *Pendleton Messenger*. The date of the paper in Dr. Sharpe's trunk was 18(?). It contained an advertisement of a lottery held at Pendleton for the relief of sufferers at Pickensville, which appears to have had a disastrous fire. The lottery was authorized by the Legislature, and John T. Lewis, Joseph Grisham, Robert Anderson, Jr., James C. Griffin and Walter Adair were named as commissioners to manage it. These two trunks seem to have been made at or near Pendleton, but there is neither record or tradition of a trunk manufacturer or maker in the district.

Some early lawyers were Pickens & Farrar, Warren R. Davis, Lewis Taylor & Harrison, Taney & Whitfield, B. J. Earle, George W. Earle, Bowie & Bowie, Robert Anderson, Jr., Yancey & Shanklin, Saxon & Trimmier, S. J. Earle, Z. Taliaferro Choice, Earle & Whitner, Thompson Tillinghast, Martin, and George McDuffie, John C. Calhoun.

The justices of the peace seem to have been paternal sort of officers. In the early days one John Ward made complaint that Samuel Lofton, through his son, James Lofton, had failed to deliver to the plaintiff three wands of tobacco entrusted to the said Lofton by Ward's mother. The complaint was very bitter and the justices before whom it was made were Andrew Pickens, Samuel Taylor, John Hallum and John Miller. They announced their decision thus: "We do award and declare the said charge to be frivolous, and that as the accusation was made publicly, the reparation should be also. We therefore award that said Ward do publicly acknowledge that he is sorry he made such a complaint against his neighbor, Mr. Lofton." Signed with the names of the peace commissioners and the seal.

The acknowledgment was made as follows: "State of South Carolina, Pendleton County. I, John Ward, of the said county, having brought malicious and unjust charge against James Lofton, youngest son of Samuel Lofton, Esq., sheriff of the county, a charge of such an abhorrent nature as should not even be mentioned among men, do confess myself to have been deceived, and am most heartily sorry for my conduct, and do promise for the future to conduct myself agreeable to good neighborhood, and a good member of society, and do hereby acknowledge the forbearance, tenderness and leniency of Mr. Lofton in pardoning my offense." Signed by J. Miller for Ward, who made his mark. One suspects that he could not read, either, and that the document he signed was not read to him exactly as it appears to us.

In the streets of Pendleton indignant citizens first kindled a bonfire of abolitionary literature sent into the state.

In Pendleton's soil sleep three admirals of the United States Navy, Thomas Holdup Stevens, William B. Shubrick, and Cornelius K. Stribbling. The latter, when a boy, walked all the way from Pendleton to Charleston to get a job. He got it. He was serving as midshipman on the Macedonian when that vessel fought with and captured an Algerian frigate.

William B. Shubrick was a lieutenant on the Constitution when she captured the Cyane and the Levant. He was Commodore during the Mexican War, and commanded the Pacific Squadron. He landed and captured the fortified town of Mazattan from a superior force, and held it until the end of the war. He attained the rank of rear admiral in 1862.

Rear Admiral Thomas Holdup Stevens was born in Charleston in 1795. Left an orphan, he was adopted by General Daniel E. Stevens, and was given his name. As lieutenant he commanded the Trippe in Commodore Perry's Squadron, and took part in the battle of Lake Erie in 1813. For gallant conduct on that occasion he was presented by Congress with a silver medal, and by the citizens of Charleston with a sword.

In Pendleton is buried Alexander Worley, captain in the Confederate Navy. There also sleep General Clement H. Stevens and General Barnard E. Bee.

In 1897 Pendleton held the ninety-seventh annual ball of the Pendleton Dancing Club. An account of the fancy costumes worn appeared in the newspapers of the time. In *The Pendleton Messenger* of 1816 appears the item: "The Pendleton Dancing Club celebrated the advent of Spring with a merry meeting of the young people."

The last man to represent old Pendleton district in the State Senate was Dr. Alexander Evans. Anderson District's first senator was General J. W. Harrison.

When the district was divided there was a new courthouse in process of construction. The contractor was to be paid for any damages he might suffer from the loss of his contract. The remainder of the money appropriated for a court house was to be divided between Anderson and Pickens. The records were to remain in Pendleton until the new courthouses were finished, and court held there until further notice. Public officers living in either of the new districts were to serve out their terms in the district in which they lived.

There were some famous men who practiced law at the old Pendleton bar. Some of them were John C. Calhoun, George McDuffie, Zachariah Taliaferro, Warren R. Davis, Joseph Taylor, Armstead and Francis Burt; the latter was appointed by President Pierce governor of the territory of Nebraska.

All of the people who lived in the old district were not good. There was at least one bad man, a desperado whose name was Corbin. He had committed various crimes, among which were several murders, and had successfully defied arrest and trial. The judge knowing his desperate character had issued a bench warrant for his arrest, and placed it in the hands of the sheriff, with orders to take him at all hazards. E. B. Benson was sheriff at that time, and he learned that Corbin was expected at a certain house on a specified night. Summoning a posse the sheriff went after his man. The men were mounted, and they had to pass through a set of draw bars. All had gone safely through, and the house was almost surrounded, only one man was to pass through, but his horse stumbled, and the criminal heard and realized what had happened; he sprang out of bed and running out of the back door of the house started on a path towards the spring. He ran into the man stationed there and was shot down. The sheriff immediately gathered in his men and made them swear that nothing should ever induce them to reveal who it was that fired the shot that killed the man. This they did; all were arrested and tried. They were defended by Mr. Armstead Burt, and triumphantly acquitted. Mr. D. K. Hamilton was one of the posse that night, and many years afterward his grandson, D. H. Russell, said to him: "All of the men who took part in the affair are dead but you; it can hurt no one now for you to tell who fired that shot, and I should like to know." To which the old man replied: "You'll never know," and the secret died with him.

Among the interesting people who have lived in Pendleton at least during the summer, have been Charles Cotesworth Pinckney, to whom has been attributed the reply to the representative of the French government in negotiation over Algerian matters: "Millions for defense, but not one cent for tribute." Mr. Pinckney said that he never made the remark, but nevertheless it goes down in history as his, and if he did not say it, he ought to have done so. It is much more poetic and forceful than what he always said he did say: "Not one cent, sir, not one cent."

In Pendleton, too, was the summer home of Mr. Huger, who

rescued LaFayette from imprisonment. He it was who gave to Pendleton its ancient timepiece.

And now comes the distressing statement from General Pershing that when he landed in France he made absolutely no remark to the ghost of LaFayette. If he did not inform that august spook that the Americans had come several million strong to pay him for going to the American colonies and helping Washington fight, why he ought to have said it, and so somebody kindly said it for him, and we'll go on teaching our children for countless years that Pershing touchingly remarked: "LaFayette, we're here!"

FORK.

Fork Township lies between the Tugaloo and Seneca rivers. Its boundaries form an almost equilateral triangle about eleven miles in length, with Andersonville at its apex, lying in the fork of the rivers; the name of the section was inevitable, and antedated the subdivisions of the county into townships by many years.

The first settlers in the region were David Sloan and his wife, Susan. The young couple came to try their future in the newly opened highlands of South Carolina. They pitched their tent on the west bank of the Seneca river, at a point subsequently known as "Sloan's Ferry." The exact date of their coming is unknown, but they obtained a grant of 1,500 acres of land from the State, and one chimney of their old home bore the date 1794. It is safe to conjecture that they must have been there ten years before becoming able to erect a dwelling that should be occupied as long as the family held together. It was standing in 1896, at that time the property of J. S. Fowler.

They acquired what was wealth for that time, and tradition represents Mr. Sloan as very kind and lovable, and Mrs. Sloan, who was Susan Major, as a woman of unusual intellect. They brought up a large family of sons and daughters. Their eldest son, William, died in 1804, at twenty-one years of age. The second child was a daughter, Elizabeth, who married Jesse Stribbling. The next were twins, David, who married Nancy Trimmier, and Susan, who married Robert Bruce. The next daughter, Nancy, married Joseph Taylor. Next came a little girl named Mary, who lived not quite a year. Rebecca, the next, married Dr. Joseph Berry Earle; Benjamin Franklin married Eliza C. Earle; Thomas M. married Nancy Blassingame; Catherine married J. P. Benson; J. Mattison married Rebecca Linton. The children and grandchildren of these sons and daughters married into families bearing the most respected names of the section. Their descendants are numbered among the best people of the county.

Some of the other early settlers in the section bore the names Farrow, Anderson, Earle, Holland, Guest and Maxwell.

Colonel Farrow, a soldier of the Revolution, lived in what was known as "The Red House." He was living there in 1793. The house was built on a high hill, had a piazza running all around it, and was painted a bright red. The gay dwelling was the scene of many youthful frolics in old times, as Colonel Farrow loved company, and was a violinist of no mean ability. He was a man of ample means, and his home was a favorite gathering place for the young people.

About 1790 John Anderson, of Maryland, came to South Carolina with his family and settled on Seneca river about a mile below Sloan's ferry. He had been educated for the Presbyterian ministry, in what is now called the Associate Reform Presbyterian church, then known as "Seceders;" but he abandoned the idea before obtaining a license. The Dickson family of the Fork are descendants of John Anderson.

William Guest settled in that part of the Fork lying between Big Beaver Dam creek and Tugaloo river known as Cracker's Neck. He was a justice of the peace. The Hollands also settled in Cracker's Neck. They were Virginians. A father and several sons determined to make a home in the newly opened part of the country. They traveled about looking for a spot that appealed to their fancy and one night pitched their tent in that locality; when morning came and they looked about them, they decided that there could be no more pleasing part of the world, and there they remained. Theirs became a large family connection in the community.

Townville is the metropolis of the Fork. There is a tradition that gold is to be found in its soil. The place was founded by Mr. Samuel Brown, and its original name was Brownville, but when a postoffice was to be established there, it was found that South Carolina already had one of that name, so the postal authorities called the new office and its locality Townville.

One of the original settlers in the county was Matthew Dickson, a Scotch-Irishman from County Tyrone, Ireland, who, in 1750, emigrated to Pennsylvania. With the great wave of Scotch-Irish people who swept from Pennsylvania into North and South Carolina and Georgia just before the Revolutionary War came Mr. Dickson. He went first into what was then Camden district, and lived just about where the town of York now stands. He bore an active part in the patriot army during the Revolution, and a few years later emigrated to Pendleton district and bought land on Six-

and-Twenty creek. Matthew, Jr., Walter Carson and James Dickson, sons of the Revolutionary patriot, enlisted in the company formed by Mr. Alexander Moorhead and went to fight Indians under Jackson in Alabama territory. During their absence, while the country was embroiled in its second war with England, Benjamin Franklin Dickson, son of Matthew, Jr., was born. That boy lived to become Captain of Company E, State Reserves, in the War Between the States. His service was along the coast of North and South Carolina. It was said of him by his contemporaries that he knew Macomb's tactics by heart, and that he could handle a company or a battalion with the ease and skill of a West Pointer. Under the old militia regime he commanded a company in the Fork for many years, and was a conspicuous figure at battalion and regimental musters. In 1828 he became a citizen of the Fork, where he spent the rest of his life. He married Miss Matilda J. Gantt, of Anderson county. The only children of this marriage were Reverend J. Walter Dickson, a prominent Methodist minister, long a presiding elder, and Mr. W. A. Dickson, for many years a conspicuous teacher and newspaper correspondent of the Fork.

A Presbyterian church was organized in Townville about 1803. It stood near where the old Mahaffey home is now, and was called Nazareth on the Beaver Dam, to distinguish it from Nazareth in Spartanburg county. In 1877 it was moved into the village. Some of its pastors have been William McWhorter, J. B. Adger, D.D., J. D. Riley, D.D., and T. C. Ligon, who served there many years.

In 1851 a Baptist church was organized in the town. Some of its pastors have been David Simmons, E. L. Sisk, J. R. Earle and J. D. Chapman, as well as others.

The Methodist church was some miles out of the village, though its parsonage was in the place. The Wesleyans had a small church just outside of the town limits.

Townville was incorporated by the Legislature in 1871, but in a few years the charter was suffered to lapse. In 1862 the place suffered a scourge of smallpox, brought by returning soldiers.

Townville furnished the Confederacy with three colonels: J. N. Brown, D. A. Ledbetter and F. E. Harrison; three captains: R. O. Tribble, Samuel Lanford and B. F. Dickson; one major, D. L. Cox.

The echoes of war had not ceased to reverberate when the people of Townville took up the duties of life. As he trudged homeward from Appomattox, Mr. R. O. Tribble secured the services of B. F. Gantt, a fellow soldier, to teach school when he should reach home. Mr. Gantt taught very successfully for six or eight years. In 1872 the people built an academy commensurate with their means, and employed Reverend E. F. Hyde to teach it. Some years later another academy was erected on the Anderson side of the line, and Mr. J. M. Fant taught there for several years.

Broyles is the most thickly settled portion of the township. It has a handsome school building well equipped.

The Farmer family, so well known and highly respected in Anderson, came from the Fork. Boggs is also a Fork name.

In early times Jesse Dobbins moved from Newberry to the Fork section, and soon became a man of property and note in the locality. He acquired a number of slaves, but like many other Southern men, he was not satisfied as to the moral right to own them, and disposing of his slaves, invested the proceeds in land. Mr. Dobbins was a Universalist in religion. In that early day there were quite a number of that faith who became residents of Anderson county. His wife was Miss Mary Mills. The Dickson and McCarley families are descendants of Jesse Dobbins.

The Fork has furnished Anderson county and city with some of her best citizens.

WILLIAMSTON.

In this, as in some other cases, the township took its name from the largest and most important town within its borders.

Back in the third decade of the nineteenth century there lived in the locality, which has since become the town of Williamston, a wealthy planter whose name was West Allen Williams. He owned several thousand acres of fine fertile land, and there has grown up a pretty tale about how he found on his possessions the wonderful spring of mineral water which has made Williamston famous. The story runs that one autumn day Mr. Williams mounted his horse, intending to ride over his land and make plans for plantation work. But much of Mr. Williams' possessions was primeval forest and his ride was long and hard. Becoming weary, the horseman dismounted in a cool, dark, quiet spot to rest. Tying the animal, he threw himself upon the brown earth and lying gazing up to the patches of blue sky discernible between the leaves of the trees, lazily watching the birds flit from bough to bough, he fell asleep and dreamed —or perhaps he had a vision.

At his feet purred a silver stream, which gushed in crystal cascades from the ground just beyond him. It spread around until its waters covered much of the surrounding land. Hundreds of pale and feeble persons passed before his wondering eyes. They stooped and drank from the gushing spring, and lo! they were restored to health and strength. The waters were magic.

The vision passed, or the sleeper awakened. Behold! the ground about him was wet. Urged by the spell of his dream, he pushed aside the tangled growth and plunged into the heart of the dense woods. There before him gushed the crystal waters of his vision; held back, it is true, by debris and tangled weeds, but still flowing through.

Another story, not so picturesque, is that a woodcutter named Zahra Kelly found the spring and often drank from it. He is said to have told Mr. Williams of its existence. However, he found it, he tried it and proved its qualities.

In a short time the spring became famous in the region. People came from miles away to try its waters. Tents were pitched about the surrounding woods, then huts began to supplant the tents, and later cottages succeeded the huts. Finally three men from Abbeville bought the property and put up a mammoth hotel. Its cost was a hundred thousand dollars—no mean sum even in this day of inflated prices—and an enormous sum in the thirties; it was the largest building in the State, and became known as "The Mammoth Hotel." It was equipped with all of the conveniences known at the time, even gas, and its rooms were always full.

There gayety, mirth, fashion and frivolity as well as health-seeking held full sway. For years it was popular and remunerative. However, in 1860, the big wooden hotel was burned and its glories became but a memory.

On the same site, using much of the brick which had formed the chimneys and pillars of the former building, a new all-brick structure took its place, much smaller, however, than its predecessor. But war had laid its cruel embargo on all the pleasure or health resorts, and no longer was the little village which had grown up around the spring thronged with visitors. Its men enlisted in the army and its women lived the war-time existence of their sisters throughout the South.

In laying off his projected town, Mr. Williams had apportioned two good lots for schools, one for boys and one for girls. The high school for boys was from the first successful. The girls' school, however, languished and soon died. Not until Dr. Lander opened his college in 1871 did Williamston have a satisfactory school for its daughters.

With such a start as a wonderful health resort, fashionable hotel, two good schools and flourishing churches, a town was obliged to develop along good lines. Williamston has done that very thing.

Among its prominent citizens have been G. W. Sullivan, a man of means, who has filled many public offices in the county; Reverend John Lander, missionary to Brazil; James P. Gossett, mill man and financier; Dr. Ben Brown, beloved physician; the Hortons, the Crymes family, the Prince family, the Ackers, and numerous others.

The war furnished many men who were brave and deserve to be remembered, and in the community have been some brave women who have "carried on" amid difficulties; such people are to be found throughout the county and the State, but Williamston township has a girl who ranks with the bravest. She was only twelve years old in 1915 when Eva Dessie Hand rescued three smaller sisters from death by fire. The country home caught and this girl was the first to be awakened by the smoke and smell. She ran downstairs and aroused her parents, who rushed out of the house; then she returned to the second floor and awakened three little sisters whom she handed down from a piazza roof to her father, who caught them; after that the brave child started across a hall to wake a sleeping brother, but the flames beat her back. Again and again she struggled to reach the boy, but was finally compelled to jump to safety without having been able to rescue the boy.

Dr. W. B. Milwee married in 1848 and built the first house in what became the town of Williamston. It is the house long known as the "Dr. W. W. Wilson Place." It has been much repainted and rearranged, but it is the same house erected when young Dr. Milwee married a daughter of " 'Squire Williams."

Dr. Milwee is authority for the statement that on the day that his father-in-law deeded the spring park property to the public, his three sons-in-law offered him $5,000 for the land, and that he refused to sell it, saying that he intended the mineral spring to be a benefit to the public forever.

MARTIN.

Martin Township embraced the old Ebenezer Church neighborhood. From very early days a school has been located there. Varennes Presbyterian Church and Bethel Baptist Church are within a short radius from Ebenezer, all of long standing.

In this instance a man was honored in the naming of the township, and the fact of his name being chosen testifies to his popularity. He was Colonel John Martin, born September 1, 1793, on the place where he lived and died, about half a mile from Ebenezer church. His father was Roderick Martin, one of the pioneer settlers of Varennes section. His mother was a widow, Mrs. Taylor, when she and Mr. Martin married. John was their only child.

When only nineteen years old John Martin volunteered in Captain Thompson's company, made up of Pendleton and Abbeville district men, and served through the War of 1812. At the time of his death in 1880 he was probably the last survivor of that company. As long as he lived he drew a pension for service in that war.

John Martin married Cynthia Rutledge, daughter of another pioneer settler. To this couple were born sixteen children, eleven of whom lived to be grown—eight sons and three daughters.

Mr. Martin's early experience in war gave him a taste for the military, and in early life he became captain of "Bear Creek Company," and later colonel in the Fourth Regiment of South Carolina Militia. In 1832 he represented the county in the Legislature. In 1836 he became ordinary of the county. In 1846 he was elected sheriff, and again in 1854 he held that office.

He was a delegate from Anderson county to the State Convention which passed the Ordinance of Secession. When in 1860 volunteers were called for, he enlisted in Captain Anderson's company and went with them to Columbia, taking with him his old rifle, which he called "Old Friday." The authorities appreciated his patriotism, but decided that he was too old for service, being at that time 67 years of age. It was with difficulty that the old man was persuaded to return home and leave the fighting to younger men.

Colonel Martin was a great sportsman and hunted often, especially wild turkeys, which were abundant in his day.

Although a man of fine moral character, for many years he belonged to no church, and was on that account a source of grievance to the preachers of the locality. At old Ebenezer the earnest and consecrated Mr. Hodges was pastor. After long thought on the subject, and probably heart-felt prayer, the good man decided that it was his duty to go and talk to Colonel Martin about his soul, and urge upon him the propriety of becoming a church member. One of Colonel Martin's customs was to invite visitors to walk down to his mother's spring, a cool and beautiful spot. It was there that Mr. Hodges broached the subject near his heart. The minister put all of his eloquence into his fervid speech. After his impassioned talk he paused for a reply. Colonel Martin was silent a few minutes, then in a most interested manner said: "Mr. Hodges, do you see that tall pine over there? Well, sir, on that tree I once killed the biggest turkey gobbler you ever saw."

That was the end of Mr. Hodges' attempts to convert "the old sinner." However, whether in consequence of Mr. Hodges' talk or for some other reason, Colonel Martin later became a member of Ebenezer church.

His kindness of heart and sympathy led him on several occasions to give his signature as security for friends, and the result was the usual one—he had the money to pay. When he was sheriff he was sometimes known to pay unfortunate people out of debt, rather than sell them out of home. In spite of, or perhaps on account of, these kindly losses, Colonel Martin became for his time and section a man of wealth.

Another of the early settlers in the locality was Elijah Brown, also a man of means, and one who believed in education. He belonged to Ebenezer church and was a prominent supporter of the adjacent school.

In Martin Township before the War Between the States there was a young couple who fell in love with each other and planned to be married. They were Newton W. Parker and Miss Kay, daughter of Francis Marion Kay, a faithful member of Ebenezer church. But war was declared and in place of getting married young Parker went with the army to Virginia. In 1864 the young soldier got a furlough and came home on a visit, and while there married his sweetheart. The couple lived to be very old; they not only reached their golden wedding day, but passed it by ten or more years. Mr. Parker had two sisters who lived to be over ninety years old.

The family of Mr. J. F. Clinkscales, of Anderson, belonged to Martin township.

BRUSHY CREEK.

Called for the picturesque little stream which bears the same sylvan name, probably bestowed upon it by the earliest settlers in the section. The man to whom was given the contract for building Anderson's first courthouse lived in that part of the county. His name was Denham. He sublet the contract to Mr. Robert Wilson, of Greenville. It is said that some of the material for the building was hauled from that neighborhood.

The old Pearl Spring School was located in what later became Brushy Creek Township. The Anderson side of Piedmont lies in the same township.

A prominent family of the section is that of Wigginton. Mr. John E. Wigginton is one of Anderson's best newspaper men. He began his journalistic career when a boy with the publication of *The Brushy Creek Banner*, of which he was sole proprietor, editor, reporter, printer and publisher.

A resident of Brushy Creek of the long ago was James F. Wyatt, who was at one time colonel of the old Fourth South Carolina Regiment. He lived first near Belton, but moved later to Brushy Creek. His son, Redman Foster Wyatt, was one of Anderson's early newspaper men, having come to the town when he was sixteen years old

HISTORY OF ANDERSON COUNTY

with Mr. Reed, for whom he worked on *The Highland Sentinel*. Later he and Mr. Todd were editors and proprietors of *The Gazette*.

Somewhere in Brushy Creek soil, in a lonely and forgotten graveyard, lies the ashes of a Revolutionary heroine. Her grave is marked, "Here lies the body of Mary Smith, a heroine of the American Revolution, who died August 17, 1829, age 92 years." Surely her blood runs in some of the people of the township who can tell what particular heroic thing she did in that long past time.

The Mountain Springs School in Brushy Creek Township was organized before the War Between the States. J. N. Bramlett was teaching there when the war broke out, and many of his students enlisted in the army. There were some fine teachers at that school who left a great reputation in the locality. Among them are Joshua Smith, Strawther Reeves and Major Wales Smith.

Some years ago a "home coming day" was organized to be an annual event at Mountain Springs School. The yearly reunion has been an event eagerly anticipated and long remembered by those who attend. Among the men who have served the organization as officers were President Charles Smith, Vice-President Dr. W. A. Tripp, Secretary John E. Wigginton.

The first jury of women to serve in the state was in Brushy Creek Township. A negro was brought before Magistrate H. A. Foster on a charge of petit larceny. He demanded a trial by jury and the magistrate ordered his constable to go out and summon a jury. Judge Foster was amazed when the constable returned with a jury of women. They were Mrs. Lula Ellison, Mrs. Jeff White, Mrs. G. N. White, Mrs. H. R. Tripp, Miss Ethel Foster and Miss Nannie Foster.

The judge, however, proceeded with the trial and later expressed himself as greatly pleased with the attention shown by the women, their dignity, and the order and dispatch with which they returned a verdict of guilty.

Among other talented citizens, Brushy Creek has a poet whose verse is graceful and pleasing. He is S. A. Long, one of the many natives of the section who have proved that her people are educated and cultured.

Rock Mills.

So called from the settlement started there by Lewis and Maverick and the great merchant mill with its solid rock foundations which they erected at the place. Rock Mills is one of "the dead towns" of the county. It was at one time a flourishing little village. It was there that the well known Lesser merchants, of Anderson, started their career in the Piedmont.

Miss Dora Geisberg, for years the popular woman merchant of the town, is a granddaughter of the original Lesser who kept a store at Rock Mills.

GARVIN.

Named for Thomas Garvin, prominent in Pendleton district when the division was made, a soldier of the Revolution and one of the commissioners appointed to divide the district, the other two being Colonel Kilpatrick and Major Lewis. It lies close to Pendleton and many of the men who were active in the early days of the district lived in what has become Garvin Township.

When Robert Anderson settled on Three-and-Twenty Creek he became one of the first residents. Later there came to the same section Job and Benjamin Smith, Alexander Oliver, Peter McMahon and Thomas Hamilton.

The original owner of the Fort Hill Farm, afterwards the property of John C. Calhoun, was Reverend W. M. McElhany, who was an early pastor of Mt. Carmel Church, which was organized by the first residents of the locality.

Probably the most interesting part of the township from an historical point is Slabtown, a village lying on the public road between Pendleton and Greenville. It received its name from the slabs used in the construction of several of its buildings. The first structure erected was a mill on Six-and-Twenty Creek, built by a man named Rankin. It was long known as "Rankin's Mill." For more than a hundred years it and much of the surrounding property remained in the Rankin family.

Across the creek was erected a store built of slabs from the saw mill, as were a number of cattle sheds and other places for rough use or storage. It is said that the name was given by a party of emigrants who, when passing through, were struck with the building material so much in evidence, and remarked, "We surely have reached Slabtown." The bridge over the creek is known as "Slab Bridge." Since the War Between the States there is only one store there where two flourished before. It was long owned by T. S. and J. M. Glenn; nearby is a steam saw and grist mill.

In the early days of the nineteenth century 'Squire McCann ran a store there, and not far away was his home. As his second wife, 'Squire McCann married Miss Hamilton; their daughter married Christopher Orr. They had but one other child, a son who succeeded his father.

Ezekiel Long, Sr., and his grandson, Ezekiel Long, Jr., were for years the owners and occupants of the old McCann place.

Some of the other early settlers of the section were named Pickens, Pickle, Mullikens, Wilson, and others.

The first merchants were Ex-Sheriff James McKinney and George Rankin and William McMurray; the last two formed a partnership.

The first buggy ever seen at Slabtown was owned by Mr. Maverick and was a great curiosity. Parts of that buggy are said to have been used in 1896, and maybe later, by Warren Knight. The stage coach from Pendleton to Greenville passed through the place.

Thalian Academy was its crowning glory.

Some of the people of Garvin Township of the present day have been the Richardson family, the two brothers, Matthias and Newton, who were for many years men of influence and importance in the community; the son of Matthias, who served long and faithfully in the United States Navy, Louis Richardson, and attained the rank of captain; the Duckworths, especially Dr. J. G. Duckworth, who was the loved and trusted physician for a large section of the county, and his widow, Mrs. Nancy Duckworth, who for many years has been a leader in all of the good works of her community, a Sunday-school teacher whose lessons will live long after she has passed away, an organizer of splendid work done by the women of the section. Mrs. Duckworth's beautiful home is almost a clubhouse for the community; there women hold important meetings and plan improvements for Lebanon, and always loyally assisted by Mrs. Duckworth, the work is carried through to a successful finish.

Some of the merchants of Garvin in 1849 were John and James Smith, Thomas McCann and Joshua Smith.

HONEA PATH.

Honea Path was called from the flourishing and progressive town of that name within its borders. The town has been so called since the memory of man runneth not to the contrary and its origin is lost in the mists of antiquity, for the town of Honea Path does not owe its existence to the railroad which passes through it as do so many of the stations on its route. There has been a settlement there since white people began to come into the section and built their homes near each other for mutual protection.

Even thirty years ago the name of the place was distinctly called Honey Path. It is only of late years that the pronunciation has been according to the spelling, and the probabilities are that a confused notion arose that the village was named for the family of Honea. But it has been said that the family did not move to the section until long after the name Honey Path was established.

Naturally many legends grew up around the picturesque and unusual name. Most of them show in their structure, however, that they were suggested by the name and not the cause of it.

The most plausible meaning has been given by Dr. J. W. Daniel, the distinguished antiquarian and student of Indian lore. He says that it was a custom among the Cherokees to make a statement emphatic by repeating it. The town of Honea Path stands on the old Cherokee trail, or their great road from Keowee to Charleston. In their language the word for path is pronounced very much as is the word honey; consequently, in speaking of their great road, they would naturally say "Path Path," meaning the large or important path or trail, and that as they learned to talk with the English they would sometimes use one word and sometimes the other, honea and path, both meaning the same thing, path path or honea honea finally becoming Honea Path.

As Dr. Daniel is a scholar and has made a study of Indian languages, it seems fitting that those of us who are not scholars and know nothing of the subject, should be wise enough to accept his solution.

Honea Path has furnished Anderson with some of her best citizens, among whom Mr. J. A. Brock holds an honored place.

Among the early citizens of the section were David Green, born in Antrim, Ireland, came to America in 1779. Landing in Charleston, he drifted up-state and settled first in Newberry, but remained there only a few years. Suffering from malaria, he emigrated into what was then Pendleton district and made his home on Corny Creek, about three-quarters of a mile west of where the village of Honea Path grew up.

Henry Purdy built on the same creek, though quite a distance away. Jervey Petty and Nimrod Smith were other settlers who soon followed, also John Cullins. William Davis lived on Broadmouth Creek. He was the father of twins whom he named before he had ever seen them. They were born while he was absent from home, having gone to Hamburg to sell his farm produce. On his return he met a neighbor going on the same errand who informed him of the arrival of the two boys at his home. He immediately called them Moses and Aaron. What Mrs. Davis thought of the names history sayeth not. If she objected it had no effect, for so her sons were known through life.

The little settlement remained but a tiny village until the building of the Greenville and Columbia railroad in 1853. It passed through the place and gave it an impetus toward larger life.

Others of the early settlers were Obediah Shirley, Ansel Massay, O. M. Gent; the locality where he settled became known as "Gentsville." "Old Uncle Neddy Hull" lived where "Due West Corner," now Due West, grew up, and owned the land on which the town is built. He and David Green married sisters, Peggy and Polly McCormick.

Mills were very important and centers of industry in the pioneer days. There was one where Gambrell's Bridge used to be on Saluda River. One was built by "Uncle Dicky Smith" on Broadmouth where Davis and Bigby long had one. Mr. Smith sold it to Isaac Clement, who built it over in 1835, and years ago boys playing about the old mill were familiar with a stone in the formation wall bearing the inscription, "B & I C 1835," Benjamin and Isaac Clement.

In 1869 Davis and Bigby built a mill on the site of the old one.

One mill could grind for half a district in those early times. Little wheat was planted in 1792 and what was made was threshed out with a flail. Five or six bushels was a day's work for one hand to clear. Some people constructed rude machines for cleaning away the chaff. Most people "made wind" by using a sheet or large cloth handled by two persons, a third holding the grain in a basket above his head and letting it fall slowly on a cloth spread on the ground. The swaying sheet fanned it clear as it fell. Others had horses "tread out" the grain.

The first seed corn that old David Green got, he planted in drills like wheat, expecting to have to reap it. He was accustomed to reaping his wheat with a hand scythe and tying it up. He thought that corn would grow on top of the tassel, and was greatly astonished when he made no corn at all.

Mr. Green was the first settler in the locality and he outlived all who came later among his generation. He died in 1855, one hundred years old.

CORNER.

Corner Township took its name from the old current appellation of the section as "Dark Corner." Why the epithet dark, is one of the unanswered conundrums of the county history. Many stories were made to fit the name; one of the most probable is that it was bestowed by Colonel Elias Earle when he was told about an experience of his friend, Squire Andrew Liddell.

Squire Liddell was tax collector for that part of Pendleton district which afterwards became Dark Corner. On his rounds as tax assessor he rode up to a very humble log cabin. Its furniture consisted of a straw bed, three home-made stools and a broken oven. The man of the house was not at home and the visitor spoke with his wife. She asked him what he wanted with her "ole man." He replied: "I only want to ask him how much he is worth."

"Well, who sent you here to fin' out what we's wuth?" she indignantly demanded.

"Congress," replied Mr. Liddell.

"Whar do Mr. Congress live?"

Colonel Earle, member of Congress, was living at Centerville, so Mr. Liddell replied: "He lives at Centerville."

She told him that her "ole man" would go up there and "whup" Mr. Congress for meddling in their affairs. Consequently when the assessor saw Colonel Earle he laughingly warned him to beware of the indignant old man who was coming to whip him. Colonel Earle was greatly amused and said that must be the dark corner of the district. He said he would dodge the whipping by denying the name of "Congress."

Corner township was settled by people bearing the names of Tucker, Thompkins, Jennings, Blackwell, Pickett and Searl. They organized a beat company and Tucker kept a bar room. A story is told of him which is also offered as an explanation of the epithet dark in connection with the name of the locality.

The court house was at Ninety-Six and there was a small newspaper published there. On one occasion old Mr. Louden Tucker was at Ninety-Six attending court. He saw one of the newspapers and it pleased him so much that he bought a dozen or more copies to distribute among his neighbors, thinking they would be as greatly pleased with it as he was, and that several of them would subscribe for it. It was a weekly publication and Mr. Tucker's idea was to get as many subscribers as possible in order that there would be a number of them to take turns in going after the paper, which was the only way of getting it at that time, and if there were a large number interested in receiving it, the turns would come seldom, occasioning little loss of time to any one man. But to his disgust not a single member of the company would take the paper. Failing to persuade them he angrily exclaimed: "How long shall we live in this damned dark age and day!" and the name stuck to the place. It is said that one old man of the community named McKinney remarked that the Dark Corner was good enough for him and would remain so if people would only keep out books, newspapers and foreigners.

However, it was at Dark Corner that one of the finest of the early schools flourished—Moffattsville Academy.

Iva is a flourishing town in Corner Township. It sprang up as a station on the Savannah Valley railroad, and was first called

Cook's Station as the charming country home of Dr. A. G. Cook was the most prominent feature of the landscape. But Dr. Cook preferred to have his little daughter honored rather than himself, so at his request the place received the name of Iva. Miss Iva Cook in later years became Mrs. David Bryson.

SAVANNAH.

Named from the great river which is its boundary. It was in that section that the old Earle home "Evergreen" was located with its enlightened community and its busy enterprises.

In that township now lives Mr. Paul Earle. His beautiful home is as hospitable as was the old Evergreen place of his ancestors, and his cultured wife wields a wide influence in the community. Mr. Earle's remarkable marksmanship has made his name and his home known very widely. He has numerous beautiful trophies of his skill.

The old Evergreen home of Mr. Samuel G. Earle was in Savannah township, and the old Shockley Ferry Church was also located in what was afterwards laid off into that township. The preachers of long ago—James Burriss, Cooper Bennett and Richard Madden— are a part of the history of this township.

Dipping Branch and Hollands are points in the township. A family which moved to that section soon after Anderson was established was that of Thompson. The founder of the family in South Carolina was John Thompson, who came from Pennsylvania before the Revolutionary War, and settled in Union. He suffered imprisonment in Ninety-Six at the hands of the Tories, and after his release walked to his home in Union. It was his son, Addison, who emigrated to Anderson in its early days. He had just graduated from the Charleston Medical College when he came to begin his practice in Anderson District. He lived for a time with his uncle, John Thompson, when he first arrived. Mr. John Thompson had a daughter, Elvira, who was married about that time to Dr. William C. Norris. That was a very fashionable and elegant wedding. The father of the bride was well-off, and the family wished to have the marriage of the only daughter a very brilliant event. The bride's trousseau was bought in Charleston, and a wonderful feast was prepared. All of the elite of Anderson District were invited to the wedding festivities.

The bride had a friend who was also first cousin to the man she was about to marry. Miss Jane Swain Norris was the young lady. She was to be bridesmaid. The girl friends of the bride gathered at the home several days before the wedding, and one day

Elvira said to her friend: "Janie, I have a charming young cousin who is coming to see me married. He is a doctor, too, just as your cousin, my bridegroom, is. I will give him to you, and we will exchange names. I shall become Mrs. Norris, and you take my cousin and become Mrs. Thompson." Miss Norris laughingly accepted the gift, and on the evening of the wedding she met Dr. Addison Thompson, who really fell in love with her at sight. The affair terminated in her acceptance of her friend's proffered gift, and actually becoming Mrs. Thompson. The young couple lived for a time with the bride's father, 'Squire Ezekiel Norris, who afterwards gave them a home near his own where they spent their lives.

The young doctor soon became a popular physician and had a practice which covered twenty miles around. The roads of those days were too bad for vehicles, so the doctors rode horseback, carrying their medicines in their saddlebags. Those old doctors were soldiers of duty. They never stopped for weather; through storm and sunshine, bitter cold and intolerable heat they rode faithfully, night or day, often remaining away from home for several days at a time. It is no wonder that the family physician of those times was like a beloved member of every home.

The eldest child of Dr. Addison E. Thompson and his wife was Richard Edwin, who also became a physician. When a little boy "Dick" was started to school to Weston Hayes, who taught in a log house near Bethesda Church. That church was built on land given for the purpose by Mr. Baxter Hodges, a devoted Methodist, and a Methodist church was built. When it was finished it was found to be on land owned by Dr. Thompson, who was a devoted Presbyterian. The mistake brought to his attention, he immediately deeded a sufficient part of his property to the church to set the matter right.

Young Dick's next school was at Cross Roads, now the town of Starr. It was taught by a man named Jerry Yeargin. Young Thompson was finally sent to Anderson to attend Hall's Military Academy and he boarded at the hotel kept by Mr. Christopher Orr. Miss Jane Orr was the proud possessor of a piano, the first to be brought to the town of Anderson.

Finally Dick was sent to Erskine College where he was a student at the outbreak of the war. He enlisted in 1862 and served until the end. After returning home he attended medical college in Charleston, and upon his graduation settled in Varennes township where he practiced. Dr. Dick Thompson lived to be quite an old man, dying just a few years ago.

He had two brothers younger than himself who enlisted in the army, but both died of disease before seeing any service.

Dr. R. E. Thompson and Mr. Tyler Gambrell, two young Confederate soldiers, were put for a time to guard the Confederate treasury in Anderson. They were also put on duty guarding cotton on the Savannah River.

In his old age Dr. Thompson was a familiar figure for many years at all reunions of Confederate Veterans, or dinners given by the U. D. C. to the Veterans.

HALL.

Hall township was the home of a large family of that name and lineage. The first to come to the section was Nathaniel Hall, who emigrated from Virginia and settled about where Storeville grew up. He was a Baptist minister, and the first of that faith in the locality. He found the people of the community greatly prejudiced against his religion, so much indeed that when he held baptismal services according to the practice of his church, it was necessary to provide guards to prevent interference.

John Hall, a son of Nathaniel, gained the soubriquet "Stone Fence Hall," as he was the first and a most ardent advocate of using the stones found in abundance about the farms, for making stone fences, thus preserving to some extent the timber.

Zachariah, great grandson of Nathaniel, was, however, the outstanding member of the family, and in his honor was the township named. Mr. Hall was a man of large means, and of education, and he did a great deal for his locality, in a mental, moral and financial way. He was a magistrate, and for twenty-five years a deacon in the First Creek Baptist Church.

Some of the oldest churches in the county are in Hall Township. First Creek and Rocky River are very old Baptist Churches, and Hebron is an old Methodist Church.

Carswell Institute was located in Hall Township. After the War Between the States the veterans of Company F, S. C. Volunteers, held their reunions from place to place all over the county. Mr. Martin Hall believed that a permanent meeting place was a thing to be desired for the company, and he donated to it a half acre of land adjoining the school grounds of Carswell Institute, and for many years the annual reunion at Carswell was an event anticipated with pleasure by the old soldiers.

Storeville is one of the points of trade in Hall township. In 1849 Enoch Benson and Theodore Trimmier were merchants of that section. Other men have followed them. In the days of rural postoffices there was one at that place.

The Milford family belonged to this township. The late Mr.

John B. Leverette of Starr was born in Hall township, and his distinguished uncle, Stephen Leverette, is buried in an old family graveyard in the township.

HOPEWELL.

For Hopewell Church, which applied for a charter in 1841.

Septus, better known to some of the older people as Five Forks, is located in this township. Once it was an ambitious dream to build a town there. Dr. Gailliard owned much of the property, and he had it marked off into lots and sold at auction by Colonel W. S. Pickens.

Before the War Between the States there was a postoffice established at a point in what is now Hopewell township, named Piercetown, for a prominent family of that name. A little village grew up around it, and there were several enterprises. In the stirring days of war preparation there was a great public gathering at Piercetown and one of the young ladies of the community presented one of the companies, about ready to leave, with a handsome flag. She made a presentation speech, too, although it was unusual for a woman to speak in public at that time. But though she might stand up on the speaker's platform and make her few remarks, her name could on no account appear in the newspaper, so the journalistic account of the time mentions her only as "Miss E."

The place flourished until ruined by the war. The postoffice was moved to Watkins' Mill, on Six-and-Twenty Creek, and took with it the name. The present locality, known as Piercetown, is not the ante-bellum village. Some years after the war the community wished to establish again a postoffice, and it was necessary to find a new name for it, so it was called Guyton, for a well-known family of the section.

Another well-known locality is Septus, probably better known as "Five Forks." It was once marked off into lots for a prospective town, by a large landowner of the community, Dr. Gailliard, and sold at auction by Colonel W. S. Pickens.

There used to be a section known as "Lick Skillet." The reason for the queer name is lost, so imagination has run riot. Pioneer wagons have been pictured, oxen drawn, slowly dragging a weary way over tractless wastes, where passage had to be blazed ahead of the procession as it crept along. Finally, provisions giving out at this spot, the hungry family had to lick the skillet in order that nothing should be wasted; or, a scarce time may have come to the early settlers, crop failure, or other misfortunes making it a time of scant living. Whatever may have been the reason the locality bore the name from very early times.

The first authentic records show a wagon shop kept by a man named Gid Land, and a nearby smithy. That was nucleus enough for a gathering place, the social club of the country side, that is, for the masculine portion of it. The women had no recreation except going to church, consequently in almost all family records great-grandpa was a muchly-married man, his wives numbering first, second, third and even fourth, and sometimes fifth.

Professor John G. Clinkscales, of Wofford, when he was Anderson County School commissioner, changed the name of the place to Eureka.

One of the first settlers in that neighborhood was Daniel Campbell, a Scotchman, who had settled first in Newberry, and moved on to this section when the Cherokee lands were opened up for occupation. The government sold the land for 50 cents an acre, and Mr. Campbell, in partnership with an Irishman, took up 132 acres. For one time a son of Erin outwitted a canny Scotchman in a money transaction, and it somehow transpired that Mr. Campbell paid $1.00 an acre for his share, and the Irishman paid nothing.

Storeville was a settlement on the Generostee Road made by the Thompsons. Near their home place is an old Indian graveyard where an Indian chief was buried.

Sandy Springs gets its name from a beautiful spring surrounded by snowy sand. When the religious people of the section were looking about for a suitable place to hold camp meetings, a man named Smith came forward and donated that beautiful spot. For very many years the wonderful camp meetings held there drew people from far as well as near. A town grew up around the church, and the place received further notoriety when it became the camp where Orr's Rifles were organized, drilled and prepared for war. It is now one of the most flourishing small towns of the county. It is also the home of "Uncle Dave," otherwise Mr. D. A. Taylor, whose wise, witty and charming letters to the newspapers have long been a pleasing feature. He also sometimes writes delightful verse. Mr. Taylor came from Virginia, but he married an Anderson county woman, and cast his lot among us.

There was once a Rockville projected in the county. Charles Cotesworth Pinckney and his wife, Mary, deeded 60 acres of land to General Andrew Pickens, Colonel Robert Anderson and others in 1792 to found the town of Rockville, in Pendleton District. Nothing came of the project, however.

HISTORY OF ANDERSON COUNTY

Stuartsville was an embryo town about five miles north of Belton, and until the C. and G. Railroad was built in 1853 it was quite a little center of trade. The first store in Belton was one which was removed from Stuartsville. It was run by J. B. Lewis and Dr. W. C. Brown. Holland's store, Craytonville, and other places bearing the names of people, speak for themselves.

There was once a corner of Anderson county that got lost. It was lost a long time, but just a few years ago, W. H. Shearer found it.

In 1827 the line between Anderson and Pickens counties was surveyed, and a corner established in the middle of Eighteen-Mile Creek, right in the center of a road which ran between Pendleton and Central. But if there was ever an official record of that survey made, it was destroyed or misplaced so long ago that it has been entirely forgotten.

Some few years ago there arose a question of building a bridge across Eighteen-Mile Creek, and Pickens claimed that the site of the proposed bridge was in Anderson county, therefore Anderson county should bear the expense of the bridge. Anderson, on the other hand, maintained that the site was in Pickens County, and that Pickens should erect the structure.

W. H. Shearer was appointed civil engineer for Anderson, and F. V. O'Dell for Pickens, to determine where the boundary line was located. The two engineers disagreed, and a third surveyor, R. E. Dalton, of Greenville, was added to the committee. Mr. Dalton agreed with Mr. Shearer's decision.

The original survey was made on May 3rd, 1827, by Thomas Garvin, Thomas Lamar, and James Gilmer, starting from the mouth of George's Creek on Saluda River, running to a point where Eighteen-Mile Creek is crossed by the road leading to Hagood's Store, thence to the mouth of Cane Creek, on Tugaloo River. The old ford where the road crossed Eighteen-Mile Creek has been discontinued for many years, and the road has been changed in many places, but by the help of old maps and examination of many papers connected with the adjacent lands, Mr. Shearer finally found and fastened down the long lost corner of Anderson County.

CHAPTER XVI.

The War Between the States.

In 1860 Anderson was as deeply interested in politics as any part of the country. On December 13, the people elected as their delegates to the Secession Convention J. N. Whitner, J. L. Orr, J. P. Reed, R. F. Simpson, B. F. Mauldin and John Martin. That document was signed in Charleston, December 20th, 1860.

Hostilities actually began in April, 1861, with the firing on Fort Sumter by Citadel Cadets. The late Captain P. K. McCully, of Anderson, was a student there at the time, and was always proud that he participated in that affair. Another Anderson county student who took part in that first skirmish was Samuel B. Pickens, of Pendleton, who was afterwards known in the state as "the boy colonel," being only twenty-one years of age when he attained that rank.

Almost immediately Governor Francis Pickens issued a call for military volunteers, and practically every young man in the county responded. The Fourth South Carolina Regiment was organized Sunday, April 14th, on North Main Street, about opposite to where the postoffice is located. J. D. Ashmore was its commander. Colonel Ashmore lived in the house now occupied by Mr. W. A. Watson in North Anderson, then a handsome country residence, now a beautiful city home.

However, on the afternoon of the next day Colonel Ashmore had a quarrel with Scott John Wilson on the square just in front of the court house, which resulted in a fight, and after that he felt it incumbent upon him to resign his command. He was succeeded by Colonel J. B. E. Sloan, of Pendleton. In that regiment there were three companies, composed almost entirely of Anderson men. The Palmetto Riflemen consisted from first to last of one hundred and forty-five men. Ten were discharged from disability, wounds or sickness, thirty were transferred to other commands, thirty-four killed in battle, fourteen died of disease while in service, thirty-four were wounded more or less seriously, thirty-nine survivors surrendered at Appomattox.

Its captains were: First, James H. Whitner. promoted to Major of the Fourth S. C. Vol.; second, William W. Humphreys, promoted to Major; Third, Thomas Prue Benson.

Lieutenants: Claudius E. Earle, died 1861; Amaziah Felton,

killed in battle, 1862; Mike McGee, Joel H. Gleason, James H. Hoyt, Newton A. McCully, William Poe.

Sergeants: R. E. Sloan, Thomas McGill, S. A. Langston, J. P. Sullivan, R. L. Keys, R. C. Nevitt, J. T. Skelton, O. N. Hall, T. O. Jenkins.

Corporals: E. B. Rice, B. S. Smith, James Thompson, J. F. Clinkscales.

Among the private soldiers of this company are to be found most of Anderson's best known names.

Company D of the Fourth Regiment had for its officers: Captain, James Long, of Brushy Creek; First Lieutenant, John Long; Second Lieutenant, M. A. Cason; Third Lieutenant, V. B. King; Fourth Lieutenant, J. W. Bramlett; Sergeants: J. W. Orr, B. W. Mitchell, J. N. Wardlaw, B. F. Mullikin, J. H. Laboon.

Corporals: J. A. Monroe Smith, J. E. Hembree, William H. Fielding, M. L. Mullikin, A. F. Martin, G. A. Rankin.

In this company, too, appear many of Anderson county's oldest and best names.

Another company of the Fourth was formed around the Dean section of the county, and one of the Deans was its captain.

On April 15th the regiment started to Columbia. They stopped in Belton for the night, and reached their destination on the afternoon of April 16th, with Sam Elrod and his corps leading the procession. It remained in training in Columbia only six weeks, then was ordered to Leesburg, Va. While in that town the regiment was presented by the ladies of the place with a flag, one of the first made for the Lost Cause. Sergeant Warren D. Wilkes, of Anderson, a gifted speaker, received the flag for the regiment, and the address he made on that occasion was to the day of their death considered by the members of the regiment the finest speech ever made by anybody at any time.

The Fourth Regiment was ordered to Manassas, where it was placed on the left wing of General Beauregard's Army, Evans' Brigade. In connection with the Louisiana Tigers, it did some of the fiercest fighting of the First Battle of Manassas, holding the field for a time against tremendous odds.

The Fourth was the largest regiment sent by South Carolina, which sent a goodly number.

Some of the other captains of the county were Watkins, of Pendleton; F. W. Kilpatrick, of Pendleton, who rose to be colonel of his regiment. He was killed at the Battle of Lookout Mountain.

J. L. Orr organized a regiment at Sandy Springs, where it trained for service. For many years after the war the regiment held yearly reunions at that place, and its most honored guests on those occasions were Mrs. J. L. Orr and Mrs. D. A. Ledbetter, widows of two of its colonels. This regiment was ordered to Sullivan's Island July 21, 1861, with Foster Marshall, of Abbeville, brother of Mrs. Orr, as its Colonel, and D. A. Ledbetter, of Townville, Lieutenant-Colonel. It was attached to McGowan's Brigade, and being found larger than army regulations allowed, some of its men were sent home to organize a new company, which they did, making P. K. McCully its captain. This nucleus grew into the Second South Carolina Regiment of Rifles, commanded by Colonel John V. Moore and assigned to Jenkins' Brigade. Colonel Moore was killed at Second Manassas.

Colonel Orr, after having formed the regiment, and bestowing upon it his name, was induced to retire from the army to serve in the Confederate Congress. Colonel Orr was a far-seeing man, and a shrewd politician. He was opposed to secession, fought it with all his strength until it was an accomplished fact, then he is said to have remarked to a group of his hot-headed friends: "Well, boys, you are headed for hell, but if you are determined to go, I'll go with you."

Company K of Orr's Rifles had as Captains: G. W. Cox, wounded at Gaines' Mill, resigned; R. S. Cheshire, promoted from Corporal at Spottsylvania.

Lieutenants—James A. Bigby, George M. Bigby, promoted from Sergeant; W. C. Norris, wounded at Gaines' Mill; James A. Lewis, killed at Battle of Jones' Farm; D. R. Geer, wounded at Fredericksburg, promoted from Sergeant, at one time color bearer of the regiment, G. B. Rollins, killed at Jones' Farm.

Sergeants—John T. Green, wounded at Fredericksburg; J. M. Harper, died at home; L. N. Green, died in Richmond; Perry Gaines, wounded at Spottsylvania; W. B. Cox, wounded at Fredericksburg; W. S. McDavid, killed at Spottsylvania; T. F. Milwee; Robert C. Telford, wounded at Chancellorsville; W. P. Wright, wounded at Fredericksburg, discharged.

Corporals—G. W. Wasson, wounded at Battle of the Wilderness; Enoch Gambrell; J. M. Cox, killed at Wilderness; G. M. Harper, wounded at Chancellorsville; John R. Harper, wounded at Spottsylvania; James Robinson, S. H. Stone, J. J. Poore.

There were other companies also in this regiment which contained many Anderson men; all saw hard service.

Company F, of the Second Regiment, had as officers: Captain John V. Moore, promoted to colonel and killed at Second Manassas;

Captain D. L. Donald, the man for whom the town of Donalds was named; Captain James A. McDavid.

Lieutenants—A. W. Vandiver, killed at Lookout Mountain; F. A. Deale, W. Y. Sherard, W. H. Wauley.

Sergeants—Samuel Agnew, J. W. Rowland, R. D. Newell, Reuben Tucker, W. J. Stevenson.

Corporals—Bastle Hall, W. D. Hall, J. N. Barrett, L. E. Campbell, Press C. Moore.

Company G, of the Second Regiment, had as Officers: Captains, Peter K. Norris, discharged at Gordonsville, Va.; William P. Strange, died from wounds received at Wilderness.

Lieutenants—John M. Cox, killed at Frazier's Farm; Alfred M. Ayers, captured; Elijah C. Horton, promoted from Sergeant; John L. Humphreys, promoted from ranks, wounded at Wilderness, captured; Major L. Keys, wounded at Second Manassas; Augustus A. Dean, promoted from ranks to Corporal, Sergeant, Lieutenant; Elisha W. Byrum; John J. H. Hall, wounded at Manassas; Hampton Poore; Henry N. Breazeale, promoted from ranks to Corporal then to Sergeant; John W. Poore, ranks, Corporal, Sergeant; James P. Cox, ranks, Corporal, Sergeant; Chamberlain J. Mattison, ranks, Corporal, Sergeant, wounded near Richmond; Reuben B. Kelly, ranks, Corporal, Sergeant, captured; William McClinton, ranks, corporal, Sergeant, wounded at Frazier's Farm.

Corporals—J. Thompson Norris, Anderson Brock, A. R. Newton Gilmer, died of disease in Charleston.

In various regiments there were companies either composed entirely of Anderson men, or which numbered many Anderson men in their ranks. One of these was Company E, 20th South Carolina Infantry.

Captain— J. A. Cowan.

Lieutenants—J. J. Shirley, J. A. King, W. C. Pruitt, J. F. Mattison, J. J. Copeland.

Sergeants— W. A. Shirley, William Brown, William Smith, J. P. Parker, Luke Hanks, William Cowan, A. M. Hall, Isham Taylor, C. M. Kay.

Corporals—W. C. Hall, J. M. Hanks, Jesse Robinson, R. E. Parker, T. C. Pruitt, W. C. Pearman.

Company D, 18th South Carolina—Captain, J. W. Bramlett.

Lieutenants—B. C. Martin, John C. Bryant, J. F. Stone, J. A. Moore.

Sergeants—D. E. King, A. E. Spearman, W. J. Moore, W. F. Bryant, B. R. Bryant, John E. Wigginton, J. F. Clardy.

Corporals—John W. Spearman, Jasper King, J. C. Martin, W. L. Murphy.

HISTORY OF ANDERSON COUNTY

About two years before the war the young men of Williamston formed a company of militia, which they named Gist Rifles, in honor of the Governor of the State, States-Rights Gist. When war was declared the company, though always retaining its own name, became officially Company D, Hampton Legion. It saw hard service. Its first captain was Henry Julius Smith, who was killed at Sharpsburg. He was succeeded by J. A. McNeely, who was killed at Biddles Shop. The next captain was W. H. Austin, who survived the war. Its lieutenants were R. R. Hudgens and E. H. Acker. Its Sergeants were J. W. Crymes, William Gibbs, R. C. Kennedy, Thomas Crymes. Its corporals were W. C. Burdine, J. H. Burdine, J. W. Lawson, A. H. Kohler. R. V. Acker was the company drummer.

In 1864 the young men of Anderson and Pendleton who had been too young to go into the army, formed an independent company of cavalry scouts, which was later attached to the Second Regiment S. C. V., Kershaw's Brigade. Its Captain was Doran Kay; Lieutenants, Verner, Tribble, L. W. Harris; its Orderly Sergeant, Russell; Corporal, S. Looper.

Probably the soldier from Anderson county whose name is best known throughout the South was Barnard E. Bee. He was really a Charleston man, but he had a summer home in Pendleton, and his body was returned to Pendleton for burial, so he must have given that as his home town when he enlisted. He was a brave soldier and not only fought well, but gave up his life for the cause. But he is remembered for words and not for deeds. His career was very short, but brilliant. For three long hours he had been fighting McDowell's great army at Manassas, with a pitiful small body of men. Finally, almost exhausted, they were giving back when Thomas J. Jackson with his brigade came to their aid; it was then that Bee, rallying his discouraged men, pointed to Jackson and exclaimed: "Look, men, where Jackson stands like a stone wall! Follow the Virginians!" Those words, spoken on the spur of the moment, were to become immortal, and were to give to the greatest soldier of the century a name which should almost entirely supersede his baptismal one. And they were the last the young soldier was to utter, for he fell, shot to death even as he spoke.

There were a number of Anderson men members of Brooks' Cavalry, of Greenville; among them was Dr. Hiram Cooley, first surgeon of the company.

At the expiration of their first term of service some of the county soldiers formed a new regiment known as "The Palmetto Sharp Shooters;" it became a part of Jenkins' Brigade.

Still another Anderson company was commanded by Captain Hill, and belonged to the Twenty-fourth Regiment, S. C. V. It served under General Ellison Capers.

Anderson men fought at First and Second Manassas, Williamsburg, Seven Pines, Gaines' Mill, Frazier's Farm, Boonsboro, Sharpsburg, Fredericksburg, Chickamauga, Wilderness, Spottsylvania, Chancellorsville, Petersburg, Gettysburg, Franklin, Atlanta, Bloody Angle, The Crater, Lookout Mountain, and stood with Lee at Appomattox. They were in every Northern prison, and every hospital. They left limbs on many a battlefield; they fought, bled, suffered, died, starved, froze, scorched wherever the Demon of War placed his foot.

To Company F, First S. C. Cavalry, belonged the notorious Manse Jolly, who served faithfully during the war, but would not accept conditions of peace. He and his fine grey horse, Ironsides, were well known figures, and he kept up single-handed a guerrilla warfare for several years after peace was declared. The stories told of his daring are picturesque, and for that reason he has appealed somewhat to the popular imagination. But when one comes to examine the actual record, horror takes the place of admiration. Stories were told of his taking captive unoffending travellers who happened to be Yankees and after robbing them, throwing their bodies in a well on his place. An old negro used to tell a story which people hesitated to believe of his bringing a captive to his home one day, and the man, when he found that he was really in the hands of a desperado, took his watch from his pocket with some other trifles and handing them to Jolly's sister, said: You are a woman; surely you have some mercy, I ask that you send these things to my wife." But Jolly informed him that his wife would never see them, then he shot his prisoner and threw him into the well. Once he captured five Yankees near Townville and marching them to the home of Mr. Burket, a place still standing in Townville, and a very pretty and attractive old home it is, asked Mrs. Burket to give them a good dinner as it would be their last; and after he had eaten, whether his prisoners had or not, he actually took them out to a knoll several hundred yards from the house and shot each one of them. Such stories offset the glamour which gathers around the tales of his hairbreadth escapes, and his daring appearances in the very presence of the Yankee officers who were stationed in Anderson, and asking them if there were not a reward offered for the capture of Jolly, telling them he could deliver him into their hands, then telling them that he was Manse Jolly, deliberately walking out of the officers' presence and riding unharmed away.

HISTORY OF ANDERSON COUNTY

The county did, however, finally become too hot to hold him, and he went to Texas, riding Ironsides. Both man and horse were drowned soon after he got there attempting to swim a swollen river at night.

A few years ago an old well on the farm once owned by Jolly was cleaned out, and a number of human bones were taken out of it, giving color to the wild stories that used to be told about what went on at Jolly's home.

A very different Anderson soldier was Joseph Newton Brown. To many who knew Colonel Brown only in his old age, when he seemed just a very quiet, gentle elderly gentleman, the story of his courage and actual achievements in war comes as a surprise.

He responded to the first call to arms, enlisting as a private, and going to Charleston that he might be present at the capture of Fort Sumter. From there he returned to Laurens, where he was living at that time, and raised a company of which he was elected captain. He fought with conspicuous bravery in both Battles of Manassas, in the Battle of Chancellorsville, was with Jackson at the capture of Harper's Ferry, and also with Jackson in the Shenandoah when news came that Lee was hard pressed at Antietam, and in the terrific march Jackson then made, when he covered thirty miles in less than fifteen hours. Forming their line of battle when crossing the river, they saved Lee's army. In the return to Shenandoah, Captain Brown was given command of the rear guard, with orders to hold the enemy off until the army had crossed the river. This he did without the loss of a single man; for which he received personally the thanks of General Lee. A few days later he was promoted to Lieutenant-Colonel.

Colonel Brown again distinguished himself in the first days fighting around Gettysburg. His regiment took active part in the strenuous contest which so nearly drove the Federals from the field. The cannonading was terrific, but the brave boys never flinched; they pressed on under a rain of bullets, their colonel in the lead. There he lost two-thirds of his men. The third day, at Gettysburg, Colonel Brown was seriously wounded in the shoulder, having assisted in that wonderful charge of Pickett's men, the most glorious episode of the war. After that battle Lieutenant-Colonel Brown was promoted to Colonel.

The most sanguinary episode of the entire war was that known as "The Battle of Bloody Angle." Owing to wounds, illness and death, Colonel Brown's superior officers in McGowan's Brigade were all incapacitated just at that time, and the command of the brigade fell for that historic day upon Colonel Brown. Nobly it

HISTORY OF ANDERSON COUNTY

bore its tragic part in the fierce slaughter of that awful fight. For twenty hours it lasted without cessation. The Federals were repeatedly reinforced, fighting in relays, but the Southern men had no reserves, and for the entire time the same men carried on. The dead were piled on that battle field in layers three and four deep, great trees were cut down by the bullets as though laid low by axe or saw; darkness fell, but the mad fighting went straight on for nineteen hours, the Confederates having neither rest nor food during the entire time. It is said that during that battle the Federals used in all 40,000 men; Colonel Brown had but 6,300, but he refused any suggestion of surrender. It has been told that during the day there was at one time a white handkerchief accidentally displayed, and the Northern army thought it a flag of truce, and a Federal officer went forward to receive the surrender. Somehow he succeeded in reaching the commanding officer. Colonel Brown turned to receive him, and asked in his peculiar rather high voice his business. When the visitor gave his reason for his approach, Colonel Brown said: "Well, now, young man, you'd better get back to your lines; you might get hurt." In that battle the men of the two armies were sometimes separated only by a parapet, and their muskets actually at times touched. "The Bloody Angle" was a section of the Battle of Spottsylvania. Fighting began at 10 o'clock May 12, 1864, and lasted until four o'clock on the morning of the 13th. The Colonel used to talk proudly of the men who fought that battle, saying that after dark fell many of them could easily have slipped away undetected, but that not one did.

From Colonel Brown's own section of the country, the "Fork," one hundred and seventy-six men went into the army of the south. Daniel A. Ledbetter entered the service as Major and attained the rank of Colonel. Frank E. Harrison and D. L. Cox went in as Captains and rose, Harrison to Colonel and Cox to Major. B. F. Dickson entered as Captain; P. S. Lanford, W. L. Grubs, W. F. M. Fant and John Grubbs as Lieutenants. Lanford became Captain. Of all those commissioned officers Colonel Ledbetter alone was killed; none of the others was even desperately wounded. One day on the anniversary of the first Battle of Manassas Mr. N. O. Farmer, of the Fork, who served in Co. D, Hampton's Legion, fell into reminiscent mood, and told of a raw company's first experience of real war. He said there were about six hundred men who boarded the cars late that Saturday afternoon at Richmond for Manassas Junction. They traveled all night, reaching the junction a little before day, and were at once put in motion for the battle field, about six miles away. They did not know where they were going, but most of them had an idea there was a fight somewhere.

As they approached the battle field, well up in the morning, they could hear the booming of cannon and the rattle of small arms. That sounded like business. The heat was awful and the men were very weary, for they had slept none the previous night, and the sound of battle at hand produced a sort of sinking sensation. As they toiled painfully along the road in columns of four, anxious and silent, but steady, the ominous sounds grew more distinct.

Colonel Hampton halted, and riding in front of the command, faced them and made the men a speech. He did not say much, but it was to the point. He wound up by telling them that any who did not feel able to face the music might march three paces to the front, and go to the rear. To the surprise, not to say consternation of the whole company, several men gravely stepped forward and walked out and back. Not a word was uttered, and the troops marched on. Mr. Farmer said: "No doubt most, if not all of us, would have been glad to have gone back with them, but pride held us to the scratch." He also said that the very men who that day showed the white feather, afterward retrieved themselves and became gallant soldiers. He said, too, that as they looked over their company with its bright muskets glittering in the morning sun, they thought in their ignorant vanity that with this body of men between it and the Yankees, Richmond was safe. However, he remarked, "the experience they got soon took the conceit out of them."

As they moved onward, and it became certain that they were to take part in the fight, they became more and more serious; no man spoke aloud, when suddenly Bill Green called out: "Boys, it's my opinion that we're driving our ducks to a damned poor market." That lightened the tension somewhat. Bill got wounded that day, and was sent home. In the beginning a wound was equivalent to a discharge; later on a man had to be shot literally to pieces before he was dismissed.

At one time during that battle this company was lying down in support of a battery of artillery. A shell from the enemy's guns burst immediately over the line, killing and wounding several men and stampeding probably a dozen more. One of them, a strapping six-footer, had got well on a run for the rear when he came across an artillery officer in the act of mounting his horse, where he had tied it in a depression behind the lines at the beginning of the fight. With drawn sword the officer tried to bring the bleeding soldier about face, but the six-footer was on the go, and with a lunge of his bayonet he sent the officer sprawling upon the ground and kept right on. He, too, in after days became a good soldier.

Mr. Farmer was promoted to a lieutenancy in Company D for

conspicuous gallantry long before the war was over, but he would not accept his commission unless permitted to carry his gun and fight among the men. Once, with a mere handful of men, he rescued Colonel Alexander Haskell from the enemy among whom he had fallen terribly wounded and insensible.

On Monday morning, April 3, 1865, upon the evacuation of Richmond, Lieutenant Farmer captured and disarmed, single-handed, two Federal soldiers, and compelled a non-combatant to ferry the party across the James, when he turned his prisoners over to the proper authorities, and was himself captured by Sheridan's scouts disguised as Confederates.

W. T. Grubbs lost an arm in the war, and after he returned home he used to have the stump bound to a plow handle, and in that way he ploughed his little farm.

J. T. C. Jones joined the army at fifteen years of age. He, his father and his grandfather were all serving in the Confederate ranks at the same time.

At the Battle of Frazier's Farm five Anderson county men were killed. They were Lieutenant Milton Cox, Silas Crow, Jim Telford, "Beau" Cox and J. V. Jones, color bearer. A. H. Osborne, at the age of eighteen years, joined the Palmetto Sharp Shooters. Judge J. N. Whitner had five sons and three sons-in-law in the army. One of the sons, J. H. Whitner, was captain of Company A, Palmetto Riflemen, and was promoted to Major in the Fourth S. C. Regiment.

W. W. Humphreys was a great skirmisher, being nearly always in command of skirmish and picket lines. J. Pink Reed entered the service in Company G, Palmetto Riflemen, after being in several battles. He contracted typhoid fever and was taken with some wounded men from Lookout Valley to a field hospital. Mr. Tolly was his nurse. The hospital was taken by the enemy, and the prisoners carried to Rock Island. Mr. Reed was a prisoner there for fourteen months.

Mr. Fleetwood Clinkscales belonged to Company D, 20th S. C. V. He served as a non-commissioned officer for eighteen months, when he joined Captain Keith's company of mounted Cavalry, 19th S. C. Battalion. He served as lieutenant to the close of the war.

Anderson county furnished approximately 5,000 soldiers to the Confederacy.

Some of the ammunition used by the military companies of Anderson was made near Slabtown. There timbers were burned and the ashes collected, put into a large pot, made into potash and used for powder.

HISTORY OF ANDERSON COUNTY

Most of the men who went from the county reflected credit upon their home, but there are other tales of some. Mr. Bailey Breazeale used to tell a number of stories of the different soldiers that he knew. In his company was a boy named Sam, who before the regiment was called to the front used to boast very greatly about how he was going to kill the first Yankee slain by his regiment. When the firing actually began, Sam darted behind a tree, took off his cap and put it on his musket, holding it out; when a bullet whizzed through it he let the cap fall, and kept running until he had left the bullets a long way behind him.

It is said by some that Wilton Earle was the first Anderson man to be killed, by others that it was Sam Wilkes. It may be that Mr. Earle was the first county man to go, and that Sam Wilkes was the first man from the town. Certainly his funeral was the first to be held in the town, and it was a notable occasion. He, with his brother, Warren, formed a brilliant law firm in the town before the war. He left a young widow, who had been Louisa Webb, daughter of Mr. Elijah Webb, and a baby boy who grew up to be a well-known young man in his town, but who moved to Atlanta soon after he was grown.

One of Anderson's best known and loved Confederate Veterans for many years was Mr. "Wood" Fant. He had been a good soldier, and he was an inimitable raconteur. Children and grown people alike listened entranced when Mr. Fant would tell them stories. He enlisted at the beginning, was in many of the biggest battles always doing his part, but he came through without a scratch. He was about the only man who maintained that he really liked the hard tack and salt meat that were the soldiers' rations. Like most of the boys, he was probably always hungry, and he remembered only how good it was to get anything to eat without regard to what it was.

Dr. Divver, one of the few veterans left among the living now, tells sometimes of some of his experiences. One of his stories is that on one occasion he was behind a good gate post, from which vantage point he was firing. Another soldier coveted his retreat, and did not hesitate to push him out of it. The doctor was very indignant and expressed himself in no uncertain terms to the usurper, but to no effect, as the other man had proved himself to be the stronger, he held the post, and the discomfited young doctor had to seek another point from which to pour fire into the enemy. After the battle he passed the spot, and to his horror found the man who had taken it from him lying dead; the post had not saved him.

Tally Simpson, whose name the camp of Confederate Veterans

at Pendleton honored by bestowing it upon their organization, was killed at Lookout Mountain. There, too, Robert Maxwell, who had assisted in taking Bee's body off the field of battle, fell. Lieutenant Augustus W. Vandiver was also killed there. His body was found well in advance of the spot where his company halted. He was buried with a great number who fell in that bloody battle, and his family could never after the war locate his grave.

Clifton A. Reed joined Company A, Rutledge's Mounted Riflemen. For a year his company did service on the coast, then was ordered to Virginia. In the battle of Haw's Shop, Mr. Reed was loading his gun, when the fire from the enemy caught him in both hands. His right hand was amputated, and the doctors thought that the left should also be taken off, but he resisted so strenuously that they let it alone for "a time," and it got well. In his latter days Mr. Reed, as commander of the Confederate Veterans of South Carolina, became General Reed.

Dr. W. H. Nardin volunteered as a private in Orr's Regiment, but was rejected upon the ground that being a physician, he was more needed as army surgeon than as a soldier. He was appointed surgeon to the Twenty-Fifth South Carolina Volunteers, where he healed wounds in place of inflicting them.

Among the first county boys to respond to the call for volunteers were T. H. Williams and J. V. Jones. The young men had been intimate friends from childhood, but a short time before there had been a bitter quarrel between them and each refused to speak to the other or to recognize his existence in any way. At the Battle of Frazier's Farm, Williams saw one of the color bearers reel; without hesitation he sprang forward and seized the flag, and upholding its bearer, fought his way to a place of safety. Weak from wounds that he himself had received, he dropped his burden and looked for the first time at the face which had been resting on his shoulder. At the same time the exhausted color bearer regained consciousness and the two old friends gazed into each other's eyes. Jones raised his weak hand which was taken by his former playmate. The sorely wounded man was taken to a hospital where his early friend remained beside him until the end, which occurred six weeks later, when he passed out, clinging to the last to the hand of his boyhood friend.

Mr. Lewis E. Campbell, long one of the county's best known veterans, was rejected when he first volunteered because he was too small. It was only after Congress passed an act enabling men who had been considered undersize to enlist that he became a soldier and proved that a small man can fight just as well as a big one. In his old age Mr. Campbell was very proud that he remembered the whole manual for drilling Confederate soldiers and liked very much to go through with the drill.

At the beginning of the war there was of course great excitement. On one occasion a band in front of the court house was playing martial music with so much spirit that a young married man who had been sent by his wife to get some onions from Benson's store was so inflamed with patriotic ardor that, forgetting his errand and his waiting wife, he enlisted and immediately went away with his company. Two years later he asked for a furlough and told his captain the incident. The captain told him he would grant the furlough on condition that he get the onions and carry them to his wife. That he did. When he entered the house he handed them to her, saying: "Well, Mary, I was a long time getting onions but here they are at last."

Anderson county furnished practically two whole regiments to the army and a number of soldiers who belonged to other regiments. Ten of her men became colonels; they were J. D. Ashmore, J. C. Kilpatrick, J. B. E. Sloan, D. A. Ledbetter, T. F. Watkins, J. L. Orr, J. V. Moore, F. E. Harrison, C. S. Mattison and J. N. Brown.

The first child born in the town, Ben Brown, a first cousin of Colonel J. N. Brown, had grown to manhood when the State seceded and he offered his services, enlisting as a private in Company G, Second South Carolina Volunteer Rifles. Four days later he was detailed to assist as surgeon and not soldier.

General Stephen D. Lee bought a farm not far from Starr, in Anderson county, and lived there several years after the war. Then he moved to Mississippi.

The Confederate States had in Anderson one of its largest commissary depots; it was in charge of Mr. Sylvester Bleckley.

When Sherman's vandals started their incendiary march through South Carolina the branch of the Confederate treasury was hastily removed from Columbia, which everybody realized was inevitably on Sherman's route, and sent to the upper part of the State. A part of it, in charge of W. N. Leach, of Charleston, was committed to Anderson and lodged in the old University buildings which were at that time owned by Frazier Trenholm & Co., of Charleston. The Treasurer-General of the Confederate States, George A. Trenholm, was a member of that firm.

When the raiders reached Anderson in their search for Confederate treasure, they looted what was left of the outfit at the University buildings and scattered it over the streets. The girls of the town had been very much distressed all during the war by the scarcity of writing paper; any old discolored piece was treasured, and when the nice white paper used in making the money was blown about the streets there was almost a scramble for it. The young ladies secured as much as they could and saved it for their very best correspondence.

CHAPTER XVII.

War Time at Home.

WHILE the men served as soldiers the women at home did their part toward maintaining the families and sending supplies to the front. In the first years it was not hard, but after a time things on hand when the war started gave out and so close was the blockade that little could get past. The spinning wheels of former times were brought out of garrets and girls and women learned to use them. They planted cotton and flax, then spun it into cloth and made garments. Many of them became expert in making pretty dye from roots, herbs and berries. Little wheat could be raised, so corn bread was the usual food. Substitutes for coffee were made of parched grain or okra seed ground up.

One of their greatest problems was getting salt. The earthen floors of old smoke houses were scraped and the dirt boiled out and strained off, then the water left, and the salt would settle at the bottom. Corn cobs were burned to make soda substitute. Homemade molasses was used almost entirely as sweetening. Hats were manufactured from plaited straw, covered for winter with scraps of wool or silk goods if one were fortunate enough to have any. Old curtains were used, the tails of men's broadcloth coats which were too worn to be of further use as coats. Mrs. Garrison, who lived on the southeast corner of Main and Church streets, was the city milliner. She had two styles, one was a "droop," the other a "boulevard." The droop was a hat with a wide brim strapped down with ribbon or pieces of silk from old dresses. The boulevard was a small round hat that turned over the head like a soup plate and was usually trimmed with palmetto rosettes. Pins and needles were scarce, and carefully treasured. Lent sometimes to a neighbor as a great mark of favor. Shoe blacking was made from elderberries cooked and strained with a little molasses stirred into it. Candles were made by pouring melted tallow into moulds made at a tin shop. The best "parlor lights" were made by taking a long cord made from several strands of thread, stretching it across the yard, then passing a saucer of melted wax under the cord backwards and forwards several times until it was about the size of one's little finger. The long waxed cord was wrapped around and around a bottle, up and down and across in a fancy design, the wick fastened in an upright position on top, then the candle was ready and placed on the "parlor" mantel for company, for not even war could destroy the Southerner's love for visitors nor kill his hospitality. Sad as were the times young people were cheerful, and had their parties whenever it was possible to seize upon a soldier home on furlough or sick leave.

Candy pullings were popular, molasses candy pulled until it was a lovely straw color or mixed with peanuts or pop corn, made delightful refreshments. "Confederate" fruit cake was by no means bad. It was sweetened with molasses and its fruit consisted of dried apples and peaches, peanuts, watermelon rind preserves, cherry preserves and hickory nuts or walnuts.

The women and old men supervised the negroes and continued to raise crops and vegetables. Domestic animals were carefully cared for so milk, cheese, butter, meat, eggs and chickens were plentiful.

Life was so full of work that in spite of anxiety about the boys at the front and the outcome of the desperate fighting, time flew by.

Women organized societies for war work. There were two principal ones, The Hospital Club and The Ladies' Aid. Mrs. Rosa Webb was president of one and Mrs. Munro of the other.

In Pendleton there was one of which Miss Harriet Maxwell was president. Smaller societies were formed throughout the country districts wherever a few women could get together. Bandages were rolled, home-made remedies packed, as medicine was a contraband of war and could not be procured. Clothing was made for the soldiers, boxes of food packed and sent whenever it was possible.

During the last two years of the war the women established a hospital in the old Masonic Hall. When troop trains passed through, they were met by committees carrying refreshments for the soldiers.

Near the railroad station in Pendleton stood a little one-room house which was converted into a wayside hospital where many a suffering soldier received good nursing. There were no Red Cross societies or nurses then, no Salvation Army, no Y. M. C. A. or Y. W. C. A., and all the comforts and conveniences the soldiers got were supplied by the women who in that way were responding to the country's call.

The Ladies' Aid Society of Anderson held its meetings in the old Temperance Hall over the store of Mr. A. B. Towers, which stood somewhere about where Woolworth's Ten-Cent Store is now. The president, Mrs. Webb, with her sister, Mrs. Daniel Brown, used to spend three days cutting out garments and when the society met each woman was given a garment to make.

Knitting was the fashionable employment and all manner of knitted garments were sent to the front.

Of course there were no shoes from great shoe factories, so the people of Anderson got theirs from an old colored shoemaker, Elias Caldwell, whose shop stood about where the buildings of the Farmers' Oil Mill are located.

Tea was made from various leaves and roots; sassafras was preferred but any spicy roots or leaves were used. Buttons were made of persimmon seed or pieces of gourd cut out the desired size and shape and covered with bits of cloth. Ink was made of oak balls or the mashed out juice of green walnut hulls. Paper was greatly treasured, any old yellow piece was put carefully away. A letter from the front was handed all through the town.

Then on that long past May day the raiders came! Yelling and screaming, they charged upon the public square. The audit department of the Confederate treasury was located where Evans Pharmacy No. 3 now stands. They ransacked it, tearing into bits all the records and papers of every description. The drunken, rowdy soldiers entered every house, taking whatever of value they could carry away, and wantonly destroying much that they could not.

Among things sent to Anderson for safekeeping was a large stock of fine liquor which was stored in the cellar of the B. F. Crayton building, which stood on the corner occupied for many years by the Bank of Anderson. It was soon discovered and the marauders reeled around the streets cracking the necks of bottles against door posts, house corners and every other place that would crack glass. While pandemonium reigned, three young men, J. A. Hoyt, P. K. McCully and a young Charlestonian named Parker, were standing together in front of the court house. As the Yankees came riding madly into the square from East Benson street, these young men started across towards Crayton's corner, probably intending to leave by South Main street; as they reached the corner the invaders fired and young Parker fell dead. The tragedy naturally added horror and fear to the emotions already felt by the inhabitants.

Among the outrages perpetrated by these men was the torture of citizens in an attempt to make them tell where money, their own or anybody else's, was hidden. One of the refugees to Anderson was an old man who for some reason the raiders believed to be wealthy, and they actually hung him by the neck until he was almost dead in an effort to make him disclose the hiding place of the money that he really did not have.

They also tied a rope around the neck of Mr. Daniel Brown and, throwing it over a tree with him seated on a horse beneath, threatened to strike the horse and make it bolt from under him, and all in the presence of his little daughter who was screaming "My papa, oh! my papa!" all the time.

Dr. A. P. Cater was hung up by his thumbs and when he would make no disclosures, he was left hanging that way. Some time later when he was completely benumbed, his two aunts and an old colored woman cut him down.

Mr. C. A. Reed, hearing that the Yankees were coming, went to his home. He was not long married then and living with his young wife at his father's home, Echo Hall. He hastily gathered up what silver and valuables he could and buried them on the place. He had scarcely finished when the raiders rode up, just as he was attempting to leave. They halted him at the front gate and demanded that he go with them. They trained their guns on him. When he held up his empty right sleeve and, calling them cowards, told them to fire if they chose, one of them jerked off his nice new felt hat and, putting it on his own head, replaced it with his filthy Yankee cap which, although the young man had but one hand to work with, he immediately caught hold of and pitched as far as he could send it. He was taken to the court house where they were imprisoning as many men of the town as they could, and ordered to go to the second story. But, noticing that the attention of his immediate captor was distracted from him, Mr. Reed stepped behind one of the big columns of the court house where he was completely concealed and the captors, evidently thinking that he had obeyed orders and gone upstairs, did not look for him.

Major Thomas Lee, an Anderson man, was in charge of the penitentiary in Columbia when the radicals took control and they trumped up a charge of cruelty against him in order to have him removed. One of the witnesses called against him openly said that he knew nothing of any harsh treatment of the prisoners, but his were Jacksonian principles, to the victors belong the spoils. The Republicans were in power in South Carolina and their friends should hold the offices. A cloud of witnesses were invoked and the trial lasted ten days. During that time those who were bringing the charge against him sent a messenger to tell him if he would divide the money appropriated for the maintenance of the institution with them they would let him alone. He ordered the messenger out of the house and in a short time it was surrounded by a howling mob of both whites and blacks who threatened him with violence. Fortunately they lacked the courage to carry out their threats. Major Lee's wife and four small children were in the house at the time. The investigation committee happily, was honest, and Major Lee was completely exonerated from the charges brought against him and retained his office for some time longer.

Where the Republican officers were reputable, which some of them were, things were not so bad.

The raiders who preceded the garrison in Anderson were composed of the riffraff of the army and in the three days that they remained in the town there is not one tradition of them that is not as bad as it can be. They had no respect for anyone and regarded no man's property.

Rumors of Confederate gold had attracted the ruffians, who claimed to be a part of Stoneman's command under an officer named Brown. The United States War Department, however, asserted that the army register showed no such command as Brown's when Governor Orr later tried to identify the troops which raided Anderson.

Two days they held high carnival when, suddenly, boots and saddles was sounded, and in great haste they departed. General Stoneman, with his troops, passed through Anderson in the dead of night with the flag of truce at their head. It was a beautiful moonlight night and they rode so quietly it seemed as though the horses' hoofs were muffled; they almost seemed to be phantom horsemen. They stopped only to inquire their way, took nothing, paid for what they got. It was the approach of Stoneman's men that caused the hasty exit of the Brown crowd.

As for the gold, it was phantom, too; at least it disappeared as though it might have been. It was started away from Anderson to be taken to Davis on his flight, but it completely vanished and no man has ever been able to tell where it went or who saw it go.

Numbers of legends grew up around that gold. Stories were told of boxes of it being hidden under the long dining table in the Benson House dining room while the raiders sat around the same table and ate. They must have been much more quiet than they have been represented to have been if not one foot kicked those boxes under the table. Also a pretty story is told of a box of it being in the home of one of the government officials which, being unable to hide, his wife with her baby in her arms sat on while the raiders searched the house. It was said that she was ordered several times to get up and let the searchers see what was there and that she quietly arose, saying that they had left her nothing to sit on except a rough box, and that they kicked the box, but she seemed so indifferent that they concluded there was nothing valuable there and let it alone. Again they must have been less eager for treasure than they have been represented if they let a fastened up box upon which a woman determinedly sat to go unexamined.

Also wild yarns grew up as to where the money went. In whispers, every prominent man or every man who seemed to get somewhat ahead financially or any man who offended anybody else, was accused of knowing something about where that gold went. Truly it became one of the unsolved mysteries of history and gathered about it legend and story as time went on.

Stopping at the Benson House were several gentlemen from Pendleton and Charleston and some other places who had some pieces of jewelry and other valuables which they were anxious to save from the clutches of the raiders and they were at a loss to know how to do it. Finally somebody suggested trusting them to an old negro chambermaid whose name was Martha Walker. The trust was not misplaced. Martha took them and, placing them in the bosom of her dress, managed to drop them undetected into the well as she drew water. Afterwards they were recovered. There were also two negro men employed at the hotel who were supposed to know where valuables were concealed, and especially that elusive Confederate gold. Those men the raiders questioned, cajoled and threatened, but faithfully they kept their knowledge to themselves. The raiders got no help from any of the Anderson negroes.

Anderson, being far removed from the actual scene of strife, was selected by many low country people as a suitable place of refuge during the war. There were about seventy-five Charleston families living for the time in the town and some from other parts of the coast country. It was a convenient point for cavalry troops from the west to stop for a short rest on their eastward journeys and in these passing companies the quiet people of the up-country village saw battle-scarred soldiers and war weary men before their own survivors returned.

In 1864 when clouds were lowering blacker and lower over the stricken South, President Davis ordered a day of fasting and prayer and all the churches in the little town observed it. A lady who was a girl in Anderson then has preserved an account that she wrote of one of those services at the time.

It was held in the little Episcopal church which saw its brightest days during the time when so many Charleston people made their homes in Anderson. She wrote:

"Just at that time Martin's division of Alabama Cavalry was passing through Anderson and the little Episcopal church was filled with soldiers on that day. Our rector, the Reverend John H. Elliott, who afterwards became D.D. and attained a reputation as a literary man, preached a most eloquent and touching sermon. He, like ourselves, was a refugee, and freely gave his services to the little church. At the conclusion of the sermon there was sung the metrical psalm, 'When we our weary limbs to rest, sat down by

Euphrates stream, We wept with doleful thoughts oppressed, and Zion was our mournful theme." Those weary-looking, ill-clad, ill-fed men took up the singing and in the mournful, droning way peculiar to them, sung the psalm. The choir seemed to drop out; it was too much for the self-control of the congregation and in a few moments sobs were audible on all sides. I am sure that among those present it has been a lasting memory." Then she goes on with other matters.

It was in the winter of 1862 that Morgan's men seemed to find it most convenient for some unknown reason to make Anderson their headquarters until one day a quiet looking man appeared in their midst and was greeted by them with wild enthusiasm; it was the great John Morgan who, having escaped from the Ohio penitentiary, had arranged to meet the members of his command at this point. General Morgan was a handsome, dignified looking man, with dreamy gray eyes, very retiring in manner, by no means courting the ovations his presence seemed to evoke wherever he went. In looking at him one could hardly realize the dare-devil he was. He again visited Anderson on his return to Tennessee when he met his death, betrayed by a woman.

As soon as it became known in the town on that day in 1863 that General John H. Morgan was at the Benson House the citizens, men, women and some children, flocked to the hotel to see the great man and to have the honor of shaking his hand. Some of those children are old people now, but each retains a vivid memory of the splendid, kindly soldier who once graced the streets of Anderson by his presence.

Wheeler's Cavalry frequently passed through the place and although they were very often just as much dreaded as the enemy, the only traditions of them in this town are favorable; it is said "they always conducted themselves with decorum here." There were many rumors afloat of approaching raids but as time passed on and they were unfulfilled and Sherman's army of destroyers had left Columbia in ruins the Anderson people came to believe that they would escape entirely, though when a branch of the treasury was brought to the town from Charlotte, many people felt that its presence would certainly draw the dreaded invasion upon them.

The great storm in February, 1865, had cut Anderson entirely off from the rest of the world; letters and papers were of ancient date before they reached the people. In April, after the assassination of Lincoln, rumors were vigorously renewed. About 500 of Wheeler's Cavalry, cut off from their command, had located themselves in Anderson and the inhabitants felt their presence a protection. Great then was the amazement and consternation when, on the first day of May, 1865, rumors of raiders being rife, the Confederate soldiers mounted their horses and rode away by one road as the raiders rode in by another.

The war was over, both Lee and Johnson had surrendered, but on that historic May day there were two skirmishes fought in Anderson county. The people of the vicinity long believed them to have been the last and rather boasted that "the last shot of the war" was fired in Anderson. That has been proved to be fallacious. But the little fights were the only ones that took place in the county and for that reason are interesting.

A body of Arsenal Cadets, commanded by Colonel Thomas, had been defending some fortifications above Greenville and there was in Greenville a military company which had been organized to guard life and property, Captain A. D. Hoke, of the Butler Guards, its captain. Dr. John A. Broadus, afterwards a prominent Baptist preacher, president of the Southern Baptist Theological Seminary, and W. P. Price, later a member of the South Carolina Legislature, its lieutenants.

Mr. Price had opened the state armory in Greenville and equipped the company with arms. On account of this act which might bring down vengeance on his head, Mr. Price, at the approach of a Federal company from North Carolina, left the city, accompanied by a small party of civilians, all armed. They soon overtook the Arsenal company, which was also retreating before the advancing enemy, and the two united. They traveled the highway between Greenville and Anderson and camped near the home of Mr. Thomas Moore, northwest of Piedmont. There they stacked their arms near a well and, being very tired, threw themselves upon the ground to rest, many of them falling asleep at once. Coming from Pickens on that same road was a party of Yankee cavalry on its way to destroy a railroad bridge over the Saluda River, just below Piedmont; they were also in search of horses. Fearing no danger, they came yelling and firing pistols, awakening the sleeping Confederates. A few of the younger Arsenal boys, in their sudden alarm, ran away, leaving their guns. The greater number, however, stood their ground and fired such a continual volley into the approaching party, not having to stop and reload, because, as their charges were exhausted they threw aside their own guns and picked those abandoned by the fleeing cadets, that the Federals retreated, turning into the White Plains road, and were soon out of sight, giving up their plan of burning the bridge.

They left behind them one man badly wounded, who would have been dispatched by the maddened boys except that some of the women of the community came upon the scene and begged for his life. One of them, Mrs. Moore, took him into her home where he was carefully nursed until he was able to be carried to Greenville to a hospital.

The Anderson boys who took part in that scrimmage were James L. Dean, D. S. McCollough, F. A. Silcox, J. B. Lewis, G. W. Sullivan and E. A. Smyth, who has become an Anderson county man by virtue of his mill property in the county.

In this skirmish James Spearman, of Newberry, was slightly wounded in the hand by a slug fired from a shotgun in the hands of a negro who was piloting the Yankees. That negro was Mose Jennings, a slave, belonging to Mr. McElroy Jameson. Frank Blakely, a notorious outlaw and deserter from the Confederate army, had enticed the negro from his master's home and had him then as an aid in guiding a band of thieves and cut-throats through the section. Blakely had terrorized the country during the war when most of the men were away from the state and had been hunted more than once by bands of Confederate soldiers detailed to capture him. He had, in consequence, made many threats against the lives of some Southern men. South Carolina had become too hot to hold him and he had kept out of the state for a time, but finally had secretly returned and begun again his career of crime. In the fall of 1865 a party began a determined search for him and he was captured and dispatched without ceremony.

The Monaghan Cotton Mills now occupies the former site of the armory from which Mr. Price supplied his company in Greenville.

The other engagement in Anderson county on the same day was participated in by a company of young boys commanded by Captain Jones and stationed as a home guard in Pendleton. They learned that a detachment of Federal soldiers was en route towards that town and the captain ordered his company out to meet them. A skirmish took place near Pendleton Factory, now Auton.

These two scraps were the only battles fought in Anderson county, but they were not the last of the war. One took place in Georgia several days later and a whole month after there was a small fight between Confederates and Federals in Texas.

Anderson has not been wanting in appreciation of what her men and women did during the war. A Survivors' association was formed as soon as the county had time to recover somewhat from the desolation which followed the long struggle. Later it was superseded by camps of Confederate Veterans. The first organized in the town was named in honor of one of Anderson's soldiers, Camp Benson. It did not, however, seem to take deep root, and died. It was succeeded by the present Camp Stephen D. Lee.

There was a camp in Pendleton for a number of years, Camp Tally Simpson. That is now extinct.

The United Daughters of the Confederacy organized a chapter in 1897 which they named Robert E. Lee. It was soon followed by two others, the Dixie and the Palmetto. There was in the early days of the new century a chapter of the Children of the Confederacy called The Bonnie Blue Flag Chapter. It lasted until its girls got old enough to go away to boarding school, then passed out. In very recent years two new chapters of the children have been organized, both named for splendid Anderson county soldiers. One, W. W. Humphreys; the other, Joseph N. Brown.

The teachers in the Anderson schools are and have always been largely Southerners, sons and daughters of Southern soldiers, and Southern history and patriotism have been instilled into Anderson children.

Both Pendleton and Starr had short-lived chapters of the Daughters of the Confederacy, but they found that it was more satisfactory to belong to the Anderson chapters after automobiles annihilated space.

One of the pleasantest obligations assumed by the Daughters of the Confederacy is the entertainment of the Veterans; and greatly have they been rewarded for any attentions they have shown the old soldiers by the charming stories they have gathered of war days and war experiences from the lips of those who participate in them.

Squire Acker, of Williamston, was a veteran of intelligence and it was a pleasure to listen to the old man talk when he was in reminiscent mood. He was a member of Company D, Hampton Legion, having enlisted in June, 1861, when he was 19 years old. He remained there until after the Battle of Seven Pines, when Hampton took charge of a brigade of infantry, and the company known as Hampton's Legion was assigned to a Texas brigade, of which J. B. Hood was commander. However, they were later brought back to South Carolina. Mr. Acker was with Lee at the surrender and kept as long as he lived a piece of his battle flag, which he esteemed one of his greatest treasures. One of his brothers, E. H. Acker, was killed during the war; two besides himself came through to the end. One was in a Northern prison and the other in a hospital when hostilities ceased.

After the Battle of Manassas, Mr. Acker, with W. C. Burdine, was detailed to go and bury the dead of their company. While digging a grave under an apple tree on the Henry Place, a comrade approached and asked their assistance in burying his brother. They offered the grave they had just dug, which was gratefully accepted, and together they interred the dead soldier, then they placed another body in the same grave, putting a plank between the two. Many years after the war Mr. Acker wrote an article for *The Confederate Veteran* telling about that double interment, and asking if the man who had asked their assistance should chance to read it, would he reply. An answer came and the writer proved to be the author of the once popular book, "Four Years in Stonewall's Brigade," J. B. Casler. The two old soldiers then agreed to meet at one of the Confederate Reunions which took place in Little Rock, and their pleasure in each other was great.

It was not always those who had fought side by side who met with pleasure when the din and tumult were long over. About thirty-five years ago an article appeared in *The News and Courier* from a Northern soldier in which he stated that after the Battle of Lookout Mountain, he had taken from the dead body of Lieutenant A. W. Vandiver his watch. He knew his name from a letter in his pocket which he had that day received from his wife and that if any member of Lieutenant Vandiver's family cared to have the watch he would be glad to surrender it. Lieutenant Vandiver's son, James R. Vandiver, replied, and the watch was sent to him. Not a great while after that Mr. Vandiver was going to New York and arranged to stop in Philadelphia long enough to meet the man who for so many years had been in possession of his father's watch. The meeting was a very pleasant one and the old time foes became friends.

C. S. Milford was another Confederate soldier who was with Lee at Appomattox. He enlisted in Company F, Orr's Regiment, under Colonel Ledbetter, and took part in the battles of Gaines' Mill, Cold Harbor, Chancellorsville, Gettysburg, The Wilderness, Spottsylvania, Second Cold Harbor, Petersburg, Reams' Station, Jones' Farm, Southerland Station and many minor engagements. He was wounded once, losing a finger at Bloody Angle. He always took pride in saying that he was never captured.

Once when the color bearer, Kyle, was shot down, Mr. Milford seized the colors and carried them to the end of the battle. After the surrender he made his painful way home in company with ten members of his own company and three men who belonged to other companies. The members of Company F were, besides Mr. Milford, Captain Billy Terrell, whom Colonel Miller had promoted from sergeant to captain for distinguished gallantry; M. A. Terrell, James Dickson, T. A. McElroy, Dan Hull, John Hull, two Honea brothers and Charles Starke Milford. The other three were Chappell and Mitchell, of Georgia, and Corn or Kuhn, of Abbeville. The party walked from Appomattox to Greenville, rode to Anderson, then walked again to Pendleton. Their intention had been to go home with Tom McElroy, who lived on the railroad two miles above Seneca. But when they got to Pendleton on May 1st the town was in an uproar of excitement from a threatened Yankee raid, and the commander of the Home Guards tried to induce Captain Terrill to stop and help him fight, but that war-worn officer replied that he and his men were paroled prisoners and were through fighting. The party then left the town, still walking, crossed the Seneca River on the railroad bridge as the freshet of the previous January had swept away Cherry's bridge. They reached the house of Mrs. Patterson who had kept the bridge, where they got the "rations" of "seconds" which they had drawn in Anderson made into bread. They spent the night of May 1st at the home of Mr. Moore, who lived on a hill just north of Conneross Creek, the last night the battered little party spent together. The next day they reached the old muster ground where most of them had volunteered and there they separated.

When Mr. Milford reached the old Ward house within sight of his own home, he saw his little boys, the older of whom was but ten years old, hoeing corn. He felt, as did many another Confederate soldier, that it was time for him to be getting back to take care of his family.

CHAPTER XVIII.

Reconstruction and the Aftermath.

IN the unfortunate years between 1860 and 1876 hatred grew like a weed in the hearts of the American people and its noxious odor dulled the moral sense like a deadly anodyne. We of the South did not believe that the loathed Yankees were really human beings, loved and loving just as were our own glorified Southerners who, however, in turn appeared to the distorted vision of the virtuous North not the genial, kindly people we knew them to be, but monsters of wickedness, conscienceless slave drivers. Each section misunderstood the other and believed that to exterminate such depraved creatures was as necessary to public weal as the killing of rattlesnakes.

In the process of reconstruction a Yankee garrison was stationed in Anderson and cordially were they hated by Anderson people. For a short time there was a garrison of negro soldiers in the place, but so many of those niggers disappeared and could never be accounted for, nobody had seen them at all, that the garrison was removed and one of white men substituted. The white soldiers did not disappear as the black ones had, but they were bitterly disliked.

At the close of the war there was a company of Home Police organized for the protection of the citizens. Its captain was James A. Hoyt; first lieutenant, B. F. Whitner; second lieutenant, M. L. Keys; and citizens at large were invited to become members. There was an interested response; men felt the necessity of having some protection for their families. However, there was no serious clash between the citizens and the soldiers, with the exception of the affair at Brown's Ferry.

Jolly and his confederate, Sargent, stirred up some mischief and there were several clashes in the country between these guerrilla bands and the Yankee soldiers. In one of these skirmishes a soldier was killed and the enraged company set fire to the nearest house, not waiting to find out whether or not it belonged to any of the offenders. The two leaders of the lawless bands were the especial objects of search to the garrison and both of them had some hairbreadth escapes from capture. Between them they kept the community in a state of apprehension and unrest, and there was general relief when the two desperadoes left the county and went to Texas, where Jolly was drowned and Sargent soon died of tuberculosis.

That gang of ruffians kept in a large body of woods a store of stolen horses, wagons, cotton, provisions and anything else that was salable. When they had accumulated enough, a member of the gang would take it to Hamburg or Charleston and dispose of it. None knew of their rendezvous until one day a young lady, daughter of a prominent citizen of the county, who was out horseback riding, took a short cut through the woods and came upon a sort of camp. Several horses were eating, there were a number of heavily loaded wagons, but no living man in sight. She rode swiftly home and reported what she had seen. The next morning a posse went out to the place, but everything was gone.

The garrison used the Johnson University buildings as headquarters, some of their officers roomed there, and their property was kept in the buildings. The men camped on Fant street between the old mattress factory and Orr street. Some of the officers boarded at hotels.

Samuel Lord was referee for the Federal Government in the adjustment of property claimed by the government just after the war. These adjustments were made with Trenholm & Frazer, appointed by those who represented the interests of the sympathizers with the Confederate Government. The old house standing on the northeast corner of Benson and McDuffie streets, long known as the Robert Keys place, was one of the pieces of property which passed through their hands. When Mr. and Mrs. Keys lived in the house it was a charming cottage home. The flower garden at the east end was must luxuriant and beautiful, and over the front piazza grew rose vines whose blossoms brushed the hair of one entering the house.

The first Yankee garrison sent to the town was the Fifteenth Maine, and its members behaved so well that upon its departure the one weekly newspaper in the town complimented them upon their quiet and unobjectionable conduct. Their successors, however, were of a different kind. The next was the negro one under Colonel Trowbridge, of Massachusetts. That created so much friction that it was soon replaced by one composed of white men, but scarcely less objectionable. Its commander was Colonel Smith. One day as he rode into the square from East Benson street, two young men fired on him entirely without provocation. They were never apprehended. Official regret was expressed by the town, but nobody could ever identify those young men.

Among the objectionable negroes who were in Anderson during "the days of good stealing" was one Prince Rivers, formerly intendant of the good town of Hamburg. He had sought the promising town of Anderson for his home and one Sunday during the morning service he entered the Baptist Church, the largest both in point of building and of congregation in the town. He strode about half way up one of the aisles and took a seat about the middle of the church. Carpetbaggers, scalawags and negroes were in the ascendant, and the congregation did nothing to resent the indignity.

Before the war almost every church had its colored as well as its white members and the bond of Christian brotherhood united them, but Northern interference in Southern affairs killed, and it is greatly to be feared killed forever, that kindly spirit. Openly the white people could do nothing. Nevertheless these indignities were not allowed to go unchecked. Masked men frequently stopped with no gentle hand negro depredations. When Rocky River was dredged and straightened some few years ago, probably about 1920 or 1921, an old citizen wtih a grim smile remarked: "It's a wonder that the work on the stream has not revealed a lot of hidden bones of many a coon that disappeared while that Yankee garrison stayed in Anderson."

On the same Sunday that Prince Rivers decided to associate with "the quality," some of the negro soldiers took horses belonging to their regiment to the intersection of Market street with Whitner's Creek, now a thickly built up part of the town, then well in the woods. As the horses were drinking three men disguised by having their faces smeared with blue mud crawled from behind bushes and, covering the soldiers with guns, demanded and obtained the horses. It has been whispered that Sam Jones, once a noted evangelist of the section, was one of the three; his home was just across the river on the Georgia side, and Sam dearly loved adventure.

But such a state of things could not go on forever. In 1876 the disfranchised people, which class included practically all of the educated, respectable white men, determined by fair means or foul to wrest the state of South Carolina from the hands of the Republicans who had held high carnival since 1868. For once the oft-reviled doctrine, "the end justifies the means," was devoutly endorsed by the respectable people of the state. The beloved Hampton was chosen standard bearer and grimly the sons of the Palmetto State determined that he should be their governor. Not even the war had brought men's blood to the fever heat evolved by the historic campaign of 1876. Insult and oppression had been borne as long as Anglo-Saxon blood would stand for it, and though the Federal Government should by its soldiers who overflowed into the state shoot and imprison the "rebellious Southerners," yet were they determined to free their state from the intolerable incubus.

The means taken to win the bloodless victory are known to every one.

Probably the first meeting of Reformers held in 1876 was at Geer's School House in Broadaway Township. It was held one night in January and some of the men present were James B. Moore, Joseph B. Moore, Samuel E. Moore, S. N. Pearman and probably a few others. These men were deeply interested. They had been impressed by the sentiments expressed by a citizen of Broadaway who on the occasion of the last election had remarked that he was disgusted at casting such a mixed vote, that hereafter he would vote a straightout Democratic ticket or none at all.

That first small meeting encouraged the men who were present to call a larger one, which they did, a number of men of the town were interested and the meeting at Holmes' Shop, Lick Skillet, was well attended. A call was issued for all citizens of Broadaway Township to meet at Neal's Creek on Saturday, January 29th, for the purpose of reorganizing Broadaway Democratic Club. And a suggestion was made that other townships follow suit. The suggestion struck a sympathetic note in the public heart and Democratic clubs sprang up all over the county and the state.

The officers of that first post-bellum Democratic Club were: President, Thomas Erskine; vice-presidents, Lewis E. Campbell, William Shirley and Jasper N. Vandiver; corresponding secretary, Joseph B. Moore; recording secretary, J. B. Carpenter. Delegates elected to the county meeting were: J. Willet Prevost, Joseph B. Moore, S. M. Geer, Thomas Erskine and Joshua Holland. The Broadaway Club determined to celebrate Washington's birthday by a picnic dinner. Major John B. Moore, of Anderson, a native of the Broadaway section, was invited to speak. Also Mr. Edwards B. Murray, editor of *The Intelligencer*. The general public was invited and a brass band from Anderson furnished music. The Reform movement was born, and it proved to be a lusty infant.

On the 7th day of February was held a county meeting in the court house to which all of the country clubs sent delegates. James A. Hoyt was elected chairman; John B. Moore, M. C. Parker and J. B. Sitton, vice-chairmen.

The Broadaway delegates were instructed to urge upon the convention the nominating of candidates by primary elections in place of the convention system.

There was a large and enthusiastic meeting of the members of the Anderson Democratic Club held in the Masonic Hall early in February. After they had attended to business, Major John B. Moore suggested that they hold a celebration in the court house on the night of February 22nd. Delegates elected to the county convention were Messrs. John B. Moore, N. K. Sullivan, E. B. Murray, A. J. Watt and James Wilson. The new ideas spread like wild fire, democratic clubs were organized from the mountains to the seaboard. The newspapers were enthusiastic and fiery speeches vied with fiery editorials to arouse any who might be lethargic in the matter.

Then the men of Broadaway initiated a movement which added much to the desired effect; they organized a mounted rifle club and gave it the name, "Broadaway Mounted Hampton Riflemen;" officers, captain, Joseph B. Moore; lieutenants A. C. Wardlaw, L. E. Campbell, J. W. Erskine; sergeants, W. H. Geer, S. N. Pearman, C. B. Wardlaw, E. L. Smith; corporals, J. D. Warnock, E. L. Clark, J. M. Elgin and H. C. Erskine. This club was organized August 12, 1876.

There seems to have been another organized in the same neighborhood on the 18th of the same month with J. N. Vandiver, captain, and A. A. Carpenter, first lieutenant.

During the remaining months of the year rifle clubs were organized throughout the county.

On September the second, 1876, Hampton formally opened his campaign in Anderson. There was the biggest crowd on the streets that the town had ever seen. The exercises were to be held at the old Johnson University grounds. No house was large enough to hold the people and a stand for the speakers was erected out of doors. There were elaborate decorations. Above the stand were in evergreen letters the words: "Hard Money and Plenty of It—Tilden and Hendricks—Peace and Protection to All Classes—Hampton and Simpson—Retrenchment, Reconciliation and Reform." The stage was smothered in flowers and bunting, and Old Reformer bellowed its joyful note; it is said that its voice was heard and recognized in Abbeville. The speakers were Hampton, Simpson, Gary, D. Wyatt Aiken, William Wallace and others. Suspended in front of the court house was a large flag under which the procession passed on its way from the fair grounds, about where Mr. J. M. Paget now lives, to the school grounds, about where Mrs. C. S. Sullivan lives. And the procession didn't lack much of filling the whole space at one time. It was over a mile long. And there for the first time the famous red shirt made its appearance.

On August 23, 1876, a few active members of the Democratic Club of Pendleton met at Anderson to discuss and formulate plans for the campaign. It was decided that mounted parade companies would be organized to take part in the great march and a costume was desired. Something that would be conspicuous and distinctive, yet inexpensive. Finally the bright idea of red flannel shirts struck some one. Perhaps the familiar phrase, "Bloody Shirt," suggested it; at any rate, there it was, the great idea, and the men adopted it with delight. A. J. Sitton was captain of the company, but when the great day came he was ill and could not be with the boys. They were led by J. C. Stribbling. Mounted on prancing steeds they careened into Anderson. The news of their coming clad in red had been telegraphed from Pendleton when they started and some conservative Anderson citizens met them outside of the town, and urged them not to attend the meeting in such battle array. But the councilors were old, and the red-shirt boys were young. They had come to accompany Hampton, and they would not be deterred. They were so brilliant that they were given a place of honor in the parade, riding next behind the speakers.

This was really the second appearance of the red shirt men in Anderson. A few days before they had come down from Pendleton to assist in breaking up a radical meeting in the court house. They came whooping into the town and conceived the idea of riding round and round the court house where the Republicans were holding their meeting. This they did for half an hour or more. An old negro standing on a street corner watching them was heard to say: "There's mor'n a thousan' ov 'em, an' mo' a comin'." As they entered the court house the negroes in attendance at the meeting fairly fell out of the windows getting away—their white leaders couldn't hold them.

The red shirt uniform appealed to the public and in a short time every man in the state was arrayed in scarlet.

For years there was, and it still crops up at times, an acrimonious dispute between Anderson and Edgefield as to which county originated the famous uniform. The Pendleton men were perfectly sure that when they adopted it they had never heard of its being worn anywhere else, and Edgefield gave a date prior to the one claimed by Pendleton as that on which they had adopted it.

The truth seems to be that Edgefield had originated a bloody shirt costume which became confused with the red shirt uniform.

Senator Tillman in a speech in Anderson about 1892 or 1893 explained the whole matter. He said that he was in Hamburg at the time of the famous Hamburg riot. A band of young men, among whom were, besides himself, his brother, George Tillman, and Mart Gary, as well as other eager young men, had gone to the town with the determination to terrorize the negroes into behavior. Some kind of a costume was desirable. They could not use that of the Ku Klux as that organization was under indictment at the time to appear before the courts for alleged complicity in a number of outrages. Those were the days when Blaine was widely waving "the bloody shirt" in the United States Senate, and the suggestion came that the oft-mentioned garment should be the insignia of the goaded Democrats, or rather should be adopted by that special band of them to wear at their "trial." The idea met with approbation and B. R. Tillman was one of two young men sent to procure material for the bloody shirts. He said they bought a great quantity of yellow homespun, and that the women of the vicinity went to work immediately to make it into garments for the men by the next day, when the "trial" was to take place. Also one huge shirt was to be fashioned, to be stretched across a gigantic frame with arms extended and to be surmounted by two negro mask faces turned back to back, then of course facing both ways, topped by a kinky negro wig; this herculean figure to be carried as a sort of banner. The shirts, as soon as finished, were splotched wtih great red spots, some made with paint, some with polk berries and other crimson dyes. That was the first uniform worn by any of the South Carolina men soon to become known as "Reformers"—theirs was the "bloody shirt." That of the Pendleton men which became the official uniform of the Reform movement was "The red shirt," a simple red flannel blouse.

It was very effective, and gave enthusiasm to its wearers. The names of the officers and the members of that Red Shirt Brigade are carefully preserved in the annals of old Pendleton.

General Hampton in recognition of what the Red Shirt Brigade accomplished, made Colonel Sitton aide-de-camp when he became governor.

When the Democrats stormed the state house in Columbia and marched in, taking seats in defiance of the Republicans already in session there, keeping that incredible situation of two legislative bodies in the same hall almost at each other's throats for three days and nights, it was an Anderson man, J. Lawrence Orr, who, with his strong young shoulder, forced open the door of the legislative hall so that the reformers might enter.

With the election of Hampton, reconstruction days were over, and Anderson, along with the rest of the state, began her new life, which has come to be known as "The New South."

Anderson suffered many indignities and felt greatly degraded by the events of those days, but it is very probable that she would have had more and worse things to endure had not John Cochran been intendant of the town the whole time. There were negro aldermen and negro policemen. Negroes filled most of the offices, but Mr. Cochran could and did hold them pretty well in hand. Having entered the Republican party, he was greatly anathematized; no white man could become a Republican in South Carolina and fail to be heartily condemned by the majority of the people; though it is more than probable that some of them really went into it with the idea that it was the only way that white people could obtain any share in the government. J. L. Orr also became a Republican, and was governor of the state under Republican rule. But though before the war he had been a popular politician, he was from that time dead to his own people, and sought and obtained an appointment abroad. He became United States minister to Russia, but died within a few weeks of his arrival in the country. His body was returned to Anderson, and death restored him to the good graces, for the time at least, of the Anderson people. His body lay in state in the old Masonic Hall for some days and, as the art of embalming the dead had not reached then the perfection of the present time, the sickening odor of that room is a memory that has outlasted the years to a very small girl who was taken to the hall with her elders. The funeral, which took place in the Presbyterian church yard, was largely attended. Colonel Orr's sons never became Republicans. In fact, there is a tradition that J. Lawrence, with some other young men, attended one of his father's meetings in order to create a disturbance when he was speaking.

Colonel J. P. Reed also tried his luck in the Republican party for a short time. He, however, returned to the Democratic fold. The same thing happened in the case of Reverend J. S. Murray. They were probably making an honest effort to restore the reins of government to their own race, but finding that it would not work, and the only result was a coldness on the part of their friends, they retracted.

After the heated campaign of 1876 was safely over, the people of Anderson presented their adored Governor Hampton with a fine horse. He was a peerless cavalryman, and he looked his best, and a very good best it was, on horseback.

The presentation was made on the lot opposite the First Presbyterian church, which had once been a part of the Female Seminary grounds. The horse was a powerful thoroughbred black, and General Hampton mounted on it was a magnificent sight. The animal was bought from John B. Adger, near Pendleton, and the price paid was $300. The occasion was the sixtieth birthday of the beloved governor.

The speakers were, of course, Hampton himself and Lieutenant-Governor Simpson, who later became chief justice, Circuit Judge Cook and Circuit Judge Mackey. For a time after that festive day the vacant lot which had been used was dignified by the name, "Hampton Park."

CHAPTER XIX.

THE MIDDLE YEARS.

THE war was over, the Yankees were gone, and the negroes had settled back into their position of subservience to their former masters. Life in the little town resumed its wonted way. Many who had been leaders or prominent in the years preceding the storm were dead, but quite a number still remained, and others had grown up or moved in.

Anderson people have always been given to amusements, even though at times they have worked hard over them. In 1867 there was a Farmers' association formed, and it held fairs which were preliminary to the later ones when a regular fair grounds and building were provided. In the lists of prizes for domestic articles occur names of women who fifty and sixty years ago were the prominent women of the community. Mrs. W. W. Humphreys, Miss Fannie Earle, Mrs. C. A. Reed, Mrs. J. B. Skelton, Mrs. J. N. Brown, Mrs. J. A. Hoyt, Mrs. B. F. Whitner, Mrs. Love Gentry, Miss Alice Russell were a few of those busy women who made cake and bread and pickle, and quilts, and "tattin'," and wax flowers, and garments of various kinds. They may have had a lot of fun, but they worked hard to make those fairs successful.

The live stock was, of course, what interested the men, and they were chairmen of one and another of the exhibits, and some of them took prizes for horses that could trot, and horses that could run, and pigs and chickens, and everything that breathes on a farm.

Interest in horse racing did not die on the battlefield. As soon as good horses could be obtained the races began again.

The first race course in Anderson of which there is any record was about where the Anderson Cotton Mills are now located. It was probably established as soon as Anderson became a village, as it was in active operation in 1835, and was not new then. Benson's field track was where the railroad crosses the creek, the grandstand was on the southwest corner where the mill is now located. There was a row of about thirty or forty stables for keeping race horses about where the jail is now.

The second race track was near Orr Mill. It had a great circular track a mile around. It was there that the races were held until they became illegal.

When one hears of the reading clubs, debating societies, learned lectures and abstruse books that formed the recreation of the city's forbears, one is inclined to exclaim and admire and consider them a very cultured people. But just when the mind has settled to that conclusion, some old newspaper gives a detailed account of a hanging, and tells about the throng of people who witnessed it. It seems also to have been one of their recreations. The first hanging ground was about where Mrs. J. S. Acker's garden is now, its successor was outside of the town, near the old Bell home in North Anderson. It was to see a negro hanged there that Mr. Hall dismissed school in about 1864. Another was on South Main street. It was there that the last public hanging occurred in 1870. After that the people had really become too civilized to make an entertainment of such horrors.

A more interesting form of entertainment was the celebration on June 24, 1866, of the festival of St. John Baptist by the Masons. The exercises were held in the Baptist church, the largest building in the town. There were speeches, a parade, music and all the adjuncts of festivity, in spite of the gloom of war, which had not yet lifted.

In 1869 the old debating societies were revived and people flocked to their public meetings. The same year the first Survivors' Association was formed. The organization had been formed in Charleston in November with Wade Hampton, president; R. H. (Fighting Dick) Anderson, first vice-president; J. B. Kershaw, second vice-president; Samuel McGowan, third vice-president; T. G. Barker, fourth vice-president; A. C. Haskell, secretary; W. K. Bachman, treasurer. Executive committee, Edward McCrady, William Wallace, J. H. Rivers, C. Irvin Walker, J. McCutchen, Ellison Capers and James Conner. Delegates to the meeting which had been called in Charleston sent by Anderson were J. A. Hoyt, A. J. Sitton and E. M. Brown.

So thrilled was an old soldier by that memorial association formed in Charleston that he called a meeting in the Anderson court house of Anderson county veterans on November 15. An Anderson branch was formed.

The doctors of the county formed a medical association very soon after the war. About twenty-five of the physicians of the county met and organized. For the first time fees were definitely agreed upon, and other matters incident to their profession discussed and arranged. Dr. Alexander Evans was president; Thomas Lee, vice-president; Dr. W. H. Nardin, secretary and treasurer. The other members were M. L. Sharp, T. J. Pickens, E. M. Brown, S. R. Haynie, W. W. Keith, S. M. Brown, W. C. Brown, J. G. Knight, John Wilson, R. S. Cheshire, W. T. Holland, George W. Earle, T.

A. Evans, D. M. Russell, H. R. Rutledge, A. E. Thompson, P. A. Wilhite, A. P. Cater, A. G. Cook, John Hopkins, J. H. Reid, H. C. Cooley, John H. Maxwell and W. S. Jenkins. These were among the leading doctors from all over the county, and others joined at later meetings.

Dr. Webb, Dr. Cater and Dr. Alexander Evans were the earliest physicians in the town of whom there is any record. The account of them continues: "They were calomel doctors." Later doctors were Wilhite, Scudday, Holland, Tom Evans, nephew of Dr. Alexander; Nardin & Divver, Dr. Duckett, Dr. E. C. Frierson, Dr. Harvey Todd.

To Dr. Philip A. Wilhite belongs the honor of having discovered the properties of ether. It was in the days when he was a young apprentice to Dr. Crawford Long, of Athens, Georgia. For some reason there was ether in the office, and the young medical student got to playing with it. Finding that sniffing it had curious effects, he used to administer it to his companions for the fun of seeing what they would do. Finally one night, for the amusement of a party of his young friends, he administered it to a negro boy. He gave him more than he had ever given before, and the negro became insensible and helpless. The boys finding that they could not arouse him, went for Dr. Long, who also tried without avail, but after a time the negro recovered of himself, with apparently no ill effects. Dr. Long was so impressed that he began to experiment with it, and finally to use it in his practice. There has long stood in the public gardens of Boston a memorial to a Boston hospital which it claimed was the first to use ether. After a long, hard fight, and the presentation of irrefutable evidence, the name of Dr. Crawford Long, of Georgia, was finally added as having been the first person to have used it in his practice, but of Dr. Wilhite, who actually discovered its properties, nothing is said, and no credit is given except in some old musty out-of-date medical journals which nobody will ever read.

Dr. Wilhite was a native of Carnesville, Georgia, but he attended medical college in Charleston, and graduated in 1852. In 1853 he located in Anderson. He had been married several years earlier to Miss Cora Hillis. When they first came to Anderson they lived in what came to be known as "The old Towers House" on Whitner street. Later he bought a lot on McDuffie street, where he built a handsome house, and there his family has dwelt ever since, the place now being the property of his daughter, Miss Mary Wilhite. Dr. Wilhite soon became a popular physician. He opened a drug store on Brick Range, with a Harrison as his partner. At one time Dr. O. R. Horton was Dr. Wilhite's partner. "Wilhite & Harrison" was an Anderson firm until 1861. In 1874 Dr. Wilhite entered into a partnership with Major John R. Williams, and they bought the drug business of Benson & Sharpe on Granite Row. In 1878 Mr. Williams sold his share, and Dr. Wilhite took into partnership his eldest son, Frank T. Wilhite, and the business continued under the name of Wilhite & Wilhite. Later the younger son, Dr. J. O. Wilhite, also became a member of the firm. It did business in the town until both Dr. P. A. and Mr. F. T. Wilhite were dead.

In 1878 the State Board of Health was created, and Dr. P. A. Wilhite was appointed a member, and continued in active service until his death in 1892. When he died Dr. Wilhite was the oldest Mason in the upper part of the State, and was for years Royal Arch Mason. He was also a member of the United States Medical Association, and at one of the meetings of that body in New Orleans he was acknowledged to be the discoverer of anesthesia, and it was determined that his services ought to be recognized by the government.

Dr. Wilhite was a member of a commission sent by the State Board of Health of South Carolina to investigate the cause of yellow fever, and suggest means of preventing its introduction into the State. When he died he was the last member of the original Board of Health for the State.

Dr. Waller H. Nardin was born in Charleston, but his father dying in his infancy, he was brought to Anderson by his mother, who came with her sisters and father to make it their home when two of the sisters were made teachers in the Johnson Female University. The young widow married Mr. Daniel Brown, when her son was still a boy.

"Mark the perfect man, and behold the upright; for the end of that man is peace." Had the psalmist known Dr. Nardin he could not have formed phrases more perfectly fitting him. His was the perfect and unconscious dignity that comes alone from birth and breeding. Gentle, sympathetic, courteous and kind, he was generally beloved. He married Miss Lucy Hammond, and their home on Fant street across from the old railroad station, set back in its great oak grove, was a center of hospitality. As the years passed and five attractive daughters graced the home, it became also a center of gayety. Three sons followed the girls; one of them is Dr. Waller H. Nardin, of the present day. Dr. Nardin had a large practice. He went through the war as army surgeon.

Dr. Richard Furman Divver was born in Charleston, where he

spent his boyhood. He was one of the band of boys who marched through the streets of that city with a banner bearing the words: "Welcome Home," in honor of the soldiers returning from the Mexican War.

When a young man he was one of the bodyguard of honor appointed to accompany Jefferson Davis and stand around the platform when he made his inaugural address. In his boyhood Dr. Divver was thought delicate, but he has outlived all of his family, most of his early friends and most of his war comrades, being now over eighty-seven years of age. In his youth he was placed under the supervision of Judge John Belton O'Neall, living for a time in Judge O'Neall's home, and the strongest sentiment of his life seems to be his reverence and admiration for that remarkable man and his teachings.

Dr. Divver served all through the war, and is at present commander of the Anderson camp of Confederate Veterans. He married Miss Frances Simpson, a descendant of Reverend John Simpson. They lived for a time in Newberry, then came to Anderson, where he has ever since resided. For several years he practiced medicine, and was considered a fine physician, but his heart was always in machinery, and in the early eighties he opened the Anderson Foundry and Machine Shops, which he managed for a number of years. He was once a locomotive driver on the C. and G. railroad, and was master mechanic at Helena where the shops were located.

Dr. Divver has a remarkable memory, and it is to him that all students of local or Confederate history turn for help and information. He has known many of the foremost people of the State in his eighty-odd years of life, and he has an inexhaustible fund of anecdote and reminiscence. Dr. Divver has been a prominent Mason for many years. A firm and loyal friend, an open and fair enemy, Dr. Divver made an impression on the town of his time which will not soon be effaced.

Dr. Samuel M. Orr was younger than the doctors just mentioned; during the war he was only a boy. After he graduated in medicine, he entered into partnership with Dr. Nardin, and Nardin & Orr were the leading physicians of the place after the elder Dr. Wilhite's practice began to wane, and the younger had not started. In Dr. Orr's ability as a doctor, people had the strongest faith. He was rough in his speech, but tender in his manner and dealing. On entering a sick room he might swear at the patient for being sick, but touch him with fingers softer than a mother's with her baby. Often he sat beside a sick bed all night long, and by sheer will pulled a very ill patient through a crisis. Though he was an able physician, and one greatly beloved, his heart, too, was elsewhere. He was interested in electricity, and soon took over from Mr. Will Whitner, who founded it, the Anderson Water, Light and Power Company. He greatly improved and extended the system, and soon Anderson was using electricity for many of her enterprises which before had been dependent upon steam power. It was when Dr. Orr was in charge of the electrical supply of the town that Anderson received the name, "The Electric City."

In later years the doctors in Anderson have been and at present are: Dr. Louis Gray, Dr. B. A. Henry, Dr. J. O. Wilhite, Dr. Halbert Acker, Dr. Harrison Pruitt, Dr. Olga Pruitt, the first woman to venture in the field; Dr. Land, Dr. Herbert Harris, Dr. J. C. Harris, Dr. J. R. Young, Dr. C. H. Young—the last three especially surgeons—Dr. Anna Young, Dr. Daniel, Dr. Breeden, Dr. Smethers, and before her marriage Mrs. M. L. Bonham was Dr. Lillian Carter, a successful osteopathist; Dr. Wade Thompson, Dr. J. E. Watson, child specialist; Dr. Barton, Dr. McWhirter, Dr. W. H. Nardin, and Dr. Campbell, specialists, eye, ear, nose and throat; **Dr. J. O. Sanders, Dr. Latimer, Dr. Clinkscales, Dr. Bennett Townsend, Dr. Ashmore.**

With the exception of Dr. J. O. Wilhite these are all living to speak for themselves, or rather to have their patients speak for them, for each of them has warm friends and admirers among those who have been helped by their faithful ministrations.

Some of Anderson's early lawyers were, first a stately Judge, J. N. Whitner, "Father of Anderson;" Tyler Whitfield, B. J. Earle, J. W. Harrison, John V. Moore, Warren Wilkes, Samuel Wilkes, J. L. Orr, Sr., J. P. Reed, Sr., J. S. Murray, Peter Vandiver, E. M. Rucker, Sr., Ibzan Rice, J. H. Creswell, E. M. Keith, W. W. Humphreys, William H. Trescott, W. D. Evins. Some of these men came with the formation of the town, others only a year or two after, and most of them have left enviable reputations in the place where they served.

Then came lawyers who were young when the first were growing old: John B. Moore, John C. Whitfield, J. N. Brown, A. T. Broyles, Sanford Brown, B. F. Whitner, J. L. Orr, Jr., J. C. C. Featherstone, J. H. Earle, R. W. Simpson. As these grew old they were followed by E. B. Murray, J. L. Tribble, M. L. Bonham, George E. Prince, J. R. Vandiver, C. C. Featherstone, T. J. Mauldin, J. E. Allen, W. H. Frierson, J. E. Breazeale, H. H. Watkins, H. G. Scudday, E. F. Cochran, J. W. Quattlebaum, J. K. Hood, E. M. Rucker, Jr., J. M. Paget, G. H. Geiger and J. F. Rice. Many of these are still in active practice in Anderson, some have moved away, and some are dead. Among them are six who have risen to the bench, G. E. Prince, M. L. Bonham, C. C. Featherstone, T. J. Mauldin to the Circuit Court, and H. H. Watkins and E. F. Cochran to the Federal.

There are a number of young lawyers now in practice in the town; among them are C. B. Earle, J. L. Sherard, A. H. Dagnall, T. F. Watkins, G. C. Sullivan, Curran Cooley, Leon Harris, Rufus Fant, K. P. Smith, Leon Rice, Thomas Allen, T. P. Dickson, R. E. Wilson, J. A. Neely, S. D. Pearman, O. H. Doyle, J. O. Havard, H. B. Watkins, Harold Major, Harold Dean; Ezekiel Major was a bright young lawyer just starting practice when death took him several years ago; S. M. Wolfe, H. C. Miller, S. L. Prince, G. B. Green and John K. Hood, Jr.

In all, Anderson has had fourteen judges to whom it was for a time at least "home." Three of them left the section long ago and became judges in their new localities. They were Judge Archer, of California, grand-uncle of Mr. William Archer, the railroad man. Judge Archer grew up in Anderson, and went west when he became a young man. Judge Jehu Orr, of Mississippi, was a brother of Judge J. L. Orr, born and bred in Anderson county. Judge J. H. Earle, who once practiced at the Anderson bar, then went to Sumter and later to Greenville. He ran for Governor against Tillman in 1890. Later he was elected to the bench, and afterwards to the United States Senate. When Anderson was his home he lived at the place which later was General Ayer's Seminary. Judge C. C. Featherstone, of Greenwood, was an Anderson boy, a pupil of Mr. W. J. Ligon. Judge Munro lived in Anderson for several years just after the war. Judge T. J. Mauldin lived in Anderson for a time in his young manhood, and was "Tom Joe" to the Anderson boys and girls of the time. Judge Orr, Judge Reed and Judge Murray belonged to the older time, and Judge Whitner was at the very beginning.

One of the most interesting men who ever practiced at the Anderson bar was William Henry Trescott, who lived in Pendleton, and came to Anderson daily to his office. He was in partnership with W. W. Humphreys, and their office was in the second story of the building now occupied by the Penny Store, then the mercantile establishment of N. K. and J. P. Sullivan.

Mr. Trescott had specialized in the study of international law, and his skill in diplomacy was very remarkable. Much of his life was spent in positions where his knowledge of international law made his services very valuable. James G. Blaine regarded him as the ablest lawyer in his special line that he had ever known. When he was thirty years of age he became Secretary of the Legation in London, and he was selected by General Cass for Assistant Secretary of State under President Buchanan, and was acting Secretary when the war broke out.

Mr. Trescott represented Anderson county in the Legislature during and just after the war, until the reconstruction period set in.

A few years later he went to Washington to live. In conjunction with General Grant he made a treaty with Mexico. With Caleb Cushing he made a treaty with China. He and Charles A. Dana made a treaty with England. In all of these transactions he represented the law for America's interests. They were all ratified by the Senate. He was connected with the Department of State as special councillor for a number of years, including the incumbency of Hamilton Fish and James G. Blaine.

He was a prominent figure in diplomatic circles in Washington, and remained in active life until a few years before his death. He was quick-witted, and could argue ably on either or both sides of any matter. One of his friends once undertook to warn him of the instability of political position, saying: "You had better look out or some day you'll be stranded with these sudden changes of administration." To which Mr. Trescott laughingly replied: "No administration can change any quicker than I can." One of his daughters says that it was in the drawing-room of her father's home in Washington one Sunday afternoon that the Democratic and Republican parties made the compromise that enabled the reform movement in South Carolina to become successful. Hampton should become governor and the carpet-bag administration in the State should be scrapped, provided South Carolina agreed to the Hayes administration in Washington. Hard it was on Mr. Tilden, but the country could not have afforded a Democratic government at that time, and South Carolina badly needed one, so the compromise was best for all parties except cheated Tilden.

Mr. Trescott was a versatile and highly accomplished man. His graceful pen proved him a master of literature. His fine English is unsurpassed. The Confederate monument in Columbia bears an inscription which comes from his head and heart, and is considered a masterpiece of composition, while expressing the noblest and most patriotic sentiments.

It is said that when he belonged to the American Legation in London that he was once dining with a company of which Lord Macaulay was one. In the course of conversation Mr. Trescott made a quotation which he said was from Scott. Macaulay asked from what book it came. "Woodstock," replied Trescott.

"Oh, no!" replied Macaulay, who was noted for his reading, his memory and his accuracy, "I think you must be mistaken; I do not remember any such passage in Woodstock."

Mr. Trescott asked for a volume of Woodstock, and found the passage. In London, where a knowledge of "polite literature" was almost an open sesame to polite society, the incident established the position of the young American.

The inscription on the monument in Columbia runs:

>This Monument
>Perpetuates the Memory
>of those who,
>True to the instincts of their birth,
>Faithful to the teaching of the fathers,
>Constant in their love for the State,
>Died in the performance of their duty;
>Who
>Have glorified a fallen cause,
>By the simple manhood of their lives
>And the heroism of Death;
>And Who,
>In the dark hours of imprisonment,
>In the hopelessness of the hospital,
>In the short sharp agony of the field,
>Found support and consolation
>In the belief
>That at home they would not be forgotten.
>Let the stranger
>Who may in future times
>Read this inscription
>Recognize that these were men
>Whom power could not corrupt,
>Whom death could not terrify,
>Whom defeat could not dishonor,
>And let their virtues plead
>For just judgment
>Of the cause in which they perished.
>Let the South Carolinians
>Of another generation
>Remember
>That the State taught them
>How to live, and how to die,
>And that from her broken fortunes
>She has preserved for her children
>The priceless treasure of these memories,
>Teaching all who may claim
>The same Birthright
>That truth, courage and patriotism
>Endure Forever.

Among the earliest lawyers in the town were several who were noted for brilliant oratory. That was especially true of Warren Wilkes and J. H. Creswell, though there were other fine speakers among them.

In later years General M. L. Bonham has carried off the palm as a speaker in Anderson. For more than thirty years he has been asked to make an address whenever Anderson wished to make an especially fine impression, and he has always been accommodating, not only on political occasions, and men's meetings of every kind has he been asked to speak, but the women have demanded his services without mercy, and found him always courteous and ready to assist. General Bonham's speeches were always delivered in a most graceful manner, and were gems of polished English, abounding in interest and information.

The first merchant in Anderson to open a modern store for ladies' goods only was W. A. Chapman. He was for years the leading merchant of the town. His first store was in the hotel block on the north side of the square. Mr. Chapman is a Confederate veteran. His wife was Miss Jennie Keith, daughter of one of Anderson's brilliant lawyers, Elliot M. Keith.

Some of the familiar places and people in those days just after the reconstruction period were Mr. Osborne and his tan yard out Whitner street, which was then called Tan Yard Street; Ed Anderson and his little white horse, Mack; Joe Martin, with a smile that would not wear off, and always a hearty welcome to his harness shop which stood somewhere on Granite Row; Newt Scott, the town marshal, Anderson's sole policeman, at once the guardian of the village and the friend of all the boys; Davy Woodson, printer, called by one old Andersonian, "a ray of sunshine of a peculiar kind." Long, tall, rather sombre looking, but so friendly that never man, woman, child nor dog passed within his radius that he did not call out hearty greeting. He lived out of town then where West Franklin Street is now.

One of the notable characters who used to come frequently into the village from his cabin home up in the Fork, was Steve "Chattine," or more correctly Chastain, a short, strong-built man somewhat gray, full of self-confidence and much palaver, good-hearted, but with an imaginary enmity always against the town marshal and the "a'istoc'acy," and a notion that his visit to the village was a failure unless he was arrested, or had been engaged in a scrap. He was afflicted with an insatiable thirst.

Another character of those days was Silas Massey, of notorious fame, one of the few slave owners who was unkind to his servants. His cruelty consisted rather in starving than in beating them, but as he nearly starved himself, he probably did not know that he was mistreating them. On his visits into town he used to buy old-time hard tack crackers and cheese for his lunch, and it seemed to him such a delicacy, that he could not wait until his usual dinner time to enjoy the feast, but ate it at once with tremendous relish.

Old man Billy Holmes, once town marshal, later court cryer, was long remembered for the unction with which he called "Oh, yes, oh, yes; the court is now opened!"

Lute Braddy was a well-known tinner. He mended everybody's tinware for nothing, and was a better friend to everybody else than to himself, for he remained always a poor man. His successor in the tin business was Mr. L. H. Seel, who, to the indignation of his patrons, charged them for repairs. He was always met in the first days of his business in Anderson with the remonstrance: "Why, Lute Braddy used to do such jobs for nothing." To which Mr. Seel pertinently replied: "That's what kept him poor, too; I'm working for a living."

A list of the town characters of the time would be incomplete without mention of Grant Fant, an old negro who was everybody's friend and everybody's servant, everybody's chum. He belonged before the war to the mother of Mr. Wood Fant. That was before the days of ice cream, but the children did not miss the fun of buying goodies. Grant made boiled custard, and all of his patrons were not children, though they could never let him pass if they could coax the pennies from their mothers to indulge in his delicacy. Grant's custard was the best ever made, according to those who ate it, and many were the inquiries for his recipe. With arms akimbo and thumbs in his vest armholes he always made the same reply: "I never tells nobody how I makes me boiled custard." His regular calling was helper in the marble yard.

Where the city hall now stands Alfred Moore kept a blacksmith shop.

Cricket Hays was another character who delighted the boys of fifty years ago. His favorite throne was a seat on the iron steps of the courthouse. There he loved to bask in the sunshine, with an old vest for an overcoat. Hezekiah McGee, who stood on his head in front of the courthouse and spelled, pronouncing by syllables: "Abominable big bumble bee with his tail cut right short, smack, smooth, big, little, square toed-off," and reciting all of the books of the Bible, and the stations on the C. and G. Railroad.

Some of the business houses were Leavell & White, marble yard, and furniture store in the second story of the Masonic building;

John M. Partlow, confectionary; Samuel Owen, repairs clocks; John Milwee, photographer, pictures made for fifty cents; Bewley & England, merchants; Sharpe & Watson; D. A. Keasler, Bleckley & Crayton, Sloan, Sullivan & Co., Sloan & Towers, J. T. Horne, dentist; B. M. Frost, dentist; Evans & Hubbard, drugs; Cater, Gailliard & Hammond, sewing machines; J. W. Bohannon, cabinet maker; Wilhite & Harrison, drugs.

A few years later the firms are: N. K. & J. P. Sullivan on the north end of Granite Row; W. F. Barr, Wilson & Reed, A. B. Towers, Wilhite & Wilhite, Bleckley & Brown on the south end of Granite Row; the others all came on the same Row. On Brick Range was the old National Bank; Julius Poppe's store, where there were the most delightful dolls and other toys at the front, whatever may have been in the back in the funny stone bottles, half white and half brown. He had the flower beds in his charming little red brick Dutch-looking home grounds bordered with those same bottles stuck in the earth. Fant's book store and post-office, Miss Charlotte Daniel's ladies' store, Mr. Bostell's jewelry store. On the north and south sides of the square there were a few buildings, but the whole space was not built up. J. R. and L. P. Smith's Tailor shop stood where Theo Fant's store was so long on the corner; A. P. Hubbard kept a toy shop further down, and the only sodawater fountain in the town, and no ice. Tolly's furniture store, Moss & Brown, a sort of general store; McCully & Cathcart, J. B. Watson & Son. Where Plaza Hotel stands, the old Waverly House. On the south side, the Centennial boarding house about the center, Crayton's store on the corner, the Masonic Building where the present one stands, and possibly one or two others.

On sales days old Mrs. Gambrell used to be close at hand with a little covered wagon from which she sold ginger cake and cider.

When the long summer days came these merchants attended to business in the mornings, and after their midday dinner they gathered in front of one or another of the stores on their own row usually, and seated on upturned boxes or tilted back in split bottomed chairs they listened and shouted with boyish laughter to the inexhaustible yarns of Messrs. N. K. and J. P. Sullivan, Mr. Bleckley, Squire Whitfield, or some of the other raconteurs of the time, for the town of the seventies was rich in good story-tellers, and the men had time to live, not merely exist.

Some other business houses of the time were S. M. Pegg, who ran his advertisement upside down, "Pegg, always topsy-turvy;" John R. Cochran, general merchandise; W. M. McGukin & Co., groceries; Simpson Hill & Co., drugs, in the hotel corner next to Main street, the same site which in Hotel Plaza is occupied by Evans' Pharmacy; M. Lesser, on Granite Row: McGrath & Byrum, bar room and family grocery.

In the hotel block about this time a young jeweler set up a modest shop. A genius at repairing and making things was John M. Hubbard, C. A. Reed's Emporium, a sounding title that commanded respect. The people didn't know what it meant, but they liked to say it. Further down were Cunningham & Prevost, then M. Kennedy, bar room.

Mr. A. B. Towers, Mr. A. P. Hubbard, Dr. Divver, Mr. Crayton and Mr. Luther P. Smith were the leading spirits in prohibition work in that day. It is a pity that none of them, except Dr. Divver, lived to see the whole country go bone dry, legally at any rate.

The men of the seventies made the Anderson we know today. They picked up the threads broken by war and knitted them together again, and being what they were as a rule, high-toned, honorable, fair-minded and industrious, they laid well the foundations of the city which has grown from the village of their day.

Leaving the square going north and south there were residences on both sides of the street. Between the Bleckley home, and the old Anderson house which stood where Mrs. Frank Johnson's home is now, there were no houses at all, only fields of cotton. Then the Watson house, and the old E. A. Bell house, which Mr. Bell used to call "The Bishoprick," because it was there that Bishop Capers lived when he made Anderson his home, and it was to that place that the first load of commercial fertilizer ever brought to Anderson was carried, leaving in its wake such an odor that the town council debarred any other from passing through the village streets.

Going south from the square there were a few inferior store rooms occupied by small businesses, as far as Church street, where on the corner stood the Garrison house; a brick building was next, then the old Elijah Webb house, standing right on the street, but with a pretty flower garden at the south end. Stephens' carriage shop was a big square brick building which stood where Stephens' shop is now, and the dwelling was the same which is still back of it, but remodeled. Judge Reed's beautiful home came next.

In those days McDuffie street stopped at Earle street. The Earle residence stood at the head of the street. It was burned, and Mr. David Taylor bought the property and built the Taylor house, where his family still lives.

There were few residences on Calhoun street. Dr. Frierson's home stood about where Dr. Watson's house is now. Mr. A. P. Hubbard lived for a time in a house that stood about where the Barton house is. Another home stood across the street further down occupied by Mr. W. F. Barr. On Orr street the home of Mrs. Orr, widow of the Governor, it was the same house now the home of Dr. Louis Gray. The old Hill house is still standing, not greatly altered.

On Whitner street the old Tolly house, still standing, was one of the first built in the town. The Humphreys home was built by Major B. F. Whitner, and that was where he brought his bride, Miss Church, of Georgia. He lived there until after his father's death, when he went to live in the old Whitner home, "Rose Hill." The Ligon home, across the street, was built by Colonel Rucker when he married Miss Sarah Whitner.

River street was a long waste from the old square red brick house which stood where the Felix Watkins home is now, out to the home of Mr. Jesse Smith, which was the house now the residence of Mr. Walker, with the exception of the residence of Mr. G. W. Fant, which was the same now occupied by his daughter, Mrs. J. S. Aker, and a small house which stood where Mrs. Bigby's home is now, which was the place where Colonel and Mrs. J. N. Brown began housekeeping. There were no buildings on the west side of the street. About 1880 Mr. Kennedy built the house now the home of his daughter, Mrs. Barun O'Donnell.

Beyond the Smith house the next was the home of Mr. Sam Brown, a big unfinished old place which stood somewhere out towards Buena Vista Park. Beyond that the next was the home of Mrs. Georgia Brown, a widow with three sons. They lived somewhere out in the country, then toward Rocky River, and not far from Silver Brook.

On Greenville street, Mrs. Betty Moore, widow of Colonel John V. Moore, lived in a charming old house which stood where the Girls' High School is now located. Old Mrs. McKinney lived across the street and had in her front yard the loveliest snowball bush that ever grew. Mrs. Carrie McCully lived where the Duckett house is now. Captain P. K. McCully lived in the house which is still standing, though much altered, which almost faces the end of McDuffie street. The Cook house used to be the old Murrah Place. The two Cater homes were very much as they are now.

In 1870 Anderson was only a village; it has grown with giant strides. About 1890 it began to feel the stirring of new life, and with the building of the new hotel and the new opera house, and soon the new graded school, the town woke up and began to grow; since that its development has been rapid.

The first restaurant ever run in Anderson was opened in 1867 by Mr. A. P. Hubbard just back of the Bank of Anderson, on Main street. He also manufactured candy.

Circuses began coming again as soon as peace was declared, and somehow the people got the money to go to them; there disfranchised gentlemen and loathed Yankees mixed together, and for one day forgot their animosity. The first balloon ever seen in Anderson accompanied a circus in about 1867. The show grounds were where the Blue Ridge freight yards are situated, and that was their favorite site for many years.

Until well up into the eighties stock companies came to Anderson and gave theatrical performances every night for a week or more, and no Broadway favorite is more royally treated than were the young actresses who appeared in those plays. Many of them became well known to the people, and the return of a favorite was looked forward to with great delight. Maybe their acting and singing would not interest a Broadway audience, but the Anderson people felt that they were keeping well up with the fashionable world. They saw many of Shakespeare's dramas and all of the plays and musical comedies or operettas that had pleased New York just a year or two before. "Her Majesty's Steamship Pinafore" was given in Anderson in the seventies for a week, and everybody was singing and whistling its catchy airs.

Social life never stopped; everybody in that dear old town will be dead and buried before Anderson ceases to entertain.

Just after the war the home of Judge Reed was filled with girls, and from the Judge down to the small grandchildren who were beginning to make music in the house, they all loved company. His two older daughters had married before the war—Emelia, the eldest, was Mrs George Miller. Her eldest child was named for the South's chieftain, Lee; he died long years ago a little child. Two other little boys also were hers in the years that followed the war, Will and George. Both grew up to be musical, as were the twin girls who followed them, Carro and May, but it remained for her youngest child, Reed, to become widely distinguished as a singer. Her own voice was very beautiful, and it made rich music at the social gatherings in her father's home.

The next daughter, Julia, married John Peter Brown, brother of Colonel J. N. Brown, and in those post-bellum days some of her children were always at their grand-father's home; there was no lack of children in the gracious house. The other daughters who were young ladies in the seventies were Mary, who became the wife of B. Frank Mauldin, so long president of the Bank of Anderson; Eleanor, who married first William Davis, and after his death Mr. J. A. Brock. She was first a young lady and later a young widow, in the home. The next two sisters were quite young girls, but one of them was endowed with a lovely voice, and her music added to the gayety. She was Miss Cora, who married William Ligon. Her voice has been a source of pleasure and pride to the people of Anderson for many years. There has never been an occasion when the town wished to make an especially good impression with a musical program that Mrs. Ligon has not been asked to assist, and she has never refused if it was possible for her to be present. The next daughter was Lucy, who married Arthur Ligon, and spent her married life in Spartanburg. The youngest daughter was a small child in the seventies, Teresa, who became the mother of Lily Strickland, who has shed luster on her native town by her nationally recognized musical compositions. Colonel Reed had but two sons who lived to manhood. The elder was Clifton A., who lost his right hand in the war. A story is told of that day when young Reed had been detailed to hold horses during the fight at Haw's Mill. As he stood attending to the duty assigned him, a young comrade approached and said, "Reed, my gun's got out of order, lend me yours." To which the youth replied, "I won't let any man have my gun; here, you hold these horses and I'll take your place." The exchange was made, and while young Reed was in the act of loading his gun, he was wounded. After his return home, at the age of nineteen, he was married to Miss Fannie Kingsley. He describes his wedding suit: "You know it was impossible to get anything but homespun then, so my mother had woven by the women on the plantation a beautiful piece of jeans, which was dyed black. Of this I had made a long-tailed coat and a pair of trousers. I borrowed white kid gloves and a white satin vest from Dr. Nardin, and these, with a pair of cowhide, home-made boots, constituted my wedding garments." Those who knew Mr. Reed are sure that when dressed in his marriage outfit, he looked well-dressed and immaculate, because he always looked that way—there are some fortunate people who somehow wear their clothes in such a way that everything they put on looks well, and Mr. Reed was one of those happy mortals.

The old Judge was always well dressed; in those days of the seventh decade of the nineteenth century, he was an elderly man of florid complexion, stout, but tall enough to carry it well. He always wore expensive clothes, and a tall silk hat, and carried a gold headed cane; a very dignified figure. Yet he was often the life of the parties given by the young people of his home, and not one of his children or grand-children could make better music than the judge could when he got a violin in his hands.

The only other son was a bright, handsome boy, quite a few years younger than all of his sisters except the baby of the family. J. P., for he was called only by his initials, was a popular and a brilliant young fellow. When he was about fourteen years old he one day took a gun, which his father had forbidden him to touch, and went out shooting. In climbing over a fence the gun was discharged and the boy was shot in the left hand; the wound was so severe that amputation was necessary. When he grew up, he and his brother bought a pair of gloves between them. He attended the University of Virginia and began the practice of law in Atlanta in the eighties. Very soon after he was attacked by typhoid fever and died in his brilliant young manhood.

Judge Reed married Miss Caroline Hammond, of Dalton, Georgia, a near relative, however, of the Hammond family of Anderson. Mrs. Reed was a tiny, quiet, elegant lady in the full sense of that word as used by Carolinians of two generations ago, one of the people whom everybody loves.

Another place of the mid-years which was a center of gayety was the Bleckley home. There were five daughters there, ranging in age from two grown young ladies to one tiny baby, but the merriest, brightest, liveliest of the crowd was then and remained until 1914 the brilliant mother, Mrs. Elizabeth Hammond Bleckley. In many ways the most remarkable woman that Anderson has ever produced, and her like has not been found elsewhere.

She was born in 1837 at her father's country home, "Rosewood," several miles north of Anderson, the daughter of Colonel Frank Hammond, a man foremost in the affairs of his time and community, and his big two-story white house, set back in a flower garden, was one of the show places of his time. She was a student at Johnson University and some of the old school catalogues and stray numbers of the school magazine, "La Bas Bleu," show that she was foremost in the literary affairs of the school. From that institution she graduated at the age of seventeen, in 1853. At twenty-two she married Sylvester Bleckley, who had recently come to Anderson and opened a mercantile business which was destined to become one of the largest of the place. They began housekeeping in a modest cottage which stood where the Simpson home is now, opposite the Market Street School. From the start the Bleckley home was a social center, for both Mr. and Mrs. Bleckley loved people and liked to have them about them. Mrs. Bleckley has been heard to say that she had heard people say they were bored, but that in her whole life she never was bored, that she always had good times wherever she went. The great beauty of that statement was that where Mrs. Bleckley was nobody else was ever bored either; she carried a good time with her. She was gifted as an impersonator, and her rendering of both negro and mountain dialect was fine. To hear one of Mrs. Bleckley's recitations was a real treat, even to persons who had formerly thought that they did not care for recitations at all. She wrote essays that were not only rich in local history, but were always amusing, too. When she was a young woman there was in Anderson a dramatic club and Mrs. Bleckley was star actress. She loved bright colors and always wore them. She has been an invaluable member of the various women's organizations of the town, and her house was always open for the use of her societies if they needed it. Mrs. Bleckley was a fluent and witty talker but quick as her wit was she was never heard to say an unkind thing about anybody. She was a firm and benevolent friend to the negroes, and was the first person to show any interest in their schools. When she was president of the W. C. T. U., that organization through her efforts offered a medal to the negro students for the best recitation at their commencement on the subject of temperance. She always attended those exercises and encouraged in every way any effort that the negroes made towards improvement. When she lay for long weeks ill before her death, one of the pathetic sights was the visit every day of her old cook, who had been for some time too feeble to work, and lived in a house in Mrs. Bleckley's yard. The old woman would hobble in and Mrs. Bleckley, though suffering greatly, never failed to greet her with a cheery word. She was once in a railroad accident; fortunately it turned out to be slight and nobody was hurt, but Mrs. Bleckley's quick wit and action averted a panic. It was in a tunnel, and all of the lights went out after the dreadful jar which shook the passengers out of their seats. Some started to push out, some were hysterical, when Mrs. Bleckley raised her voice and began to sing: "There'll be no dark valley when Jesus comes." It quieted the crowd at once, and in a short time all was adjusted. At women's conventions or at other public gatherings her quick wit and funny remarks have caused shouts of laughter and she always did those things with an absence of self-consciousness that was amazing; she never did anything to attract any attention to herself—she just thought of something that was apropos or funny and she simply handed it on. She was the life of every party she attended; but a personality cannot be described and it was her remarkable personality that made her what she was and prevented her from ever getting old; nobody ever thought of Mrs. Bleckley as old—she was an ageless person. Those who knew her will not forget her and to those who never knew her it is impossible to convey any idea of what she was.

Mrs. Bleckley's daughters were Josephine, married John E. Peoples; Mary, married Joseph J. Fretwell; Ella, married William Laughlin; Anne, married Albert G. Means; Zoe, married Frederick B. Maxwell.

Joseph Younger Fretwell lived in a beautiful grove about three miles west of Anderson and he was generally to be found somewhere on the place. His house was a comfortable, hospitable country home and his friends loved to visit there. Captain Fretwell was an interesting talker. He enjoyed a joke and could tell one well. He married rather late in life. It is said that when he was a young man, a friend, proud of his new baby daughter, laughingly told Mr. Fretwell that he would give her to him if he would wait for her. He did not marry and when the little girl, Louisa Russell, grew up, he demanded of her father that he fulfill his promise. The young lady being willing, Mr. Russell gladly entrusted her to his early friend. This couple were good neighbors, kind and sympathetic, and always ready to help where help was needed. Captain Fretwell was the father of Mr. J. J. Fretwell, Mr. A. G. Fretwell and Mrs. Carrie McCully.

Another of Anderson's early citizens was Joseph La Boon Byrum. His house was a mile and a half west of the city. It is a substantial brick building and when a few years ago it was bought for the Anderson Country Club, a little remodeling made of it an ideal clubhouse.

Mr. Byrum was a successful farmer and raised large herds of sheep, cattle and hogs and owned a number of slaves. He was a native of Hart county, Georgia. Once in his young manhood, when visiting Anderson, he made the acquaintance of Miss Peggy Burriss and fell in love with her. Whether the young lady made any stipulations regarding her place of residence is unknown, but as soon as he married her he came to Anderson to live. He cared little for his personal appearance or for the conveniences of life, but he was a man of stern integrity, the kind whose word is as good as his bond. He gave full measure of wheat and corn for the money paid and put honest lumber and honest work into every plough stock and wagon wheel that went out from his shop, for he was a mechanic as well as farmer. Mr. Byrum made few visits but gave a hearty welcome to every one who entered his house.

Mr. Byrum's shop was a veritable paradise for small boys and the good-natured mechanic allowed them many privileges. He was a fine shot and possessed the full outfit of a hunter. He was a powerful man and reached an advanced age before there was any perceptible waning of his vigor.

His wife, commonly called "Aunt Peggy," was a great nurse and was often called on by her neighbors to take care of their sick, and she never failed to respond willingly.

One of the wealthy and influential men of Anderson in the years preceding and just after the war was Mr. O. H. P. Fant. For several years he was depot agent, after Mr. Rice, and was succeeded by his son, Mr. H. B. Fant, who was agent for many years. Mr. Fant accumulated a good property and he bought the handsome place which Judge Orr had built a few years before the war and lived there a long time. Mr. Fant had a large family of sons and daughters and his home was always gay.

Mr. S. N. Pearman, who lived a few miles west of the city, represented Anderson in the Legislature for several terms. He had been a Confederate soldier and was one of the most progressive farmers of the county. His sons are Benjamin, "Chess," Frederick and Dean, all prominent men in the community. Mr. Benjamin Pearman is a successful politician. His daughters are Miss Carrie, who has been a popular teacher, and Mrs. Samuel Moore (Maggie). One of his grand-daughters, Miss Carrie Moore, is one of the best known teachers in the city schools.

CHAPTER XX.

SOME PUBLIC BUILDINGS.

THE first public building was, of course, the court house. The one built of logs by Mr. Robert Wilson served for a few years until the new town showed that it had come to stay, then the primitive structure gave way to one of brick. It is probable that Mr. Wilson built that one, too. It was an unpretentious square house with a small court room and a few offices.

In 1850 that building was remodeled and beautified. It must have been a stately edifice when it first graced the public square, for even in its old age and decline it was dignified and architecturally good. The old red brick was plastered over and painted white, a belfry was added at the western end. Four large columns were erected on a portico at each end, giving it a decidedly Grecian air. There were two curving flights of ornamental iron stairs at both entrances running from the ground to the second story, which was the court room. There were doors beneath the stairs opening into the first floor which contained offices. The windows were large and arched. Then the crowning glory was added, a bell, a big bell that could be distinctly heard for some distance outside of the town.

Up to that time the largest bell in the village had been the clanging little market bell which announced on the early morning air— "fresh meat," its voice barely reaching the residents on the edge of the town.

Small as it was the market bell long rang the curfew at nine o'clock, warning all negroes to retire to their homes and not to appear on the streets again until day. That bell is now owned by Mr. J. S. Fowler and used on his farm. It now tells the negroes who work for him when to go to work and when they may quit.

But the new bell! the big mouthed bell! how the hearts of the citizens swelled with pride as its deep tones boomed on the air. Judge Reed, having been the most eager and determined in urging the people to buy it, was given the privilege of being the first person to ring it, and as its clear notes sounded out, he threw his hat in the air and shouted "Hurrah for Anderson!" After its installation it rang the curfew warning until the end of the war; and in reconstruction times again its warning notes rang out at nine o'clock, but then it was the white people who were to retire and not be seen until next day.

Dr. W. H. Nardin was out on professional business one night

and was arrested and locked up in the court house until morning. He managed after much trouble and delay to get a note to his wife to allay her anxiety at his non-appearance. Captain P. K. McCully too, was arrested one night and locked up. The captain, usually a very mild and quiet gentleman, would ruffle up and almost sputter to the day of his death whenever he had occasion to allude to the incident. Other prominent men had similar experiences.

The town marshal used to ring the hours through the night on the court house bell. During the day people were expected to keep their own time, and if the marshal went to sleep and forgot to strike an hour or, waking, found it might be half past, never mind, he struck anyhow and nobody knew any better; some wakeful soul might murmur "everything's all right, Uncle Billy's at his post."

The bell also gave the fire alarm. It is the same good bell which for years struck the hours of the clock on the court house steeple before the clock went on a permanent strike.

The brave little court house with its Grecian columns and imposing double staircases, after a time seemed to dwindle, or the town grew; anyhow, there arose new notions of architecture and the business of the county was too voluminous for the little court house and the temple of justice, once so admired, was anathematized, execrated and abused until today it is very hard to find a photograph of the building at all. When views were taken of the square it was most carefully excluded; plain, ordinary two-story stores were freely photographed and handed about with pride, but the one really beautiful building was not deemed worthy of a place in the picture.

In 1898 a new court house was erected on the site of the old one. It was of the most pronounced mid-Victorian type of architecture, but how the people admired it!

It was dedicated Monday, June 27th, 1898. The building committee was composed of Supervisor Snelgrove, J. D. Maxwell, J. F. Clardy, J. H. Jones and W. D. Garrison.

At ten o'clock the court officials with the members of the bar and representatives of the local press formed in procession and marched from Hotel Chiquola to the court house, scarcely one hundred steps, but they marched in imposing array. A newspaper of the time says: "The spacious court room was crowded to its utmost capacity, a great many ladies honoring the occasion with their presence." The Anderson orchestra played its very best and J. L. Tribble, chairman of the committee on arrangements, called the assembly to order. Reverend J. N. H. Summerell, pastor of the First Presbyterian church, made the opening prayer. Then after another musical number Mr. Tribble made an address. It was a fine and interesting speech. He wandered all around among the notable buildings of antiquity, both sacred and secular, quoted the Bible, the history and literature of Babylon, of Egypt, of Greece, of Rome, of England and America, then he said: "It has been the boast of this grand old county for years that she has outstripped her neighbors and some even dare claim for her the name 'banner county'—and I never understood why people who claimed so much for themselves were content to suffer so long the old building—a fit abode for vermin—to occupy the most conspicuous place in their chief city. But the laws of evolution are inexorable. The fullness of time came and our past chagrin at the appearance of the old gives way before our joy and admiration of this beautiful temple of justice which stands a thing of beauty and a joy forever! There are buildings more elaborate in design and ornamentation, more artistic in finish, but many of them represent useless expenditure of money without utility of purpose." He continues then to praise the committee, the architect, the commissioners and the builders, then says: "You have a building of which you may all be justly proud. It is modern—and it has no mortgage on it—tasteful and attractive, beautiful for symmetry, built out of first class materials from the first brick to the final one that crowns the tower. It is of that style of architecture somewhat of the composite order—Americanized. That is, it has all that is necessary to make it pleasing to the eye, tasteful in ornamentation, essentially useful and comfortable." Etc.

Mr. Tribble was followed by Mr. J. E. Breazeale who, on behalf of the county board of commissioners, turned over the keys to the presiding judge, Honorable W. C. Benet. Mr. Breazeale also made a fine speech, giving a history of the building from its inception to that moment.

Then followed the oration of the day, Judge Benet's speech of acceptance. He also praised and admired the new court house, he congratulated the city and the county upon its possession and complimented the people of the county, the people of the city, the commissioners, the committee, the architect and the builders. He said: "Here now it stands, a stately structure, beautiful exceedingly, with graceful turret and lofty tower, quaint gable and artistic porch, a building to be proud of, a building that does honor to its architect and builder, to the brain which conceived and the hand which constructed it." . . . "But while we stand and look and admire, memory cannot refrain from looking backward, and thinking of the old structure which stood where this now stands. Unlovely it must have been in its youth, unsightly it became in its age. The outside view revealed no line of beauty; the inside view was destitute of grace. Small, mean and squalid, its day was done; it was time that it should be demolished. And yet its demolition was not without regret. I see before me within the bar of this spacious and beautiful court room gray-haired councilors who must think of that old court room with sadness and regret. For them how many hallowed associations cluster around that building whose place knows it no more forever. Shabby were its precincts, and dusty were its purlieus, but they cannot forget that it was the scene of their professional triumphs, the arena of many a hard-fought contest. And for them the dingy old court room is thronged with the shadowy ghosts of the departed, dimly seen in the mists of the past. And as figure after figure appears within that old bar they seem to hear once more the sound of voices that have long been still. Again the bare, discolored walls seem to reverberate with the eloquence which held the listening throng in thrall.

"In that ghostly company they see several venerable men who were elevated from the Anderson bar to the judicial bench; men whose learning and uprightness shed luster on their profession and did honor to their position. They see one who graced the speaker's chair in Washington, and represented his country abroad at an imperial court. They see others who for their country's sake left their mimic strifes of the bar for the bloody battles of the Civil War, some of them never to return. Others they see who filled the measure of a lawyer's busy life and then rested from their labors.

"All are gone, the old familiar faces, but the memory of them haunts the old court room, now itself only a memory. There were giants on the earth in those days—men of great learning, men of high character, men of great ability, men who maintained a lofty standard of professional conduct. What better dedication of this new court house can be desired than that the mantles of Anderson's distinguished dead should fall upon the shoulders of the members of her bar, and that they might be baptized with the spirit of those great departed who fought their battles and gained their laurels in the old court room and made their county famous? What greater benison could be pronounced on this new court room than to express the hope and belief that this spacious bar and those lofty walls will be made familiar with the faces and the voices of a succession of eminent judges, eloquent advocates, learned councilors and courteous, honorable gentlemen, such as those whose memory has made sacred that old court room which is now no more?"

Judge Benet continued his speech by pointing toward the future and exhorting the people to press forward.

In a short, impressive speech, Mr. G. E. Prince, later himself a judge, presented the criminal code to Solicitor Ansel, afterward Governor Ansel, who responded in a very eloquent and learned speech.

Next Mr. J. K. Hood presented the Bible to the clerk of the court with an appropriate speech. Mr. E. F. Cochran, now Judge Cochran, responded on behalf of the clerk.

The presentation of the bailiff's staves was made by E. M. Rucker, Jr., afterward professor of jurisprudence at the South Carolina University. On behalf of the sheriff, Colonel R. W. Simpson responded.

Architect Milburn was called upon by the chairman and made an appropriate response.

The benediction was pronounced by Reverend W. T. Capers, rector of Grace Episcopal Church, now Bishop Capers of western Texas.

Many of the men who took part in that day's exercises are living and still useful citizens; yet now, just thirty years later, there is a wail, "the old court house is inadequate, unsuitable, dirty, ugly, an architectural monstrosity; it must go." Truly that "thing of beauty and a joy forever" did not last as well as did its reviled predecessor.

That year of 1898 saw many improvements in Anderson. The old rectangular brick jail, which must have been built sometime in the forties, as it was the successor of the first jail which was situated back of the court house, was torn down and the present jail, the front part of it looking like a nice residence, presenting a good appearance to the street, and occupied by the sheriff, was built.

Also the City Hall on the corner of Market and South Main streets was erected, and the really big bell, the fire bell, was put in its tower.

Hotel Chiquola was still in its glorious youth in 1898 and considered a very fine building.

The Masonic Temple was also comparatively new, having been erected in 1889 with ceremonies as elaborate as those attending the dedication of the new court house. Mr. R. S. Hill was Worshipful Master of Hiram Lodge at the time. Dr. Divver, Grand Master. The cornerstone of the first Masonic building was laid on Friday, October 12, 1855. When it was opened in 1889 whatever had been put into it with the exception of some silver coins, had crumbled to dust, the receptacle not having been air tight. They were not of any great interest, however, as their dates ran only from 1834 to 1853.

Hram Lodge was established in Anderson in 1848. That was a day long looked upon as a red letter one in the town's history.

There was a great crowd in the streets and many visitors came for the event. Speaking, plenty of speaking and said to be fine speaking, too, followed by a dinner at the Benson House.

The Masons used in those earlier times to celebrate with elaborate exercises the day sacred to St. John the Divine. There is a tradition of such a celebration and at the same time dedication ceremonies at Milford's Mill near the Abbeville line where a lodge was established in 1867. It was Herman Lodge No. 116, A. F. M. Speakers were Colonel W. D. Wilkes, Governor Orr and Dr. N. J. Newell.

There were Masonic Lodges at Williamston and at old Piercetown soon after their establishment.

Along in the days when the century was new, Mr. Swain Gilmer, of Anderson, married a Charleston girl, Miss Jennie Krammer, and brought her to Anderson to live. The young couple had a cottage on South Main street. There the little bride made a sweet and dainty home, but she was not too busy to see much that transpired in the streets around her and the sick, wounded and suffering people that were sometimes carried past her house with only small, stuffy and often dirty homes to be taken into appealed strongly to her sympathy.

Mrs. Gilmer was a "society woman" and an invitation to her house was always eagerly accepted. One day she invited a number of her friends for an afternoon. When they had gathered in her pretty rooms she told them about the miserable things she had seen and she said "Anderson needs a hospital, and if you women will undertake to build one, it will be done." Her earnestness and the strength of her cause struck a sympathetic note and then and there the Anderson County Hospital Association was formed. Small, almost insignificant it seemed at first, and the cause it championed was so big. Mrs. Gilmer was elected president and was untiring in her work. In the years that followed there were several other women who filled that office, for after her first term had expired Mrs. Gilmer refused re-election though she never for a moment faltered in her interest or her work.

The women worked earnestly and the membership grew. Money was raised by the time-honored methods of women's organizations and public sentiment was enlisted. After several years' work under the efficient leadership of Mrs. R. C. Webb, who succeeded Mrs. Gilmer as president and put into that work all of the energy and enthusiasm of which she was capable, and of Mrs. S. C. Baker, daughter of the beloved Dr. W. H. Nardin, who was himself an ardent member of the association, the movement had grown so big that the ladies asked the co-operation of the men of the community. A new organization grew out of the old one. Mr. R. S. Ligon was induced to become its president and faithfully he has served with time, interest and money for almost twenty-five years.

In 1907 the first building was erected on Fant street. It was a beautiful little hospital and well equipped. Several years later it was burned. A careless delivery man carried gasoline to the hospital and while smoking attempted to pour it into a tank. An explosion followed and soon the place was wrapped in flames. Fortunately there were at that time only twelve patients in the building. The staircases and elevator were burning from the start and several patients were taken out through second story windows. One little nurse, Miss Clinkscales, repeatedly climbed a ladder and brought out sick people. Other nurses also worked faithfully.

The hospital was immediately rebuilt. It had never entirely ceased functioning—a couple of houss across the street were secured and the work went on as well as the limitations permitted.

In a few years' time Dr. Singleton Breeden built a small but bautifully equipped hospital next to his home in North Anderson which has been eminently successful. It is known as St. Mary's.

In 1920 Dr. Smethers bought the old Johnson Female University dormitories and remodeled the building, making of it a thoroughly modern and well furnished hospital, "The University Hospital." It is mysterious what sick people did before these hospitals were erected, because they are all three full most of the time and often there is no room in any of them for some unfortunates.

Another need which had long been felt in Anderson was an opera house or theater. The little theater built in the Masonic temple which, in 1889, had seemed so splendid had long been outgrown. In 1913 and 1914 Mr. J. S. Fowler put up a nice, up-to-date theater building on Whitner street. It had a formal opening and the newspapers of the time are enthusiastic over the "happy culmination of dreams and aspirations of many years" and states that "the interior of the house rivals fairyland" and assures the youthful people who were fortunate enough to witness the dedication exercises of "Anderson's first real theater" that when they are old the memory of those exercises will be as "fresh and bright as the magic colors from the artist's brush that make of this superb creation a thing of bewildering beauty." Mr. Fowler, president of the Anderson Development Company, was chairman. General Bonham made a brilliant and eloquent address. Mayor Godfrey also spoke and his opening sentence was: "I suppose that February 18th will go down in the history of Anderson as one of the most notable days in the life of the city." C. H. Bleich, imported from somewhere else, was manager of the theater. He also spoke, making extravagant promises, which probably he never intended to keep. Mr. Bleich did not remain in Anderson long. The first entertainment was on February 19, 1915, a musical comedy, "The Prince of Tonight."

The beautiful little Carnegie Library on North Main street has for twenty years been a real source of strength and pride to the Anderson people. It, too, was the outcome of the work and interest of women. About 1896 or 1897 the Women's Christian Temperance Union became interested in a scheme proposed by some traveling library agent to establish a "Lend a Hand Library." Just at first the ladies thought that a small thing of that kind was about all they could manage. But when they began to talk about the matter to their friends they found that the people of Anderson were anxious for a library and that the co-operation they would receive would warrant the establishment of a real library of their own. Mrs. G. E. Prince was president of the W. C. T. U. at that time. Other working members were Mrs. S. Bleckley, Mrs. William Laughlin, Miss Ida and Miss Lois Watson, Mrs. J. H. vonHasseln and a few others, though the society was small. With the hearty assistance of other women of the town the library was started. The city council gave the use of a room in the city hall and a number of books and plain shelves were donated. A Library Association was formed. Mrs. Daisy Aldrich Bonham was its first president. At the beginning the members of the association served as librarians, but very soon the association thought that its interests would be served if it paid a small sum for the services of one capable woman to take charge of the work, and Miss Margaret Evans was selected. She opened the library on Monday, Wednesday and Saturday afternoons and on Saturday mornings. The dues were one dollar a year and a surprising number of persons became members, also a goodly number of new books were purchased from time to time. Miss Sue Whitfield became practically substitute librarian, Miss Evans calling in her services whenever she found that she could not attend to the duties of the office. That little library lasted for some years, then the members of the association began to talk about a Carnegie fund. Mr. Carnegie was written to about the matter and the result was a liberal donation provided the town would also contribute a stipulated sum every year. It was by no means an exorbitant amount, and the city council made the required promise. Then Colonel J. N. Brown, of Anderson, became interested and donated a lot and ten thousand dollars, the interest to be used. In 1904 the new building was ready for occupation and opened with appropriate but simple exercises. Miss Evans declining to become librarian of the new library which would require so much more of her time, Miss Whitfield was elected. In a short time she became Mrs. Geiger, but she continued to serve the library until her lamented death in 1927.

The library is justly an object of pride and love to the Anderson people. When the new Carnegie library was established, it was realized by the women that its affairs required the business experience of a man and Mr. J. A. Brock was made president of the association. He has served loyally and faithfully for more than twenty years.

CHAPTER XXI.

THE SPANISH WAR.

PRESIDENT McKINLEY called for volunteers against Spain in 1898, and the Anderson organization was the third to be sworn into the service of the United States. There was a little feeling of uneasiness and of curiosity concerning the attitude the South might take should the country get into war; but the sons of the Confederate fighters showed their loyalty immediately and unmistakably.

The company organized in Anderson had as its captain Henry Hitt Watkins, now Judge Watkins; first lieutenant, Joseph H. Grant, living for years in Oklahoma. He married a daughter of Mr. George W. Fant. Second lieutenant, Joseph Newton Brown, nephew of Colonel J. N. Brown; first sergeant, William P. Nicholson; second sergeant, Edward L. Johnson; other sergeants, Stephen E. Leverette, Benjamin M. Sullivan, John C. Acker, Charles W. Gentry; corporals, John Scott Murray, Richard Furman Divver, Jr., Henry C. Martin, George F. Baker, Charles F. Power, Luther E. Tate; musicians, Joseph J. Trowbridge, Leon P. Brock; artificer, John F. Tatum; wagoner, John C. Robins; mail carrier, Victor Cheshire; privates, Newton Acker, Samuel Adams, Paul E. Ayer, Thomas H. Bigby, James H. Brown, Prue H. Burriss, Walter C. Burriss, Robert B. Cheshire, Will M. Cochran, Daniel P. Coley, James A. Dillingham, afterwards Anderson chief of police and popularly believed to be afraid of nothing under the sun; John Dodd, Joseph B. Dodd, Adolphus A. Duncan, Baylis D. Earle, Preston C. Fant, Clyde N. Fant, Robert T. Feltman, Alfred N. Fortune, Jefferson Gambrell, Ira C. Giles, Edward O. Gordon, Guy T. Grove, Almon C. Hall, James L. Hall, Samuel D. Harper, Romus D. Henderson, Steven F. Hoover, William M. Jolly, James P. Killebrew, George W. King, Larious O. King, Thomas B. Lee, Jr., Jay W. Madden, John W. Martin, Reuben M. Martin, Wade H. McGee, Jacob R. Miller, Hamilton C. Moore, Butler T. Norris, Thomas M. Norwood, Benjamin B. O'Shields, Charles Poore, Ernest H. Poore, Walter B. Pratt, Frank J. Rhody, John T. Rose, E. P. Ruidaeal, Edgar M. Scott, Noel B. Sharpe, William S. Sharpe, Rufus C. Sherard, Milledge L. Bonham, Jr.

Most of these men were from Anderson, both town and county. There were a few from other places. There were also a few Anderson men in other companies. But this Company C was Anderson's own. Among the young men who enlisted in the army in other companies was G. Cullen Sullivan, who was quartermaster in the Second South Carolina Regiment, and Crayton Cummings, who went to Cuba with a Georgia regiment.

James P. Killebrew from Edgefield, who had been a printer on a newspaper, was appointed correspondent to the Anderson paper from the camp. Some of the items he sent were:

"I did not write you last week as Captain Watkins said he would prefer to wait until this week before sending any news from camp. Well, to begin at the beginning, the boys remember the parting scene at Anderson, often speaking of it, and will remember it as long as life lasts as the greatest day in their career.

"Upon our arrival in camp, affairs were in rather a chaotic condition, but as soon as possible everything was put in shape and we spent some very pleasant hours at the auditorium at Hyatt's Park, where we were encamped at first.

"The company eats its meals at a table which is long enough for over a hundred people to eat at comfortably. The fare is plain, but it's wholesome and there is plenty of it."

This was written when the boys first went into service. As everybody knows, that condition did not last long and the food given the soldiers during the Spanish-American War became a national scandal; and some of the men who were in that army, though they got no further than the camps in the United States, were never again well people. Some lived for ten, twelve, fifteen years or more, but were never in good health after that camp life.

The notes from camp continue: "J. B. Dodd, of Charleston, formerly of Anderson, came up here on the eleventh and became a member of the company.

"We took the oath of service to the United States on the 12th of May, and as one private recently put it: 'Uncle Sam will be our daddy for the next two years,' and a braver or better set of boys I venture to say he will not find in his whole army. Our officers and our men are being complimented on all sides.

"Camp life seems to agree with the boys; so far none of them have been seriously sick; on the contrary, nearly all of them claim that they have enjoyed better health than ever before since they have been in camp.

"Lieutenant Grant on his return from Anderson, where he had been securing recruits for our company, was cheered over and over again when he made his appearance in camp.

"Our company was mustered in with 81 men upon its roll.

"On the 4th we were moved to tents, and the boys seem to like it better than sleeping in the auditorium. The boys are now anxious to secure their uniforms and guns.

"I have not time to write a long letter now, but will try to do better in my next.

"Our company is about the only one in the regiment that has not a company flag. This company is now Company C, and is color company of the regiment."

In his second letter Mr. Killebrew says that there were yet three companies lacking to complete the regiment, also that Captain Newman in charge of the commissary department said the uniforms and equipments would not be furnished the soldiers until the entire regiment had been mustered in, it might be a month before they were supplied. Some of the boys expecting to be furnished at once brought only the clothing they were wearing. He tells of several men from each company being detailed to "learn the culinary art;" mentions those sick from having been vaccinated, and tells of the enthusiasm with which a box of eatables sent by the Anderson ladies had been received. "We now drill three times daily, with the exception of Sunday, upon which day we are excused from everything except guard duty and roll call."

"A good many amusing things occur daily. The other day Governor Ellerbe attempted to pass a sentinel, but was peremptorily commanded to halt. He informed the sentry that he was the governor of South Carolina, but it made no difference, until the corporal of the guard was called who of course passed him through the line."

In Anderson life moved along without interruption, not enough men were gone from the town to create any great enthusiasm, and war seemed too far away to affect the people of the Piedmont to any great extent.

The box, or rather boxes of eatables mentioned by Mr. Killebrew were sent at the suggestion of Mrs. Annie McFall Harris, first wife of Dr. J. C. Harris. A number of ladies were interested and a great many good things were prepared and sent to Columbia to the Anderson company. The temporary camp at the capital was named in honor of Governor Ellerbe. After they had been brought up to their full quota and furnished with equipments and uniforms the boys were sent to Chickamauga, and after remaining there for a time were transferred to Florida, whence they hoped soon to cross to Cuba. But the Anderson boys never got into the thick of the fight, the war was over before they received the coveted call.

J. Scott Murray, son of Major Edwards Murray, who had been

drowned some years earlier, died in camp from disease. When his body was brought home for burial, war seemed to have come closer, and there was widespread sorrow, for the young man was generally liked, and his family had many sympathizing friends. He was buried at Silver Brook Cemetery.

Though the boys never left the United States, yet some who left home privates returned as officers. They had seen some real military life, if not any fighting.

When Company C returned to Anderson they were met by the Patrick Military Institute Cadets, and the Minstrel Band of Barlow Brothers escorted them through the square to a vacant storeroom on the west side where General Bonham made a beautiful address of welcome. A tray of flowers was presented to Captain Watkins, who accepted it with an eloquent speech of thanks. The colonel of the regiment, James Tillman, accompanied the Anderson boys home, and he made one of the speeches that he was famous for on that occasion. He was immensely popular with the soldiers.

The boys of Company C showed their affection for Captain Watkins by presenting him with a handsome sword.

At least one colored man from Anderson was connected in some capacity with the Spanish War. He knew well many of the soldiers in Company C. But he got to Cuba and they did not. He is John E. Sherard. John can talk quite a lot about what went on in Havana, and says he has often seen Roosevelt and his Rough Riders.

CHAPTER XXII.

MANUFACTORIES, MILLS AND OTHER INDUSTRIES.
INVENTIONS AND INTERESTS.

THE real beginning of the cotton mill industry in the Piedmont section dates back to 1820, when William Bates, a native of Massachusetts who learned his trade in the Arkwright Mills near Providence, came to Carolina at the instance of the Lesters, and finally built Lester's factory on the site of what is now Pelham. The machinery for that mill was bought in Philadelphia, second-hand, shipped to Charleston by water, and hauled from there in wagons over 300 miles. Mr. Bates was a thoroughly practical man, and his influence and handiwork was felt in all the small mills—about half a dozen in number—that were put up in the next twenty years, and had a more or less successful existence—such as Batesville, named for him; Bivingsville. Fingerville, Lesters, a mill at Greensboro, and a few others. The progress of these mills from 1840 was slow, and at the outbreak of the War Between the States, the Confederate Government took charge of all cotton mills in the south, and detailed officers to run them, using a large part of the product for army purposes.

The oldest cotton factory in the county is Auton. It was one of the few operated all through the war of the 60's.

The land on which the factory stands was bought by Benjamin F. Sloan, Enoch Berry Benson, Thomas M. Sloan and John T. Sloan, from Joseph Grisham, on the 20th of July, 1836. They formed a company and were chartered as a cotton manufacturing company with Benjamin F. Sloan as president. The building was of brick 50 feet wide, 150 feet long and two stories in height. The machinery—10 combination roller and flat cards with 960 flyer spindles etc., for manufacturing block yarns—was bought in Paterson, N. J., shipped by water to Charleston, thence by rail to Hamburg, and hauled from there on wagons to the site of the mill. It was set up by John Kershaw and William A. Bradley, of New Jersey, and commenced operating in February, 1838. Kershaw and Bradley remained long enough to teach and train hands to run the machinery. This company kept the spindles in motion until the 9th of January, 1866, when the president, Benjamin F. Sloan, sold it for $28,000 to John W. Grady, O. Hawthorne, and William Perry, a manufacturing firm of Greenville County, known as Grady, Hawthorne and Perry. On the 30th of May, 1866, this firm was by mutual covenant dissolved and William Perry was deeded the mill as his portion of the assets of the firm. Perry operated the factory until the 7th of November, 1868, when he deeded one-half interest to James W. Crawford ($10,-000); A. J. Clinkscales, ($7,000), and E. G. Roberts ($5,000), retaining one-half interest himself, and then operated under the firm name of William Perry & Company, until the 29th of January, 1884, when they conveyed to the Pendleton Manufacturing Company, an organization composed of the same individuals with the same interests but chartered by the state under the new name. On the 19th of August, 1875, William Perry deeded to J. W. Crawford and A. J. Clinkscales all of his interest in the Pendleton Manufacturing Company, likewise all the interest of Mrs. Margaret Perry and Miss C. L. Perry. The company having issued $30,000 in bonds and secured them by mortgage of all assets, and being sorely pressed by outstanding debts, John B. Sitton, of Pendleton, was appointed receiver by the court. After advertising fully, the property was sold at public outcry at Anderson, and bid off by Colonel J. N. Brown for the bond holders, who then organized by electing Augustus J. Sitton, president, and he was employed to run the mill until such time as they should agree to sell.

After keeping the factory in operation for fifteen months he asked for $2,500 to buy new machinery and change product, which was refused by the bondholders; then he advised its sale. It was advertised and sold at public auction in Anderson, and bid in by O. P. Jackson, for himself; Isaac Bell, of New York, and Arthur Barnwell, of Charleston. These men failing to take the property, Colonel J. W. Norris, Augustus J. Sitton and D. Sloan Maxwell asked the privilege of doing so at the same price bid in for by O. P. Jackson. The bondholders, at a full meeting, agreed that they should have it and authorized receiver to make titles to Augustus J. Sitton for two-thirds (he having bought D. Sloan Maxwell's interest), and Colonel J. W. Norris for one-third interest, which was done on June 3rd, 1879. Since that time the property was owned and the mill run by the same persons with A. J. Sitton as manager, under the firm name (without letters of incorporation) of the Pendleton Manufacturing Company. After the death of Colonel J. W. Norris, October 10th, 1899, Augustus J. Sitton bought his third interest for $21,500.

The postoffice at the mills was known for years as Pendleton Factory. Colonel Sitton married late in life, Miss Aull, and he combined her name with his, Au-ton, and had the place so christened. It has since that time been known as Auton, and the factory as Auton Mills.

Mr. Sitton died March, 1909, and the plant became the property of his heirs, Eugene N. Sitton and Mrs. Cema Sitton Chreitzberg, and has been managed by Mr. E. N. Sitton ever since. Very recently it has been bought by a northern company.

The Piedmont Mill was projected and successfully carried out by Colonel H. P. Hammett, a son-in-law of Mr. William Bates. That mill was started in 1873. Proving successful, in 1882 the Pelzer and Clifton Mills followed and proved to a skeptical world that cotton goods could be manufactured in the South as cheaply, if not actually cheaper, than in other sections of the United States.

South Carolina ranks third state in the Union now in cotton goods manufacture, being surpassed only by Massachusetts and North Carolina. In 1890 she stood next to Massachusetts, but has been surpassed by the old North State since that time.

For labor, the South Carolina Mills have depended almost entirely on the natives of the region, who are quick to learn, and generally honest and industrious, and not affected to any great extent with the grievances and unrest which afflict the foreign-born workers of the North.

In 1882 Mr. F. J. Pelzer, Mr. William Lebby, and Capt Ellison Smythe, of Charleston, organized the Pelzer Manufacturing Company. The site selected for their cotton mill was on the Saluda River, in Anderson County. Several shoals of the river were considered, and that known as Wilson's Shoals finally selected. The original capital was $400,000. By 1888 the paidup capital had been increased to $600,000. The company bought several shoals on Saluda River, and combining, secured the development of 5,000 horsepower by building a dam of stone two and a half miles below the Pelzer Mills. In August, 1894, it was decided to develop this property and build additional mills. In the fall of 1894 the capital of the company was increased to $1,000,000, the new stock being placed at 25 per cent. In 1882 there was not even a flag station on the C. & G. road at that point. In 1895 the town was a regular station, and the company paid the road nearly $200,000 a year in freights.

Captain Smythe was president and treasurer from its organization. Mr. Pelzer furnished much of the capital, and the town and mills were given his name. Captain Smythe at once established a model town. There was a good school running ten months, free to all children of the town. The place had also from the first a lyceum course and reading rooms which, in 1895, contained 3,000 volumes and subscribed to 25 newspapers and magazines, all free to the people. There was a successful savings bank started, known as the Chicora Savings Bank, Captain Smythe its president. The company built ten stores which were rented to as many mercantile concerns. Both the town and the mill have continued to grow in every respect in the years that have passed.

In the mill town of Piedmont, lying partly in Anderson and partly in Greenville counties, there is a little museum which would do credit to a large city. It is the work of Mr. Rowell. There he has collected Indian relics and work, interesting specimens of Carolina ore, pictures of old time places and people, curiosities from many foreign countries, although the collection is chiefly local, and it is marvelous how much he has found in the locality that is worth placing in the museum.

In 1888 the city of Anderson caught the spirit of the new South, and begun to think and dream of whirling machinery, of busy communities where Anderson cotton could be manufactured into yarn and cloth and not have to be sent to some distant state.

The first mill in the town was Anderson Cotton Mill, now located near where the old Blue Ridge Car shed had stood so long. The capital was $100,000. Mr. J. A. Brock was its first president. The formation of that mill company was one of Anderson's red letter days. There were speeches by home people and people imported for the occasion. There was a dinner prepared by a large number of women of the town, served in a big brick warehouse belonging to Bleckley, Brown and Fretwell, on Benson street, people from the country and people from the town all united in the great celebration of the birth of Anderson's first cotton mill. The successive ones have been launched without so much fuss. Mr. R. E. Ligon, then a very young man, was elected manager and treasurer. The mill was incorporated in 1889 and began business in the spring of 1890. Steam power was used at first, but in a few years abandoned for electricity. It was purely a home concern.

Anderson has always been one of the best cotton markets in the state, and has handled much of the product grown in Georgia. Some of the best known cotton buyers in the place have been P. K. McCully, F. E. Watkins, E. W. Brown, J. G. Cunningham, F. G. Brown, W. A. Vandiver, W. H. Smith, D. P. McBrayer, F. G. Rhody, Frank Cary, Wm. Stringer, A. B. Rivers, Joe Bell, and R. S. McCully, and every year adds new names.

Orr Mill was the next factory to be built. It was incorporated in 1899, capital $800,000. J. L. Orr, formerly of Anderson, but at that time living in Greenville, was its founder and first president.

Riverside, incorporated in 1899, D. P. McBrayer its first president; Toxaway, 1902; Brogan, Equinox and Gluck and Conneross followed quickly. These mills have repeatedly been enlarged and their capital increased. Also the officers have changed so often that to attempt a list of them would inevitably be to leave out some who should be included. They are most of them now largely owned by northern concerns.

However, the operatives are almost entirely southern people, and there has been almost no trouble between the workers and the managers and owners. All have good schools. Superintendent McCants said once: "We have no mill schools, we have schools at the mills." There are two or more churches at every mill village, and several stores. At some there are municipal playgrounds.

Anderson is justly proud of her mills and of her mill people.

The year of 1889 witnessed an industrial awakening in Anderson. It was then that the first ice factory was organized by Mr. J. B. Townsend. Then began the first agitation about lighting the town with electricity. In 1890, Mr. W. C. Whitner established the Anderson waterworks, and lighted the city with 750 incandescent lamps, generating the electric current by steam power. He was faithfully and efficiently aided by Mr. Reuben Long, who managed the machinery, and was identified with the business until 1921, when he left Anderson to go to Richmond to be again associated with Mr. Whitner. Mr. J. L. Mauldin was superintendent of the plant.

In 1894 Mr. Whitner conceived the idea of utilizing some nearby water power to operate the electric light plant and the waterworks. He was convinced that the transmission of electric power was a success, and wanted the company to buy Portman Shoals, on Seneca River, ten miles away, for the purpose. But his associates did not agree with him, nor was the Anderson Cotton Mill ready at that time to make the contract for electric power to operate the mill, a condition that was necessary in so large an undertaking. Mr. Whitner, however, felt so sure of his position, that the development of Portman Shoals was the proper step, he commenced to buy such parts of this shoal as he could secure, as a private investment. In the meantime his company signified their willingness to try the long-distance transmission of electric power on a small scale, and for this purpose authorized Mr. Whitner to lease High

Shoals, on Rocky River, six miles distant, and with an investment of $25,000, a part of which was Anderson money, he developed and successfully transmitted 200 electrical horsepower. The incandescent lights were increased to 2,000, and 70 arc lights were put in. The large power pumps at the waterworks plant were operated by this power, and the balance was distributed to various smaller industries in the city. The Anderson Cotton Mill soon decided to use electric power rather than steam, and many other industries began doing the same thing. Then the company determined to develop the power at Portman Shoals. A meeting was called, and Anderson subscribed $50,000 of the bonds to be issued. The company was re-organized as the Anderson Water and Light Power Company, with Dr. S. M. Orr as president, and a number of the leading business men as directors. In a short time $100,000 was raised outside the city. Dr. Orr showed his faith in this enterprise from the beginning, doing everything in his power to convince the people that the development of Portman Shoals was what was really needed to give Anderson a new start, and make it a manufacturing center. The interest he manifested and the work he did, played an important part in bringing about the success which attended the enterprise.

The plant established at High Shoals was the first long-distance transmission power established in the South, and the electric generator then used was the first alternating current machine in the world to be built and operated for an initial voltage of 5,000 volts. It was considered impracticable to operate this type of dynamo at so high a voltage. The alternating current was comparatively new, and high voltage was an experiment, and considered dangerous. Running the machine at low voltage, and using step-up transformers to obtain the high voltage required was considered the only practicable method, and when Mr. Whitner, who is justly entitled to be considered the pioneer in the use of high voltage machines and long distance transmission, visited the manufacturing companies with the object of having this machine built, his views were regarded by many as impractical and visionary. The Stanley Manufacturing Company, of Pittsfield, Mass., agreed with Mr. Whitner, and encouraged him to try this voltage. They built the machines, and since that time the building of generators of high voltage has been adopted by all the manufacturers.

When the plant at Portman was established, Mr. Whitner decided to use generators giving 11,000 voltage, which were operated with perfect safety, and most satisfactorily. The Anderson plant was at that time the only plant in the world where alternating current generators were operated with so high a voltage as 11,000 direct on the generators and switch boards.

In the fall of 1901 a great freshet swept down the big dam at Portman Shoals. Industry in Anderson was almost paralyzed. Until that occurred the people did not realize how many industries depended upon the electrical current. From the great wheels that set in motion the machinery at Anderson Cotton Mills to the sausage grinder of the butcher shops, all kinds of work came to a stop. The streets were in plutonian darkness. People rummaged among abandoned trash and fished out oil lamps to light the houses, and public buildings, such as churches, stores, opera houses, etc., had to buy lamps big enough to give them light.

At the Anderson Cotton Mills most of the operatives were thrown out of work, though by the help of steam engines a part of the machinery was kept going. To add to the misery of the situation, that winter was one of the most severe the section has known, and an epidemic of measles and pneumonia broke out among the mill people. Actual privation was felt among them, and it became necessary that the people of the city go to their relief. The Anderson ladies formed themselves into a relief association, and certain of them were appointed to go to the mill village with medicine, food and other necessities every day. Many of the people of the village died during that dreadful winter.

In September, 1902, the new dam was completed, and on the evening that the lights were turned on for the first time in so many weary months, grown people behaved like children at Christmas time.

The electric power and water plant continued to flourish and grow. It became some years later the Southern Public Utilities Company, under the management successively of Dr. S. M. Orr, Mr. H. A. Orr and T. F. Hill. In 1920, after various improvements from time to time, new street lamps were installed, and it is an interesting fact that the new lights which approach as near perfection as artificial lights have attained, are an adaptation of the very type first used in Anderson in 1890, just thirty years before these were adopted. The lights of 1890 were the old incandescent lamps with carbon filament, which shed a pale and rather sickly shade of illumination over a comparatively restricted area. But in their day they were the wonder of the times, and the "great white way" of any big city never shone brighter than seemed those old carbon lamps just hitched on the top of a pole, and scattered about the city. While the new light is as much an improvement over that old type as electricity was over oil, the change is not so radical; it has been effected through years of work and invention. The first departure from the original system was made about 1895, when arc lights were put in. The brilliancy of those queer old flickering globes of blue pink light was amazing for a time, then about 1900 another improvement was effected, and the lights removed in 1920 were installed. At the time they were the brightest type and were greatly admired. Now instead of the arc system, which held sway for about twenty-five years, the type has reverted to the incandescent globe, but the old carbon filament with its many deficiencies has been supplanted. A metal known only to the makers of mazda lamps is used, and by its use brilliancy superior to that of the arc light is secured.

The Anderson Spring Bed and Mattress Factory, founded by Mr. O. B. VanWyck about 1890, is still a successful concern. It is now owned by Tolly & Son.

While all of these various enterprises were starting along about the same time, Anderson decided to give her dead more commodious quarters. The Presbyterian and the Baptist church yards had been the only burial places until about 1898, when the city bought a large tract of land about the pretty little stream, Silver Brook, which had for years been a favorite play ground, and made of it a beautiful City of the Dead.

The first planing and lumber mill was organized by J. E. Barton in 1887. Jesse Smith was a well known contractor. H. C. Townsend established another lumber mill in 1891. Sloan's was another. W. L. Brissey has probably made a greater success of the lumber business than any other who has engaged in it. He was a progressive citizen and his recent death leaves a vacancy in the business life of Anderson that will long be felt.

The Masons organized Hiram Lodge in Anderson in 1847, the Knights of Honor were organized in the town in 1896, A. O. W. W. in March, 1888; Knights of Pythias, Chiquola Lodge, 1890; Elks and Red Men more recently. Rotarians and Lions have appeared in the past few years. The Elks own a nice building on N. McDuffie street, built in 1913.

Anderson has not lacked for inventors. Long ago Mr. Scott John Wilson invented an iron loom which Mr. Borstel bought from him, paying for it the lot on which Mr. Felix Watkins' house now stands and where Mr. Wilson lived for years.

An Anderson man designed and built the first horseless carriage ever built in America. It was in a small machine shop, the power for which was supplied by a small creek near Westminster. Colonel John V. Stribbling, for years a resident of the city of Anderson, and a native of the county, took out a patent on January 13, 1882; its number was 259600. Though rather crude in appearance this vehicle embodied many of the ideas used in the construction of the present automobiles. It was built before the day of gasoline engines, and Mr. Stribbling's car was propelled by steam. A small upright boiler was used so pivoted that it would remain in an upright position, regardless of the position of the car. Colonel Stribbling was probably the first man ever to make and use the differential gear on a road machine. He says that the idea of this complicated gear construction was original with him, but that after he had made his, he later found that a similar construction had been used on a spinning frame in a cotton mill. Until Colonel Stribbling made his road carriage all vehicles had used wheels that turned on the axle, but his was constructed with wheels fastened to the axle and the driving axle and differential gears were enclosed within a hollow shell just as is used on modern cars. Colonel Stribbling applied the power to all four wheels of his carriage, and some of the truck manufacturers have recently employed this idea in their construction.

Colonel Stribbling's patent rights covered a period of seventeen years, and it was five years before the expiration of his patent that Mr. Selden applied for the patent for the use of a gasoline engine in a motor vehicle. The cost of building a steam propelled vehicle at that time was prohibitive, and as gasoline propelled vehicles did not become popular during the last five years of Colonel Stribbling's patent rights, he allowed his patent to expire, and then it became public property.

Colonel Stribbling was thirty-five years old when he secured his patent. When he showed his invention to an uncle, the older man exclaimed: "Johnny, the world is not ready for the horseless carriage; you are just fifty years ahead of your time." The first silo in South Carolina and the third in the United States was built by Colonel Stribbling on his farm.

The first automobile ever owned in Anderson was the property of Claude Townsend, about 1889 or 1890. A queer, high concern which was forever stalled in the road as his laughing friends drove past him in carriages or buggies.

The first woman to drive an automobile in Anderson was Mrs. Henry Orr.

It is said that the first automobile wreck in Anderson happened to a "turtle back" style Ford driven by Mr. Fred Maxwell. The car struck some sand in the road, skidded into a ditch and bent up some tin. The wreck was then regarded as very serious, and was for a long time detrimental to the sale of cars in Anderson.

Mr. J. C. Stribbling is the original automobile dealer in Anderson. In 1905 he declared his intention of opening an automobile business in the city. Friends advised against it, considering the risk too great. There were only three or four machines in the county, and horses were deathly afraid of them, consequently owners of horses and carriages cursed them most fluently. However, Mr. Stribbling persevered, and opening a small shop did quite a lot of work on the few machines in the county. In 1906 he made an order for a car load of Reos, the first car load of automobiles ever received in Anderson. They were one-and two-cylinder cars. They were bought by Mr. W. L. Brissey, Claude Townsend and Ben Fant. Fords were the next sensation in the automobile business, and Mr. Stribbling sold a Ford car to Dr. Ashmore, who has said that he had to give himself plenty of time to make a call in his car, as he spent much of the time in leading people's horses by his car, or sometimes he unhitched a horse from its vehicle, then drove slowly by him, then of course went back and harnessed him up again.

About 1907 or 1908 Mr. Albert Farmer created a furor in the town by the purchase of a brilliant red car which he proudly drove and when that Red Rambler appeared, men, women and children and horses gave him the road. It finally took fire and burned up.

The year 1916, Saturday morning, May 13th, people on the square saw a wonderful vehicle roar its way into Anderson. Sylvester Williams, a country negro living near Denver, with his wife and daughter, entered the city in a blaze of glory, riding in a buggy neither drawn by horses nor propelled by gasoline, neither did it owe its locomotion to electricity. Steam was the moving power. Fed by coal furnished from the front seat, and water from a ten gallon keg attached to the back of the concern, the contrivance steamed noisily along, belching smoke from a smoke stack, which the irreverent whispered would have to be removed to the cooking-stove before Sylvester and family could eat their next hot meal.

A newspaper reporter accosted the proud owner and inventor as soon as his triumphal car came to a stand. He told the reporter that he had built the thing in two weeks, he fed it only coal and water, had used the remains of a Buick. To the wheels and body support he added a boiler from whence he hardly knew. "I gathers up all kinds of old throwed away things." He fitted a buggy body to the frame, placed the keg tank, and sundry screws, brakes, pistons, taps, etc., turned the juice on and waved good-by to his admiring friends. With the musical apparatus of a calliope, the coal-eating, horseless buggy would have made a street parade attraction that would put to shame some pretentious shows. The contrivance traveled twenty-five miles an hour. It drew about it admiring and wondering crowds of both blacks and whites as long as it adorned the streets of the city.

Mr. J. M. Payne manufactured a bridle which the Tate Hardware Company took over and at one time sold as many as twenty a day. They changed the name from the "Jim Payne Bridle" to "The Anderson County Bridle."

G. W. King invented a cotton planter, fertilizer and cultivator all in one. Mr. King demonstrated that the thing would work, and a company was formed to have it manufactured and put on the market.

Thomas Carter, of Belton, invented a number of labor-and fuel-saving machines, among other things a fireplace heater and cooker which will heat two rooms, and answer the purpose of a cook stove.

F. T. Currie invented a timepiece made from a foundation of an 18-jeweled watch, the dial so arranged as to show at a glance the time of day in ten different cities. The section for Anderson is at the top edge of the dial where the figure twelve would appear on an ordinary clock and the other sections are labeled London, Paris, Rome, Tokio, Hong Kong, Greenwich, and Honolulu. The clock has two dials which turn, an hour dial which makes one revolution every twelve hours corresponding to the hour hand of a clock. The minute dial is a smaller one set over the hour dial, and makes one revolution per hour.

H. L. Meisser made a perfect "Electric City" in miniature at his home. The little city was erected on a raised platform which took up half of his parlor. There was everything complete, an electric street railway, the P. and N. station is represented and the houses across the street are lighted. Thre is a barn-yard scene, an old-fashioned farm house, with animals grazing behind the barn. There is a park in the center and a lake on which there are boats and swans, and beside it bath houses. There are roses and other flowers in the park, also tables and chairs. It is a remarkable piece of work.

Mr. Arthur Wilson invented a phonograph which changes its own needles and records automatically, and one after another will play any number of pieces. It is self-winding, and will play indefinitely without being touched. He actually seems to have produced perpetual motion.

Mr. M. M. Jarrett has invented an anti-theft device for automobiles.

But Mr. Osteen is the most versatile inventor that Anderson has ever had. His inventions are not only one or two, but number so many, in fact, that he has probably forgotten some of them himself. Among others is the automatic winder which he claims the Ansco Photo Products Company, of New York, infringed upon after having seen and refused to consider his invention. Another of his inventions was a coupling device for fire hose. Beside these his busy brain has produced many others.

Mr. J. Whit Moore, of Pendleton, world war veteran, has made a number of inventions, some of which he has had patented. Some few years ago he refused an offer of $50,000 for his invention of a valve lock for use on steam boilers. Mr. Moore was at one time clerk at the Plaza Hotel. He spent about two years perfecting this lock, and it promises to be a great success.

In 1922 a negro, whose name is W. H. Kay, was employed by Mr. James Dobbins, whose business was threshing grain. The negro, who was called "Red," having one day finished a hard day's work threshing grain fields, and expected on the morrow to begin just such another day, dreamed a dream. He thought he was seated upon a towering threshing machine, which was mounted upon a huge truck, and the truck was being run into a great grain field. He dreamed of dismounting and pitching thousands of forks of grain into the maw of the thresher, until he beheld two gigantic black monkeys with vermilion tails hopping about the thresher, then Red fled. When he awoke the memory of the dream haunted him, and he told his employer about it. Mr. Dobbins had been in the threshing business for several years, and he realized the possibilities of the idea. Not having to take an engine along with the thresher would cut down the number of hands required, and having the whole equipment in one piece would mean fewer delays. Decidedly impressed, he applied to W. A. Nixon, a skilled mechanic, to assist him in working out the idea. An industrial invention born in the brain of a sleeping negro.

The Conneross Yard Mills is one of only three mills in the South which manufactures asbestos. During the World War this Anderson asbestos plant played an important part in the ship industry in the United States by producing an asbestos material made from raw materials from South Africa, which made possible the welding of seams of boats instead of the tedious process of riveting, and was used for manufacturing big shells. This was the only asbestos plant in the United States producing this particular article, which is strictly an English production.

Mr. Albert S. Farmer is president of the Conneross Mill. Before 1915 the mill manufactured in addition to asbestos yarns, rope and mop yarns. These were not manufactured after 1915.

Mr. I. G. Watson has patented one of the most economical and simple canning outfits on the market, and has also invented a most successful washing machine, which can be converted into a canning outfit.

CHAPTER XXIII.

Highways and Byways, People and Things.

MUCH of the bygone life of countries and cities is embalmed in their roads and streets. Walk about the streets of London, and you find yourself, though treading stone and asphalt, yet marching along "roads," "lanes," even "fields," and the old-time sylvan names lend a touch of poetry and romance to the dull streets. So it is also in Boston, in Charleston, even in New York.

Anderson is not a large or widely known city, yet some of its history also lies in the names of its highways.

When the village was projected in 1828 there ran through the very center an old wagon road bearing the euphonious and appropriate title, "The General's Road," it lay between the residence of General Pickens, in what is now Oconee county, and Abbeville. The General's Road lay straight through the projected town, but the forefathers failed to see the beauty of retaining the name, consequently the first thoroughfare of the town bears the same name that is borne by hundreds of other streets throughout the country, and since Mr. Sinclair Lewis' widely-read novel of a few years ago, it has come to be a synonym of the absolutely commonplace. Main Street means nothing, the General's Road would be distinctive, and also historic.

When the town was laid off there were four boundary streets, just two or three blocks around the square marked off for business. North and South Boundary streets soon lost the name, but until a very few years ago East and West Boundary were the familiar names of Fant and Towers Streets, then the council decided that they were obsolete, and changed the names in honor of two of Anderson's oldest and most highly respected citizens who had lived on the streets, and had been dead but a short time. The home of Mr. George W. Fant is now the residence of his daughter, Mrs. J. S. Acker; it stands at the fork of River and Fant streets, the home of Mr. A. B. Towers is still standing, one of the oldest houses in the place, on West Whitner street. Towers street, the old West Boundary, is one block west of the old Towers residence.

North Boundary street was where the railroad cut was afterwards made, and South Boundary has become River street after it turns and runs so that it will cross Main.

Main street, after leaving the square, became hilly towards the south. There was once a deep depression running back of the row of buildings where the C. and W. C. Railroad has offices. A brick wall was erected there to support Main street. When Mr. John Cochran was mayor he either built or strengthened the wall, filled in much of that section, elevated Main street for quite a distance, and planted the beautiful oak trees that were long the pride of the community, but which fell a victim of the speeders.

At first in the little town the few stores were on the west side; the east was shut off by a high fence which ran back from the court house enclosing the jail and some city stables. After the big fire of 1845 the stores rebuilt on the west side were of red brick, and the proud inhabitants began to call that little line of business houses "Brick Range." After a time the fence was torn away from about the court house, and a line of brick stores built on that side also. They were plastered over and painted grey, and became "Granite Row."

Benson street, which bounds the square on the south, was named from the hotel which, though it faced Main street, yet abutted on the square on its north side. That old hostelry was connected with much of Anderson's early life. Among its proprietors was at one time a Mr. C. C. Langston, not the editor whom many remember, but his uncle, who had been employed as manager by Mr. Benson. He bought the place in 1854 and he and his wife, who was Miss Annie Fant, sister of Mr. O. H. P. Fant, kept the hotel for a long time. The house never changed its name, however, it was always the Benson House. In 1872 Mr. Langston went to Georgia, and Mr. Thomas M. White, who married Miss Benson, became its proprietor. Mr. White is remembered by many people, but best and most affectionately by those who were children when he was landlord of the Benson House. He was a joy to children, and to be invited to join him and his young folks for an outing was bliss indeed. His children, who were small in those days, were Kitty, who married Mr. Eagle and left Anderson; Leila, who became Mrs. Clarence Tolly, and Mort, who is Mrs. Raymond Beaty. They were the little ones. Mr. White, however, had two older children of his first marriage; they are Mr. Walter White, who succeeded to his father's marble business, and Alice, who married Mr. E. P. Sloan. She is the mother of Mr. Mortimer Sloan.

Mr. White was the last proprietor of the old hotel. In the early eighties it was torn down for modern buildings to take its place.

The street which bound the square on the north was called Depot street on the east side of Main, and first Tan Yard, and later

Whitner on its west side. Some fifteen years ago it was determined to call the whole street Whitner.

McDuffie, which was a very short street in the thirties, started at Earle street where the old-fashioned house of Miss Fannie Earle stood across the head of the street, and it stopped at the property of Mr. Daniel Brown, whch began about Hampton street, or very near it. When after the war Mr. Brown opened up the street through his property as far as the Fulwer Watson place, there was a movement to change the name of the street to Brown. But it was never done. Governor McDuffie was very popular in Anderson, and the people had long before called that one of their earliest streets by his name, and preferred to keep it as a memorial to him.

Manning street was named from a citizen of that name, a cabinet-maker who lived where Mr. Malcolm McFall's house is now. Small as the town was in the beginning, Mr. Manning shared the furniture trade with a Mr. Johnson, who lived where Judge Reed afterward built his home, "Echo Hall."

Morris street was named from the family of ladies who have lived for many years in the house at its head. John street was so named when Mr. John Cochran was mayor, in his honor. Mr. Cochran was a member of the Legislature as well as mayor when that street was opened sometime in the early seventies. Capt. Sam Pegg was in charge of the street work and wished to call the new street for the mayor. However, when he mentioned the matter to Mr. Cochran, he objected to having it called for him while he was in office. As he refused his consent to its being named Cochran, Captain Pegg called it John. It has somehow added a letter in the years that have passed, and is now universally called Johns. Reed street ran beside the home of Judge Reed and received his name. Breazeale street for Mr. John Breazeale, Broyles street for Dr. O. R. Broyles.

Hampton street was opened up in 1876, and naturally called Hampton. The people thought in that year in terms of Hampton.

Franklin street was so named for a little son of Mr. and Mrs. B. F. Wilson, who lived on that street; McCully for Mr. Stephen McCully, who gave the land on which it and Franklin were both opened. Wardlaw street was cut through the property of Mrs. Columbus Wardlaw, who was a daughter of Mr. Daniel Brown, and inherited his home. Cleveland street was opened during President Cleveland's administration, and given his name. Thomas street is named for a respectable colored tailor who lived in the old two-story house which stands on its corner. "Jule" was head workman for Mr. Jesse Smith, and made most of the wedding suits and other finery of the beaux of the seventies and eighties. When he built his two-story house, it was the only building in that section, and by far the most pretentious colored home in Anderson.

White street, from Mr. W. W. White, whose house was the first built on the new street. Sayre street from the home of Mrs. Jane Sayre, which was the first built on it. Norris street from the Norris family, whose home stood beside it. Ligon for Mr. W. J. Ligon; it ran back of his school. River street appears in some of the old maps as Belton street, but the boys wouldn't call it by that name; it ran to the river, and to their "wash hole," and it mattered little to them where else it led; to them it was the River road, and finally older people also adopted the name, though they would say street, and not road.

Elizabeth street was named for a bride whose home was near when it was opened, Mrs. John Cochran, Jr. Jefferson and Washington streets, in a patriotic burst when they were opened, for the early presidents. Bell street, from the residence of Mr. Joe Bell, which stands beside it. Sullivan street, for Mr. J. M. Sullivan, who was mayor when it was opened. Coughlin avenue, for the man who came to Anderson from Indiana and started the street railway, and also the interurban. Kennedy street, for Mr. Mike Kennedy, through whose property it ran. Brissey street, for the well-known builder, Mr. W. L. Brissey. Church street takes its name from the Baptist church, which stands at its head.

The first market and the only building ever put up expressly for a market stood, when it was built in Anderson's earliest days, on what is now Whitner street, just back of where Penny's store is located, just outside of the court house fence. Later the building was rolled from that place across the square, down south Main street. It was hauled by two four-horse wagons, followed by an escort of shouting boys, its bell cord vigorously pulled by Mr. Ezekiel George, whose furniture shop had stood almost across the street from it when it was on Whitner street, for he was the father-in-law of Mr. Tolly, who came a few years later to work in his shop which stood just where Tolly's business has always stood.

Colonel John McFall, for the sum of ten dollars, superintended the removal. The caravan rested in the middle of the street where Market street crosses Main and there for years was Anderson's meat sold. Mr. T. J. Webb, who lived to be Anderson's oldest citizen, was a son of Dr. Edmund Webb, and he said in his boyhood he was often aroused early in the morning to go to the market when it stood on Whitner street and buy meat. When there was fresh meat the bell pealed forth the joyful news and to get good cuts one had to respond promptly. Later, when the market stood on Market street, Mr. L. P. Smith, son of Mr. Jesse Smith, who lived at that time in the Garrison house on the corner of Main and Church streets, said that it was his duty when that bell rang to get up and go for meat. Those early buyers saw others come laden with baskets, gathering from every direction. Those who were not fortunate enough to have boys or servants to send had to go themselves.

Earle street bears the name of a family which was prominent in many sections of the county. But it takes its name directly from Miss Fannie Earle, a woman of great force of character, who lived on that street at the head of McDuffie. Orr street from J. L. Orr, whose beautiful home was built just outside of the town on what is now Orr street.

Society street! Why have not the residents of that perfectly good street of perfectly good homes not rebelled long ago? Main is bad but Society is worse. It is an insult to the intelligence of the people who live on it. It must have been named by some blunderer when somebody who lived on the street entertained her friends, and probably did not invite the said blunderer.

Marshall avenue was cut through the Orr property, Mrs. Orr giving the land. There was already an Orr street, consequently the new street was given her maiden name. Sharpe street runs through the old Sharpe estate. Captain W. F. Sharpe was one of Anderson's principal merchants years ago, and a wealthy man.

Wholesale Row takes its name for the character of its business houses. Calhoun street bears South Carolina's proudest name. Greenville street is a continuation of the high road to Greenville. The Bleckley Annex was so named because it was cut from the estate of Mr. Sylvester Bleckley. His home, Bleckley Place, stood well out of town, and there was quite a little farm all around it. Ella street was named for Mr. Bleckley's daughter, Mrs. William Laughlin, whose first home after her marriage stood on that street and Greenville street. Crayton street, because the home of Mr. T. S. Crayton was the first house to be erected on it. Cater street, from Mr. A. P. Cater, through whose land it was run. Roberts street runs through the property of Colonel James Roberts. Clinkscales street, from the adjacent property of Mr. Fleetwood Clinkscales, who served the South throughout the war bravely and well. He was born near old Ebenezer Church but came to Anderson when a youth. He was connected with newspaper work all of his active life, being for many years editor of *The Intelligencer*. When Mrs. Clinkscales lived, her flower garden seemed in full bloom all of the time.

West End avenue, like the old Boundary streets, once seemed the farthest limit of Anderson. The city, however, has grown beyond it. Peoples street is named for Mr. J. E. Peoples, who once owned that whole section of the town. Webb street faces the last home of the venerable T. J. Webb, now the home of his daughter, Mrs. E. F. Geiger. Tolly street for Mr. G. F. Tolly, beside whose home it ran. Fair street runs back of the old Fair Grounds. Munro street for Judge Munro, whose home faced the end of the street. Brown street for its first resident. Prevost street runs by the side of the lot where, in 1876, America's centennial year, Mr. S. H. Prevost built a beautiful home said to have been modeled on a small scale on one of the centennial buildings. It was always far back from the street in an immense lawn, which has been sold off into building lots and a whole street of houses has been built in front of it, forcing it to face Prevost street. It is the home of Mrs. Oscar Dean and the curving approach has been made very attractive. Murray street from the beautiful home of Major E. B. Murray, which was for years hidden from the world in its almost country solitude, yet within a hundred yards of Main street. Major Murray had a fish pond made on the place which was a source of delight not only to his family but to all of the young people of the town. Boating and bathing were two popular pastimes. One afternoon his daughter, having a party of young visitors, went out in a boat on the pond and in some way the little skiff overturned. Major Murray sprang in to help the girls who could not swim and in some way never understood sank almost immediately and was drowned. The girls got safely to the shore. He was in the prime of life and was considered a brilliant lawyer and newspaper man and his tragic death was a grief to the whole town.

Townsend street, so named from the home of Mr. J. H. Townsend and the lumber business of his son, Mr. Claude Townsend, which were located on that street. Tribble street, from another brilliant Anderson lawyer, Mr. J. L. Tribble, whose house stood where the P. and N. station is located, on the corner of Tribble street and Main. Spring street, because it passes near the old spring known successively as Poole's, Harrison's and Murray's.

Glenn street, from the home of the late Mr. Lawrence Glenn which was located on it. Maxwell avenue, from the home of Mr. J. D. Maxwell, beside which it ran. It is now the home of Mr. A. S. Farmer. Broadwell street, from the name of Mr. W. C. Broadwell near it.

In North Anderson, "Mr. John Lindley's town," the streets are mostly named from their first residents. However, it has one, Holly street, named for a wonderful holly tree that stands on it where it runs into Main street, unless the speed fiends have "got it" in the past two years. Arlington avenue, from the name Mr. M. C. Dicken gave to the beautiful home built by Judge Orr and which has been successively the home of Judge Orr, Mr. O. H. P. Fant, Mr. Will Brown, his son-in-law, and Mr. M. C. Dicken, who came to Anderson to take charge of Chiquola Hotel, fell in love with the beautiful old place, and bought it. After painting and freshening it up, and installing modern conveniences, he furnished it throughout—and lived at the hotel, keeping Arlington, as he called the old place, shut up except when he chose to take parties of his friends out there. It was always immaculately kept and he could serve refreshments whenever he felt disposed. After a few years in Anderson Mr. Dicken returned to Richmond, whence he had come, and sold the place to the late W. R. Osborne, whose sisters still live there.

Evins—not Evans—street was named for Captain William Evins, who gave the ground for the street. He was a merchant in Anderson in the seventies and his home is still standing on Evins street, an old fashioned, two-story house which was the only building anywhere about that locality fifty years ago. He married a daughter of the brilliant lawyer, J. H. Creswell, for whom Creswell avenue is named. Green street and Forest avenue on account of the beautiful trees which adorned them when they were first made.

Boulevard was christened by Mrs. Elizabeth Hammond Bleckley. When that broad, beautiful street was laid off and trees planted on each side she named it Boulevard, hoping that it would some day be equal in beauty to some of the lovely Paris boulevards.

Pecan street and Pecan Grove named from their trees. Welch avenue for Mr. Alonzo Welch who, of his own accord, opened a street through his property and presented it to the city.

Woodrow circle was laid off the first year of Woodrow Wilson's administration and named for him. Osborne street and Dicken avenue both run by the Arlington place and take their names from those two former owners.

Mr. Creswell lived in the country and on his place was a negro graveyard. Some of the dwellers around Woodrow circle, Summit avenue and College Heights lead their daily lives over the bones of many an old time slave. Fortunately for them if now and then a stray dusky ghost shall arise about their dwellings they need have no fear; the gentle spirit of the old time "mamma" or "uncle" will never hurt or disturb the "white folks." It is just looking about the world to see why so many spirits of the later generations of its race are such "ornery" ghosts.

Toxaway is called from the pretty Indian name of the mill at which it terminates. Nardin avenue for the dearly loved physician who for so many years lived beside it.

Hornet street is one given over to the colored population and its name must indicate its character. Bee street may be so called for the same reason, "hot times." But as it became confused with B street at one of the mills the name was changed to Gray, the name of one of its inhabitants. Lee street, near North Anderson, is another given over to colored people, but it was named for Major Lee, whose property was near it. There are probably many streets not mentioned. This data was collected a number of years ago. Most of the streets have been called for some family and as after a time some of the names once familiar disappear, it is a just and beautiful thing to preserve them in places where those people lived and served.

The country roads are almost altogether named for the places to which they run and called according to which end is nearer. Long ago, however, there was a road in Anderson county named for a woman, the only one so distinguished, and with time it has disappeared. It was called "Aunt Betsy's road." Mrs. Elizabeth Burriss rode horseback over that road every time her church was opened and she became such a well-known figure that the road by degrees took her name, the affectionate one by which her friends called her. Her church was Mountain Creek.

Most of Anderson's streets are paved; at one time the city was said to have more miles of paved streets than any town in South Carolina, and they are well kept. Indeed, one of Mayor Fant's specialties is neatness and cleanliness; he sees to it that his is a thoroughly clean town.

There is an interesting old character on the street cleaning force, "Uncle Barbus Frazier," who for more than forty years has cleaned up the streets of Anderson. When Uncle Barbus began to work for the city its entire street cleaning force consisted of himself, one two-wheeled cart and one mule. He used the cart to haul dirt and rock to fill the holes in the streets. In the forty-odd years that the old man has worked he has not lost six days from sickness or any other cause; he is always the first of the hands to arrive and the last to leave the city barns where the street tools are stored. When he began his wages were fifty cents a day, now he draws $3.00 every day. Uncle Barbus is as black as the proverbial ace of spades, a big man weighing 300 pounds. A faithful servitor.

Many people remember well the negro drayman, George Caldwell, who wore a smile that would not come off. But few who knew him were aware that once George was one of Anderson's policemen.

HISTORY OF ANDERSON COUNTY

Another well-known negro in Anderson a few years ago was Joe Cannon, a brick mason. Many people employed Joe for sundry small jobs but never knew that he had once joined an expedition of his race to go to Africa, there to establish a colored man's country. Joe was young at the time and went with an uncle who had accumulated some property. They sailed on a crowded vessel from Charleston. Joe's uncle had more judgment than many of his people display—he did not burn his bridges behind him—he left some money safe in South Carolina. When they finally got there after a long and miserable voyage, when many of their fellow passengers died and were buried at sea, they did not like their ancestral country and decided they would be more comfortable under a white man's government, so they came back as soon as the old man's money could be sent him. Thereafter Joe was quite content in Anderson and had many friends among the white people.

In the contemplation of roads and streets the late Edwards B. Murray cannot be overlooked. He represented Anderson in the Legslature in the eighties and his good roads bill, upon which he spent his energy and talents, became a law in 1886. It provided for wider road beds and an increase in the number of days' work required on the roads and provided for a tax of one-fourth of a mill to be set aside for road work. After his time the roads in the State were greatly improved. Captain W. P. Snelgrove has continued the good work begun by Major Murray.

The man for whom Towers street was named, A. B. Towers, was for many years one of Anderson's leading merchants, a rigid Presbyterian, a man of high character and great influence. Yet fully appreciating fun, he was always one of the group surrounding Messrs. Sullivan and Bleckley when jokes were being told and it is said he even contributed some occasionally. Mr. Towers had but two sons, both of whom died in young manhood; the elder, John, graduated from West Point in the class with General Pershing and seemed to have a bright career before him when death took him off. The younger, "Bob," died from typhoid fever while a student at the South Carolina University. The daughters of Mr. Towers are Mrs. Mary Ligon, Miss Annie Belle Towers and Mrs. Nelle Townsend. Another daughter, Martha, who was the wife of Dr. E. C. Frierson, died years ago.

CHAPTER XXIV.

Later Times.

IN the early days of the new century Anderson honored herself by honoring her Confederate soldiers.

For years Miss Leonora C. Hubbard had been trying to awaken interest in the matter and her school raised the first money towards a Confederate monument. Later she organized a Ladies' Memorial Association, whose object was to raise such a monument. In 1901 her efforts were crowned with success and the marble shaft surmounted by the figure of a Confederate soldier was placed on the public square.

The day of the unveiling was a great occasion; the ceremonies were in charge of the Masons, Dr. Divver in command. In the march from the Masonic Hall to the monument he was accompanied by young ladies who, by their relationship, represented past grand masters. They were Miss Gertrude Hoyt, who represented her father, J. A. Hoyt; Misses Louise and Nell Humphreys represented their father, W. W. Humphreys; Misses Mary and Lydia Orr their grandfather, J. L. Orr; little Miss Elizabeth Divver, a tiny child, represented her grandfather, R. F. Divver, who was present himself also; Miss Martha Clark, her grandfather, J. B. Clark; Miss Annie Prevost, her father, J. W. Prevost; Miss Mary Lee Breazeale, her father, J. E. Breazeale; Miss Bess Tolly, her grandfather, G. E. Tolly; Miss Bessie Tribble, her father, J. L. Tribble; Miss Edna Broyles, her grandfather, Jephtha Wilson; Miss Lois Hill, her father, R. S. Hill; Miss Bertha Duckett, her father, Dr. J. P. Duckett; Miss Nellie Watkins, her father, J. C. Watkins; Miss Annie Boleman, her father, G. N. C. Boleman; Miss Lizzie Smith, her adoptive father, J. N. Vandiver; Miss Mary Lewis, her father, J. B. Lewis; Miss Annie Farmer, her father, J. L. Farmer; Miss Fannie Earle, her relative, T. B. Earle. There were two little boys in the procession, their fathers having at that time no daughters who could represent them; they were Tom Hill, son of T. F. Hill, and William Hood, son of J. K. Hood.

A number of veterans of the army were represented by a daughter or a grand-daughter, and the girls were all dressed in bright colors, making a gay scene. There was music and speaking and general rejoicing and to Miss Hubbard the honor was duly given of having caused the memorial to be erected.

In 1903 Anderson, for the first time, organized a Chamber of

Commerce. F. G. Brown was the president and the moving spirit. Mr. Brown was a grandson of Judge Reed and he had much of his grandfather's public spirit and enterprise. He entered enthusiastically into anything which would promote the interest of his town and likewise of his church, though he made no pretense of great religion, yet he showed his love for and pride in his church by leaving it a generous bequest at his death. He was on the building committee of Grace church and when ordering material or church furniture nothing would answer for him but the best.

Probably Mr. Brown did more to put Anderson before the rest of the world than any citizen she has ever had.

Among the men who have been secretaries of the Chamber of Commerce, Mr. A. P. Fant stands out in the work that he did. He and Mr. S. M. Byers organized the great and successful county fairs which have been the event of the fall for the past few years. Mr. Byers is county demonstration agent and he has few if any equals in the State.

The street railway system was inaugurated about 1903. The late Rufus Fant was largely instrumental in bringing street cars to Anderson. He aroused interest in the project and was instrumental in securing the services of Dr. Caughlin, an Indiana man, who came to Anderson and took charge of the building of the tracks and securing cars. He ran both the street and the interurban cars for a time.

Mr. Fant was greatly interested in horticulture and it was his care that kept the pretty plaza a beauty spot in the midst of the business section of the town. The Department of Agriculture of the United States gave Mr. Fant credit for having the only grove of edible bamboo in the United States. So much faith had the Department in the bamboo grove that a few years ago it commissioned Francis Fant, a son of Mr. Rufus Fant, to propagate 1,200 plants to be transplanted in Washington and from there disseminated throughout the various States of the Union.

Probably the largest business concern that Anderson ever had is that of the Sullivan Hardware Company. In the last years of the nineteenth century J. M., H. K. and N. B., sons of N. K. Sullivan, opened a hardware business on a modest scale. Later a younger brother, Charles S., was taken into the firm and after a time the oldest of the brothers, Mr. J. M. Sullivan, withdrew. The venture prospered, the brothers proved themselves to be shrewd and versatile business men. They branched out and by degrees took in other members of the Sullivan family, which was a large one, until now there are innumerable brothers, nephews and cousins connected with the concern which has grown to enormous proportions and has numbers of branches. H. K., N. B. and C. S. Sullivan died some years ago and so well organized was the business it continues a prosperous firm under the guidance of Mr. W. W. Sullivan.

Other prominent business men and houses of recent years have been R. S. Hill, J. A. Brock, B. F. Mauldin, J. D. Hammett, D. C. Brown, J. D. Brown, R. E. Ligon, R. S. Ligon, D. A. Ledbetter, W. L. Brissey, J. E. Barton, Malcolm McFall, the Hortons—father and several sons; H. G. Anderson, J. J. Fretwell, G. H. Bailes, John M. Hubbard, S. O. Tribble, H. A. Orr, J. J. Major, D. S. Vandiver, E. P. Vandiver, A. S. Farmer, G. W. Evans, B. O. Evans, J. L. Orr III, Marshall Orr, M. M. Mattison, J. W. Dickson, the Townsends, O. D. Anderson, S. A. McCown, D. S. Gray, T. Q. Anderson, T. B. Fant, S. R. Parker, Harvey Todd, W. H. McLeskey, G. F. Bigby, W. H. Harrison, the old firms of G. F. Tolly & Son, now managed by the son, G. M. Tolly, and Fant's Book Store, now run by grandsons of the original Fant; the Moore Wilson brother and sisters, John T. Burriss & Son, Keese and Cochran, Miss Dora Geisberg, the Lessers, Thompson's Shoe Store, J. D. Rast, McDougal and Bleckley, the Farmer Brothers—Frank, Jim and Joe; T. F. Hill, R. S. Hill and many other promising young men.

And in other parts of the county some of the leaders have been J. P. and B. B. Gossett, Walter Geer, T. C. Jackson, Claude Jones, Paul Earle, the Tuckers, the Pearman brothers, W. Q. Hammond, W. G. Watson, Dr. D. S. Watson, Boyce Burriss, A. A. Dean, W. T. Dean, S. A. Dean, R. B. Dean, J. T. Rice, John A. and T. T. Wakefield and many others.

The first fire company in Anderson was purely voluntary. Cisterns were dug in various parts of town and a little fire apparatus bought, then the boys organized their company. That was some time in the last years of the nineteenth century. When the fire bell rang the members of the company dropped whatever they might be doing and ran for their engine. At first they dragged it themselves and they used to meet and practice running with the fire machinery.

The negroes also formed a company which was called the Black Paddies.

But though willing the voluntary fire companies were found inadequate, even after they were furnished with horses to pull the paraphernalia, and in the course of time were replaced by a paid and trained company which has living quarters in the city hall; the horses were replaced by motor trucks and Anderson's fire department put on a plane with the best in the State.

And the police force has grown since the days when Marshal Newt Scott could unaided keep order in the town. Now Anderson has a chief and a number of assistants who do efficient work. W. W. Driskoll is the present incumbent; he has held the office for years and by his courtesy and efficient work has gained the respect of the community.

Anderson is an agricultural county. It has more farms than any other county in the state. In the value of its agricultural products it leads the southeast, is second in the South and twenty-third in the Union. It was the first to introduce alfalfa and it is believed that in the planting of alfalfa it was not only the first in the state but also the first in the Union. The first champion corn grower was an Anderson county boy. While cotton is the staple crop, there are many other things grown and raised in the county. It has the only tea tree in the country. Tea plants are usually small but this one, planted years ago on the McFall plantation at High Shoals, was tended and allowed to grow as it would and it developed into a large tree.

Anderson has always raised fine horses, and after Colonel Crayton years ago introduced fine blooded cows and hogs, they, too, have been used by the farmers of the county.

Bees have always been kept to some small extent but a few years ago Mr. Ned Prevost began to raise them scientifically and with modern methods of culture.

The women of the county have not shown any great interest in their political privileges. But one of the first, if not the very first woman to cast a ballot in the state was an Anderson county woman, Mrs. Inez Callaham, of the Oak Grove section, who voted for an additional school tax. Mrs. Callaham was a childless widow, but she was greatly interested in the welfare of her community and particularly of the schools.

Mrs. R. A. Gentry has been a leader of ability among the farm women of the county. And Mrs. Henry McFall has proved herself a wonderful organizer. She has had charge of the woman's department of the county fairs from the first, and has not only made them successful, but has made herself liked and trusted by the women who work with her.

Mrs. Carrie McC. Patrick is the leading woman politician. She belongs to the League of Women Voters and holds important office in the organization. Being an efficient newspaper woman, she is well fitted for the work that she likes.

The women of the town have been interested in the various phases of women's clubs, and have done some good work. They have formed several patriotic chapters of both the Daughters of the American Revolution and the Daughters of the Confederacy.

They have had a number of literary and musical clubs and study clubs of all kinds.

In April, 1924, the beloved regent of Cateechee Chapter, D. A. R., Mrs. J. D. Rast, was killed by the awful storm which early in the morning swept over the northeast section of the town. Ten other people lost their lives, and the destruction was appalling.

In 1904 Mrs. Rufus Fant organized a Civic Association of which she was the president. It has done good work in beautifying the city and in creating a sentiment for civic improvement.

An Anderson girl once accomplished a very astonishing feat of memory. Miss Cora Wilhite, daughter of Dr. P. A. Wilhite, memorized the entire poem, "Lady of the Lake." To recite it required five hours. She became Mrs. Baker, and died young, leaving two small children.

When in 1916 Mexico seemed to threaten trouble and the president thought it wise to send troops to the border, Anderson boys were not backward. A company was formed with R. D. Henderson, a Spanish War Veteran, as its captain. It went to El Paso and remained for several months. As there was no fighting there were no casualties. Reverend R. C. Jeter, for a number of years rector of Grace Church, was chaplain of the First South Carolina Regiment and while on the border he became ill and died. Mr. Jeter was greatly liked in Anderson and his death cast a shadow over the town.

Later when real war came practically all of the young men in the county either enlisted or were drafted. Most of the Anderson boys were in the Thirtieth division, which was stationed at Camp Sevier in Greenville until they were sent to France. Anderson had three companies, B, C and K, and a machine gun outfit. They were attached to the 118th infantry and P. K. McCully, of Anderson, was their colonel. Company C was commanded by Captain Jesse Crawford, Company B by Captain Louis Ligon and Company K by Captain Basil Vandiver. The machine gun company was commanded by Captain R. J. Ramer. After the command had been organized several months some changes were made.

To Anderson the great figure of the war was her own son, N. A. McCully. He was sent to the United States Naval Academy by appointment of Congressman D. Wyatt Aiken. He graduated with high standing and has since served his country in her navy. From the first he received promotion and when the world war broke out he was a captain. Then he was sent in command of the United States fleet in European waters and after the conflict was sent to Russia as a diplomat and protector of United States property. One who served with him in Russia tells of his kindness and consideration towards the Russians while on that mission.

While serving on the sea during the war he held the rank of vice-admiral and later attained the rank of rear admiral. While serving in Russia his sympathies became so enlisted by the miserable condition of the people that he adopted as his own seven little stranded orphans and brought them to America. Several years later he married a Russian lady.

N. A. McCully, for he was always called by his initials, was liked when he was a boy growing up in Anderson and on his various visits to his old home he showed as much interest in his old friends as though he had never lost touch with them. And thrown as he was among the foremost people of the country, he could and did return to Anderson and recognize the humblest people whom he had ever known with as much cordiality as though they were to him the most interesting friends. No matter how long since he had been in the town when he met any one whom he had ever known there was never one moment of hesitation. He would extend a hand and say, "Why, how do you do, Mr. Blank? I'm glad to see you again." In short he was so utterly unspoiled by success that everybody rejoiced in his success.

No sooner were the boys gone than the home people went to work. A Red Cross unit was formed with Mrs. W. H. Nardin at its head. Miss Bessie Carlisle was the efficient and hard worked secretary.

Mr. J. J. Fretwell gave the ladies the use of one floor of the Bleckley building and there every day they gathered for all manner of Red Cross work. And they knitted everywhere and at all times. There were several sewing machines put at their disposal and not one was ever idle. Numbers of boxes of war supplies were sent by the organization.

Mrs. J. R. Vandiver was appointed by Mr. Hoover head of the woman's department of food conservation for Anderson county. Mr. R. E. Ligon was the official representative to whom all reports on food supplies and prices were made.

There were speeches made on every possible occasion to keep people interested in saving food and other necessaries for the army. Wheatless days and meatless days and sweetless days and gasless days were religiously observed. In short the people at home were doing their part toward winning the war.

General M. L. Bonham was chairman of the local board of the selective draft and his was a busy office. Several times he called for volunteers among the women, for there were few men to assist in the work, and he never called in vain.

HISTORY OF ANDERSON COUNTY

The Thirtieth Division, to which most of the Anderson boys belonged, sailed from New York May 11th, 1918, for Liverpool. From there they were taken by train to Dover and across the channel to France. On returning to the United States they embarked from St. Nazaire on March 15th, 1919, on board the Mercury and had a quick passage home.

The first Anderson man killed was Claude Stephenson. When, after the war, his body was sent home he was given a great military funeral. There were a number of the Anderson boys killed. Some were brought home for burial, some were not.

The men who came home went to work and seemed to try to forget the horrors they had known. People got back to normal living as far as possible.

Since that time Anderson, like the rest of the world, has had some dreadfully depressing times, but the people have carried on, the town is worthy of its progenitors, and now in this year 1928 it is celebrating with joy its one hundredth birthday and preparing to make its next hundred years a period of even greater growth and progress.

Traditions *and* History *of* Anderson County, S.C.

ABBOTT, Mary S. 126
ACKER, ...149,208
   Alexander 137,138
   Amos 137,138
   Belle Fant 156
   Dearborn 137
   E.H. 227,246
   Elizabeth 137,138
   Frances 138
   Halbert 138,262
   H.H. 163
   John 137
   John C. 286
   J.J. 104
   Mrs. J.S. ...258,270,303
   Joel Milton 138
   Joseph 137
   Joshua 138
   Lucinda 138
   Mahala 137
   Mary 137,138
   Nancy 137
   Newton 286
   Peter 75,137
   Peter, Jr. 137,138
   Rhoda 24,137
   R.V. 138,227
   Squire 246
   Susan 137
   Teresa 138
   William 137
   William V. 138
   W.S. 15
ADAIR, Walter 200
   Adams, ...197
   Jasper 57
   Joseph M. 116
   Samuel 286
ADDIS, Miriam 140
ADGER, ...197
   John B. 205,256
ADKINS, Mr. 125
AGNEW, Samuel 226
AIKEN, D. Wyatt 253,316
AKERBURG, Mrs. Knut ...120

   Verna Ayer 89
ALDRMAN, ...29-31
ALEXANDER, Ruth 137
ALFORD, A.N. 171
   Mr. 171
ALLEN, Pet 123
   J.E. 262
   Thomas 263
ALLGOOD, Elizabeth 103
ANDERSON, ...192,269
   Andrew 68
   Anne..........65,68,70
   Capt. 209
   Caroline............70
   David...............132
   Edward E. 70,266
   Elizabeth 65,70
   Female Seminary .117,120
   Gen...10,32,69,161,195,
  196,198
   Georgia Ann 61
   Henry 70
   H.G. 123,314
   Jane 64
   Jim 62
   John..........64,70,204
   John R. 186
   J.F. 104
   Jule 35
   Mrs. Jule 191
   Julius 70,96
   Lily Strickland ....
  29,90,272
   Louise 106
   Lydia 65,68,69
   Maggie 108
   Martha 70
   Mary 65,68
   O.D. 314
   R.H. 258
   Robert.......64,66,167,
  212,212
   Robert E. 70,200
   Sam 125
   Tennie 167

Traditions *and* History *of* Anderson County, S.C.

Thomas 70,195
T.Q. 314
Mrs. Walter 106
W.F. 61
William...68,70,108,199
ANDREWS, Mannie 94
ANSEL, Gov 281
ANTHONY, Whitfield 50
    Capt. 117
ANTIOCH, ...59
ARCHER, Judge 263
    Miss. 22
    William..13,143,187,263
ARNOLD, Helen 103
    Hendrix.............54
    Lawson T. 29
ARTHUR, T.S. 81
ASHLEY, Joseph M.H. 13
ASHMORE, Dr. 262,299
    J.D. 223,235
ATKINSON, Sarah 119
AULL, Miss. 291
AUSTIN, ...171
    W.H. 227
AUNT Margaret 39
AYER, Alfred M. 226
    Gen 120,124,127
    Hartwell 120,123
    L.M. 89,117-120,123
    Lula 119
    Marie Louise 120
    Paul E. 286
    Thomas R. 123
    Verna 120
BACKMAN, W.K. 258
BACON, James 112
BACOT, Mrs. 123
BAGBY, Bessie 119
    Mary 119
BAILES, G.H. 314
BAILEY, W.T. 31
BAIRD, Thomas 35,105
BAKER, Eva 152
    George 152
    Helen 152,286

John 56,152
J.J. 120
John T. 30
Mrs. 316
Robert 152
S.C. 123,125,282
BALDWIN, Lizzie 120
BANKS, Professor 125
    William 85
BARKER, T.G. 258
BARNEY, Mr. 193
BARNWELL, Arthur 291
BARR, L. 15
    LeRoy 19,92
    Matilda Ann 92
    W.F. 13,120,268,270
    Mrs. W.F. 114
BARRATT, ...104
    J.N. 226
BARTON, Dr. 262
    J.E. 30,95,297,314
BASS, Smith 180
BATES, Misses 95
    William 290,294
BATTLE, Professor 69
BEATY, Raymond 304
BECK, J. Mack 31
BEE, ...197
    Barnard E. ..57,201,227
BELCHER, ...100
    R.E. 83,116
BELL, E.C. 19,38,269
    ISAAC ,,,,,,,,,,,291
    J.M. 121
    Joe 293,306
BENET, W.C. 279
BENNETT, Archibald 73
    Cooper..........44,217
    Egloe..............175
    Elisha.......73.175,175
    Mitchell...........175
    Sarah..............175
BENSON,............22,304
    Catherine 203
    Catherine Sloan ...203

Traditions *and* History *of* Anderson County, S.C.

Enoch 159,219
Enoch Barry .199,202,290
Eugenia.............121
Evelyn..............154
J.P......14,81,159,203
Kitty................37
Mary.,.........23,235
Store...............235
Thomas Prue 157,223
BERRY, David 139
William.............139
BEWLEY,.............82,268
BIBB, Eliza 101
Sam................102
BIGBY,.................215
G.F................314
George M. 225
James A...............225
Mrs..................270
Thomas H. 286
BLACK, R.F. 15
BLACKWELL, ...216
BLALOCK, ...107
BLAINE 255
James G. 263
BLAKELEY, Frank 245
BLASSINGAME, Nancy 203
BLECKLEY, Anne 128,275
B.B. 30
Elizabeth 127
Elizabeth Hammond .....
..............90,273,309
Ella................275
John................115
Josephine 275
Mary................275
Sylvester ..29,120,235,
........268,269,273,307
S.M. 284
Zoe 275
BLEICH, C.H. 283
BOGGS, ...206
Julius............86,88
BOHANNON, Misses 174
J.W.................268

BOLEMAN, Annie 312
G.N.C. 312
BOLT, Hiram 100
William L. 16
BONHAM, Daisey A. 284
M.L. Jr. 90,286
M.L. 262,263,266
Mrs. M.L. 262
BOONE, Bishop 56
BOROUGHS, ...147
BOSTIC, J.N. 56
BOX, Joseph 196
BOWIE,.............104,200
BOYD, John 142
BRADLEY, William A. 290
BRADY, Lute 267
BRAG, David 259
BRAMLETT, J.N. 104,112
J.W. 224,226
BRATTON, Eliza 158
John................141
BRAZEALE, K. 22,208
BREAZEALE,.........132,159
Bailey............2,233
B.B................108
J.E.....120,262,279,312
Henry N. 226
John................305
Mary Lee 312
BRECKENRIDGE, ...96,105
Billy...........97,108
BREEDEN, J.K. 126
Singleton 262,283
BRESTLING, Col. 158
BRISSEY, W.L. ...30,297,299,
..............306,314
BRISTOW, J.L. 30,126
BRITT, Edward J. 50
BROADUS, John A. 244
BROADWELL, W.C. 30,308
BROCK, A...............226
J.A. 17,154,214,
........272,285,293,314
Leon P. 286
BROOKS, ...227

321

Traditions *and* History *of* Anderson County, S.C.

BROWN, ...107,268
  Amelia 62
  Andrew...............35
  Anna................121
  Ben.........24,137,235
  Betty...............139
  B.F. 29
  B.F. Jr. 29
  Carroll 194
  C.C. 126
  Daniel 15,16,24,26,
   31,47,58,110,111,
   156,157,159,180,
   182,192,239,260,305
  Mrs. Daniel 57,238
  D.C. 314
  Elijah......49,62,117,
   137,210
  E.M. 258
  E.W. 29,293
  F.G......30,58,293,313
  George 152
  Georgia 270
  G. Ernest 30
  Gov. 47,96
  J...................15
  James H.............286
  J.D. 314
  J.J. 157
  John 156,192
  John Peter 82,271
  J.N.............45,291
  Mrs. J.N. 257
  John N. ...21,26,27,45,
    ...126,154,157,192,205,
   235,270,271,284,286
  Josephine 194
  Joseph N. 88,229,
   246,262,286
  Joe........8,96,138,148
  Mable 88
  Martha 152
  Miss 193
  Nancy...............192
  Nardin 157
  Nellie 124
  Newton 156
  Olive 123
  Pierce 85
  Samuel 26,74,108,
   137,139,156,157,
   172,192,240,270
  S.M. 250
  Sanford 262
  Teresa 110,174
  Varina ...19,88,121,158
  W.C. 222,258
  W.D. 30
  Will............209,226
  William Penn 171
BROWNLEE, ...20
  James 111
  S.C. 30
  William A. 36
BROYLES, ...116,132
  Aaron ...96,148,151,157
  Abel 148
  Augustus T. .149,150,262
  A.R. 151
  Cain............148,151
  Clara...............152
  Claudia 149
  Dudley Hammond 149
  Edna 312
  Edward 149
  Fannie 105
  G.N. 110
  George.........121,152
  Mrs. George 11
  Gus.................163
  John T. 148,149,151
  Julius J. 149
  Lula 152
  Maggie..........68,151
  major 152
  Marie 151
  Mary 152,155
  Miss 193
  O.R.............105,305
  Oze 148-151

Traditions *and* History *of* Anderson County, S.C.

Robert 151
Wit. 151,152,194
Zoe 151
BRUCE, Elizabeth ...139,158
  Julian 17
  Robert.............203
  Susan Sloan 203
BRYANT, B.R. 226
  John C. 226
  W.F. 226
BRYSON, Mrs. David 217
BUDDS, Joseph 60
BUFORD, Thomas 191
BUIST, Dr. 36
  E.T. 38
BURCH, Henry 196
BURDINE, J.H. 227
  W.C. 227,246
BURKET, ...238
BURNETT, Elijah 41
BURNS, ...77
  Miss...............102
BURR, Aaron 68
BURRIS, Bertha 106
  Boyce........26,148,314
  Mrs. C.D. 106
  Elisha..........146,147
  Elizabeth 146,310
  Elmira 106
  Jacob........46,147,173
  James .45,46,146,147,217
  John............146,147
  John T. 314
  Joshua 146,147
  J.T................30
  Julia 106
  Kittie 123
  Lawrence 106
  Luter Rice 86
  Marcus.........118,148
  Mary 146
  Nancy...............146
  Peggy 275
  Prue H. 286
  R.E. 31

Reuben...............106
R.H. 106
Thomas..........146,147
Toccoa 106
Walter C. 286
William 147
BURT, ...197
  Armstead............202
  Francis.............202
BURTON, H.M. 101
  Orma...........137,139
BUTLER, Julia 16
BYERS, S.M. 313
BYRUM, ...1,47,269
  Elisha W........170,226
  Joseph LaBoon 275
  Peter 143
CAESAR 42
CAGE, Susan 45
CAIN, Susan 146
CALDWELL, Georgia 310
  Mrs................138
  Samuel 159
CALHOUN, D.H. 50
  Kitty 68
  J.C.........87,148,198,
 200,202,212
  J.E. 57
  Mrs. J.E. 57
  Rachel 169
CALLAHAN, ...7
  Inez...............315
CAMAK, M.B. 90
CAMERON, Duncan 159
  Mary...............159
CAMPBELL, ...197
  Alexander 59
  Daniel.............221
  Dr.................262
  L.E. ...226,234,252,253
  Lena 106
  Thomas 59
  Zella..............106
CANNON, Joe...........311
CAPERS, Ellison 58,102,

Traditions *and* History *of* Anderson County, S.C.

............228,258,269
W.T. 58,281
CARLISLE, ...106
   Bessie 317
   Townsend 107
   William...........36,37
CARPENTER, A.A. 253
   Alfred 191,193
   A.M................85
   J.B. 252
CARSON, Walter 205
CARSWELL, E.R. 106
   Georgia............106
   Institute ...97,106,219
   L. 106
CARTER, Lillian 262
   R.L.................31
   Thomas 300
CARUTH, Louisa 70
   Mr. 70
CARUTHERS, John 159
CARY, Frank 293
CASKIN, Theodore 102
CASLER, J.B. 247
CASON, M.A. 224
   William............102
CASS, Gen. 264
CASTLEBERRY, Asa 146
CATER, ...12,268
   A.P........23,240,307
   Dr..........22,198,259
   Edwin...............37
   Helen...............93
   P.A. 29
   Postelle...........198
   Richard 35
   Sallie...........37,38
   Thomas 194
CATHCART, Emmie 142
CATLIN, Seth 178
CHAMBERLIN, ...195
CHAMBLEE, Lewis 146
   Mary...............147
   Moses...........14,147
   Sarah..............146

Z. 11, 13
CHAMBLESS, J.A. 126
CHAPIN, Mrs. 89
   Sallie 51
CHAPMAN, James 199
   J.D................205
   William A. ...15,169,266
CHAPPELL, ...247
CHASTAIN, James 48
   Steve 266
CHERRY, ...197
   Henry C. 160
   John C. 160
   Samuel 22,199
   Tom................198
CHENAULT, ...31
   Mrs. 150,174
CHESHIRE, Robert B. ...286
   R.S.............225,258
   Victor B. 85,226
CHEVES, ...197
CHOICE, Z.T. 200
CHREITZBERG, Cema S. ..292
CHURCH, Miss 270
CLAMP, W.A. 13
CLARDY, J.F. 226,278
CLARK, Betsy 143
   Bolin..............159
   Col. 77
   David..............159
   E.L................253
   Henry 195
   J.B. 29,312
   Jonathan...........159
   Martha.............312
   Matthew.........52,75
   Mrs. 149
CLARKSON, William 57
CLAYTON, Miss 58
CLEMENT, ...137
   Benjamin...........215
   Isaac..............215
CLEMSON, Col. 57,198
CLEVELAND, ...104
   Benjamin...........195

Traditions *and* History *of* Anderson County, S.C.

William..............199
CLINKSCALES, A.J.......104
   Dr. 262
   Fleetwood ...82,83,142,
  232,307
   J.F..........29,210,224
   John G. ...87,89,142,221
   Lizzelle.............174
   Miss.................283
COBB, Elizabeth 139
COCHRAN, ...255
   Dan...................19
   D.H. 15
   E.F.........262,263,281
   Grace............13,123
   John......13,28,304,305
   John Jr. 306
   John R. 268
   Will M. 286
COLEY, Daniel P. 286
COLSON, D.C. 103
CONNOR, James 258
COOK, ...270
   A.B.............217,259
   Iva..................217
   Judge................256
   Thomas 48
COOLEY, Curran 263
   H.C. 259
   Hiram 171,227
COOSEY, ...165
COPELAND, J.J. 226
CORBIN, ...202
   D.T..................188
CORNISH, A. 58
   Andrew 57
   Elizabeth 58
   Kate 90,123
   Lizzie 90,121,123
   Mrs. 57
COTE, Miss 112
COUGHLIN, ...306
COWAN, J.A. 226
   William..............226
COX, Beau 232

Billy 193
D.L. 205,230
G.W. 225
James P. 226
James M. 225,226
Judge.....19,23,115,116
Miss 137
Thomas 195
W.B. 225
W.F. 17,30,194
CRAIG, John 64
CRAWFORD, James W. 291
   Jesse 316
   Miss 83
   Samuel 111,116
CRAYTON, ...222,268,269
   Bayliss..............152
   Bayliss F. ...50,159,188
   B.F.....12,17,28,46,239
   Col..................315
   Frank................152
   Kate.................155
   Mr...................134
   Mrs..................155
   Samuel 155
   T.S.......29,30,159,307
CRESWELL, ...82
   John Hunter 29,122,
  262,266,309
   Mrs. 37
CROMER, ...61
   John S. 31
CROW, ...104
   Silas................232
CROWDER, James 159
CROWTHER,..............115
CROZIER, Calvin 186
CRUGER, Col. 186
CRYMES, ...208
   J.W. 227
   Thomas 227
CULLINS, John 214
CULNER, John 214
CULNER, Ada 126
CUMMIN, Harmon 71,72

Traditions *and* History *of* Anderson County, S.C.

CUMMINS, Crayton 287
    Francis 33
CUNNUNGHAM, ...269
    Alexander 8
    Bill...............73
    Jane..............143
    J.G..........17,30,293
    Joel J............159
CURRIE, F.T. 300
CUTHBERT, ...197
DAGNALL, A.H. 263
DALTON, R.E. 222
DANIELS, ...25,172
    Charlotte 93,268
    J.W. ..2,13,120,214,262
    Mrs. J.W. 14,156
    Maggie 106
    MaryE.......112,113,127
DANNALLY, James 52
DAVIS, ...215
    Alice 106
    Aaron 214
    Eddie 106
    Elizabeth 146
    Jane 146
    Jefferson 261
    John 62
    Miss 137
    Moses 214
    N.L. 102
    W.C. 33,34
    Warren R. ...57,200,202
    William........214,272
DART, Dr. 57
DAY, Billy 74
DEALE, F.A. 226
DEAN, ...224
    Augustus A. .72,226,314
    Eloise 88
    George.............108
    Harold.............263
    james L............245
    Moses 72
    Oscar 308
    R.B. 314

Samuel 71
S.A. 314
Thomas 135
W.T. 314
De FOUNTAIN, ...51
DELAREAUX, ...56
DENHAM, ...210
    Benjamin............11
    Miss...............127
DENSON, Jesse 48
DERIEUX, Samuel 90
DICKSON, M.C. 309
DICKENSON, Rodolphus ...56
    Thomas Wells 56
DICKSON, ...197,204,206
    Benjamin Franklin......
   139,205,230
    J.W. 314
    James..........205,247
    J. Walter 205
    Major 32
    Matthew.........78,204
    Matthew Jr. 205
    T.P. 263
    W.A. 102,105,200,205
    Walter C. 12
DILLINGHAM, James A. ...286
    W.R. 30
DIVVER, ...233
    Dr. .259,261,269,281,312
    Elizabeth 312
    Emily 94,124
    Grace Carter 126
    Richard Furman ..94,120,
   142,260,286,312
    W.S. 31
DIXON, J. Herman 31
DOARK, Samuel 148
DOBBINS, ...104
    James 36,301
    Jesse 206
    J.D.M...............13
DODAMEAD, Col. 183
DODD, John 286
    Joseph B. 286,287

DODGE, Witherspoon 60
DONALD, D.L. 104,226
DOUGLASS, Anna 167
   Archibald 167
DOUTHIT, J.B. 61
DOW, Lorenzo 49
DOYLE, O.H. 263
DRAKE, ...177
DRENNAN, Amanda 122
   Marie..................143
   MaryAnn.............143
   Mr. 26
   W.F..................31
DRISKOLL, W.W. 315
DUCKETT, ...270
   Bertha................312
   Dr..................259,312
   J.P. 30
DUCKWORTH, Annie 141
   Elizabeth 141
   J.G. 213
   Nancy................213
   Ruth 141
DUFF, Father 60
DUGGAN, Lillian 126
DUMAS, Fannie 101
DUNCAN, Adlophus A. 286
   B..................15
   William 159
DURHAM, Anderson 106
   B. 15
DURST, J.K. 126
DWYER, Thomas 73
EAGLE, ...304
EARL, ...269
EARLE, ...22,86,133,
..............150,197,204
   Adolphus 163
   Anna Sorrel 162,166
   Baylis D. 286
   Baylis Wood 167
   Bayliss J. 12,162,
................200,262
   Bettie 106
   Carolina 167

C.B. 263
Claudius........161,223
Edward Hampton 167
Elias ...15,159,161-163
....166,167,179,189,215
Elizabeth Hampton ..70,
................166,167
Eliza 167,203
Fannie.....167,257,307,
................312,315
Georgia W. .167,200,258
Hannah 167
Harriett 167
James Hampton 167
John 162,163,167
John Baylis 163,166,
..........167,172,190
J.H. 262,263
Joseph Berry 203
Joseph Taylor 167
J.R. 163,205
Mary 167
Mary Prince ...70,71,167
Morgan P. 167
Nancy 166
Nellie 167
Paul 167,271,314
Preston 84,167
Robinson M. 166
Samuel 12,31,149,
................161,162
Samuel Girard ..164,166,
................167,217
Samuel Sydney 167
Sarah 163,166
Sarah Anne 167
S.G. 59,70,71,79,163
S.J. 200
Susan E. 203
T.B. 312
Thomasina 167
Wilton Robinson .167,233
EARP, Miss 164
EASLEY, Col. 185
EAST, Emma 122

327

EASTERLAND, Col. 158
EATON, William 12
EBENEZER, ... 49
EDWARDS, Agnes 119
    Carrie 113
    Claudia 119
    Elizabeth 112,119
    John 62
    Miss 112,122
ELGIN, Clarence 106
    J.M. 253
ELLIOTT, ... 197
    John H. 242
ELLISON, Lula 211
ELMORE, E.E. 31
ELROD, Sam 224
EMBERSON, Robert 145
EMERSON, James 177
EMMERSON, James 177
ENGLAND 82,268
    J.E. 29
EPPS, R.D. 121
ERSKINE, ... 132,159,192
    H.C. 253
    J.W. 253
    Thomas 195,252
ERWIN, T.D. 106
ESKEW, Thomas 61,174
    William 100
ESTES, Lottie Crosby . . . 126
ETHER, ... 259
EVANS, . . 82,114,224,268,269
    B.O. 314
    Dr. 23,26,159,
    201,258,259
    G.W. 17,30,314
    Margaret . . . 121,123,124,
    125,284
    T.A. 259
    Virginia 121,123
EVINS, W.D. 262
    William 309
FANT, ... 24,29
    Annie 304
    A.P. 313
    Ben 156,299
    Clyde N. 286
    Foster . . . 30,31,136,156
    Francis 313
    George W. 13,29,120,
    156,270,286,303
    H.B. 276
    J.M. 206
    J. Reece 30
    May 106
    Mayor 310
    Neb 156
    O.H.P. . . . 29,276,304,309
    Preston C. 286
    Rufus . . . 156,263,313,316
    T.B. 314
    Theo 156,268
    Walter 156
    W.F.M. 230
    William 29,156
    Wood 233,267
FARMER, ... 206
    Albert . . 299,302,308,314
    Annie 312
    Benjamin 159
    Emma 139
    Frank 314
    Jim 314
    J.L. 30,312
    Joe 314
    N.O. 230
    W.F. 31
FARRER, ... 200
    Field 159
FARROW, Col. 204
FEASTER, Conductor . 139,194
FEATHERSTONE, J.C.C. . . . 82
    262,263
FELCHIA, Father 60
FELTMAN, Robert T. 286
FELTON, Amaziah 223
    Emerial 159
FENNELL, R.C. 36,37
FERRIE, ... 171-172
FIELD, Cyrus 56

Traditions *and* History *of* Anderson County, S.C.

Eugene	56
John	159
Marshall	56
Thankful	56
Samuel	56
FIELDING, William H.	224
FISHER, Charles	126
Cynthia	113
R.C.	126
FLEET, Florence	119
FORBES, George	159
FORTUNE, Alfred N.	286
FOSTER, Ethel	211
G.E.W.	13,15
H.A.	211
Nannie	211
FOUCHE, L.P.	31
FOUNTAIN, Mrs.	51
FOWLER, J. Reed	31
J.S.	17,30,175, 203,277,283
FRANCIS, Allen	3
FRAZIER, Dr.	124
Uncle Barbur	310
FRETWELL, A.G.	275
J.J.	17,25,126, 164,275,314
Mrs. J.J.	317
Joseph Younger	275
FRIERSON, David E.	38,89, 118
Dr.	38,259,270,311
Janie	118,123
W.H.	262
FROST, B.M.	268
R.M.	82
GADSEN, Minnie	63,121
T.F.	58,63,123,124
GAILLIARD,	268
Dr.	220
Joshua	36
Josiah	198
Smith	36
Theodore	12
GAINES, Ella	122

M.B.	13
Mr.	107
Perry	225
GAMBRELL,	132,159
Enoch	225
Jefferson	286
Matthew	10,14,168
Mattison	194
Mrs.	106,268
Tyler	219
GANT, C.	168
B.F.	205
Matilda J.	205
GARNER, Lucy	138
GARNET, Alma	103
GARRIS, Miss	138
GARRISON,	104
Charles	139
Clemmie	128
Elizabeth	138
Henry	128
Levi	52
Mourning	138
Mrs.	237
W.D.	278
William	107
GARVIN, Thomas	10,212,222
GARY, Mart	254
Thomas W.	120
GASSAWAY, M.H.	128
GASTON, William	199
GATLIN, Mrs. Arthur	106
GAWTHMEY, Basil M.	152
GEER, Davis	191
D.R.	225
H.M.	183
Levi N.	31
S.M.	252
Solomon	159
Walter	314
W.H.	253
GEIGER, E.F.	308
Emily	75
G.H.	124,262
Mrs.	285

Sue Whitfield 55
GEISBERG, Dora 212,314
GENT, O.M. 214
GENTRY, Baker 143
    Charles W. 286
    Lewis W. 104
    Mrs. Love 257
    Mrs. R.A. 315
    Robert 102
GEORGE, Ezekiel 24,306
    John 179
    Mary Jane 24
    Thomas 147
    Vashti 106
GIBBES, ... 197
GIBBS, William 227
GIBSON, Walter M. 168
    W.B. 28
GILES, Irs C. s 286
GILLIAM, James 70
GILLELAND, James 33
GILLILAN, John 176
    Sarah 176
GILLISON, Arch 177
    Jane 177
GILMAN, ... 197
GILMER, A.R. 226
    James 222
    Jennie Kramer 90
    Swain 282
GILMORE, J. 13
GIRAND, Madam 23
GIST, Gov. 227
GLEASON, Joel H. 224
GLEN, Gov. 8
GLENN, Capt. 105
    J.M. 212
    John F. 52
    Lawrence 308
    Mell 85
    T.S. 212
    William 52
GLOVER, Dr. 163
    Tocoa 38
GODFREY, J.H. 31

Mayor 283
GOODE, L. 11,15
GOODGION, Mr. 107
GOODMAN, Blanche 120
GOODRUM Mr. 52
GOODWYN, John 159
GORDON, Edward 286
    Ellen 121
    James 143
    Robert 26
GOSSETT, B.B. 314
    J.P. 207,314
GRACE, Baylis 139
    James 137
    Mr. 139
GRADY, Henry 162
    John W. 290
    Watson 107
GRANT, Lieut. 287
    Lillie 106,156
    Joseph H. 286
    William 76
GRAY, D.S. 314
    Louis 262,270
    J. 15
    Julia 119
GREELEE, Margaret 146
GREEN, David 214,215
    G.B. 263
    John T. 225
    L.N. 225
    Mrs. 1
    Nelson R. 13
GREGG, Irving 108,164
    Mary 141
    Sarah 163
GREGORY, Mrs. 104
GRESHAM, John 138
GRIFFIN, John C. .10,12,159
    Mr. 133
    Thomas 172
GRIFFITH, James 198,200
GRISHAM, Joseph 199,290
GROVE, Guy T. 286
GRUBBS, John 230

Traditions *and* History *of* Anderson County, S.C.

W.L. 230
W.T. 232
GUEST, William 204
GUERARD, Benjamin 191
GUNNIN, Cyrus 178
   James 176
   Mary 176
GUYTON, ...220
   J.R. 102
   J.W. 13
HAGOOD, ...222
HALBERT, Arthur 138
   Enos 138
   Frances 138
   James 138
   Joel 138
   John 138
   Joshua 138
   Lucinda 138
   Martha 138
   Mary 138
   Ruth 137-139
   Sarah 138
   Susannah 137,138
   William 138,195,196
   William Jr. 139
HALE, Mary 169
HALL, Almon C. 286
   A.M. 226
   Annie Belle 119
   Asa 79
   Bastle 226
   Dr. 33,57
   James L. 286
   John 219
   John J.H. 226
   Matrtin 219
   Mr. 258
   Nathaniel 219
   O.N. 224
   Robert 33
   Thomas P. 115
   W.C. 226
   W.D. 22
   William Sanford 186

Wilton E. 85
Zachariah 177,219
HALLUM, John 200
HALSEY, Tervey 70
HAMILTON, D.K. 202
   James 159
   John 35
   Miss 212
   Thomas 35,212
   William 104,138
HAMMETT, H.P. 292
   J.D. 314
HAMMOND, ...268
   Amanda 164
   Carolina 273
   Clorinda 146
   Frank 273
   John 148
   Lucy 260
   Mrs. 121,123
   S.J. 11
   Vic 118
   William 159
   W.Q. 314
HAMPTON, Gen. Wade .75,231,
  251,254,258
   Elizabeth 167
HAND, Eva Dessie 208
HANEY, J. 15
HANKS, ...125
   J.M. 226
   Luke 226
   Nancy 135
HARBOUR, Miss 115
HARLIN, B.F. 29
HARBIN, Morgan 100
   Nat 102
HARDIN, ...107
HARDY, James 52
   Richard Baxter 52
HARKNESS, ...176
HARPER, G.M. 225
   J.M. 225
   John R. 225
   Margaret 138

Samuel D. 286
HARRIS, Andrew 77
  Annie McFall........288
  Benjamin 77
  Eliza 77
  Gillison 143
  Herbert.............262
  J.B.................102
  J.C..........30,262,288
  John.........76,77,197
  Joseph P. 70,77
  Leon................263
  L.W.................227
  Nathaniel 77
  N.H..................37
  Thomas 36
  William..............36
  W.K..................25
HARRISON, ...23,56,76,
 197,259,268
  Dr. 260
  Elizabeth 14,25
  Elizabeth Hampton ..163
  Frank E. ...161,162,167,
 205,230,235
  James............10,23,
 161-163,166
  J.W. 28,29,150
 201,262
  Nettie 167
  Nina.............68,151
  Robert H. 100
  Thomas 159
  W.H.................314
HARVEY, George 195
HASKEL, ...197
HASKELL, Alexander .232,258
HASTIE, John 160
HATCHER, Mr. 122
HAUCK, Clara 119
HAUGHTON, Miss. 113
HARVARD, J.O. 263
HAWTHORNE, D. 290
HAYES, Weston 115,218
HAYNES, Mrs. 119

HAYNIE, S.R. 258
  Sarah...............100
  W.H.................108
  William.............100
HAYS, Cricket 267
  Issac 50
  Ruth................103
HEARD, O.M. 55
HEATON, William 199
HECKLE, Newton 63
HENBREE, ...104
  J.E.................224
  J.L..................31
HENDERSON, Romus D. 286,316
HENRY, B.A. 83,262
  Place...............246
HERBERT, T.G. 50
HERRICK, H.D. 104
HERRON, John 36
HEWETT, ...152
  Cassandra 26,113
HIBBARD, Bettie 151
HIGHSHAW, ...159
HILL, Capt. 228
  Elizabeth 138
  Eunice 94
  Joshua 159
  Lois 312
  R.S. 55,195,281
 312,314
  Simpson 269
  T.F. 17,296,312,314
  Tom 30,312
HILLHOUSE, J.B. 102
  John.................36
  Joseph...............36
  Waddell.............100
HILLIS, Cora 259
HIOTT, D.W. 48
HODGES, ...209
  Baxter..............218
  Mrs. G.W. 52
HOKE, A.D. 244
HOLLAND, ...204,222
  A.M..............28,159

D.R. 116,259	Jane 83,118
John 192	John 1,26,30,55
Joshua 252	John McFall .142,269,314
Moses 41,43	Mrs. J.E. 122
William 155	Leonora 83,121,
W.T. 258	 125,171,312
HOLLEMAN, Lee G. 30	Lillie 114
William 159	Mahala 22
HOLMES, William . . . 183,191,	Nora 142
. . . . 195,267	R.H. 29
HOLT, J.P. 37	W.R. 30,136
HOLTZCLAW, Lillian 103	HUDGENS, Lucia taylor ..90
HONEA, ... 213,247	Mrs. 122
HOOD, J.B. 246	R.R. 227
J.K. 30,262,281,312	W.A. 122
John K. 263	HUDSON, Ellie 126
William 312	HUFF, ... 104
HOOVER, Steven F. 286	HUGER, ... 55,197,198,203
HOPKINS, John 259	HUGNER, John 159
HORNE, J.T. 82,268	HULL, Dan 247
HORTON, ... 127,209,314	John 247
C.E. 104	Neddy 215
Elijah 226	HUMPHREY, ... 270
Grief 132	HUMPHREYS, Anna 94,182
M.C. 88	David 35-37,68
John C. 192	John L. 226
O.A. 89	Louise 312
O.E. 7	Nell 312
O.R., ... 260	W.W. 17,30,82,120,
Thadeus 87	 223,232,246,262,312
HOWARD, Dudley 176	Mrs. W.W. 257
T.E. 13	HUNT, W.H. 126
HOWELL, ... 178	HUNTER, ... 197
HOYT, ... 84	Andrew 66
Col. 135	Anne 68
Gertrude 312	Helen F. 126
J.A. 29,82,194,239,	John 68
. . . . 249,252,258,312	Mary 68
Mrs. J.A. 257	Norton 23
James H. 224	William 68
Rebecca 14,127	HYDE, E.F. 206
HUBBARD 82,268	IRBY, J.H. 158
A.P. 268,269,270,271	IRWIN, McDuffie 31
Augusta 83,86,121	Robert 40
Billy 198	JACKSON, ... 144

    A.E. 36
    Bill 145
    D.P. 291
    T.C. 314
    Thomas J. 227
JAMES, Misses 71
JAMESON, McElroy 245
JAMISON, Miss 139
JARRETT, M.M. 301
JEFFERS, Gussie 117
    H.L. 117
JEFFERSON, Thomas 56,68
JENKINS, Micah 58
    Robert C. 58
    T.D. 224
    W.S. 259
JENNINGS, ...197,216
JETER, R.C. 56,216
JOHNSON, Allen 155
    Blanche 90
    Capt. 77
    Dr. 112,114
    Edward L. 286
    Frank 132,269
    John 157
    Judge 134
    L. 48
    William B. 38,111
JOLLY, ...249
    Manse 228
    William M. 286
JONES, Adam Crane 15
    Betty 159
    Capt. 245
    C.F. 30,123
    Charley 55
    Claude 314
    Ella 19
    J.H. 278
    J.L.E. 174
    J.T.C. 232
    J.V. 232,234
    Lula B. 126
    Mrs. 55
    Sam 251

    Thomas 159
JORDAN, Pleasant 96
JUDSON, Dr. 121
    Mary 113
JUNKIN, David 105
KAY, ...132,159
    Armand 177
    C.M. 226
    Doran 227
    Frances Marion 210
    J.D. 139
    Jesse 192
    L.W. 61
    Miss 210
    Strother 192
    W.H. 301
KEASLER, D.A. 82,268
KEATON, ...178
    Welborn 137
KEESE, Elijah 101
KEITH, ...82
    Bessie 151
    Capt. 232
    Eliot M. ...82,262,266
    Elizabeth 68
    Jennie 266
    W.W. 258
KELLY, Reuben 226
    Zahra 207
KEMP, ...7,96,168,176
KEMPER, ...118
KENNEDY, ...107,270
    A. Ross 103
    J.L. 95,103,104,110
    J.P. 78
    M. 30,269
    Mike 59,306
    Mrs. 60
    R.C. 227
KERSHAW, J.B. 258,290
KEYS, Crawford 170,181
    Della 122
    Major 226
    M.L. 249
    Peter 131

R.L. 224
Robert 170,250
W.W. 147
KILLEBREW, Jame P. 286-288
KILPATRICK, ...197
  Col. 76,212
  F.W. 224
  J.C. 10,235
KINARD, James P. 127
KING, D.E. 226
  George W. 286,300
  Guerdon...............13
  Larious O. 286
  Jasper...............226
  J.A. 226
  Peter................168
  Robert...........43,168
  V.B..................224
  W.B...................13
KINGSLEY, Chester ..193,196
KIRKLAND, Rev. 85
KITSINGER, Dick 192
  Jefferson 183,184
KLUTE, Miss 113
KNIGHT, J.G. 258
  Warren...............213
KONLER, A.H. 227
KRAMMER, Jennie 282
KUHN, ...247
LABOON, J.H. 224
LAFAR, D.X. 36,72,114
LAFOY, L.W..........183,185
LAMAR. Thomas 222
LAND, Dr. 262
  Gid..................221
LANDER, Dr. 207
  John............62,207
LANDORD, P.S. 230
LANDFORD, Samuel ...107,205
LANGSTON, C.C. 29,30,
 82,304
  S.A. 29,224
LATHAM, ...104
LATIMER, Asbury C. 195
  Col. 182

Dr. 262
LATTA, ...197
LAUGHLIN, ...118
  William 13,275
  Mrs. William ...284,307
LAWHORN, Van 12,13
LAWSON, J.W. 227
LAWTON, John S. 160
LEACH, W.N. 235
LEATHERS, W.W. 102
LEAVELL, ...267
LEBBY, William 292
LEE, Anderson 159
  Harry 66
  Major................240
  Miriam Earle 167
  Rebecca..............86
  Stephen D. 235,245
  Thomas...............258
  Thomas B. 286
LEDBETTER,.............104
  Col. 247
  D.A. 204,225,230
 235,314
LEMON, Martha 159
  Robert 159
LENDERMAN,..............59
LESLEY, William 191
LESLIE, Amandus 158
LESTER, ...290
LESSER, ...51,212,314
  M. 269
LEVERETTE, ...121
  J.B. 97,220
  Margaret 97
  Stephen 97,111,
 220,286
  Wesley.....21,22,27,97,
 107,111,118,158
LEWIS 56,118,197,211
  Berry 143,155
  Dr. 47
  James A. 225
  J.B. 86,120,131,
 163,222,245,312

335

John S. 199
John T. 12, 200
Major 10, 165, 212
Mary 312
Mollie 139
Richard 159
LIDDELL, Andrew .70, 190, 215
Margaret 97
LIGON, ... 121, 127, 270
Arthur 272
Charley 61
Cora 28
Dick 55
Helen 28
Louis 316
Mary 311
Professor 89, 120
R.E. 30, 293, 314, 317
R.S. 17, 126, 283, 314
T.C. 206
William S. 118, 272
W.J. ... 117, 118, 262, 306
LINCOLN, Abraham 135
Thomas 135
LINDSAY, Mary 138
LINSEY, J.Q. 36
LINTON, Rebecca 203
LIPSCOMB, ... 10, 15
LOFLIN, ,,,,,,,,,,,,,,, 131
LOFTON, James 200
Samuel 196, 200
LONG, ... 92, 132, 159
Berry 106
Crawford 259
Ezekiel 212
Ezekiel, Jr. 212
James 159, 224
John 224
Reuben 294
S.A. 211
LOOPER, S. 227
LORD, Samuel 250
LOTHER, Lord 299
LOVELACE, Jonathan 193
LOWREY, William 159

LOWRY, Mrs. 68
LYNCH, Bishop 60
McALLISTER, John 159
McBRAYER, D.P. ..121, 293, 294
McBRIDGE, J.L. 61
McCALEB, William 197
McCALISTER, N. 15
McCALL, Col. 77
McCANN, Robert 35, 105
Squire 78, 212
Thomas 213
McCANTS, E.C. 88, 125
McCARLEY, ... 206
McCAULEY, May 152
Mr. 152
McCHERE, C.M. 31
McCLINTON, Alec 165
William 226
McCLURE, Capt. 73
McCONNELL, J.H. 13, 123
McCOLLOUGH, D.S. 243
McCORMICK, Peggy 215
Polly 215
McCOWN, ,,,,,,,,, 106, 157
McCOY, James 192
Mary 124
Polly 192
Samuel 192
McCRADY, Edward 258
McCRARY, Mrs. 119
McCULLY, ... 24, 268
Carrie 93, 182, 270
Newton A. 224, 270,
.... 316, 317
P.K. ...30, 111, 223, 225,
.... 239, 278, 293, 317
R.S. 293
Stephen ..18, 28, 111, 156
.... 159, 182, 305
McCUTCHEN, J. 258
McDAVID, Allen 138
James A. 226
John 137
W.S. 25
McDONALD, James 143

Traditions *and* History *of* Anderson County, S.C.

McDOUGAL, Viola P. 90
McDUFFIE, Gov. 135,149,157,
........200,202,305
McELHANY, W.M. 212
McELMOYLE, Miss 107
McELROY, Mrs. 111
   T.A. 247,248
McELWEE, J.F. 120
McFALL, ...192
   Andrew 13,15,142
   Dr. 164
   Henry................1
   Mrs. Henry 315
   John 96,142,306
   Malcolm 305,314
   Samuel 142
   William 62
McGEE, ...155
   Abner 155
   Burrell........155,193
   G.W...........193,194
   Hezekiah............267
   J.B. 13
   J.L. 18,30,136,193
   Jesse 138
   John 155
   Lon 72
   Mike.......153,173,192,
  193,244
   Thomas 224
   Wade H. 286
   William 155,168,192
McGILL, Henry L. 36
   John A. 83
   Mr..................15
McGOWAN, ...225
McGRATH, ...269
   Annie 60
   John 59,172
McGUNKIN, W.M. 123,268
McHAFFY, L.M. 100,103
McIVER, Duncan 81
McJUNKIN, John 102
   Park 102
McKILLER, ...116,117

McKINLEY, President ...286
McKINNEY, ...216
   Hugh 24
   James 13,213
   Mrs.................270
   Perry...............13
McLEES, ...104
McLESKEY, ...104
   W. Harry 31,314
McLIN, D.P. 36
McMAKIN, John 159
McMULLIN, Peter 40
McMURRAY, William 213
McNEELY, J.A. 227
McPHAIL, Charles 106
McPHERSON, ...164,165
   Elizabeth G. 176
   Malcolm 164
   Mary Gunnin 176
   Phoebe 176
   William 176
McQUEEN, S. 15
   Miss 111
McSMITH, Mrs. 123
McSWAIN, ...107
McVAY, Hugh 159
McWHIRTER, Dr, ...262
   William 36
McWHORTER, William 205
MACKEY, Judge 256
MADEEN, Jay W. 286
MAGEE, William 13,15,44
MAHAFFEY, ...205
   F.A. 105
MAJOR, ...132,159
   Elijah 193
   Ezekiel 263
   Howard 263
   James 192
   J.J. 314
   John 92,102
   Susan 203
MANLEY, Charles ...121,195
MANNING, ...104,305
MARCHBANKS, G.E. 31

Traditions *and* History *of* Anderson County, S.C.

MARETT, Cleveland 100
    W.O. 13
MARSH, Mary 139
MARSHALL, A.A. 120,121
    Aubrey................117
    C. 38
    Foster...............225
MARTIN 104,200
    Abram 141
    A.F. 224
    B.C. 226
    Catherine 141
    Charity 141
    Chesley..............141
    Col. 209
    Cynthia..............141
    Elizabeth 141
    Frances 141
    Henry C. 286
    Hester...............141
    Jacob 140
    James 141,159
    J.C. 226
    Joe 266
    John W. 13,177,208,
   223,286
    Levi 77
    Louis D. 159
    Mary 141
    Miss 139
    Reuben M. 286
    Roderick.............208
    Thomas 140
    William P. 43
MASSAY, Ansel 214
MASSEY, Silas 146,266
    MASTERS, E.W. 142
    J. 15
    Roy 106
    Victor I. 89,106
MATTHEWS, Sampson 77
MATTISON, Chamberlain .226
    C.S. 139,190,235
    J.F. 226
    John 62,203

    Mamie Brown 28
    M.M. 126,314
    Raymond............1,15
    William.........138,141
MAULDIN, B.F. 12,19,26,30,
   46,152,223,272,314
    Elsie 123
    Elizabeth 27,38
    J.L. 17,20,46,
   159,294
    T.J. 262,263
MAVERICK,...65,165,211,213
    Augustus 69
    Elizabeth 68
    Joseph 68
    Lydia 68
    Mary 68
    Mrs. 65
    Samuel 15,65,68,69
MAXWELL,..........197,204
    Alice................113
    D.S. 30,120,291
    Emily 68
    Frederick 275,298
    Gen. 70
    Harriet 238
    J.D. 17,26,278,308
    John 70,167,259
    Robert 70,167,234
    Robert Jr. 70
MAYFIELD, ...192
    Ephrain 194
MEANS, A.G. 30,153,275
    A.G. Jr. 17
MECHLIN, Robert 33
MEISSER, H.L. 300
MERRIWEATHER, ...107
MICHIEL, W. 15
MILBURN,..............281
MILES, Edward R. 115
    James 116
    John 159
MILFORD, ...219,248
    A.C. 140
    C.S. 140

Traditions *and* History *of* Anderson County, S.C.

    Clayton J. 140
    Charles S. 139,247
    Eliza Jane 140
    Henry 73
    John 73,139
    Joseph 73
    Matthew 73
    Rebecca...........139
    Robert 73
    Samuel Marshall 140
    Thomas..........73,139
MILITIA, Early 155,156
MILLER, ...111,197
    A.G. 120
    Bessie 102
    Carro 271
    Col. 247
    Emilia 28
    George............271
    Mrs. George 271
    H.C. 263
    Jacob R. 286
    John........33,80,195,
   196,200
    Juklia 271
    Reed...........28,271
    Will 271
MILLHOUSE, J.B. 103
MILLS, Mary 206
MILWEE, John 82,268
    T.F................225
    W.B...............208
MINTER, Mrs............106
MITCHELL, ...247
    B.W. 224
    Ephraim 193
    S.C. 126
MOFFATT, Col. .....,,,,,141
    Dr. 124
    John 195
MORNINGSTAR, ...56
MONCRIEF, W.F. 124,125
MOORE, ...59,82,248
    Alfred..........24,267
    Betty 122,270

    Col. 76
    Eliab........75,76,179,
   191,192
    Eliab Jr. 105,192
    Gov. 8
    G.W..............51,89
    Hamilton C. 286
    J.A. 226
    James B. 252
    John B. 135,252,262
    John V. ...28,51,83,111,
   122,133,157,225,
   235,262,270
    Joseph B. 252,253
    J. Whit 301
    Leah..............169
    Press C. 226
    Rachel 169
    Robert 98
    Samuel 75,252,276
    Soencer 98
    Thomas 294
    William 75
    W.J...............226
MOORER, Ernest 124
MOORHEAD, Alexander ...11,
   130,20
    Betsy 143
    John 130
    R.L. 30
    Robert 15,40,130
    Sarah 147
MORELAND, James 159
MORGAN, Edward 159
    Gen. John 243
MORRIS, ...305
    Mrs. Edward 57
    Elizabeth 123
    E.P. 58
    Misses............114
MORSE, Professor 111
MOSS, ...268
    B.F. 30
MUIR, John 130
MULLALY, Adger 87

MULLER 107	NICHOLSON, William ,,,,286
MULLIKIN, ...213	NIXON, W.A. 301
B.F..................224	NOBLE, Capt. 77
M.L..................224	NOLAND, J.H. 120
MULLINAX, T.D. 30	NORRIS, ...104
MUNRO, James .22,23,263,308	A.C..................82
Maggie...........23,122	A.O..................29
MURCHINSON, Hugh 40	Butler T............286
MURPHY, Charles 98	D....................15
Ezekiel 141	Elvira Thompson 169
F.M. 30	Ezekiel 218
Richard 98,99	Frank 84
W.L. 226	Harriet 143
MURRAY, ...119	Jane Swain 217
Claudia.....112,118,119	J.E. 111
E.B. 308	Jesse 21,191
Edward 19,84,252,	J.J. 30
.............288,311	J. Thompson 226
J. Scott 28,46,112,	J.W. 6,105,153,
........114,262,286,288	188,291
Mrs. 121,122	Mary 142
MUSGROVE, Edward ,,,,,,,43	Patrick 36,169
NARDIN,Dr..55,120,122,124,	Peter K. 226
......157,234,258-262,	Robert 10,11
..............277,282	William C. .169,217,225
Eleanor St.C. 157	NORRYCE, L.E. 86
Eva 120	NORTH,.................197
Lucille.....121,123,124	NORTHRUP, Claudian 60
Lucy 55	Harry 60
W.H. Jr. 29,30,121	NORTON, Jeptha 145
Mrs. W.H. 317	Sarah 143
NEELY, J.A. 263	William 145
James 142	NORWOOD, Thomas 286
John 142	O'CONNELL,..............59
Miss.................74	O'DELL, F.V. 222
NEVITT, R.C. 224	O'DONNELL, Barum 270
Sallie 155	James 60
William 191	O'NEAL, John Belton 20,
NEWELL, N.J. 282	181,194,261
R.D. 226	O'REA, Miss. 139
NEWMAN, Capt. 288	O'SHIELDS, Benjamin B. 286
NEWTON,.................62	OLIVER, Alexander 212
Joseph..............157	OPIE, Sue 117
Julius R. 107	ORR,.........15,20,45,50,
Olivia 107	83,147,186

Christopher ..15-17,47,
........78,108,119,133,
..........154,212,218
Gov. 270,282
H.A. 296,314
Mrs. Henry 298
Jane 218
Jenu 77,78,178,263
J.L. ...20,21,27,28,88,
....96,141,223,224,235,
........262,263,307,312
Mrs. J.L. 93,225
J.L. Jr 27,116,262
J.L. III, ...314
J.W. 224
L.J. 109
Lydia 312
Marshall 314
Mary 312
Mill 293
S.M......17,30,120,121,
........123,261,262,295
OSBORN, A.L. 29
OSBORNE, ...134,185,266
    A.H. 232
    Andrew 38
    Emma..................123
    Lizzie 106
    Miss 38
    W.R. 30,309
OSTEEN, ...301
OTWELL, William 174
OUELLA, J. Homer 85,86
OVERBY 144
    Sarah................113
OVERMAN, Flora 169
OWENS, ...261
    Samuel 25,268
PAGET,J.M......153,253,262
    Mrs. J.M. 123
PAINE, Charlotte 112
    Phoebe 112
PALMER, B.M. 39
PARK, Hazel 126
PARKER, ...229

Capt................128
J.P. 226
M.C. 252
Newton W. 210
R.E. 226
S.R. 314
PARKS, B.M. 125
PARTLOW, John M. 268
PATRICK, Carrie 90,182,315
    J.M..............30,120
    John B. 120,121,
    R.S. 120
PATTERSON, Mrs. 248
PAUL, Thomas 48
PAYNE, J.M. ...29,30,121,300
    Misses 156
PEARMAN, ...314
    Benjamin 276
    Carrie 123,276
    Chess 276
    Dean 276
    Frederiack 276
    James 13
    Maggie 276
    S.D. 263
    S.N. 252,253,276
    W.C. 226
PEARSON, Harry 159
    J.T...............30,31
    W.F...............36,37
PEGG,S.M...........268,305
PELZER, F.J. 292
PENDLETON, J.N. 159
    Judge ,,,,,,,,,,,195
PENNELL, R.E. 103
    Thomas...............36
PEOPLES, John E. 17,30,
   275,308
PERINNEAU, Henry 116
PERRIN, ...82
PERRY, C. 291
    Commodore 201
    Margaret 291
    William 290
PEPPER, Fanny 139

Traditions *and* History *of* Anderson County, S.C.

PERSHING, Gen. 203
PETTY, Jervey 214
PHILLIPS, Reuben 155
PICKENS, Andrew 8,10,32,33,
......66,70,77,141,195,
............200,213,221
   Anne 54
   Chales C. 202,221
   Elvira 143
   F.J. 57
   Robert 54,70,106
   R.w. 106
   Samuel 70
   S.B. 223
   T.J. 258
   W.S. 153,188,220
PICKERING, Eleanor 81
PICKETT, ...216
   Mrs. 122
PICKLE, ...107,213
   Belle Mabon 86
PIERCE, ...220
   William............171
PICKNEY, ...55,197
   Mary...............221
   Thomas..........57,196
PINKIND, Mrs. 23
   Nettie 23
   Tony 23
POE, William 224
POOLE, ...23
   Betty 24
   Catherine 156
   Manning 11,19,22
   Matilda............143
POORE, Charles 286
   Ernest H. 286
   Hampton 226
   J.J. 225
   John W. 226
POPE, Sampson 50
POPPE, Julius 268
PROCHER, ...197
POSTELLE, John 159
   Miss 198

POTTER, William S. 57
POWELL, B.O. 121
   Charles F. 286
   H.A................31
PRATT, Walter B. 286
PRESSLEY, Dr. 40
   Ebenezer 111
   John S. 40,116
PREVOST, ...269
   Annie 312
   J.W................312
   Ned................315
   S.H................308
   J. Willet 252
PRICE, W.P. 244
PRIESTLY, Chalmers 107
PRINCE, ...208
   Mrs. Charles 37,38
   George E. 124,262,
  263,280
   John 162
   K. 15
   Mary 162
   S.L. 263
   Thomasina 162
PRUITT, Harrison ...106,262
   Janie 115
   Olga 106,126,262
   Sam Orr 62
   T.C. 226
   W.C. 226
PUCKETT, Coleman C. 83
   Lester 83
PULLIAM, Robert 101
PURDY, Henry 214
QUATTLEBAUM, ...134
   J.W. 262
QUIGLEY, Father 60
RAMER, R.J. 316
RANKIN, ...212
   George A. 213,214
RAST, J.D. 31,314
   Mrs. J.D. 316
RAVENALL, ...55
REAMER, Miss 73

Traditions *and* History *of* Anderson County, S.C.

REECE, ...25,67,197
   Dr. 65
   James 139
   Mrs. 65
   Thomas 32,33
REED, ...268,272
   C.A. 111,186,193,
  234,240,269,272
   Mrs. C.A. 257
   Col. 83
   Cora. 272
   Elenor. 272
   Emilia 112,271
   Enoch. 132
   Fannie. 148
   Henry. 43,118
   J.P. 7,12,20,26,27,
  46,47,80,90,96,
  109,111,132-134,
  178,223,269,271,
  272,305
   J.P. Sr. 256,262
   Julia 139,271
   Lucy 272
   Mary. 272
   Pink. 118,135,232
   Sally. 176
   Teresa. 272
REEVES, Georgia Ann 61
   John 12,192
   Noah 61
   T. Strawther . . .104,211
   Washington 61
REID, ...132
   J.H. 259
   Robert 36
   Whitelaw 132
REMBERT, Mrs. 119
RENAN, Mrs. 149
RHODES, Thomas 48
RHODY, Frank 286
   F.G. 293
RICE, ...104,192,276
   Amaziah . .46,47,167,180
   E.B. 224

E.C. 180
Fleetwood . . .28,159,180
H. 11,12,15
Hezekiah 47
Ibsen 20,83,262
J.F. 262
Mrs. J.T. 119
Leon 263
Polly L. 47
RICHARDS, J.T. 21
RICHARDSON, ...104,141
   A.N. 141
   G.N. 102
   John 12
   Katie 155
   Louis 213
   Matthias 141,213
   Newton 213
RILEY, J.D. 205
RIMMER, Miss 120
RIPLEY, N.R. 48
RISNER, Silas 192
RISER, Lucy 126
RIVERS, A.B. 293
   J.H. 258
   Prince 250
RIVES, John 107
ROBERTS, ...34
   E.G. 291
   James 307
   William. 59
ROBBINS, John C. 286
ROBINSON, Eliza 25
   Frances Wilton 166
   Horseshoe 5,78
   James 225
   Jane 25
   Jesse. 226
   Sallie. 122
   W.W. 30
ROGERS, mamie 103
ROLLINS, G.B. 225
ROPER, Delia 139
   Lillie 22
   L.M. 126

ROSAMUND, J. 15
ROSE, John T. 286
ROSEMAN, ...132,159
ROSS, ...197
   A.W. 38
ROUND, Rev. 118
ROUNDTREE, Hester 140
ROWAN, ...141
ROWELL, ...293
ROYALL, ...61
RUCKER, Col.............270
   E.M. 117,262,281
   E.M. Jr. 262
RUHAMAH, ...52
RUIDAEAL, E.P. 286
RUSSELL, ...156,227
   Alice 257
   D.H. 84,85,125,
  138,202
   D.M. 259
   Lelia 123
   Louise 275
   May 106,125
   Thomas H. 84
   W.W. 13
   Mrs. W.W. 90
RUTLEDGE, ...77
   Anne 177
   Cynthia 209
   Gov. 66
   H.R. 259
SADLER, ...23,142
   David 75,158
   John 23
SALLA, U.G. 31
SANDERS, J.O. 13,262
SATTERFIELD, ...50
SAYRE, Jane 124,306
SCOTT, Edgar M. 286
   Newton 266,314
SCUDDAY, Dr. 184,259
   H.G. 262
SEABORN, ...197
   George 197
SEABROOK, George 90

SEARL, ...216
SEARS, J.B. 61
SEEL, Carrie 121
   L.H. 267
SELDEN, ...298
SEMMES, F.W. 197
SEWERS, James 37
SHANKLIN, ...56,197,198,200
   Joseph 199
   Mrs. 122
SHARP, M.L. 258
SHARPE, ...86,116,121,268
   Noel B. 286
   W.F. 307
   W.K. 184,199
   William S. 286
SHAW, John 106
   W.S. 105
SHEARER, ...104
   Andy 172
   W.H. 222
SHELDON, William A. 101
SHELOR, John W. 101
   Joseph R. 100
   Joseph W. 102
   Thomas R. 100
SHERARD, J.L. 30,88,263
   Mrs. Reid 88
   Rufus C. 286
   William 10
   W.Y. 226
SHERRELL, John 139
SHESHANE, R.S. 59
SHIRLEY,.........132,159
   James 159
   Jennie 102
   J.J. 226
   Kyle 106
   Obediah 214
   Riley John 193
   W.A. 226
   William 252
SHUBRICK, William B. ...201
SHUFORD, ...68
SHUMATE, Miss 138

Traditions *and* History *of* Anderson County, S.C.

SILCOX, F.A. 245
SILLIMAN, C.H. 120
SIMMONS, David 172,205
SIMPSON, ...32,104
    Frances 261
    Jane 141
    James 141
    J.D. 120
    John .34,73,141,142,261
    Lieut. Gov. 256
    Maggie 120
    Minnie 120
    Mrs. 74
    R.F. 223
    R.W. 87,262,281
    Tally 233,246
    Mrs. Will 191
SIMS, Miss 155
SINGLETARY, W.H. 36
SISK, E.L. 205
SITTON, ...197
    Augustus J. .254,258,291
    Col. 255,291
    Eugene N. 292
    John B. 252,291
    Nancy 139
SKELTON, ...104
    John 15
    Mrs. J.B. 257
    J.T. 224
SKINNER, Genevieve 119
SLIGH, Uriah 77
SLOAN, ...28,82,116,197,268
    Benjamin F. .102,203,290
    Catherine 203
    David 15,78,203
    D.P. 23
    Ed 23
    Eliza C. Earle 203
    Elizabeth 203
    E.P. 304
    J.B.E. ...27,57,223,235
    J. Mattison 203
    John 160,290
    Mary 203

Mary Earle 167
Mortimer 304
Nancy 203
Nancy Blassingame ..203
Nancy Trimmer 203
R.E. 224
Rebecca 203
Rebecca Linton 203
Susan Major 78,203
Thomas M. ..160,203,290
William 203
SMELTZER, Dr. 60
SMETHERS, Dr. 262,283
SMITH,........7,26,62,76,
........107,192,197,221
Benjamin 212
Billy 186
B.S. 224
Charles 211
Claude 62
Col. 250
Dicky 215
E.L. 253
Ella 139
Father 60
Hattie 106
Henry Julius 227
J.A. Monroe 224
James 213
James D. 139
Jesse 143,255,259,
...........270,297,305
J.M. 30
Job 212
John 68,213
Joshua 104,211,213
J.R. 24,28,268
K.P. 263
Lizzie 312
L.P. 111
Luther P. 24,30,268
.............269,307
M. 48
Mary...........179,211
Matilda 143

345

Minnie 152
Nimrod 214
Peggy Blanton 90
R.E.L. 103
Robert 195
Samuel 163
Wales Major 104,211
W.G. 61
W.H. 263
William 194
SMYTH, E.A. 245
Ellison 292
SNELGROVE, ...278
W.P. 311
SNIPES, B.Crayton ...106
SOUTHERLAND, Alexander 137
Jane 137
SPEARMAN, A.E. 226
Asbury 98
C.F. 31
James 245
John W. 226
SPEER, C.H. 101
W.A. 31
SPEERY, B.W. 17
SPOON, ...62
STAUNTON, Katie 155
Matthias 79,155
William 155
STEELE, Robert 140
William 197
STENSELL, Marshall .144,145
STEPHENS, ...269
A.B. 30
STEPHENSON, Claude 318
STEVENS, ...197
Alexander 194
Clement H. 57,201
Daniel E. 201
Henry 159
Thomas Holdup 211
STEVENSON, John 88,111
Miss 137
Robert 40
W.J. 226

STOKES, Miss 125
STONEMAN, Gen. 241
STOWERS, Gaines 170
STRANATHAN, Sara ...126
STRANGE, William P. 226
STRIBBLING, Cornelius .201
Elizabeth Sloan 203
J.C. 254,299
Jesse 203
John W. 297
S.P. 102
STRICKLAND, A.C. 30
Teresa 90
William 102
STRINGER, A.J. 194
William 293
STUART, ...197
SULLIVAN, ...82,268
Ben M. 286
Charles A. 30,126,
.............253,313
Mrs. C.S. 112
G.C. 85,263,287
G.W. 207,245
H.K. 313
J.P. 117,224,
.............263,268
J.M. 30,306,313
Lila 142
Luta Bewley 90
Marty 61
N.B. 313
N.K. 29,253,263,
.............268,313
Thomas 184
W.W. 314
SUMMERELL, J.N.H. ..278
SURRATT, Jackson ...139
SYMMES, ...187
TABB, Mrs. 119
TALIAFERRO, ...56,57,197
Zachariash 202
TANEY, ...200
TATE, Luther E. 286
Robert 159

TATUM, John F. 286
TAYLOR, ...197
   Bessie 124
   D.A. 221
   David 269
   Gen. 133
   Green 195
   G.W. 194
   James 137
   John C. 13
   Joseph 93,202,203
   Isham W. 29,226
   Lewis 200
   Mrs. 206
   Samuel 159,200
   Sarah 167
TELFORD, ...176,192
   Jim 232
   Robert C. 225
   William 195
TEMPLETON, ...110
TERRELL, M.A. 247
TEW, Emmie 123
THATCHER, Daniel T. 33
THAYER, W.E. 126
THOMAS, Andrew 158
   Maria 70
THOMPKINS, ...158
THOMPSON, ..68,197,221,314
   Addison E. 259
   Anne 64
   Dr. 72,191,217,218
   Elvira 217
   James .11,15,36,158,224
   Mrs. James Sr. 36
   John 50,169,217
   Major 105
   M.A. 36,158
   Mary 50
   Matthew 36
   Mrs. 122,191
   Pearl 106
   Richard E. ..72,218,219
   Robert A. 83
   Sallie 47

Wade 262
Waddy 69
TILLINGNAST, Daniel ...166
   Thompson 200
TILLMAN, George 254
   James 289
   Sen. 254,255
TITWORTH, Isaac 159
TODD, ...156,192,211
   Adam 193
   Archibald 82,84,193
   Harvey 259,314
   Mettis 104
   R.W. 84,104
TOLLY, ...156,268
   Bess 312
   C.E. 30
   Clarence 304
   George F. .14,24,30,308
   G.E. 312
   G.M. 314
   Mayor 182
   Mrs. Mayor 25
TOWERS, ...82,268
   A.B. 29,38,268,
  269,303,311
   Alexander 159
   Joel J. 159
   John R. 159
   Martha 311
TOWNSEND, ...314
   Bennett 262
   Claude 298,308
   H.C. 30,297
   J.H. 308
   Joel 138
TRENHOLM, Frazier 235
   George A. 235
TRESCOTT, ...197
   Henry 87
   Katherine 87
   William H. ...57,262,263
TRIBBLE, Bessie 312
   James L. 17,19,30,
  88,120,186,262,

................278,308,312
Lieut. 227
Maggie 106
M.P. 13
R.O. 205
S.O. 314
TRIMMER, ...200
  Nancy 203
  Theodore 36,219
TRIPP, H.R. 211
  W.A. 211
THROWBRIDGE, Col. 250
  Joseph J. 286
  Martin 226
TUCKER, ...314
  Frances C. 128
  Reuben 228
TURLEY, Helena 158
TURPIN, William 15
TURNER, ...197
  George 155
VANDIVER, Augustus W. .226,
................234,247
  Basil 316
  D.S. 100,314
  Edward ..72,100,158,192
  Emmaline 139
  E.P. 19,100,314
  Helena..........139,157
  Hezekiah 139
  Ibzan 91
  James................139
  Jasper N. ...252,253,312
  John 43,168
  J.R. 30,120,247,262,317
  Margaret 91
  Paul 168
  Peter......20,21,27,96,
................133,139,262
  Sanford 45,46,137,
............139,158,168
  W.A. 293
VAN LAWHORN, Wilson 22
VAN WYCK, ...111,197
  Augustus 68

Bessie 169
Elizabeth 68
Lydia 68
Margaret........55,118,
................119,151
Mrs. 123
O.B. 30,297
Oze 68,151
Oze Jr. 68
Samuel M. 68,151
Samuel Jr. 68
William O. 68
Zemaly 68
VAUGHN, ...7
VERNER, Lieut. 227
VICKERY, W.V. 61
VINES, John E. 127
VON BORSTELL, Alice 26
  Christine 26
  Frederick C. 26,113
  Mrs. 113
  Mr. 297
VON HASELIN, Mrs. J.H. ..284
  Julia 14
WADDELL, Moses 33
WADE, Jane 122
WADSWORTH, Thomas 15
WAGSTAFF, William 112
WAHL, Emil 118,120
WAKEFIELD, John 31,314
  Robbie 126
  Samuel 100
  T.T. 314
WALKER, ...270
  C. Irvin 258
  Eleanor J. 106
  J.M. 107
  McElmoyle C. 106
  William 159
  Willis 61
WALLACE, William ...253,258
WALLER, ...80
  Carrie 57,113
  Mary 57,113
  Rosa 113

Traditions *and* History *of* Anderson County, S.C.

WALTERS, William 113
WALTON, T.C. 125
WARD, John 200
WARDLAW, A.C. 253
   C.B. 253
   Mrs. C.C. 31
   Columbus 305
   Hugh 191
   James 191
   J.N. 224
   John 191
   Miss 193
WARNOCK, J.D. 253
WARREN, Taber 48
WASSON, G.W. 225
WATKINS, ...20
   Baylis 141
   Capt. 224,287,288
   Fannie 125
   F.E. 293
   Felix ...30,115,270,297
   H.B. 263
   H.H. ...126,262,263,286
   J.C. 13,312
   Nellie 312
   Professor 124
   T.F. 235,263
   W.W. 120
WATSON, ...82,268,269
   Corrie 117,123
   D.S. 314
   Earle 124
   Esther 173
   Fowler...........157,305
   J.G. 302
   Ida 284
   James 33
   John B. 26,35,120
   J.E. 262,270
   Lois 121,284
   Manley 147
   W.A. 126,223
   W.B. 17,120
   W.G. 314
WATT, A.J. 253

WAULEY, W.H. 226
WEBB, Charles 13,58
   C.W. 30
   Edmund..12,13,14,28,46,
  259,306
   Elijah.....13,14,46,47,
  113,233,269
   Mrs. Elijah 57,58,
   Julia 14
   Louisa 233
   Micajah 12,15,46
   Minnie 103
   Rebecca 82
   Robert C. 58
   Mrs. R.C. 282
   Rosa...........123,238
   Samuel 36
   T.J. 13,29,50,
  156,306,308
   W.G. 36
WELCH, Alonzo 309
WELBORN, ...132,159
   Moses 138
   Thomas 141
WESTON, Anna 182
WEYMAN, ...68
WHALEY, Miss. 120
WHEELER, William 159
WHITE, ...129,137,267
   Alice 314
   Bartholomew 15
   S.N. 211
   Jeff 211
   John E. 127
   Kitty 304
   Leila 304
   Mort 304
   Thomas M. 304
   Walter 304
   W.W. 306
WHITFIELD, ...107,200
   Sue 284
   John C. ...18,46,122,262
   George 47
   Joseph Tyler ..18,21,262

Traditions *and* History *of* Anderson County, S.C.

Tyler 20
WHITNER, ... 197,200
  B.F. 249,262,270
  Mrs. B.F. 257
  James H. ...134,147,263
  Sarah 270
  W.C. 294,295
  Will 262
WHITTAKER, ... 104
  Haynes 143,190
  Hugh 50,132
  Robert 124,143
  W.H. 104
WIGGINTON, John E. ..55,86,
  210,226
WIGGINGTON, Mae 103
WILBANKS, James 141
WILBUR, W.B. 126
WILHITE, ... 268
  Cora 316
  Frank T. 17,30,260
  J.O. 111,260,262
  Mary 259
  M.P. 111
  Philip A. ..28,29,31,111,
  259,260,316
WILKERSON, Betsey 145
WILKES, ... 82
  Sam 233,262
  S.M. 27-29
  Warren 233,262,266
  W.D. 242,282
WILKISON, Betty 159
WILLIAMS, ... 151
  A. 168
  Arthur 48
  Betsey 137
  G.W. 183
  Humphrey 139
  John R. 260
  Lizzie 93
  Matilda 138,143
  Sallie 93
  T.H. 234
  West Allen 98,206

WILLIAMSTON, ... 66
  Andrew 76
  Mrs 13
  Myra 156
WILLIFORD, ... 104
WILSON, ... 197,213,268
  Arthur 300
  B.F. 30,305
  Elizabeth 144
  Elvira 145
  Emma 152
  Franklin 305
  James 253
  Jeohtha 11,143,144,
  146,152,312
  J.F. 29
  John ...104,195,196,258
  Joseph 143,144
  Minnie 121
  M.J. 183
  President 103
  R.E. 263
  Robert 11,15,143,
  210,277
  Sarah 143
  Scott John 223,297
  Susan 120
  Tandy W. 144
  William 143
  W.W. 206
WINN, Jon 159
WINTERS, J.W. 61
WOLFE, S.M. 263
WOLLING, Rev. 62
WOODALL, Joseph 159
WOODSON, Davy 266
WOOLAHAN, W.F. 140
WOOTEN, W.F. 140
WORLEY, Alexander 201
WORNOCK, John 73
WRIGHT, Della 61
  John 166
  Sallie 103
  W.P. 225
WYATT, James F. 210

    Redman Foster ...81,210
WYNNE, John B. ...21,93,161
YANCEY, ...200
YEARGIN, Jerry 218
YOUNG, Anna 262
    C.H. 262
    J.R. 262
ZEMP, ...68

www.ingramcontent.com/pod-product-compliance
Lightning Source LLC
Chambersburg PA
CBHW030543080526
44585CB00012B/235